Rediscovering the Muses

Rediscovering the Muses

Women's Musical Traditions

Edited by Kimberly Marshall

Northeastern University Press: BOSTON

Musical advisor to Northeastern University Press
GUNTHER SCHULLER

Northeastern University Press

Copyright 1993 by Kimberly Marshall

Library of Congress Cataloging-in-Publication Data
Rediscovering the muses : women's musical traditions /
edited by Kimberly Marshall.
p.   cm.
Includes bibliographical references and index.
ISBN 1-55553-173-3 (cl.)—ISBN 1-55553-219-5 (pbk.)
1. Women musicians. 2. Women composers. 3. Music and society.
4. Music—History and criticism. 5. Folk music—History and
criticism. I. Marshall, Kimberly.
ML82.R43   1993
780'.82—dc20   93-28495

Designed by David Ford
Composed in Aldus by Coghill Composition, Richmond,
Virginia. Printed and bound by Thomson-Shore, Inc.,
Dexter, Michigan. The paper is
Glatfelter Offset, an acid-free stock.

MANUFACTURED IN THE UNITED STATES OF AMERICA
99 98 97 96 95   5 4 3 2

to Shirley Anne Marshall

who first introduced me to the Muses

"I present my message in the hope
that it will remind every woman
. . . that [she has] deep, and as yet in our world,
untapped reservoirs of imaginative power."

—Sophie Drinker
Music and Women: The Story of Women in Their Relation to Music

Contents

Contents

Illustrations

Illustrations

Acknowledgments

This book represents a cooperative effort to uncover an obscure past, a history with great potential to influence the direction of the future. Artists have always looked to their ancestors for the confidence to proceed with difficult undertakings. How exciting to discover a hidden world of women making music! New facts are continually being revealed, and new creative energy is being unleashed. The proliferation of absorbing studies concerning women in music attests to that energy, and its radiance is attracting many scholars to the subject. I am greatly indebted to the authors who have taught and challenged me. To each of the ten scholars who participated in this project I extend my heartfelt gratitude. As their work has enlightened me over the past two years, I hope that it may inspire other readers to undertake new inquiries into the rich and varied cultures of women's music.

The catalyst for this book was a visit by William Frohlich of Northeastern University Press to my office at Stanford University some four years ago. He planted a seed that took root very quickly, and although there have been periods of drought (the California sun is not always conducive to scholarship) and the need for extensive pruning, he has been a constant source of new ideas and encouragement. The essays here reflect his keen interest in the subject and his scrupulous reading.

I wish to express my appreciation to the Australian-American Educational Foundation for one year of financial support while I taught at the Sydney Conservatorium on a Fulbright Senior Scholar Award. The extra time for research afforded by this generous grant was vital to my timely completion of this project.

The following colleagues have offered advice and suggested improvements: Robert Bates, J. Michele Edwards, Annette Richards, Susan Stephens, and Eve Sutton. I appreciate their assistance and believe that this book has benefited greatly from their input.

Acknowledgments

To Adam Zweiback, my deepest thanks for his help and understanding during this project. I am fortunate to have a husband who is equally at home with historical criticism, minority issues, and the formulation of concise prose. I look forward to more collaborations as we pursue our scholarly careers together.

I am especially grateful to my colleagues at Stanford University for their support of my work. The Institute for Research on Women and Gender has sponsored faculty workshops that have been of great value to me. Daily encounters with scholars like Karol Berger and Laurence Dreyfus at the Music Department have given me much food for thought. While I am responsible for any shortcomings in this tome, I hope that it may be a tribute to the stimulating environment in which it was conceived.

KIMBERLY MARSHALL
Stanford University
November 1992

Introduction

"History is the record of what one age finds worthy of note in another."

Jacob Burckhardt, *Judgments on History and Historians*

Aspiring young musicians are often greatly influenced by women who serve as role models in their work as performers, scholars, composers, and teachers. Yet when adolescents are asked to name their musical idols of the past, it is rare for a woman to be included among them. This is because their knowledge of the past depends entirely on the choices of historians, who decide which people and events are important and worthy of being immortalized in biographies and musical studies. Since historians in the past have relegated female musicians like Clara Schumann and Fanny Mendelssohn to the margins and footnotes, it is hardly surprising that women's historical contributions to music making are largely unacknowledged, even by students who have been taught primarily by women.

As the priorities of historians have begun to change, women's musical accomplishments are being inserted into the history books. The new value given to women's culture has opened many areas for research to document the work of female artists.[1] Musicologists are participating actively in this research, as evidenced by the recent proliferation of studies devoted to female musicians. Much information is being made available to modern scholars for the first time, promising an exciting future for the field. It is now clear that "the absence of women in the standard music histories is not due to their absence in the musical past. Rather, the questions so far asked by historians have tended to exclude them."[2]

Such exclusion relates directly to the historical process as described by Burckhardt, "what one age finds worthy of note in another." Until recently the historians of Western music charted milestones on the highways of stylistic evolution without studying the prevalent conditions along smaller roads, even though these were often more frequently traveled. Music historians relied on surviving manuscripts and prints to document progressions of compositional masterpieces and stylistic innovation. This approach narrowly defined what was "worthy" of preservation, leaving large gaps in our understanding of the sociology of music, the way musicians lived, the conditions of their employment, their methods of learning, and the different historical contexts for musical performance. The criteria of "worthiness" extolled certain composers, demonstrating how their works contributed to developments in musical style. Those composers who did not command pivotal positions in this narrowly defined theory of musical evolution were ignored.

The "Great Works" approach has robbed us of many interesting insights into the sociology of music making. Perhaps more detrimental has been its marginalization of music that was never notated. Despite the Western emphasis on notation, there have always been flourishing cultures where ritual and dance music was created and learned through performance, without requiring a written score. Women were often active in preparing and leading performances of such music, but their endeavors are not acknowledged because they did not produce notated repertoire.

The purpose of this book is to restore to history some of these forgotten traditions. Most of the essays concern musical cultures that have left little, if any, notated music, such as those of ancient Israel and Egypt, of Australian Aboriginals, of Central Javanese *wayang*, of classical Greece, and of the Byzantine Empire. Since musical works are lacking for these subjects, they cannot be assessed according to the paradigms of literacy that govern many musicological studies. Extramusical materials must be interpreted to provide a more fundamental view of the tradition: Who made the music? In which contexts was music performed? How were women involved in musical creation? The answers to these questions sometimes reveal important female forces in the development of musical culture.

Similar questions and interdisciplinary methods can also be adopted to find evidence for women's work in the production of notated music. The articles on European music in this collection bring together many types of sources to highlight the musical work of women. By eschewing the frequent bias that emphasizes preserved musical works, scholars of

Western music are able to uncover the contributions of European women who created music as performers, sponsors,[3] and composers.

The inclusion of these diverse topics in one book provides examples of female musical activity at many points within a continuum ranging from purely oral traditions to precisely notated compositions. The essays chosen for this book describe female musicians working in the following ways to create music:

- Organizing the performance of ritual or ceremonial music
- Embellishing traditional melodies in performance
- Improvising new melodies
- Repeating remembered improvisations
- Teaching such repeated "works" to others
- Notating music for personal use
- Making copies of one's own music for the use of students or acquaintances
- Publishing written compositions for dissemination outside one's intimate circle.

Although at first glance this list may appear to represent a progression through time, beginning with unnotated traditional music that serves a ritual function and ending with the sophisticated products of trained professionals, these musical processes are nontemporal. We typically associate the first activities with cultures in which music partakes of the supernatural and is created "spontaneously" by nonprofessionals without recourse to notation. Yet a close investigation often reveals that a great deal of preparation precedes such performances. Although the music is not notated, musicians formulate many aspects of their music making before presenting it publicly. This is true for the Australian Aboriginal and Central Javanese traditions studied by Helen Payne and Sarah Weiss in the first two essays of this volume. Western music also may not be notated, especially when it involves only one performer or improvisation around a vocal or dance model.

The scholarly bias toward notated music has resulted in the exclusion of the work of many female musicians from musicological studies. Yet even in ethnomusicology, where there is a relatively large proportion of women researchers, both male and female writers have tended to present a male-centric view of the cultures they have studied. Bruno Nettl suggests that this "may result from the dominant role of men in determining approaches and methods. . . . Male and female ethnomusicologists have described musical cultures largely as they were presented by male informants, and usually assumed that the picture was complete."[4]

Research into Western music has also tended to be male-centric because of its focus on musicians who published their music and established professional reputations. In comparison to men, women rarely did either of these, so if they are to be included in music history, the preoccupation with great works by great composers must give way to a more general interest in all aspects of musical creation. The first obstacle confronting scholars wishing to uncover the musical history of women is to find the data long ago discarded by historians whose priorities were different. Is it still possible to find information about women who created music many centuries ago? E. H. Carr's writing on history in general suggests that it is:

> The facts are really not at all like fish on the fishmonger's slab. They are like fish swimming about in a vast and sometimes inaccessible ocean; and what the historian catches will depend partly on chance, but mainly on what part of the ocean he chooses to fish in and what tackle he chooses to use—these two factors being, of course, determined by the kind of fish he wants to catch. By and large, the historian will get the kind of facts he wants. History means interpretation.[5]

Given the changing criteria used for historical interpretation, new types of fish are being discovered in the vast ocean of music history. Scholars in many disciplines are now being summoned to help locate this fascinating data. As recently as 1986, Jane Bowers and Judith Tick compiled a collection of historical studies about women, the "first written by musicologists from different specializations within the discipline."[6] By including work by scholars focusing on different time periods, the editors were able to evaluate women's contributions to Western music during the eight-hundred-year period that roughly coincides with the development of notation, between 1150 and 1950. Of the fifteen essays in the book, four are concerned exclusively with women in music before 1600, and each of these brings new data to the reader's attention.[7] The Bowers and Tick book reflects new criteria about what is "worthy" in the historical record, and it has inspired many scholars to seek out female models that have been obscured by time.

The present collection of essays owes a great deal to this pioneering work. Following the example of Bowers and Tick, I have solicited articles about musical traditions that cover a wide chronological span. But instead of confining the book to a discussion of Western music, I have included recent research about female musicians in non-Western cultures, where musical notation is uncommon.[8] Some of the cultures discussed in this book still maintain their musical traditions after centuries of transformation, while others exist only as artifacts. Although the original sounds have ceased to resonate, the activity of female musicians is amply documented in pictorial representations, written descriptions, and archival records. By analyzing the information in these different media, it becomes possible to reconstruct aspects of the most ephemeral art form.

Just as the evidence for women in music comes from varied sources, the authors presented here specialize in different disciplines. In our joint attempt to rediscover women's music, we have consulted the work of musicologists, ethnographers, classicists, and historians. We have assembled the varied materials in which this information is found to create a collage documenting the work of women in music. As editor, I hope that this book will lead the reader along new paths of musical inquiry, just as a collage directs the eye through a variety of colors and textures.

The title *Rediscovering the Muses* evokes a powerful image of female creativity. The very word *music* is derived from the Greek *mousikê*, meaning "the art of the Muse." In the mythology reported by Hesiod, the Muses were the nine daughters of Zeus and the Titaness Mnemosyne (Memory). They were conceived when Zeus shared Mnemosyne's bed for nine consecutive evenings.[9] Originally worshipped as deities of springs, the Muses were regarded as the inspiration for learning and the arts, especially poetry and music. They were for a long time considered to be one choir of voices; later a special area was assigned to each, such as flute playing for Euterpe, lyric poetry and dance for Terpsichore, and history for Clio. By the end of the twelfth century, they are pictured with various musical instruments,[10] an iconography that was maintained through the fifteenth century. (See Figure I-1.) These late-medieval depictions of the Muses show them making music, inspiring through example as mentors in the specialized disciplines they came to represent. Unfortunately, during the intervening centuries these powerful female archetypes have been reduced to an insipid allegory for artistic inspiration. The articles collected here document living counterparts to the mythological Muses, women whose work as musicians provides models for others to follow. These real-life "Muses" play active roles in developing musical culture. In rediscovering the original meaning of the word *music,* we uncover a vital female creative force.

A similar transferal of power from the archetype to the contemporary female performer is found in the musical culture of Australian Aboriginal women described by Helen Payne. These women perform music to facilitate their spiritual connection with ancestral archetypes and their ability to summon ancestral powers in private ceremonies. Female musical archetypes also continue to exert influence over music

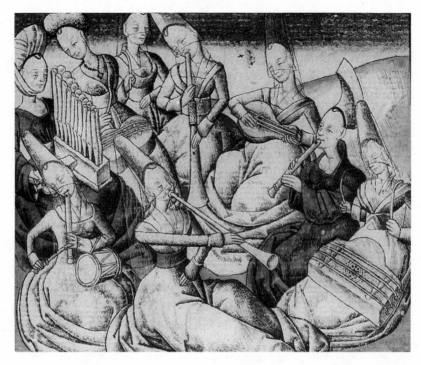

Figure I-1. *The Nine Muses Playing Loud and Soft Instruments,* by Martin le Franc, *Champion des dames.* French, fifteenth century. Grenoble, Bibliothèque municipale, MS 875, fol. 365.

produced in Central Java. Sarah Weiss demonstrates that female musicians are given special status as integral participants in a type of performance that is "largely by men, for men, and expresses the worldview of Central Javanese culture." Weiss explains this apparent inconsistency by drawing upon mythological representations of women and accounts of legendary female *gender* players. When a modern woman steps behind the instrument to play, she partakes of the creative and legitimizing powers exerted by these archetypes.

The strong links between female musicians and their mythological and historical models have gradually disintegrated in the West. Modern female musicians do not identify themselves with the Muses, since the archetype no longer evokes women's prowess in musical creation. Another obscured model for female music making is Miriam, the sister of Moses, who led the Israelite women in musical celebration after crossing the Red Sea. This biblical reference is of great relevance to women's musical history, as demonstrated by Carol Meyers in her discussion of

biblical texts mentioning the hand-drum and surviving terracotta figurines showing female drummers. From this evidence, she extrapolates
that Israelite women were trained as drummers, rehearsed together in
bands, and served important ritual functions. Meyers's documentation
of female percussionists in biblical Israel confirms the brief textual allusion to the prominent musical roles played by Miriam and Israelite
women.[11]

Like Meyers, Emily Teeter demonstrates the prestige of female musicians in an ancient culture from which no music survives. Her study
of Egyptian tomb paintings and inscriptions reveals that women who
played music were sometimes given distinction by immortalizing their
personal names in hieroglyphic captions; their high status is also indicated by the presence of many upper-class women musicians in temples
as well as in the royal residence. Teeter's assessment of New Kingdom
iconography leads her to conclude that orchestras of female instrumentalists were favored over both male and mixed-gender orchestras.

Despite the privileged musical roles of ancient Egyptian women,
modern biases and misunderstandings have distorted scholarship relating to these musicians. Their music has been demeaned by association
with female sexuality. A case in point is the Egyptian *hnr*, which has
often been translated as *harem*, a term laden with sexual overtones and
the concept of female servility to male domination. The *hnr* was actually a troupe of professional singers and dancers; originally it was composed exclusively of women, but by the end of the Old Kingdom it
included men. Another misunderstanding concerning female musicians
in Egypt is the assumption that their nudity, as depicted in pictorial
sources, indicates sexual promiscuity. Teeter argues that nudity was accepted and prevalent in women's fashion throughout Egyptian history;
she finds no evidence that female musicians in ancient Egypt were considered to be of disreputable character.

The distrust of women and their sexual powers has had great impact
on the music they have produced. Misogynist attitudes in Classical
Greece and the Byzantine Empire restricted women's musical practices,
so that female musicians were limited in the types of music they cultivated. Nancy Sultan explains the development of the ritual lament as
"a protected vehicle" through which Greek women were able to "pronounce moral judgments with political impunity." Sultan bases her arguments on a study of ritual lament forms found embedded in Homeric
poetry and classical tragedy; these texts suggest that classical Greek
women derived both public honor and private joy from their intense

expressions of grief and pain. The lament was a unique forum for female expression in a society in which women's discourse was strictly limited by law. The performance of ritual laments enabled Greek women to acquire a public voice otherwise denied to them. As shown in earlier articles, women in contemporary Javanese and Australian Aboriginal cultures are similarly empowered by their musical performances.

As in the Aboriginal rituals described by Payne, the performance of Greek laments required an intricate combination of singing, physical gestures, and emotional display. Male insecurity with the emotional intensity of women's laments was widespread, to the point that in Classical Athens women were forbidden by Greek law to perform laments. Still today the authorities of the Greek Orthodox Church frown upon the public performance of ritual laments by women, yet despite these restrictive forces, some contemporary Greek women continue the practice of public mourning practiced by their female ancestors over twenty centuries ago.

The Church's restriction of women's musical activities greatly affected the work of Greek female composers. Diane Touliatos postulates that writings by the early Church Fathers condemning female musicians as prostitutes effectively stifled the participation of decent women in secular music. By the middle and late Byzantine Empire, most female Greek composers were nuns, and a flourishing musical culture arose in the nunneries of Byzantium. The lives and work of these musicians were thus controlled by prevailing social and theological definitions based on gender.

Prevalent social and philosophical conditions centuries later fostered the development of sacred music in the nunneries of northern Italy. Robert Kendrick demonstrates how devotional themes promulgated by female mystics during the early seventeenth century found expression in a new type of motet in the 1640s. The new style was cultivated by composers in the parishes and monasteries, including one nun, Chiara Margarita Cozzolani, whose work is extant. Cozzolani's music was vital in introducing the new style to Milan, and Kendrick believes it to represent "the one form of public self-expression possible for Milanese nuns" following the restrictive ordinances of the Council of Trent. These women, like those of Classical Greece and Byzantium, were confined to socially acceptable forms of musical expression.

Important evidence for female musicians has been overlooked because of its ties to religious and domestic service. Since women's music is often integrated into spiritual activities, its creators may be primarily identified as nuns or priestesses and their musical roles ignored. As Teeter has shown, many female Egyptian musicians were associated with temples, primarily the cults of Hathor and Amon. Similarly, the terracotta figurines of women percussionists described by Meyers were originally interpreted to represent goddesses, thus obscuring their implications for the music of real women in ancient Israel.

This problem of identification becomes acute in the interpretation of medieval documents for female musicians. Women are often considered accessories to the act of musical creation: performers of music written by others, or enthusiastic sponsors, assisting composers through financial patronage or personal encouragement. My essay, "Symbols, Performers, and Sponsors," reassesses pictorial and archival documents to suggest that despite the lack of notated music attributed to women, they were actively creating music during the late Middle Ages. Symbolic depictions show women performing on instruments, an activity verified by information in payment records and literary accounts. Since instrumental music during this early time was not normally codified into musical notation, these female performers were probably inventing their own music without recourse to a score. When seen in this light, documents describing female performers suggest the types of music that women were creating. Similarly, late-medieval accounts of women "inspiring" male creativity or sponsoring musical endeavors should be scrutinized for clues to female involvement that may have been overlooked by modern scholars.

Paula Higgins elaborates upon similar problems of research bias in her article, "The Other Minervas." She gleans biographical information from French sources of the fifteenth century to demonstrate the creative activity of female poets and musicians among the literary circles of the French aristocracy. Until recently, the work of many of these women had been ignored and underestimated by historians, and Higgins signals the need for a change in perspective in order to acknowledge the contributions of neglected female poets and musicians. She urges future researchers to investigate more fully the daily musical activities in female convents, musical manuscripts destined for use by women, and court payment records of female aristocrats.

Responding directly to this call is William Prizer's discussion of female patronage in the north-Italian courts ca. 1500. Using epistolary and archival sources documenting the courts of Isabella d'Este and Lucrezia Borgia, Prizer is able to learn about the musicians they employed.

Their musical sponsorship conformed to prevailing social dictates concerning the types of music appropriate for cultivation by aristocratic women—intimate chamber music and dance music. Prizer suggests that Isabella's support of music stemmed from her active involvement as a performer; she sponsored the production of music appropriate to her musical talents, contributing greatly to the development of the Italian frottola, a type of secular song that led to the madrigal.

In addition to improving our knowledge of women's musical accomplishments at court and in the cloister, new archival research also continues to inform us about the lives of famous women composers. In her article on Francesca Caccini, Suzanne Cusick provides fascinating documentation for musical activity in the composer's later years. Historians since the nineteenth century have presumed that Caccini vanished from the musical scene after her remarriage in 1626. Troubled by this unsatisfactory ending to such a glorious musical career, Cusick uses her own experience as a woman and as a musician to help trace Caccini during her final years. She uncovers a wealth of information proving that Caccini continued her musical activity in both Lucca and Florence after her remarriage and the death of her second husband. The work is a sobering reminder of the impact historical biases continue to exert upon our recognition of women's accomplishments.

These biases often result from socially constructed gender roles. In the case of Caccini, Cusick argues that the agenda of the original biographer was to portray her as a proud and restless woman who overstepped the bounds of acceptable female behavior. His purpose was well served by a cursory account of her later years. Similarly, the musical accomplishments of aristocratic women have often been overlooked and underestimated, as shown in the articles by Higgins and Prizer. Regardless of time or place, prevailing views regarding female sexuality have shaped the creation of music by women, and this influence is reflected in the spectrum of articles included here. While Byzantine and Milanese nuns may have renounced their sexuality in order to make music, other women, such as the Javanese *pasindhen*, exploit their sex appeal in order to pursue musical careers. Such gender roles have influenced and continue to influence the paths taken by female musicians.

Music making and sexuality are intricately linked: in order to achieve musical success, "women must frequently serve the linked economic and erotic interests of a dominant culture."[12] In a catch-22 situation that still exists, the music of women who exploit their sexuality is devalued because of its association with these "economic and erotic interests," while women who attempt to pursue careers in music without recourse to their sexual allure may be considered to have betrayed their sex: "Female sexuality itself may be negated or denied as a result of musical activity."[13] Such negation of sexuality enabled nuns to cultivate musical expression within the sequestered life of the convent. Yet, because of the humility and seclusion of these women, their musical works were often marginalized. Learning about such isolated women's traditions requires great expertise and patience. Touliatos and Kendrick have combed remote archives to reveal evidence for the creative musical activity of nuns. The problem of seclusion is perhaps even more severe in the case of contemporary female cultures: Payne has devoted years of her life to gaining the trust of Aboriginal women in order to study their secret musical ceremonies.

Well before the advent of Western music, with its emphasis on notation, women thrived as creators of music, fulfilling important cultural roles. As priestesses, women created music to stir the soul; as lovers, women created music to seduce and to delight; as teachers, women created music to instruct the mind. The natural talents of women in artistic creation have always been recognized, but as art became increasingly specialized and separated from its traditional spiritual and domestic functions, women's skills were devalued. The extent and quality of their musical activities were obscured by the more widely publicized and published efforts of men. Regardless of their professional inclinations, women were conditioned to accept anonymity in the public sector so that they could devote themselves to nurturing their families and friends.

Gender is a major factor in determining an artist's choice between the pursuit of public renown and that of private satisfaction. This conflict is invoked by Milan Kundera when he discusses "graphomania," or an obsession with the published word:

> A woman who writes her lover four letters a day is not a graphomaniac, she is simply a woman in love. But my friend who xeroxes his love letters so he can publish them someday—my friend is a graphomaniac. Graphomania is not a desire to write letters, diaries, or family chronicles (to write for oneself or one's immediate family); it is a desire to write books (to have a public of unknown readers).[14]

Kundera's distinction between genders is revealing. He contrasts a "woman in love" with an aspiring male author. Although the literary quality of their love letters may be indistinguishable, they address different audiences. "Graphomaniacs" conceive their work for broad dissemination to a public of unknown consumers. Because such works are originally intended for publication, they are more likely to survive in history's record than those conceived for an intimate circle. The facility with which we can now copy documents and send them around the world may cause us to forget the many obstacles that have previously faced women desirous of entering the public realm. Publication requires financial backing and institutional support, resources often denied to those who step across lines of social order.

Perhaps more injurious to potential female creators of music has been the suppression of real-life role models through historical filtering. Instead of learning about the creative work of women, we are taught that they served as helpmates "behind the scenes," inspiring great works by their male friends and family. This interpretation reinforces the social construct of women as contented domestic partners, modestly pursuing their artistic interests to make themselves attractive to others. Consider Abraham Mendelssohn's advice to his daughter, Fanny:

> Music will perhaps become his [Felix Mendelssohn's] profession, while for you it can and must only be an ornament, never the root of your being and doing. . . . Remain true to these sentiments and to this line of conduct; they are feminine, and only what is truly feminine is an ornament to your sex.[15]

Mendelssohn's advice to his daughter was certainly intended for her own well-being in a society that was hostile to the professionalism of women. (One is reminded of the sad destiny awaiting Virginia Woolf's imagined character, Judith Shakespeare.)[16] Yet such repressive social conditioning makes all the more dramatic the recent recovery of many compositions by Fanny Mendelssohn. Modern women cannot help being inspired by the knowledge of such courageous predecessors. This book documents many more, covering a geographical and chronological gamut as extensive as women's contributions to music, from Miriam leading bands of women drummers, to Péronne d'Armentières composing *rondeaux*, to Ibu Pringga improvising for countless hours on her *gender*.

As we learn of these real-life models, we realize that women have been distanced from the public sphere through a subtle use of symbolism. Meyers's research shows that Miriam's rejoicing after the crossing of the Red Sea was not purely figurative. The Genesis account of her leading the Israelite women in song reflects a real musical tradition: female drummers played a central role in the music of the Israelites and probably throughout the East Mediterranean world. Similarly, iconographical portrayals that are considered to be merely symbolic may reflect the reality of female musicians. Stylized depictions in Egyptian tombs and Greek vases are surviving remnants of women's musical activity. When medieval artists portrayed the sixth liberal art of Music as a woman, they included details taken from real life. These symbolic representations of female musicians have strong overtones for lost musical traditions.

The active, public roles of female musicians have been omitted from the historical record as archetypal models for female musicians, such as the Muses, have been divested of their associations with female creativity. The essays in this book attempt to balance the scale, to show that the creative abilities accorded the symbols and mythologies of women musicians have been and continue to be translated into real musical cultures. By reconstructing the active role of women in music as revealed in the appended topics, we uncover many rich traditions of music making. In rediscovering the Muses, may we gain access to their artistic legacy and strive to maintain it for posterity.

1

The Presence of the Possessed:
A Parameter in the Performance
Practice of the Music
of Australian Aboriginal Women

Helen Payne

In tradition-oriented Aboriginal culture, music is commonly used in conjunction with dance steps, body movements, and painted designs to summon supernatural forces believed to be stored in environmental features such as rocks, star constellations, and so on. These powers are attributed to mythical ancestral beings who once journeyed across the earth, impregnating it with their supernatural creative forces. The release of these powers can be achieved through ritual enactments carried out by the contemporary human descendants of the creative ancestors. Once released, the supernatural ancestral powers can be used by the living descendants to change aspects of their lives—for example, to restore health or engender a sense of well-being, to avert unwanted attentions or weather conditions, or to redirect social behavior. Indeed, those enculturated in Australian Aboriginal traditions believe that there is no aspect of daily life that, given the right circumstances, could remain untouched as a result of powers "pulled" to control it during a ritual enactment. Knowledge of the ritual processes and structures integral to the release of supernatural forces is a sign of great wealth and status, and thus a highly prized acquisition in tradition-oriented society. Those possessing the most musical and ritual expertise are the respected leaders of their communities.

Identifying the musical structures and processes that serve to summon an ancestral presence for enculturated performers requires the comparison of performance practices and structures. This comparison,

1

in turn, necessitates the development of a methodology "for examining performances in themselves—and in relation to other performances (both of the same and other sorts), and as engaged in and played out in different social/material conditions."[1] The development of such a methodology should consider the "over-and-above," or the intrinsic meaning of a performance, thereby transcending an analysis that reduces the ritual to "a mechanical playing out or enactment of sign systems."[2]

The need for a "holistic perspective in the study of [p]erformance [p]ractice"[3] is echoed in Bell's caution that "unless a full analysis of the relationship between the dancers, the patterns made by the dancing feet, the orientation of the actors to the singers, the use of ritual paraphernalia and other factors are taken into consideration, the wealth of information available through ceremonial display [may] often not [be] appreciated."[4]

To respond to the pressing need for a methodology of performance practice as articulated by these scholars, I have examined and classified the women's rituals I observed and in which I participated with Australian Aboriginal women living in the Musgrave Ranges of northwest South Australia (the shaded area on the map in Figure 1-1). The majority of Aboriginal women living in this region identify themselves as Pitjantjatjara or Yankunytjatjara speakers (or both). In linguistic terms, both of these are dialects of a much larger family of dialects, including also Ngaanyatjarra, Pintupi, and others, called the "Western Desert language."[5]

Linguistic distinctions have been used by Tindale and others to categorize groups,[6] and Hamilton suggests that there is a *"de facto* relationship between a particular territory and a particular dialect."[7] Yet such distinctions serve little purpose when considering the cultural life and practice of Aboriginal women because in tradition-oriented Australian Aboriginal society, musical expression is synonymous with singing and the words of the songs are not those used in contemporary conversation. (Perhaps they once were, but "it is virtually impossible to reconstruct a hypothetical past for Aboriginal people from materials collected . . . after first contact with Europeans.")[8] I have found that song words and the musical forms to which they were so inextricably linked often "traveled" over several linguistic boundaries across Australia; the exact extent of their traveling and the degree to which they were changing *en route* is the subject of my continuing research.

My study respects the performers' categorization of their rituals into those that are intended to summon supernatural forces and those that

Figure 1-1. Map of Australia. The area of focus is indicated by shading.

are not. This division differs greatly from the categorizations of a Western perspective, in which music, body paintings, geography, and spirituality constitute distinct fields of inquiry. In the belief that the separation of these factors impedes understanding of Aboriginal ritual culture, I have organized my material according to the Aboriginal distinction and sought to isolate those processes and structural features of performances that summon supernatural forces for enculturated participants. The term *participant* denotes anyone who is present at a performance, regardless of degree of active participation. All who are present are believed to be affected by the powers generated and to derive a sense of well-being from the ritual.

Nevertheless, Béhague argues that "a possible hierarchy of levels of meaning and of structure cannot be elucidated through observation alone but through various degrees of participation."[9] My own participation in Australian Aboriginal women's life has spanned some seventeen years and has seen me cast in graded roles assigned by my

3

teachers. These teachers are knowledgeable Pitjantjatjara- and Yankun-ytjatjara-speaking women who have freely given of their time and energy to enculturate me into their ways, teaching me, an outsider, what it means to be one of them.[10] As is the custom with women's training in ritual, I have been gradually introduced to the hierarchy of levels of meaning and of structure inherent in women's "business," or the staging of ritual.[11] Concurrent with my ritual education was the expectation that I accept more responsibility in the "keeping" of this knowledge.[12] The following account reflects my insight into the distinguishing processes and structures of Aboriginal women's business that I have observed and in which I have participated.

The area of my focus, delineated by the shading in Figure 1-1, is a desert. The aridity of this land is mitigated only by semipermanent bodies of water such as rockpools that form in granitic extrusions, and seasonal reservoirs such as claypans and sandy creek beds that afford water only after rainfall. These sites sustain vegetation and animal life, and they are prized hunting grounds for the tradition-oriented Australian Aborigines. The identifying features of these sites are recorded in the rites and ceremonies practiced in the region; each item names at least one site for the trained listener-observer. As each item names a site, knowledge of rites serves as a powerful mnemonic aid in the recollection of significant economic sites.[13]

Women's Rites

In this region of Australia, Aboriginal women have a flourishing ritual life . . . distinct from, yet complementary to that of Aboriginal men. While the extreme separation of the sexes, so apparent in both the secular and ritual life practiced by the Aborigines living in the communities situated in this region, "has often been taken as an index of the degree to which women are second-rate citizens in Central Australian society,"[14] the Aborigines living in these communities speak of both men's and women's "business" and accord each an equal part in the maintenance of the "laws" governing their lives. "([B]y 'business' they mean secular and ceremonial matters governing life). . . . ([B]y 'laws' they mean those conventions or formulae ensuring the well-being of both the members of their group and of the natural phenomena, flora, and fauna on which their hunter/gatherer ancestors once depended for a livelihood.)"[15]

As practiced by Australian Aboriginal women living in the Musgrave Ranges, rites may involve the simultaneous presentation of many phenomena, such as musical forms, dance steps and actions, painted designs, ceremonial objects, the naming of topographic features or of persons, and so on. These ceremonies celebrate the lives of ancestors who existed on earth long ago and who used their supernatural abilities to create both the inanimate features of the natural world and the animate beings living in it. It is believed that the ancestors recorded their history in a series of songs, dances, and designs, and that they created objects to commemorate special events in their lives. Each song, dance, and design in the series, as well as each object, is thought to have been created at a specific geographical location. Like the site at which it was created, each item identifies the ancestor, either aurally or visually, for the enculturated listener-observer. Because each individual song, dance, design, or object is mnemonically associated with the others, *all* are to some degree simultaneously present at any single moment of a ritual performance.[16] However, at any given time, one aspect of the rite may be brought into sharper aural, visual, kinetic, or tactile focus than the others.

A ritual performance presents a particular grouping or clustering of the aspects mentioned above. The smallest unit in this grouping constitutes an "item." An item may comprise a simultaneous presentation of all, or some, of the aspects of a rite, but it always features the sounding of a publicly ratified, or previously known, text. On the average, the performance of an item lasts less than a minute, usually ceasing after about thirty seconds.

Each textual item consists of a couplet that constitutes a complete unit.[17] "Frequently two or more couplets share a common line. . . . In these common lines we have something akin to the refrain, which is a familiar feature of much popular verse the world over."[18] Moreover, "since each couplet is a self-contained unit, couplets . . . may be combined to suit any given occasion."[19]

If dancing is simultaneously presented with a sung text, one textual item may be repeated several times in succession to give the dancers time to complete their choreography. Usually a break in the performance occurs to separate the initial sounding of an item from successive repetitions, or to separate successive repetitions from each other. During this break dancers pause and rest until the singing starts again.

The singing consists of successive descents, each approximately the same in melodic range. These descents do not begin on the same text syllable, so there is overlap between the rhythmically sounded text and the repeated melodic descents. Sounded against the rhythm of the sung text is a percussive accompaniment produced by women slapping cupped palms over the hollows created between their thighs as they kneel. For a performance to be effective, all elements must be presented simultaneously. Therefore, whenever the singing and beating cease, so does the dancing. When the woman leading the performance begins the singing and beating again, she is signaling that the dancing should recommence.

Several successive performance sessions may take place before enculturated women claim to have unfolded all events in the life history of an ancestor or ancestral group, because each item unfolds only one event of the known life history of the ancestor believed to be responsible for the creation of that item. Accordingly, performances that consist of the successive enactment of items, considered to be the creations of supernatural ancestral beings, may last hours, days, or weeks.

The rites on which I will now focus are those that recount the life histories, known as "dreamings," of supernatural ancestral beings: "The ancestors, although now physically removed from the earth, are believed to have left their supernatural powers in the soil at those sites which they visited and/or created during their sojourn on earth. They are also believed to have created myths and ceremonies to tell others about their activities on earth and to have taught these to their human descendants before themselves departing from the earth. Since the time of the ancestors' departure from the earthly realm, the myths and ceremonies are believed to have been maintained and, via the process of oral transmission, passed from one generation to the next."[20] Aboriginal women are unified with their ancestors through ritual ceremonies, some of which enable them to absorb the ancestral powers and others of which are didactic in nature, ensuring the continuation of their traditions by future generations.

Performance Distinctions

Encoded within the texts of the ancestral ceremonies are the names of each of the places visited and/or created by [the] ancestors. On correctly naming a site, present-day performers believe that they can activate the supernatural powers stored in the soil at that site and then use these powers (as did their ancestors before them) to effect desired changes in both their own lives and the lives of others in their group.[21]

Aboriginal women gain control over their lives by absorbing these powers, first by drawing them out of the ground and then by attracting the powers to them. Through this process, the women actually *become* their ancestors, transcending the reality of the material world. But such strong powers can also be misdirected to bring about destruction, so their release, absorption, and manipulation are carefully controlled. Thus, women must deactivate any powers they have absorbed before re-entering the secular arena of life. Because of the intricate procedures for absorbing and deactivating supernatural powers, performances intended to summon them have some rigid requirements not demanded of other rituals. Usually, they are staged in a private space among selected individuals of one sex. Performances not intended to summon such powers, on the other hand, are given in public view so that they may be witnessed by members of either sex at a site accessible to the public. Despite the more serious intent of a power-rendering ceremony, it resembles a public performance in that hilarity and enjoyment are never lacking on the part of the performers. We are now at a point to detail the processes and structural distinctions between these two types of ritual, as observed in the performances of women living in the Musgrave Ranges.

Private Performance: Summoning the Supernatural

The announcement and organization of the performance of a rite is undertaken by the woman or women claiming authority for the items to be performed. The woman in authority, or leader, first selects a time that suits as many people as she wishes to attend the performance. It is desirable to have as many people as possible at a performance, not only to ensure a successful performance, but also to validate the power and authority of the one who organizes the ritual: "numbers are important, for in this way the leader validates her authoritative status as the widely recruited group may verify the proceedings, carry the message back to home communities, learn and be able to continue the business."[22]

Nowadays, with 9 A.M. to 5 P.M. work commitments, invitations to a performance may be issued from an idling truck, poised ready for immediate departure to the appointed site. Since few people ever turn down an offer to ride away from the hub of community life, and a running engine suggests the immediacy of such an offer, a woman issuing an invitation in this way is usually successful in coercing those whom she approaches to accompany her. Moreover, disobeying a senior authority brings severe reprimand; young women who are invited while a truckload of witnesses observe usually feel obliged to obey their elders and attend ritual enactments. In addition, if this negotiation process takes place in front of employers who would like the young women to remain at work, it assures them of a less severe reprimand from the employers upon their return, since it deflects the blame from them to others. For younger women who are able to secure access to vehicular transport, other means of persuasion must be used by the older women. I have frequently witnessed young women being told by their elders to leave their housework or schoolwork, "It will wait, but ritual will not." The senior women secure privileges from their juniors through obligations encoded in kinship.

A site may be selected after performers have been gathered by the leader, or, if the site has been previously selected, it may be changed in order to conceal the whereabouts of secret business. Women who remain in the camp when the main body of performers depart often appear at the ritual site after regular work hours, provided the selected site is reasonably close to camp. Therefore, if the leader desires the attendance of working women, she must select a site located fairly near their place of work. Notwithstanding this consideration, in the majority of cases women performing women's business prefer to go as far away as possible from others not involved in the performance.

Soft sand is the preferred medium for dancing, so performances are frequently sited in creek beds. Sometimes, however, the performance of items takes place at the actual sites named in the item texts. This latter process involves hours of traveling from site to site; as Strehlow records, "[i]n the old days . . . rites used to be practised by the totemites only at the original sites where they had first been carried out by their totemic ancestors."[23] Nowadays, however, there is rarely time for such activities. Wallace has recorded the inroads that paid work has made on the staging of men's initiation ceremonies;[24] a further complication in the case of women is the need for access to vehicles, which is rarely possible.[25] Nevertheless, women comment that the atmosphere is always most relaxed and jovial when they are performing their items at the actual sites named through the ritual. Certainly it has appeared this way to me, for I have observed that performers exhibit considerable hilarity and vigor in ceremonies conducted at the actual sites. These performances, moreover, are always rated by the performers as being more successful and exciting than those given elsewhere.

DEMARCATION AND PREPARATION OF THE RITUAL GROUND

Once at the appointed site, the leader indicates where the dancing will take place. The area assigned for dancing represents the actual ground traversed by the ancestors whose performance is being enacted by the women, and dancers are thought to move between ancestrally created sites in their traversing of it. Wild comments that among Walbiri-speakers "formal ceremonial grounds represent totemic sites and the ancestral tracks joining totemic sites, at and along which the Walbiri re-enact the events of the Dreamtime."[26] The term *Dreamtime* refers to an eternal creative period whose history is recorded in Aboriginal myths; events of that period are continually being relived through ceremonies involving music and dance.

In order to create an area comfortable for dancers' feet and knees, the leader instructs other women to clear any unwanted debris from the dancing area. To further demarcate the extremities of this area, she indicates the positioning of a fire or series of fires at one or both ends of it. Women not selected to dance will remain on one side of these fires, while those selected will move to the other side, into the area assigned for dancing. The fires serve to provide warmth and the means for cooking; on a metaphysical level that is more intrinsic to the ritual process, they create a smoke screen separating dancers from nondancers, or supernatural from natural. The leader may indicate where women should sit around the fire (A in Figure 1-2), but usually this is not necessary because the women take up their positions in generational levels such that "mothers and fathers' sisters sit on one side" and other "women and their 'grannies,' on the other."[27]

While a fire always serves to demarcate the singers' end of the dancing ground (B in Figure 1-2), a bush or bushes (C) behind which women prepare to dance may serve, in lieu of a fire (D), to indicate the other extremity of the ground. This bush is selected or constructed from nearby foliage either by the woman organizing the performance or by the first group of dancers. It is always located on one side of the selected dancing area, some fifteen to twenty meters from the fires.

ATTRACTING AND ABSORBING ANCESTRAL POWER

Women selected to dance prepare themselves behind the bush, which conceals them from the view of the singers. Here they paint their bodies and any objects they wish to utilize in their enactment. Prior to painting, the women smear their bodies and objects to be painted with fat. Fat is the sign of health and ensures that the bodies and objects appear beautiful for the ancestor whose powers the dancers are seeking to attract. Fat is also the medium through which powers pass so that it

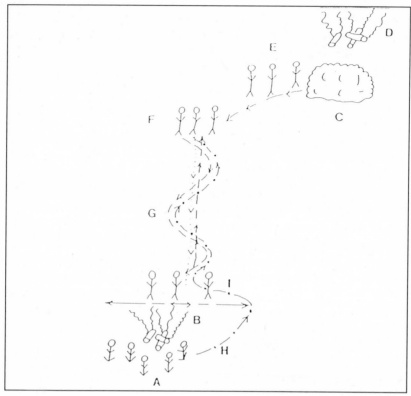

A. Singers
B. Singers' fire
C. Bush behind which women selected to dance paint and prepare themselves for dancing
D. Sometimes another fire is lit to
mark the other end of the dancing ground
E. Painted women take up their
positions on the dancing ground
F. Painted women enter the dancing ground

G. Painted women traverse the
dancing ground in the direction
of either the dotted (. . .) or
dashed (---) line
H. As indicated by the dashed and
dotted lines (- · - ·), one of the
singers moves out onto the ritual ground to smooth over the
dancers' tracks
I. Painted women, on reaching the
singers, jump in a sideways action as power is sung out of
their bodies by the singers. Dirt
is thrown over the painted
women by singers

Figure 1-2. Diagram showing the demarcating features of a ritual ground and
the relative positions of persons and activities on it.

is thought to facilitate the transformation process to be experienced by the women. As they paint, they sing to attract the desired ancestor's supernatural powers to the markings on their bodies and objects, "the song invok[ing] the spirit."[28] The painting group's singing is antiphonally answered by singing from the women seated behind the fire (B in Figure 1-2), or the two groups sing simultaneously after an initial start by one group.

The singing of the women always begins on the highest notes in the melodic range and descends via a series of terraces or steps made up of reiterated notes to the lowest note in the range. The range itself is usually an octave. The "technical musical features are interlocked with extramusical events (such as dances) and information (such as song text) which occur simultaneously."[29]

The analysis of these relationships transcends the scope of this article, but Ellis notes that through "skilful performance the interplay of patterns can highlight changes in perception which are overwhelming. The apparent casualness of the entire performance, in which one small song follows another, seemingly at random and at a time chosen by the song leader, does not in any way prepare the outsider for the pounding impact of the ceremonial climax during which all technical features are held tightly together, interlocked in such a way that the incorrect placement of one small element would cause the disintegration of the entire performance. Through correct interlocking the power of the ancestor, being drawn out of the earth by the strength of the song, is present."[30]

Enculturated performers refer to a *mayu*, or musical structure comprising at least melody, as recalling ancestral identification for them. While Ellis claims that it is the melody that is mnemonically associated with a particular ancestor, Pritam's research on melody exchange between items associated with different ancestors causes him to question this correlation.[31] My own findings point to a flexibility in the use of melodies across ancestral associations, so I do not support the suggestion that a melody identifies a particular ancestor for the enculturated listener. Rather, I believe that we have not yet completed the search to identify the structural characteristics to which enculturated performers refer when using the term *mayu*. For those not born into the tradition, this understanding requires a level of enculturation that must be painstakingly acquired over years of training and correction by patient Aboriginal teachers.

While they sing, the dancers paint themselves with their fingers or with appropriate objects such as sticks or feathers. Red, white, yellow, and black are the only colors used in painting. The red color is obtained from a mixture of red ochre and water, white from a mixture of white ash or chalk and water, yellow from a mixture of yellow ochre and water, and black from a mixture of charcoal and water. If no water is available, urine or spit is used in its place.

As red ochre is scarce and symbolizes the most secret of male rites in this region, its use is restricted to women past menopause; that is, those who have "become like men themselves."[32] Postmenopausal women may smear their hair, body, and all objects they carry or wear with red ochre. Yellow and white are the colors most often used by women enacting the part of ancestors conceived as being female in gender, while black is the color preferred by women enacting the part of ancestors conceived as being male. It is the contrast of colors that is important in painting: the female gender is represented by colors *contrasting* with skin coloring, while the male gender is represented by colors *merging* with skin coloring. As with the red ochre, only postmenopausal women use black, since they are chosen to enact the role of male ancestors, having lost the distinctive body functions that set them apart as female.

Women usually paint themselves, but may paint each other; if the latter occurs, generational levels dictate reciprocity in the painting activity. Body designs may be painted on both the front and back torso, but particularly around the navel, the seat of the spirit.[33] Designs are also painted on the breasts and upper arms, across the nose, and on the front of the thighs.[34] As the ancestor is thought more likely to be attracted to a glowing, dazzling body than a dull, visibly unattractive one, the overall aesthetic quality of the painted person and objects is of paramount importance. Indeed, it dictates many of the decisions made by the woman in charge of the painting process.

In ceremonies intended to summon supernatural forces for performers, painted women nearly always wear a white headband, thought to bedazzle those who behold them, notably the ancestor. The beholder is then believed to become irresistibly attracted to the wearer of the band. Moreover, it is thought that if striking designs are beheld on glistening skin smeared with health-exuding fat, they, too, will bedazzle their beholder. When the ancestor is so entranced, it will linger and infuse the markings on the woman's body and objects with specific powers, for the desired ancestral powers are believed to enter the body and objects through the special markings placed on them. Munn refers to these markings as "identification markings" because they identify an ancestor.[35] Sometimes the design will be the same for all items in a performance; sometimes it changes with each new item. Each part of the design encodes special information for those enculturated in women's business.

The preparation of the bodies of women selected to dance and the objects to be used in the performance is supervised by either the leader or her delegate. The woman supervising the painting commences the singing intended to summon the ancestral powers to the women preparing to dance. When preparations are complete, she aurally signals this completion to the other women, who are seated some distance away on the other side of the fire.

DEMONSTRATING POSSESSION OF ANCESTRAL POWER

IN SINGING AND DANCING

The powers absorbed by the painted women and objects are thought to transform them so that they *become* the summoned ancestors. On receiving the aural signal of readiness from the painting group, the leader (or her appointed delegate if she is among the painted women's group) commands the other women seated around the fire not to look in the direction of the painted women. If dancers have designs painted on both their backs and fronts, she may command the singers to place their faces in the sand. The leader herself may also cover their heads with a blanket. At the same time she may build up the fire with foliage to create a smoke screen through which it becomes difficult for the singers to discern anything but a bare outline. These measures are necessary because it is believed that *all* components of an item must be *simultaneously* presented in performance if the enactment is to be effective in summoning the desired ancestral powers.[36]

As the women seated around the fire bow their heads, the painted women take up their positions on the ritual ground (E in Figure 1-2). If the dancers have designs painted only on their fronts they enter the ritual ground (at F in Figure 1-2) with their backs toward the group seated around the fire, who therefore need not be so cautious about looking at them. However, if dancers bear designs on both their fronts and backs they usually assume positions facing those seated around the fire. Then it is necessary for the leader of the proceedings to guard against premature sighting of the dancers by the singers.

The dancers traverse the ritual ground (in the direction of the arrows shown in G of Figure 1-2) from their point of entry onto the ground until they meet the singing group. However, they may temporarily halt several times as they traverse the ritual ground. These halts constitute short breaks in the performance that permit both singers and dancers time to regain their breath.

Occasionally no break occurs in the singing of an item during the dancers' enactment. In such instances individual singers still pause in their singing to regain their breath, but others continue to sing the item. This form of item presentation occurs rarely in practice, and I have not had the opportunity to study the social organization of the singers relative to it. It would be interesting to know if a hierarchy of kinship determines who takes over when some singers pause. For example, do grannies take over from fathers' sisters?

As singing, beating, and dancing must cease simultaneously after the dancers have completed their movements over the ground, the leader will fade out the singing and beating, not necessarily at the same time. Sometimes, however, coordination between the dancers and singers is not achieved to end the activities. For example, the singing, which should always come to rest on the lowest note in the melodic descent, may have just returned to the start of a descent when the dancers physically reach the seated singers on the ritual ground. At these times the dancers must dance on the spot until the singing has reached the lowest melodic point.

DEMONSTRATING POSSESSION OF ANCESTRAL POWER

IN THE USE OF OBJECTS

The main object used in ritual enactment is a digging stick, which, when the ritual performance concludes, is left hidden in the bushes until the next time it is required in a ritual performance. The digging stick is used in various ways in women's business, and when placed upright in the soil at the conclusion of a performance it serves as the medium through which supernatural powers called up during the performance session are transported back into the soil. This transportation process is effected by women clasping the protruding end of the digging stick while moving clockwise around it. At the same time, they sing to deactivate the powers absorbed into their bodies during the performance. It is thought by those enculturated in women's business that during this process the powers travel through the performers' hands clasping the digging stick, down the stick, and back into the soil; the singing of those clasping the stick deactivates the powers as they travel so that on reentry into the soil they assume a latent form.

Smaller objects used in performance sessions are kept in the care of one or more of the performers. "[W]hereas men place their ritual objects in a storehouse, women, on the other hand, keep their ritual objects in their immediate care. On settlements fire risk is high as is the danger of discovery, so women are restricted in the range of objects they can maintain."[37] The objects kept in women's care may be roughly subdivided into ones that are made of human hair and ones that are not. In the former group are the head pads (hollow rings approximately 20 cm in diameter), used for carrying objects on the head while dancing, and the hairstring skirts, worn around the pubic region and/or across the forehead. Each hairstring skirt is made of a plait of human hair some 40 cm long, to one side of which are attached 4 cm-long woven hair strands at intervals of approximately 2 cm. Each woven strand of human hair is finished with an *inindi* nut. These nuts are small reddish pods obtainable from Inindi and other places to the north of the shaded area on the map in Figure 1-1. The nuts audibly knock against each other as the women move in their dancing. The hairstring skirts are knotted at the back of the body or head.

Objects kept in a woman's care that are not made of human hair include incised pearl shells, sticks, opal matrix, and the frequently worn *inindi* beads. All the nonhair objects I have seen in possession of women have been obtained by them through trade with other Aboriginal women. None were locally obtainable in the area. Buckley and her co-workers record seeing an incised pearl shell that had traveled a thousand miles or more before becoming a ritual object for women at Coober Pedy. They suggest that shell trading occurred via traditional trade routes that followed water holes and ancestral tracks.[38] They also recount that upon being shown women's sacred objects "all members of the research team were somehow made aware that to touch them or even examine them closely would not be welcomed."[39] Like these researchers, I did not wish to photograph some of the small ritual objects, even though the women showing them to me requested that I do so. However, I did feel free to examine each object as it was handed to me. While Buckley and her group list the digging stick as one of the objects they dared not touch, I, on the other hand, was instructed to clasp the digging stick at the conclusion of performances. The Buckley report includes men's ritual and hunting objects in their list of women's objects: "[T]he sacred objects consisted of a pearl shell and the lengths of hairstring worn during the dances, the women's digging sticks also used in the ceremony, and a man's boomerang, a man's shield and short pole."[40] All the objects shown to me, however, were claimed by women to be their rightful property. In addition to the objects cited above, women may use materials at hand to create other desirable objects.

NEGATING THE EFFECTS OF ANCESTRAL POWER

The ancestral powers are believed to remain in the person or object having absorbed them until special enactments take place to release them. During this time they can be used to effect desired occurrences, either benevolent or malevolent, as intended by the performers.

Immediately following the enactment of an item designed to release supernatural powers, the women who are not dancing sing a special item to negate the continuing effects of powers absorbed by the dancers and their objects. While singing the item, the singers throw dust over the dancers' bodies; one singer also moves out to shuffle over the dancers' tracks on the ritual ground (H in Figure 1-2) to remove visible marks of the ancestor(s) from the area.[41] The dust is thought to absorb the released powers and thus to return them to the soil.

While the seated women sing to release the powers from the dancers, the dancers perform a sideways jumping action (I in Figure 1-2) with their heads held low to conceal designs painted on their breasts, moving their dangling outstretched arms in front of them to conceal designs shown on their abdomen and thighs. At the end of the singing, the dancers either rub off, or smear beyond visible recognition, their body designs. They also erase any designs appearing on objects used during the dance. After making these erasures, the dancers may rejoin the seated women's group, for they are no longer possessed by the supernatural.

RETURNING TO A MUNDANE STATE

At the conclusion of a performance in which supernatural powers have been released, an additional enactment takes place not only to secure the release of the absorbed powers, but also to deactivate them and re-direct them back into the soil whence they are believed to have first issued. All women who have attended the performance are instructed to take turns at clasping the stick and, while encircling it, to sing an item designed to negate the continuing effects of their absorbed powers. Symbolically, the digging stick connects two absorbers of ancestral power, the women and the soil.[42]

After deactivating and transferring the ancestral power back into the soil through the digging stick, participants may safely return to camp in the knowledge that they no longer possess powers that set them apart from others. The digging stick, however, is left in the bushes at the ritual ground; if it should be discovered and touched by the unwary hand, it may still transfer supernatural powers to the unsuspecting discoverer. In serving as the medium for the transportation of these powers, it continues to harbor some of the powers beyond the termination of the ritual enactment. It is thus not surprising that the sight of a woman's digging stick lying in the bushes acts to taboo a locality to men and women enculturated in the traditions of the group. Naturally, such a taboo also protects women's rights to those sites at which the digging stick may be left "hidden."

Public Performance: Differences vis-à-vis Private Performance

Public performances are usually given to teach others, particularly children or visitors, about women's dreamings; no "over-and-above" results are expected to issue from them.[43] Performances not intended to summon supernatural powers are given in public view so that they may be witnessed by both males and females. The emphasis is on achieving an aesthetic quality pleasing to attendees, particularly those whom the performance leader herself has invited to attend. Accordingly, those with known skills as dancers and singers are placed by the leader in appropriate roles. By excelling in their execution of these roles, the women enhance the leader's status as a ritual matriarch.

The simultaneous presentation of all structures inherent in the ritual process enables enculturated persons to identify and summon the ancestor(s).[44] However, in performances aimed specifically at teaching others about a particular dreaming or aspect of ancestral life, some items may be omitted or presented afterwards. For example, singing may precede or follow the demonstration of a dance that it would normally accompany in performances intended to summon ancestral forces. Moreover, the dancers may not bear the designs on their bodies or carry objects to show during the dance.

In women's business enacted in public situations, items performed to absorb, release, deactivate, and redirect supernatural powers either are omitted or their functions are changed. Such items include those that accompany painting, that negate the continuing effects of the powers in dancers' bodies and ritual objects, and that deactivate and return ancestral powers to the soil.

In this article I have represented a subdivision of women's item performances on the basis of the leader's intention to summon or not to summon ancestral spiritual forces. Within each subdivision changes will occur in response to the leader's perception of the current sociopolitical climate in which she is staging the performance. Of special interest is the organization of a public performance to arrest a counterclaim to a site of considerable economic significance in the environment. While the leader might view this site as her rightful property, others may be challenging her rights to it. In my experience, the site being claimed by others will be "sung into" from multiple directions, metaphorically surrounding it with ritual (since a performance does not usually take place at the actual site being sung into, but rather at some distance). As "fertile" sites have many items that serve to "name" them for enculturated participants, the leader will have a considerable choice of items. By being seen to own an economically significant site, she will be accorded status and power in her group; this in turn will affirm her claim to that site and therefore diminish the impact of counterclaims to it. However, in order to be seen as the rightful claimant, she must invite many participants, including those challenging her land claim.[45] She will include in the selected performance group women considered to be "strong" performers by their community. "Strong" implies those whose proven executant abilities as dancers and singers favorably distinguish them from others.[46]

As the ancestors are thought to have sung with clear "high head" voices,[47] women who can sing with a "high head" voice are greatly prized as singers. Their participation accords the performance a "beautiful" rating by those present. Since such a performance is thought to be more effective in summoning the desired ancestral powers for the performers, such singers are always sought as participants.

However, while the woman who can sing with a "high head" voice is highly regarded, she is not accorded the same status in the community as the dancer who can execute a convincing performance of a dreamtime history or event. As von Sturmer postulates, "[S]ong specialists ha[ve] the opportunity to demonstrate their skill at almost any time; yet the dance specialists—those who, by their skill and brilliance, c[an] demonstrate the actuality of possession—ha[ve] few opportunities. And even when the opportunities ar[i]se it c[an] be a very hit-and-miss affair."[48]

While von Sturmer emphasizes that "[s]uccess [as a dancer] is a sure-fire route to power,"[49] I would claim that it also empowers the ritual leader. Through her issuing an invitation to dance, she directly controls if, when, and under what conditions a dancer is given the opportunity to demonstrate her "skill and brilliance" as a performer.[50] Although women are chosen to dance by the leader of the public performance, their selection usually accords with attainment of *minyma pulka* (big woman) status.[51] This status implies that the woman is ready to join her ancestors and become one of them; she does this through effecting the timeless transformation of states of being that ensures women's dreaming will continue. Indeed, a woman's excellence in being able to effect convincingly a state of transformation, as judged by those who witness her enactment, assures her of a high level of praise. Thus, a "strong" dancer is one who can capture the essence of the ancestor in the dancing act, to convince others of her transformed state so that she really *becomes* that ancestor for enculturated observers. "The great dancers are seen as [ancestral] reincarnation[s], quite explicitly so."[52] Women believe "without the slightest shadow of doubt that their ceremonies are an actual reenactment of the heroic events and that the dancers are temporarily transformed into ancestral beings."[53]

Once a woman shows particular talent in a certain dancing role it is likely that she will become the constant recipient of that role on future occasions. It is "never merely the ancestor whom the audience" sees "in a ceremony": those who are present remember "also the actor who last assumed the role."[54] As in the nonpublic ceremonies, if the role of a male ancestor is required in the public performance, only those women past menopause are selected by the leader to take this role. White notes this same practice among Yalata women; when she inquired why this was so, she was told that they were the only ones "who were really men among us."[55] This statement supports my suggestion that the selection of women as dancers is determined by their proven ability to *become* ancestors.

Women can claim sites through many means:[56] Two principal ways are through inheritance (matrilineal in the area studied here), or on the basis of length of residence and therefore knowledge of a site. A ritual leader can thus frame her claim to a site in different ways. Yet the effectiveness of her public demonstration of the claim is based upon her showing or revealing a particular ancestor in performance. This ability heightens her association with sites believed to be impregnated with that ancestor's powers. The brilliance of her public performance affirms her possession of power and hence her success as a ritual leader in her group.

The type of performances described in this article are thus interconnected in a vital way. The public's reaction to a leader's performance directly affects the status of that leader and her rights to land.[57] Given the political substance of these women's rituals, it is to be hoped that modes for analyzing actual performances will be further developed so that all the information encoded in them, both musical and nonmusical, may be appreciated by those not enculturated in their interpretation.

2

Gender and *Gender*: Gender Ideology and the Female *Gender* Player in Central Java

Sarah Weiss

Seated inside the *gender* box, Ibu Pringga slowly rolls a cigarette of tobacco heavily scented with clove. She stops to examine and expertly refine the flare of its conical shape and then inhales deeply as she lights the cigarette. She has just finished a heated conversation in low Javanese with her brother, Bapak Suparno, the *dhalang* for this evening's *wayang* performance. She leans back and smiles graciously at several of the musicians who have just arrived. As they sit down at their instruments she goads them about being late, implying they should feel guilty for being so lazy. Still tsk-tsking but grinning, she turns to adjust the suspension of several of the *gender* keys that clank against their supports as she begins to test the *gender*. She is relaxed and gregarious. Her voice is loud and boisterous, different from those of the subdued men about her. The *dhalang* signals that it is time to begin. Ibu Pringga prods the *rebab* player who has been snoozing. She glares at him for not paying attention and missing the cue. As the music begins Ibu Pringga's hands move smoothly, her wrists supple and fast. An aura of concentration and endurance settles around Ibu Pringga and the *dhalang* as they prepare to perform for eight hours, non-stop.[1]

When Ibu Pringga plays the *gender*, a metallophone with fourteen keys suspended over pitched resonators, she plays in what is known as the female style, or *gaya perempuan*. This style is subtly different from what is commonly referred to as male style, *gaya laki-laki*, or simply *genderan* (that which is played on a *gender*.)* When asked to discuss the male and female styles of *gender* performance, Central Javanese

*Some confusion may arise between the use of the words gender and *gender*. Without italics, the word is English and takes its usual complex of meanings. When italicized, the word is the Javanese name of a musical instrument.

musicians often hypothesize that the differences stem from the simple fact that women are women and men are men.

This apparently simple explanation was usually the last, exasperated attempt by many of the Central Javanese musicians I interviewed to explain to me why they thought that there was a difference between male and female styles of *gender* performance and what the nature of that difference was. Given the facts that both male and female players know the same repertoire and play in the same performance situations and that most of the performers have learned through listening to other *gender* players, both male and female, there seemed to be no other logical explanation. What made this explanation seem logical and obvious to these musicians were the assumptions about gender that derive from the dominant gender ideology in Central Javanese culture.

Assumptions about gender and gender roles are based on the gender ideology of a society. The gender ideology of a society is a fluid complex of ideas, associations, and beliefs about the nature of men and women in that society. A comparison of everyday enunciated notions of female and male attributes and characteristics to mythical, historical, or religious representations of women and men often reveals contradictions or inconsistencies. As theorized by Sanday, those two categories express different levels of ideology. By examining the relationship of these levels in a "variety of contexts, it is possible to make more sophisticated judgments about the meanings of certain behaviors and representations."[2] Sanday reiterates a point made by Schlegel in her work on the Hopi, a Pueblo Indian society: Although there is a Hopi ritual in which representations of "women are disparaged and demeaned, . . . it would be wrong to infer male social dominance from this fact because [as seen through the rest of the data in Schlegel's analysis] the Hopi believe in a balance between women and men in both behavior and symbolism."[3] As is made clear in Schlegel's essay,[4] what appears to be male social dominance from one perspective is actually a strategy designed to disparage incestuous relationships that could threaten the brother-sister relationship that is structurally important in the Hopi's matrilineal society.

The idea that there may be apparently contradictory aspects within gender ideologies is particularly useful in the analysis of the Central Javanese material I will subsequently present. When asked to discuss gender differences, both Central Javanese men and women enunciate an ideology that depicts women as less than men in all things that are valued in the dominant male worldview. Culturally perceived male attributes are more highly valued than female attributes. The areas in which women do excel or dominate are considered to be less important than areas in which it is important for men to excel. This generally accepted male-centric perspective is contradicted, however, in mythic and historical representations in which women and female sources of power are often necessary for the very existence, preservation, and legitimation of male power and culture. Indeed, in some instances, it is female attributes that are most effective in a particular situation. It should be noted that these stories and myths are part of the knowledge that is cultivated by men.

The female *gender* player provides an opportunity for an analysis of the aforementioned inconsistency between the everyday enunciated ideology and the mythic representation in Central Javanese culture. *Wayang kulit*, or shadow puppet performance, is the art form believed by many Central Javanese to capture the very essence of their culture. Playing the instrument most essential to the performance and interpretation of *wayang* (an art form that expresses the male-dominated philosophy of Central Javanese culture), the female *gender* player is perched between two worlds—male and female—and two representations—average woman equipped with inferior female attributes and powerful female figure embodying images of female potency.

Because there is a discrepancy between spoken ideology and mythic representation, it might be possible to hypothesize several separate, contradictory ideologies for women in Central Javanese culture. Anna Meigs has suggested just such a situation for the Hua of the New Guinea Highlands.[5] Through an analysis of male representations of women in a variety of different situations, Meigs has identified three ideologies ranging from "brutal chauvinism" to "egalitarianism," with one of "frank male envy of female reproductive powers" in the middle.

I believe that the notion of separate ideologies for different contexts is inappropriate for explaining the difference between the enunciated ideology and mythic representation of women, in particular the female *gender* player, in Central Javanese culture. Rather, in light of general acceptance by both men and women of the male worldview, I suggest that it is the concept of a layering of both interpretation and realization of representations over one basic ideology of women that is most useful for understanding the paradoxical role of the female *gender* player.

Wayang *Performance*

The fieldnote excerpt at the beginning of this essay describes the inter-action among the musicians moments before the beginning of a *wayang* (shadow puppet performance). In Central Java, a *wayang* performance and the accompanying festivities are an all-night affair, the preparation of which involves the cooperation of hundreds of people. As major events, *wayang* are usually hosted by either a family or a village to celebrate an occurrence such as a circumcision, a ritual cleansing of a location, or even the commemoration of the birth or death of an im-portant person.

After several days of preparation the festivities begin. The celebration may consist of several parts, each with a separate gathering of guests. A *wayang* performance is usually the last and most spectacular in this series of events. On the evening of the performance the hosts receive the invited guests in a formal manner, offering seats in straight rows of rented square-backed, metal chairs arranged in front of the *wayang* screen. These rows of chairs are interspersed with small square tables on which hot, sweet, jasmine flower tea and small fried snacks are placed.

Once seated, the guests seldom move from their chairs. After being invited to partake, they sample the tea and snacks while waiting to be served a meal of celebration fare (usually predictable). Most of the at-tending guests at a *wayang* are male—local government officials, im-portant men from the area, and family members and friends not in-volved in preparation activities. Their wives and teenaged children, both male and female, are working in the back preparing and serving food and drink for the guests and the performers.

Behind the screen the *dhalang* (puppeteer) and the musicians prepare themselves for the performance. Plates of snacks and hot tea are pre-sented to the musicians seated on the periphery of the *gamelan* (a Ja-vanese musical instrument ensemble, but the word also implies the space wherein these instruments are situated). These musicians then pass the food to musicians in the center of the *gamelan* and to the *dhal-ang* and his helpers. No one eats until well after the performance has started so the plates and glasses are wedged between instruments and humans, adding to the general clutter of discreetly placed shoes and other personal objects stashed in the usually tiny space allotted to the *gamelan*.

Clustered around the *gamelan* and reaching back into the night are crowds of uninvited guests, mostly men and children, who are the most avid fans of *wayang* performances. They will stay through the night, gradually, if timidly, moving to fill the spaces in front of the screen created as the invited guests, having fulfilled their social obligations, bid farewell to the hosts.

One of the striking aspects in this scene is that very few women are apparent. The few women seated among the guests are usually not closely connected to the families in the area and, consequently, not involved in the preparations for the event, such as the wife of a dignitary from a distant locale or the sister of an in-law and her family visiting from the city. By and large, however, the majority of visible faces are male.

Enunciated Ideology of Men and Women

Wayang is thought to be one of the most refined (*alus*) and highest forms of artistic endeavor in Central Java. Many Central Javanese believe that *wayang* is the essence of their culture. All of the attributes of human beings—or, more specifically, Central Javanese people—from the most refined and controlled to the most coarse and uncontrolled are represented in the stories. Although the *wayang* stories have their roots in the Hindu epics the *Mahabharata* and the *Ramayana*, they have been extensively developed and Javanized. Today many of the most popular stories are those classed as *lakon carangan,* or branch stories that frequently revolve around events that never occurred in the original *Mahabharata.*

Woven into the stories, through the dialogue between the puppets and the musings of the *dhalang,* are threads of the philosophy and attitudes that make up the male-dominated worldview of the Javanese. The aspect of this worldview that occupies the most space in the anthropological literature and, perhaps, in the minds of the Javanese as well is the concept of power and how it is obtained, recognized, and negotiated. Power gained not through physical strength or force but through ascetic practices—thus, spiritual strength—makes a man worthy of respect. A man has power if his world, be it a house or a kingdom, is organized, controlled, prosperous, and runs seemingly without effort. Any sign of effort or distress, financial, emotional, or otherwise, is an indication that his power is probably in decline. The respect of ever-widening circles of people who recognize his power is a man's goal. A man is worthy of respect if he can recognize and bow to others who are more powerful and thus deserving of greater respect than himself. A man who is powerful will demonstrate this through his refinement in all things, especially speech, physical movement, and an appreciation of refinement in other people and things.[6]

Javanese men are greatly concerned with their own representation as powerful persons within the myriad hierarchies of their society. If refinement in all things is necessary for one to be considered powerful, a masterful and refined use of the Javanese language is one of the most highly valued ways to demonstrate that respect is due. To successfully negotiate societal hierarchies in one's speech without incurring offense through either too much or too little respect is to speak in a refined and beautiful manner. This control over the complexities of language as well as control over one's emotions and physical movement are used in the measurement of the relative refinement and, therefore, powerfulness of men in Javanese society.[7]

I have called this worldview male-dominated not only because it describes aspects of Javanese culture that primarily concern men and their own social standing, but also because men, and to some extent women, believe that women do not possess the ability to behave in a refined manner. Women, in general, are not thought to have enough interest in personal control or patience to perform the ascetic acts necessary to gain inner strength and thus power.[8] Because they cannot become powerful, they do not need, nor are they thought able, to master the refined language and behavior that demonstrates power, in the male worldview at least. Although there are many women who are openly acknowledged for their refinement and ascetic practices, women as a group are perceived to be incapable of refinement and control, making it impossible for them to be active participants in the hierarchies of male society except through association with the power of the men in their lives: fathers, brothers, husbands, and sons. However, as will be seen below, their participation in the cultivation and preservation of male power is essential, for without women to organize and enact control, a man's world would never run smoothly without effort on his part.

Because the cultural expectations for them are so low, women do not measure their own status based on refined behavior to as great a degree as men. Since they do not worry that their standing in society will be jeopardized if they misbehave in some way and cause offense or embarrassment, they are much freer in their actions.

This comparative freedom of speech and action does not mean that women are not concerned with their own status. Rather, they have different criteria from men for showing their strength, power, and resulting status relative to others in the community. A woman is judged to be powerful by other women and, to some extent, men, if she can control and manipulate the flow of money through her household so that the family remains prosperous. For instance, if a woman is seen to spend too much for an item in the market, after she leaves vendors will gloat publicly over the price they received, and when she retells the event her friends will cluck that she has spent too much. The woman is thought to be without the strength to bargain properly. As her ability to run a household comes under scrutiny, she may fall in the estimation of the community. It should be noted that the control over household money is not something that gives Central Javanese women status in the male worldview. In fact, it is precisely because men want nothing to do with the unrefined activity of exchanging money that it falls to women to wield control over this aspect of family life.[9]

A woman is also judged to be powerful if she is a community organizer, successfully orchestrating events behind the scenes for festivals such as the one mentioned in the opening of this essay. In essence, a woman is the source of energy and organization necessary for a man's world to remain prosperous and to appear effortlessly controlled. Should an event like a circumcision or a marriage fail in some way, some will blame the failure on the inability of the host's wife to organize behind the scenes, while others will lay blame on the host himself, speculating that he did not manage to choose the day properly or that he did not ensure the proper respect due the local spirits or the local dignitaries.

I once attended a *wayang* in Klaten where the marriage of the son of a local chicken soup salesman was being celebrated. At around 10:30 P.M. I was quite unexpectedly called from my place among the musicians where I was recording the performance. Led to the back of the house through the great flurry of food preparation, I was ushered into a small room where four somewhat threatening gentlemen were waiting. After an overly gracious greeting and some supercilious niceties, the questioning took on a more serious character, centering on my proper reporting to local authorities and threats of fines and deportation. Already a veteran of many *wayang* in Klaten, I had never before reported my presence when visiting this area, where people are quite accustomed to the visitations of foreigners, nor had I ever been approached in this manner. Angry at the less-than-subtle sexual innuendos these men had mixed into their questioning, I agreed that the best thing for me to do was to go home immediately and return the next day with photocopies of the appropriate papers.

The next day brought a flurry of early morning visitors from the village to my home, some twenty-five kilometers away. Along with the news that it would not be necessary for me to return to the village, there were many apologies and a variety of explanations for the unpleasant encounter of the previous evening. The majority of reasons proposed centered on the idea that the host and his family had not obtained the proper permission for a performance from the local village head. What this meant, I was told sotto voce, was that the host had not paid the bribe necessary to receive permission, so the village head decided to cause trouble. In other words, the host had failed in his duties to appease the powers that be, spiritual or otherwise, in the proper way. Another explanation, given by a female friend from the area, was that the wife of the host had had a fight during the preparation for the event with the wife of the man at whose request I had been summoned. Thus, according to her, it was a problem in the back of the house, the domain of the wife of the host, that was the source of my problems that evening.

Whatever the real reason for the harassment, given the inordinate amount of attention and time taken subsequently to ensure that I was not offended, it is clear that it was important to all concerned, male and female alike, that the event be remembered, if at all possible, as the flawless, gracious event for which the host family had hoped. Sifting through the explanations, apologies, and humorous anecdotes of similar events in different villages, two things became apparent: everyone who had an opinion on the matter attributed the mishap to a lack of proper behavior and respect on the part of the host, and in some cases of his bad-tempered wife; and, there was obvious delight taken by people not directly involved in the situation in discussing and poking fun at the host and his family, proof that the host would be judged, and judged unkindly, because of his failure to ensure the expected order. This anecdote shows the great importance placed on the male notions of proper respect and behavior to ensure control and order. However, proper behavior must come from both male and female sources in order to ensure smooth passage through an event.[10]

Representations of Women

The enunciated gender ideology in Central Javanese society depicts women as woefully incapable of achieving refinement and thus of participating as equals in male society. In stories and myths, all of which are included as part of the refined knowledge studied and considered by men, however, the representations of women are not those of lesser beings. Rather the stories emphasize the entirely female achievements and strengths of their main characters, who in some cases can rival men. The underlying assumptions about women in these stories are based very much on an acknowledgment of the importance of women and female contributions to society.

Representations of women in *wayang* stories are not as varied or as numerous as those of male characters. However, as is true for all *wayang* characters, when they appear in performances, they tend to be exaggerations of reality. Female characters range from coarse to extremely refined. Similar in kind to the male clown figures (Semar, Petruk, Gareng, and Bagong), the mother-daughter pair, Cangik and Limbuk, display nothing but the coarsest, most humorous, boisterous, earthy aspects of women and female relations. They are extreme caricatures of Central Javanese perceptions of village women.

At the other end of the spectrum are women like Dewi Wara Sri Kandhi and Dewi Wara Sumbadra. Sri Kandhi is an expert warrior who loves battle as much as a man. In the "final battle" of the *Mahabharata*, the *Bharatayudha*, she is given heavy responsibilities by her teacher, Arjuna. Although her controlled and expert ability in battle is characteristic of the most refined male warriors, Sri Kandhi's fiery temper proves that she does not quite have control over her emotions and that she is consequently less potent than a man of her formidable skills would be. From the male perspective, Sri Kandhi can compete with men in an activity that is absolutely male, but her inability to control her anger reveals her basic femininity. A more useful perspective for the purposes of this essay is the idea that Sri Kandhi can be considered by men to be equal to men in a male activity without discarding her essentially female characteristics, which include emotional outbursts of anger.

Sumbadra, an incarnation of the rice and fertility goddess Dewi Sri,[11] is demure and refined but is thought to have great spiritual power, as represented in her will of steel and absolute loyalty. She is captured by an ogre prince in whose clutches she kills herself before she can be taken by a man other than her husband. She is ultimately loyal and so epitomizes the quintessential role of the female, that of a fertile vessel, willing to store the seed of only one man, and thus preserve purity of the family line, even if this duty results in her own death. She also has the ability to gainsay her husband.[12] The spiritual strength obtained by Sumbadra through intense asceticism is not demonstrated, as male potency would be, through power over others in her environment. Rather, her feminine power is shown through a fierceness of loyalty to her husband and her responsibilities, sexual and otherwise, to him.

Carey and Houben describe one powerful representation of women that is often overlooked in discussions of power in Central Java. Women in their role as "vessels (*wadhah*) for the seed of man" can hold "vital legitimating power for a dynasty." Carey and Houben tell of two women, Dhedhes, Queen of Singosari, and the princess of Pajajaran:

> Both these women were so "hot" in the magical sense, that flames issued forth from their wombs, and only men of unusual potency were able to possess them. . . . Even the poorest man who was able to make her his own would become a supreme ruler. . . . The point about both of these women is that their superabundant power enabled them to confer suzerainty on suitably potent partners and guarantee the legitimacy of succeeding generations. At the same time the ability of their spouses to tame the uncontrolled and excessive procreative powers symbolized by their flaming loins meant that their destructive energies could be transmuted into a fertile and beneficent influence crucial to the cosmic harmony of the realm.[13]

This discussion has outlined the contradictions and inconsistencies between the spoken ideology of women and their representations in myth and history. In the case of the female *gender* player, the contradiction is not found in a comparison of the enunciated ideology of female *gender* players and their representation in myth (although some inconsistencies do exist there as well), but resides in the nature of the role itself. Female *gender* players are exquisitely female in the male milieu of *wayang*. Their style of playing, ignorant of and impervious to male notions of order and structure, is entirely female. Yet many men will quickly tell you that a *wayang* without a female *gender* player is missing something. How can a woman, exercising all of her feminine characteristics, musical and otherwise, be the primary interpreter for the *dhalang* as he describes all that is quintessentially male in Central Javanese culture? I believe that it is precisely the contradictory nature of the role that makes the female *gender* player, at least in the minds of some, an essential element in the performance of *wayang*.

Representations of Female Gender Players

The idea that women have wild uncontrolled powers that, when tamed by a sufficiently powerful male, can be turned toward creative endeavor has bearing on this study. Female *gender* players are usually married to the *dhalang* who use them as their primary accompanists. Although the *gender* player is serving the *dhalang* both as his wife and as his chief musician, her female presence as *gender* player can be seen to legitimate the power of the *dhalang*. His potency is shown to be great enough to control the creative drive, both sexual and musical, of this female musician. He thus "transmutes" her otherwise destructive powers and turns them toward artistic endeavor.

If this analysis seems extreme in the first instance, it is helpful to look at the similarities between stories told about three legendary female *gender* players and those about other mythical spiritually charged women in Central Java. I have chosen to use versions of stories as told to me by people rather than as taken from manuscript sources. The subtle shadings laid on the female characters by the tellers of these stories give important clues to how these women are perceived and what they represent.

THE STORY OF THE FIRST WIFE OF KYAI PANJANG MAS

This story about the first wife of Kyai Panjang Mas was told to me by Bapak Naryacarita, a *dhalang* from the area of Makam Haji, Kartasura. One evening after a discussion about the nature of female-style *genderan*, I asked him if he knew any stories about Nyai Panjang Mas, a famous female *gender* player credited with the preservation of Solonese[14] *wayang* as we know it today and who, I was subsequently informed, was actually the second wife of Kyai Panjang Mas. Bapak Naryacarita peered at me with eerie eyes, deep brown with misty grey-blue around the edges, and said with utmost seriousness, "I am descended from the first son of Nyai Panjang Mas, but let me first tell you of the Kyai Panjang Mas and his first wife."[15]

> Kyai Panjang Mas was the famous *dhalang* who served in the court of the most famous ruler of Mataram [a kingdom that covered most of the island of Java], Sultan Agung [ruled 1613–46]. Before he began to serve in the court of the sultan, Kyai Lebdajiwa, for that was his name at the time, was married, appropriately, to a talented *gender* player. Kyai Lebdajiwa and his wife performed frequently in the villages of the kingdom of Mataram for they were extremely popular. There was only one problem. Kyai Lebdajiwa was unable to consummate his marriage because his wife was so talented and so powerful that she had flaming loins. One evening, on one of his many expeditions into the villages within his domain, the sultan came upon Kyai Lebdajiwa in performance. The sultan fell instantly in love with Kyai Leb-

dajiwa's wife, the *gender* player, and he was suitably awed by the performance of Kyai Lebdajiwa. Both were immediately ordered to appear at the
court and to enter service there. Lebdajiwa was appointed *dhalang* of the
court. After this the sultan asked for Lebdajiwa's wife. Lebdajiwa agreed immediately because he was scared of her magical heat. In exchange, Lebdajiwa
was given a girl, already skilled at playing the *gender*, but still young enough
for her talent to be molded and shaped by Kyai Lebdajiwa.

Although he loses his wife, Kyai Lebdajiwa comes out as an extremely potent figure in this story, second only to the sultan himself.
The fact that Kyai Lebdajiwa was powerful enough to use (control) this
spiritually "hot" woman as his *gender* player is enough to prove his
considerable abilities as a *dhalang* and legitimates his assumption into
the service of the court. That he could not consummate his marriage to
the *gender* player and that he willingly gave her up to the sultan proves
both the spiritual strength and legitimacy of the sultan as well as the
refinement of Kyai Lebdajiwa. It is appropriate for Kyai Lebdajiwa to
demonstrate his refinement by recognizing and deferring to the greater
power of the sultan. Similarly, it is expected that Lebdajiwa would fail
in a situation that requires the spiritual strength of one as powerful as
the sultan. Were Kyai Lebdajiwa to have had the spiritual strength to
consummate his marriage to the *gender* player with the flaming loins,
surely the balance of power in the kingdom would have been threatened
and the rule of the sultan brought into question.

THE STORY OF NYAI PANJANG MAS

Bapak Naryacarita continued his story of the *gender*-playing wives of
Kyai Panjang Mas with the history of the girl, later to become Nyai
Panjang Mas, who was given to Lebdajiwa in exchange for the *gender*
player with flaming loins. Nyai Panjang Mas proved herself to be of
great importance not as legitimator of kingly power, but in the role of
mother and preserver of culture.

> Nyai Panjang Mas was taught everything concerning *wayang* and *karawi-*
> *tan* [music played on a *gamelan* ensemble] known to Kyai Lebdajiwa. She
> learned to accompany Kyai Lebdajiwa with excellence and she also became
> the first female *dhalang*. She is responsible for preserving the knowledge of
> *gamelan* and *karawitan* as it is known today in Surakarta and Jogyakarta, or
> the area of old Mataram.
> During the coup against Sultan Mangkurat [ruled 1646–76], son of Sultan
> Agung, Nyai Panjang Mas and her two sons were abducted by the rebels
> and taken to East Java. Nyai Panjang Mas performed frequently, keeping

alive the Mataram tradition as well as teaching her sons and other local children the arts of *wayang* and *karawitan*. Kyai Panjang Mas [Kyai Lebdajiwa became Kyai Panjang Mas after his visit to Nyai Lara Kidul's kingdom in the South Java Sea] married another *gender* player but apparently there were no children.

Nyai Panjang Mas was released when her sons were nearly grown. On her return to Mataram, she carried a collection of *wayang* stories that are now called *lakon timor*, eastern stories, or *lakon perempuan*, women's stories. [These stories are said to have more structure (*balungan*) than other *lakon* (stories). That is, more events are specified in the story outline and, because there is less time left for improvisation, the *dhalang* does not have to worry that he will not have enough material with which to fill up the night until dawn.][16] She also is said to have introduced one of the clowns used in Central Javanese *wayang* today.

Although the story is told differently in the *Serat Sastramiruda*,[17] according to Bapak Naryacarita, prior to the return of Nyai Panjang Mas from her captors in the East, Central Javanese *dhalang* used only three clowns: Semar, Petruk, and Gareng. When Nyai Panjang Mas was in East Java, she taught her children and other students to use only the two clowns who were popular in the East, Semar and Bagong.[18] When she returned to Central Java, Nyai Panjang Mas brought with her stories that included Bagong in the clown family. Bapak Naryacarita's summary statement on the issue of the clowns was that because Surakarta is in the middle between East Java and the rest of Central Java, it is appropriate that *dhalang* from this area use all four clowns. "It's like the marriage between Kyai and Nyai Panjang Mas," he concluded definitively.

Bapak Naryacarita continued his tale with a brief description of the fate of the sons of Kyai Panjang Mas.

Nyai Panjang Mas sent one son to follow in the footsteps of Kyai Panjang Mas and serve in the court of the descendants of the sultan and she kept one son with her. This is the son who later entered service in the palace that was subsequently built in Kartasura. She asked to be given land as compensation for the loss of her husband and this was granted by the sultan. I am descended from the first son, the one who followed in the footsteps of his father, Kyai Panjang Mas, and entered into the service of the sultans of Mataram.[19]

Bapak Naryacarita finished the telling of this extended story by drawing a genealogy that traced his ancestry to the first son of Kyai Panjang Mas. He made sure I had the correct spelling of all the names in the list. As I wrote, he sat nodding his head while thoughtfully and somewhat reverently repeating the list of names. Bapak Naryacarita is not alone in seeking legitimacy through a connection with this family of performers and, by extension, with the potent Sultan Agung. As the only sons of the most famous *dhalang* of the most powerful sultan, these are the talented *dhalang* to whom nearly all *dhalang* today in Central Java try to trace their ancestry and thereby legitimate themselves as carriers of the true and ancient tradition of Central Javanese *wayang*.

THE STORY OF NYAI JLAMPRANG

Undoubtedly one of the most powerful women in the mythology of the Javanese is Nyai Lara Kidul, the goddess of the South Seas. Associated with both life and death, regeneration and destruction,[20] Nyai Lara Kidul is the mistress of the rulers of Central Java. Their relations with her are granted the highest importance, as an appearance by Nyai Lara Kidul is often a sign of the legitimacy of the ruler. In stories about *gender* players that involve her, Nyai Lara Kidul is herself said to be a fantastic *gender* player. Here is the story of Nyai Jlamprang, the *gender* player who journeyed to the kingdom of Nyai Lara Kidul, as told to me by Bapak Kris Sukardi, the husband of a female *gender* player.

> During the reign of Sinuwun Pakubuwana the Fourth, there was a terrible epidemic. People struck ill in the morning were dead in the evening. Those who became ill in the evening were dead by the next morning. Scores of people fell victim to this terrible disease. One of those struck down was a *gender* player who served in the court of Sinuwun Pakubuwana. Her name was Nyai Jlamprang.
>
> It was believed that the spirits of all those who died in that epidemic were taken by the goddess of the South Seas, Nyai Lara Kidul, so that she could populate her undersea kingdom. When Nyai Jlamprang arrived, she met with Nyai Lara Kidul, who asked Nyai Jlamprang how she had served previously in the kingdom of Sinuwun Pakubuwana.
>
> Nyai Jlamprang answered in a straightforward manner that she had been a *gender* player for Sinuwun Pakubuwana and that she wished to be returned there immediately. Nyai Lara Kidul, herself a *gender* player, thought that it would be good to have another woman who could play *gender* in the kingdom. She endeavored to persuade Nyai Jlamprang that life would be good if she stayed in the undersea kingdom. She told Nyai Jlamprang that serving in the court of Nyai Lara Kidul would be the same as serving in the court of Sinuwun Pakubuwana because, after all, Nyai Lara Kidul was (and is) the most important mistress of Sinuwun Pakubuwana. Nyai Jlamprang would see Sinuwun Pakubuwana everyday.
>
> Realizing that she had not yet been sufficiently enticing, Nyai Lara Kidul began to teach Nyai Jlamprang to play the *genderan* for *gendhing ladrang*

Gadhung Mlati, one of the sacred pieces associated with the kingdom of the South Seas. Nyai Jlamprang, who was very clever, quickly learned the piece offered by Nyai Lara Kidul but still insisted that she wished to return to the service of Sinuwun Pakubuwana.

Understanding that she had not been able to persuade Nyai Jlamprang to stay with her, Nyai Lara Kidul conceded and allowed Nyai Jlamprang to return to her world. Before leaving, Nyai Jlamprang was given tumeric and ginger as provisions for the journey back.

Like a *wayang,* these events occurred in the time of one full night in the kingdom of Sinuwun Pakubuwana. Nyai Jlamprang's family had finished the ritual washing of her body with flower-scented water. As they prepared to take her to the burial ground, suddenly Nyai Jlamprang's body shuddered ever so slightly and she awakened. Her family was stunned and frightened yet happy to see that Nyai Jlamprang had returned to life. As she sat up, Nyai Jlamprang found that the provisions supplied for her journey had miraculously turned into gold and silver.

When Sinuwun Pakubuwana heard that Nyai Jlamprang had awakened from the dead, he called her for an audience so that he could question her. She explained that she had been called by Nyai Lara Kidul to become a servant at the court in the undersea kingdom. Nyai Jlamprang explained that she had been loyal to Sinuwun Pakubuwana and that she had learned the *genderan* for *gendhing ladrang Gadhung Mlati.* Sinuwun Pakubuwana urged Nyai Jlamprang to play the piece and he was duly impressed.

To this day, because of its associations with Nyai Lara Kidul, the kingdom of the South Seas, and Nyai Jlamprang, the performance of *gendhing ladrang Gadhung Mlati* is considered a serious event and is preceded by the presentation of offerings and the burning of incense.[21]

During her sojourn to the kingdom of the South Seas, Nyai Jlamprang exhibits attributes similar to those of Sumbadra and other strong-willed women of refinement. She is absolutely loyal to her ruler, Sinuwun Pakubuwana the Fourth. No amount of persuasion from Nyai Lara Kidul is enough to convince Nyai Jlamprang to remain and revel in the delights of the spirit world. She insists in a polite but straightforward manner that she will return to the service of the Sinuwun. At the same time she does not return home empty-handed. She brings wealth of both musical and monetary worth. In this sense she is the bearer or preserver of music and wealth, both of which are creations of the goddess, who is herself associated with creation as well as with preservation and destruction.

Another interesting interpretation of this story springs from conversation with Bapak Kris Sukardi about his analogy of the events in this story to those of a *wayang* (see above). The events in this story are said to have taken place during a single night. Nyai Jlamprang dies and by the next morning, as her family prepares her body for burial, she awakens. During the night she works continuously in an effort to gain her release. She neither eats nor drinks during her stay or on her return trip to life. And, when she finishes the night's ordeal, her provisions have turned to gold and silver; in essence, she has been paid for her efforts. In the telling of this story, Bapak Kris made sure that I understood the gold and silver were a great boon: "Think of all the food that could be bought for that amount of gold and silver!" (*Emas, peraknya banyak, bisa beli makanannya, kok banyak!*).[22]

In some ways this version is a hungry man's interpretation of a story that if told by a wealthier, more historically concerned person might have included discussion of the importance of the realm of the Sinuwun as represented in the presentation of the gift of a piece of music created by Nyai Lara Kidul, the bestowal of wealth on one of the subjects and the testing of the loyalty of that subject to the ruler, and, consequently, a testing of the power of the ruler. In his telling of the story, Bapak Kris brings the story down to the ground and enunciates the attributes that are valued in a female *gender* player of Java today. She must work continuously (that is, accompaniment must be played throughout the *wayang*); she must not eat, drink, or socialize in any way; and then she must collect the payment for the performance. (It is frequently the wife of a *dhalang* who negotiates date and price for a performance as well as collects payment after the performance.)[23]

All three stories emphasize the role of the female *gender* player as one that is filled by extraordinary women endowed with all the attributes of female potency. How do these mythical representations relate to the ethnographic reality of the female *gender* player today and the nature of the female style of performance? Why is female-style *genderan* preferable to that played in male style in the opinion of many performers and observers?

Musical Accompaniment for Wayang

The *gender* is the only instrument that is essential to the performance of *wayang*. Many of the musicians I spoke with agreed that although it would sound strange and incomplete, a performance of a *wayang* with only *gender* accompaniment would be possible. Considering the fact that in Balinese *wayang* the musical accompaniment consists of two *gender* and nothing else, it is not difficult to imagine that Central Javanese *wayang*, too, may once have used only the *gender*. In Central

Javanese *wayang* the *gender* should be played continuously as it is responsible for keeping the mode and the scale in the ear of the *dhalang*, who orients both his speech and sung recitation to the *gender*. The music played on the *gender* should reflect and enhance the mood or feeling (*rasa*) evoked by the *dhalang* through dialogue and narrative. "Without the *gender* the performance is naked and must run from the audience,"[24] is the way one musician imagined the proposition of *wayang* without *gender*. In the words of an old *dhalang*, "The *gender* makes the spirit of the story come alive."[25]

The musical accompaniment for a *wayang* performance consists of several kinds of music. Only one of these, *gendhing* (in its most general meaning), requires the use of the entire gamelan. There are three different types of *gendhing*. There are long, quiet pieces in several forms (*gendhing, ladrang,* and *ketawang*) during which the *dhalang* typically speaks in narrative style to move the plot forward or to wax philosophical. He may also use this time simply to rest while the music keeps the attention of the audience. There are short, repetitive pieces (*srepegan* and *sampak*)[26] to accompany large-scale movement of puppets on the screen (walking or journeying), battle scenes, and other tense moments. Last, there are playful melodies (*dolanan*) and other forms featuring vocal melodies (*jineman* and *palaran*) to entertain the characters in the story as well as the audience, who may sometimes request specific songs.

The two other kinds of music used in the performance of *wayang* are *suluk,* the songs sung by the *dhalang,* and *grimingan. Suluk* are accompanied by some combination of the elaborating (*panerusan*) instruments, which include the *rebab,* a two-stringed, bowed lute related to the *rebec;* the *gambang,* a xylophone; the *gender;* and the *suling,* an end-blown bamboo flute. Although there is room for embellishment and elaboration, *suluk* generally have fixed text and melody. There is, however, no fixed tempo. And, while there is an internal pacing for the melodies that is dictated by convention and feeling, the pace in a particular performance is set by the *dhalang*. The players of the accompanying instruments must be flexible and react to the mood and musical choices of the puppeteer.

Grimingan is the musical accompaniment played on the *gender* whenever there is no other music required by the *dhalang*. As the *dhalang* spins out the tales of great warriors, their victories, their temptations, and their failures, the *gender* player must enhance the feeling of each scene while she keeps the mode in the ear of the *dhalang* and the mood of the moment in the ears of the audience. Although there is no space for an involved discussion on the nature and definition of improvisation, I suggest as a working definition that improvisation is the creation of music in a particular style at the moment of performance. This style must be recognized and defined through a collection of assumptions that are agreed upon by at least some of those who are familiar with the music. In terms of this definition, the performance of *grimingan* is a kind of improvisation.

If a *wayang* is an eight-hour event, the *gender* player will have to create *grimingan* for about four of those eight hours. In constructing *grimingan* the *gender* player can choose from a variety of sources. Each of the three modes around which the *wayang* performance is structured has at least one *grimingan* melody which is specific to it.[27] The *gender* player will usually start with this melody. As she must always be attentive to the mood or feeling created by the *dhalang*, the *gender* player can also choose to use parts from the accompaniment to a particular *suluk* (song) associated with an appropriate mood, or she can improvise in the mode by using melodic units that are predictable within the mode but whose overall order is not derived from any particular song. In *grimingan* and *suluk* the melody is structured around a series of pitches or arrival tones. A *gender* player expresses her creativity in the way in which she moves from one arrival tone to the next, tailoring her musical ideas to the dictates of mode, convention, and personal taste.

Male and Female Styles of Genderan: *Descriptions and Differences*

The differences between male and female styles of *genderan* are most strongly heard in *grimingan*. Female *gender* players are said to be more attentive than their male counterparts to the musical needs and emotional impetus of *dhalang*. They are said to be better at interpreting and enhancing the scene, while the music they play is more evocative of the spirit of the overall performance. When asked about how she created *grimingan,* one female *gender* player I interviewed said that she looked at the screen, felt the mood or feeling of the scene created by the *dhalang,* and then played without thinking about melody or mode. It was in this way that she could best accompany the story.[28] According to many of the people I interviewed, it is because of their attentiveness to the thoughts of the *dhalang* as demonstrated through the excellence of interpretation in their *grimingan* that female *gender* players are pre-

ferred by some connoisseurs of *wayang*. *Grimingan*, inspired as it
should be by the mood or feeling of the performance, conveys the very
essence of the story.

The following generalizations have been culled from interviews and informal discussions with a variety of people, including *dhalang*, male
and female *gender* players, musicians from STSI (the government con-
servatory in Surakarta), RRI Surakarta (the government radio station
in Surakarta), the Mangkunegaran Palace, and several villages (Gom-
bang, Manjungan, and Dlimas). Female-style *genderan* is characterized
by an abundance of melodic ornamentation and elaboration in both the
left and right hands.

> During the *wayang* on 2 July 1991, "Ibu Pringga played continuously
> throughout the night, ceaselessly stringing together *kembangan*. At times,
> eyelids drooping heavily, her body leaning ever so slightly to the left, she
> appeared to sleep, but she never stopped playing."[29]
>
> "When women play they use lots of melodic ornamentation. When men
> play they do not use any."[30]

Javanese refer to these ornaments as *kembangan* or *bunga-bungaan*,
both of which can be translated as "flowers" or "flowerings." Because
of the ebullience of this ornateness, female *genderan* is not considered
to be *alus*, refined and controlled. Female playing is highly valued for
its continuousness, a result of the abundant *kembangan*. Female players
are thought to be diligent and hardworking in their support of the *dhalang* as they strive constantly to interpret the mood of the scenes he
creates. Female-style *genderan* is believed to emerge from the depths of
the woman, directly from the source of her emotions as a reaction to
the feeling (*rasa*) of the scene or the piece of music (*gendhing*).

Whatever the actual state of their knowledge of modal theory
(*pathet*), it is hypothesized that women are not able to understand the
orderly modal rules that help a male player control and perfect his playing. It is assumed that a male player has the same feelings and reactions
to a scene or *gendhing* that a woman would have, but he has learned to
control his feelings and to express them in a controlled and beautiful
manner dictated by learned rules. There is great admiration for male
players who manage to express themselves beautifully with full feeling
on the *gender* because this means that they have advanced to such a
degree in their understanding of mode that the true essence of the
mode is expressed as if there were no order imposed upon it.

Javanese musicians usually describe male-style *gender* performance as the antithesis of female style. While female style is full of *kemban-gan*, male style is less ornamented. The left and right hands bear equally the melodic distribution, frequently reaching arrival points together. In female style the left hand usually plays extended melodies that span the entire range of the *gender* and the right hand plays intricate time-keeping patterns. The two hands rarely reach arrival points together. Because the melodies are not overly ornamented in male style, the listener can more fully appreciate the melodic and modal intentions of the *gender* player. According to most players, the *cengkok* (movement from one arrival point to another), *wiletan* (melody used for the *cengkok*), and *garapan* (interpretation of these melodies) are clearer in male style.[31]

A variety of reasons are given to explain the relative lack of melodic ornamentation in male-style *genderan*, ranging from an overriding concern for modal clarity to conjecture on the relative suppleness of male wrists. Whatever the reasons for this lack of ornamentation and however beautifully they may play, male *gender* players do not create a flowing, ceaseless line of melody as women do when accompanying *wayang*. The atmosphere that they create is neither as rich nor as evocative of the feeling of the story spun out by the *dhalang* as that of female performers. Because of this and because a male player may occasionally stop to eat and smoke or be obliged to break concentration for an exchange of pleasantries with passing visitors, male players are not thought to be as attentive to the needs of the performance as female players.

> The difference between the male and female styles of *gender* performance is that male style can be notated. Female-style *genderan* cannot be written down. If a woman is playing, her attitude is playful and flirtatious. Men cannot do this.[32]

> When women play *gender* they are diligent and zealous, knowledgeable, enthusiastic, they play continuously. If a man is playing, he will stop and eat or smoke. If a man is playing, *dhalang* do not like it because they do not use special melodies for *grimingan*.[33]

Unlike female players, male players pride themselves on a knowledge of the *pathet* system and the characteristics of the individual *pathet*, which female players rarely find necessary to consider beyond its importance to the structure of *wayang*. Male players vigorously discuss various interpretations of pieces in which the modal orientation is not immediately clear. Male players who do not have some understanding of the intricacies of the *pathet* system frequently apologize for this, often implying that they are not yet complete musicians or that they hope to study and become so in the future. Many male *gender* players also either spend time thinking about the seldom-performed, esoteric pieces from the court or speak in awe of those who do command this knowledge.

Along with knowledge of the system used to classify and organize mode comes the notion of learned knowledge. It is certain that a person who speaks easily about *pathet* or knows the interpretations (*garapan*) of the esoteric pieces mentioned above has had some training or has made an effort to learn about these concepts. They are not concepts that are necessarily included in the knowledge of a person who has learned through a lifetime of immersion in the world of *wayang* or *gamelan*, a state referred to as "still natural" (*masih alam*, that is, unschooled).

Female *gender* players are rarely able to discuss their reasons for choice of a particular melodic or modal interpretation beyond the inimitable notion of feeling, or *rasa*. They seldom use words like *cengkok* or *wiletan*. They pride themselves on the fact that they have learned everything they know by ear through listening to other musicians. They are *masih alam*.[34]

Another means of showing learned knowledge is an understanding of and ability to use notation. Women players rarely can read notation of any kind. It is commonly believed that female-style *genderan*, unlike that of male players, cannot even be notated with accuracy.

> In male style there is no inner essence (*intisari*) nor are there any ornaments (*sari-sari*, another Javanese word for flower). It is too simple. It can be notated and it is more regular and ordered (*diaturi*). In the past my mother was my favorite accompanist. Now I have to use a male player because there are no women left who know my style.[35]

In actuality, neither style can be notated accurately with the cipher notation system commonly used for Central Javanese music. That, however, is not the point.[36] Rather, what emerges from this comparison between what is said or believed about male and female styles is the clear tendency to connect men and male style with the notions of order, control, refinement, learned knowledge, the court, and its rules of hierarchy, aspects that are valued by men in the male world. Women and female style are associated with uncontrollable disorder, untaught knowledge, and expressed emotions, aspects that are frightening to men precisely because of their unpredictability. It is because women are not concerned with their status vis-à-vis the male valuation system or any of the other structures designed for the imposition of order that they are not constrained by the notion of refinement nor do they worry about musical order beyond the rule of *rasa*. Although they are playing music in a male environment, among men, they are not personally controlled by rules of male social or musical order.

Female Gender *Players and* Dhalang

To return to the description of the opening moments of the *wayang* on 2 July 1991, Ibu Pringga herself behaves in an entirely unrefined manner. In the first instance she is smoking. Women in Central Java are not supposed to smoke, as it is considered unrefined. On a more general level, Ibu Pringga addresses the *dhalang* in low Javanese. Although this man is her younger brother and so in a relaxed home setting they might speak low Javanese together, the fact is that they are adults in a public place and that Bapak Suparno is in his role as a *dhalang*—a respected, learned man, preserver and teacher of all important Central Javanese cultural ideas. Were Ibu Pringga a man, younger or older, an awareness of the public situation would almost certainly demand that she address him in some form of high Javanese. Because she is a woman and, consequently, not concerned with status (his or hers) she addresses him in the language that is most comfortable. Her relaxed manner, the loudness of her voice, the maternal chidings and teasings of fellow musicians and, more importantly, the seriousness with which she turns to the *gender* when it is time to play are all essentially female or, more explicitly, nonmale characteristics in the dominant male perceptual realm of Central Javanese society.

Ibu Pringga approaches the performance of *gender* with the same sense of freedom she shows in social interaction. She is not bound by the rules of *pathet* or the need to be *alus* in her ornamentation style. She is free to interpret the feeling and mood of the *dhalang* as the spirit moves her. In her *grimingan* or accompaniment of the spoken sections of the *wayang* she is free to invent musical ideas for specific actions and moods. According to Bapak Kris Sukardi, the fact that male *gender* players do not do so is reason enough for some *dhalang* to prefer female *gender* players. Ibu Pringga is able to immerse herself in the *wayang*. She is not bound by convention as a man would be to stop and chat and acknowledge friends who want to greet her. If she is concentrating and ignores someone who tries to get her attention, she will be excused because she is not absolutely expected to play by the rules of etiquette. However, Ibu Pringga does have the reputation of a female *gender* player to uphold. She will not stop playing for the purposes of eating or conversing and she will play continuously and mellifluously, committing herself to the expression of the spirit of the story through music.

Female *gender* players have a vitality and an energy in their perform-ance that is lacking in the playing of male players. *Dhalang,* although they themselves are greatly concerned with respect and refinement, are primarily performers. They understand that the spirit of a *wayang* per-formance lies in the interplay between the music and the story. The *dhalang* needs smart musical people in his orchestra, people who can react in an instant to his every thought and wish. A *gender* player who is sensitive to the mood of the story, one who is free to devote herself to the performance and who is free to be creative in improvising accom-paniment—one whose existence is not bound by the ordered conven-tions of Central Javanese culture—is indispensible. One could argue that it is precisely because women do not have to be *alus* that they are highly valued as *gender* players.

But can it be only musical freedom that, in the ears and minds of the male connoisseurs of Central Javanese *wayang,* justifies the presence of a woman instrumentalist? Why is it that the female *gender* player is given special status as shown through her inclusion among men as an integral participant in an event that is largely by men for men and ex-presses the male worldview of Central Javanese culture? The only other female performers included in every *wayang* performance are the *pas-indhen,* or female vocal soloists. At each *wayang,* and indeed in most performances of Central Javanese *gamelan* music, *pasindhen* are the stars of the show. Displayed prominently in front of the *gamelan* dur-ing musical performances or just to the right of the *dhalang* and close to the screen during *wayang* performances, the *pasindhen* are designed to be lusted after in both a visual and aural manner.

Dressed in elaborate and tightly wound traditional dress, bedecked in gold and sparkling rhinestones, *pasindhen* are flirtatious and delectable in every sense. Although today it is usually the case that a *pasindhen* will be more successful if she is attractive physically, it is still possible for a *pasindhen* to be successful if she is unattractive, especially if her voice is exquisite. It is said that the mere sound of a skilled *pasindhen* is enough to evoke the essence of the refinement and charm of a beau-tiful woman. Whatever their own thoughts on this topic, these singers are an object of sexual desire for every male within earshot. In the male worldview, *pasindhen* are sexual creatures, mysterious in their own way, but entirely controllable as sexual subordinates.[37]

In contrast to the *pasindhen*, female *gender* players dress in neat but ordinary traditional dress. Occasionally they may add a necklace or bracelet but it is not a necessity as is the bejeweling of a *pasindhen*. The nature of the way in which she sits at the *gender* and the technique used to play it dictate that a female *gender* player not wear rings or other heavy ornaments on or near her hands and that she not wrap her *kain* (lower portion of the traditional dress) too tightly. More important than the simply functional limitations on her dress, the female *gender* player does not dress to be noticed. She sits among the male musicians where she works harder and is more closely connected with the performance than any of the other musicians.[38] If she wishes, she may cultivate a quiet reserve in her role as *gender* player, although she usually establishes a mood of joking camaraderie with the other musicians. But there is no sexual tension. A respectful distance is kept between the female *gender* player and the male musicians.

This lack of sexual tension between men and women is rare in Central Java (or even elsewhere in the world!). In the case of the female *gender* player, there are several possible explanations. From a purely locational perspective, the *gender* player, sitting behind a horseshoe of chest-high *gender*, is visible only from the neck up. She is simply out of reach and almost out of sight. Still, distance does not prevent musicians and even audience members from a bit of innocent flirtation with the *pasindhen*. From the point of view of male-male relations, it would be audacious, not to mention disrespectful, to lust openly after the *gender* player, as she is usually the wife of the *dhalang* or at least a member of his family. However, when it is a *pasindhen* who is married to the *dhalang*, flirtatious advances may be dampened but are not absent. It is also possible that, as the female *gender* player is the *dhalang's* main musical support, she is never idle or looking around for someone with whom to chat. Constantly playing, she has no time for the empty sexual banter that frequently occurs between the *pasindhen* and the musicians or, more publicly, between the *pasindhen* and the puppets (that is, the *dhalang*).

Rather than any of the reasons proposed above, I suspect that the lack of sexual tension is a reaction to the perception that female *gender* players, unlike *pasindhen* who fit into a known and safe role in the male social order, are not sexual creatures, subordinate to or controllable by men. The female *gender* player is, in fact, a paradox. She is utterly female: unrefined, emotional, capable of intense concentration and endurance, and subordinate to the *dhalang* musically and sometimes socially as his wife. Yet, she is the *dhalang's* primary interpreter. She, a woman, understands more about *wayang* and the subtleties of the stories than do most of the men at the performance. It is through her that the essence of all that is exquisitely male and refined in Central Javanese culture is evoked.

If we look back at the myths offered above, they are not necessarily about female *gender* players. They are about legitimation: of the sultan, who shows his power by quenching the flames of the womb of the magical *gender* player, and of *dhalang* families in Central Java who can claim descent from one of the sons of the greatest *dhalang* who served the greatest king of all of Mataram. They are about the male power of the sultan, who can have the dark, powerful Nyai Lara Kidul as a mistress. They are also about the power of Nyai Lara Kidul, who, from the swirling, dangerous waters of her kingdom in the South Java Sea, can take away and restore life. They are about women so powerful and so talented that their wombs, the center of fertility and creativity, cannot be subordinated by any but the most powerful of men. And, these men, without the opportunity to control these powerful women, could not demonstrate the essence of their true potency nor could they legitimate their rule.

These myths link female *gender* players with the sources of female power in Central Java. Female power is dark (under the sea), emotional, unrefined, a mixture of evil and good, passionate, intense, loyal, and uncontrollable by all but the most powerful of men, and even they must be careful because of the great unpredictability of women. (Nyai Lara Kidul thinks nothing of causing a plague in her lover's kingdom to repopulate her own.) Female power is an essential balance to male power that is light (on earth), calm, refined, and controlled. Beyond the obvious need for women in reproduction, they are a major element of the structure supporting male power. Although she may begin as the vessel for the seed, musical and sexual, of the great *dhalang,* Nyai Panjang Mas is essential in both her legitimating and preserving capacities. She is the bearer of the seeds of Central Javanese *wayang* as we know it today. Nyai Jlamprang was the bearer of both riches and music. Brought to the kingdom through the sheer strength of Nyai Jlamprang's loyalty and her ability to gainsay her captor, *gendhing ladrang Gadhung Mlati* is one of the most sacred and important pieces used in rituals in the sultan's palace in Surakarta today.

It is in the performance of *grimingan* that the female *gender* player distinguishes herself from male *gender* players. Constantly attuned to the musical and emotive needs of the *dhalang*, her *grimingan* can be passionate, worried, delicate, love-stricken, enraged, or victorious. The *dhalang* depends on her creative reaction to and interpretation of his story. Through his refined understanding of language and his skill in moving the puppets, the *dhalang* can evoke all moods, thoughts, and actions, things verbal and visual, but it is through the *grimingan*, through the emotionally guided playing of the female *gender* player, that the essence of the puppets is lifted off the screen into the imagination, beyond the controlled, order-conscious mind of the listener, into the emotionally charged and essential realm of *rasa*.

When Ibu Pringga turns and begins to play her first notes of the *wayang*, to the person steeped in knowledge of Central Javanese stories and myths as all old-style *dhalang* and *wayang* lovers are, her presence as a female in a male world is not at all contradictory. Rather, she is the female element essential to the legitimation of male power, the *dhalang*, the potentate who controls the words and the puppets through which is displayed all that is important in Central Javanese culture. She is the subordinate, loyal support for the *dhalang*, the person who can anticipate his thoughts and needs, musically and otherwise. Yet without her, the story is only male, cosmically unbalanced and ungenerative. She is the embodiment of fertility and creativity, musical and sexual. She is dark and emotional, unrefined and intuitive, dangerous to the male world and its refined order, but absolutely essential to it aesthetically, and otherwise.

A Layering of Representations

I was once seated on the periphery of a performance in Surakarta at the Taman Budaya Siswa where I observed the following scene. Two city youths arrived on a motorbike to watch the performance because they had heard that the *dhalang* was tremendously funny and talented at performing exciting fight scenes. Standing in front of me while combing back their hair, imperceptibly ruffled by their helmets, they had an extended conversation about the women on the stage. They first discussed the five *pasindhen*, arguing about whether or not any of them were attractive. After looking around some more they expressed surprise at seeing a woman behind the *gender*. They shrugged their shoulders in disbelief and left to saunter around to the side of the performance space to flirt with the daughter of the noodle vendor. These boys were not well versed in *wayang* lore and tradition, and their expression of surprise at seeing the female *gender* player, in ignorance of tradition, demonstrates in a direct way the notion of the layering of gender representations. To an observer who does not know the context, a female *gender* player in the largely male milieu of a *wayang* performance is a puzzling sight. Without knowledge of the history of the *wayang* tradition as well as the accompanying stories and myths, a female *gender* player is simply a woman as defined by the ideology of the male worldview.

Because of the omnipresence of the male worldview in Central Javanese culture, it is possible to recognize one dominant ideology for women. In casual conversation with both men and women, this ideology will be enunciated. Women run the household; they are good with money; they are coarse and unrefined because refinement makes it impossible to do what they need to do to run the house properly. But, more importantly, they do not usually have the spiritual strength to deny themselves anything so that they can perform ascetic acts and thus gain power and refinement; they rule their husbands in the house but they are loyal and serve their husband's needs and desires; and they are not generally interested in the cultural traditions of Central Java.

Over the surface of this general ideology are placed a variety of representations, depending on how deeply one examines the woman and the role she is playing. An hour before a *wayang* performance, a *pasindhen*, hair awry and garbed in the bleakest of housedresses, could be having an extended argument with her husband about the whereabouts of his last week's pay while boiling yet another pot of rice for the five children clambering at her feet. However, the moment she steps onto the stage and assumes her role as *pasindhen* she becomes an object of desire for all. She is beautiful and glamorous, capable of arousing sexual desire in all men. The fact that she is a mother and has a husband is well known but is treated as a given because all women have these things. In some ways it makes her representation as sexual object all the more delicious, knowing that she is sexual and fertile and that her sexuality belongs to someone else. Longing for her from a distance, in full knowledge that one can not have her, only increases her delectability.

The layering process is similar for the female *gender* player. She is known by the villagers and the performers to be mother, sister, aunt, or cousin to nearly all of the members of the ensemble. Her role as guardian of the finances and schedule of the *dhalang* are acknowledged. However, to a connoisseur of *wayang* and *wayang* tradition the moment she steps behind the *gender* she is associated with the destructive and recreative power of Nyai Lara Kidul, the loyalty of Nyai Jlamprang, and the preserving, legitimating powers of Nyai Panjang Mas. She is unconcerned with, and therefore subtly threatening to, the refined, ordered, controlled male world.

Conclusion

In the dominant gender ideology of Central Java, female attributes are considered to be inferior to those of men, and women themselves to be subordinate. But as seen in the representations of women and, more specifically, in the performance role of the female *gender* player, women and female attributes are recognized as essential to the balance of social forces in the world. Female *gender* players exhibit female characteristics in both their behavior and their playing. Instead of being excluded from the *wayang*, in which male values and philosophy are expounded, female *gender* players are seen to be essential to the performance precisely because of their femaleness. They are in the contradictory position of being both subordinate to and yet empowering male authority. It would seem that in the Central Javanese myths about male and female empowerment, there is usually a balance, not a competition between male and female for power. If such a balance is woven intricately into the culture, it is probably not the case that subordination of women and female attributes is based on an inherent, Central Javanese male "fear" of female power. The contradictions in female status that exist in Central Javanese society today may result from the confrontation between new views and traditional ones, when colonialization and modernization clashed with the balance of power as reflected in the Central Javanese myths.

3

The Drum-Dance-Song
Ensemble: Women's Performance
in Biblical Israel

Carol Meyers

The mention of drummers in today's world inevitably evokes an image of male musicians. Certainly female percussionists exist; but, whether for rock combos or symphony orchestras, we tend to think of men, not women, sitting with drumsticks in hand. Has it always been this way? And is it this way in other cultures?

Such questions are evoked by feminist considerations of gender roles. Investigating the roles of women and men in society involves discerning which tasks become identified in specific cultures primarily with one gender rather than the other, and determining whether there are any cross-cultural patterns in such identification. It also means seeking to understand the significance of gendered behavior, and establishing the meaning of specific activities for the lives of those who perform them.

In the case of ancient Israel, such issues arise specifically in relation to musical traditions because of the existence of certain data that confict with contemporary notions of percussionists and gender. These data consist of archaeological materials—Iron Age terracotta figurines depicting women drummers—and references in a number of biblical passages to women playing drums. These artifactual and textual sources have long been known to archaeologists and biblical scholars. However, if examined in the light of scholarship that explores the dynamics of performance in relation to the gender of the performers, they are a source of new information about women's lives in ancient Israel. They offer the possibility of recognizing that women played a prominent and formative role in the musical traditions of biblical antiquity.

The Terracottas

Long before pottery was invented at some point in the Neolithic period, figurines of clay were being produced at widely scattered sites in the ancient Near East. The tradition of fashioning terracotta figures—of animals and humans and, probably, of deities—was evidently such a familiar aspect of life in antiquity that the biblical imagery of creation includes God forming a human figure from a lifeless earthen lump. The ancient art of coroplasty (the modeling of clay figures or statuettes) seems to have flourished in Palestine in the biblical period. Although an up-to-date catalogue of Palestinian terracottas does not exist, it is well known that small terracotta figures have been discovered at virtually every site with Iron Age settlements.[1]

Among the corpus of ceramic renderings of humans from Palestinian sites, figures of females are far more numerous than those of males. The identity of these female figures is difficult to establish. Many archaeologists have been quick to label them as fertility figurines; others see them as deities, a view that current feminist adherents of goddess worship would espouse. However, such statements about the nature of these terracottas must be seen as speculative.[2] Indeed, within the general category of small clay statues of female figures, there are wide variations of manufacture, style, decoration, pose, accompanying objects, and other aspects of form. Subtle differences in any of these variables must be taken into account in analyzing these artifacts. The issue of identity—calling them deities, priestesses, female votaries, or ordinary women—as well as that of function is far from being resolved for the terracottas unearthed in Palestine and elsewhere in the ancient world.

Within the plethora of terracottas depicting females, one type is notable for its possible connection with several biblical passages dealing with women and also with music. This type, a group of clay statuettes representing female percussionists, constitutes archaeological evidence that can be examined, in conjunction with analysis of biblical texts, to provide information about the role of women in the apparently rich musical tradition of ancient Israel.[3] These objects (see Figures 3-1 and 3-2), like almost all of the larger group of terracottas to which they belong, are relatively small, ranging from eight to twenty centimeters (three to eight inches) in height. They feature a female standing and holding a disc-shaped object in front of her, usually perpendicular to her body. The object rests on one of her hands, and her other hand is pressed against the flat side of the disc.

Figure 3-1. A typical terracotta figurine depicting a female musician playing the hand-drum. This example, featuring a hand-modeled head attached to a wheel-made base, is approximately 8.5 in. tall. The disc the woman is holding is a hand-drum, which is supported by her left hand and struck with the open fingers or palm of her right. This particular statuette was acquired in Palestine in 1907 for the Harvard Semitic Museum, where it is now on display. Presumably it is Palestinian in origin, although its place of discovery is unknown. Photograph by Sharon White.

Figure 3-2. Another example of a ceramic figurine depicting a woman holding a hand-drum, this terracotta is from the excavations at Amathus in Cyprus. Approximately 9.5 in. high, it is buff-colored with simple painted markings. The woman's hair is thickly braided. She holds the hand-drum in her left hand and is striking it with the flat palm of her right hand. Reproduced by permission of the Director of Antiquities of Cyprus and the Cyprus Museum.

Many similar terracottas depict figures holding recognizable musical instruments, such as a lyre or double flute.[4] Therefore, these females holding discs can be identified as musicians with considerable certainty. Furthermore, the discs held in the manner described[5] no doubt represent a kind of percussion instrument known as a membranophone, the term for instruments, such as drums, made of stretched hides that produce sound when struck.[6] Because these statuettes show a woman holding a small disc in one hand, the instrument can most accurately be called a hand-drum, that is, a hand-held version of a frame drum. The latter term designates a percussion instrument made by stretching a hide or skin (membrane), or two parallel hides, over a hoop or frame made of wood or metal.[7] A frame drum, as a type of membranophone, is thus distinguished from a tubular or vessel drum, which is made by stretching a skin over a hollow body of any shape or size.

The hand-drum represented in the terracottas should also be distinguished from a tambourine, which is in fact a combination membranophone and idiophone, the latter an instrument, like a rattle or bell, that produces sound by itself when moved. None of the hand-drums represented in these statuettes show any renderings of the small metal plates that would indicate a tambourine. Indeed, such attachments would not be expected, since the tambourine apparently cannot be authenticated as a musical instrument before the thirteenth century C.E.[8] Furthermore, in these terracottas the woman's hand is shown flat against the circular drum to indicate that she is striking the instrument with her palm or fingers. This pose could not signify the playing of a tambourine, which is typically played by striking or hitting it with the knuckles. Thus, although many excavators and art historians refer to these terracottas as "woman (or goddess) with tambourine," such labels are technically incorrect.[9] Similarly, the term timbrel, insofar as it designates a type of tambourine, is also a misnomer when used in reference to these ancient terracottas.

The hand-held frame drum is quite uniformly depicted in these figures, but the renderings of the women holding the instruments vary significantly. The variations include the way the figure is made, the kind of decoration that has been applied, and the style of dress or hair. In addition, there is a noticeable range in the level of artistry, with some figures being rather crude and unattractive, and others being quite finely modeled. The individual differences among the existing examples are critical for questions of provenance, of origin, and even of function. However, since those questions will not be of paramount importance for this discussion, the variations can be set aside; a general description of these objects, highlighting their characteristic features, will suffice.

Most examples of Iron Age terracottas of female frame-drum players are constructed of a wheel-made base, which forms a sort of trumpet-shaped skirt as pedestal, to which is attached either a hand-modeled or mold-formed head. The figure's arms, hands, and musical instrument are all formed by hand. Some small, rather crude, examples are entirely handmade, but most feature the composite technique. This composite technique may be an indication that the terracottas are the result of the workshop production of quantities of such artifacts rather than of individual artistry.

The hand-drummer terracottas are made of the typical buff or reddish clays of the east Mediterranean. Some examples are undecorated; others show evidence of simple black and/or red painted lines to indicate stripes or patterns on the skirt, sleeves, or bodice of the woman's dress. Her face is often colored red, as is the drum. The hair, which is sometimes painted black, may be braided, or it may be loose, full, and shoulder-length. Typically the bangs fall evenly across the forehead. The hairdo is quite simple, probably indicating that the woman's own locks and not a headdress or hairpiece are being represented.

The simplicity of the woman's garment is noteworthy, the few painted stripes notwithstanding. There are apparently no flounces, ruffles, pleats, appliques, bangles, or any other elaborate drapings or embellishments in the rendering of the hand-drummer's dress. Similarly, there is a marked absence of other decoration. These women musicians do not wear hats, crowns, wreaths, or other headpieces. Nor do they wear bracelets, necklaces, earrings, or any other items of personal adornment. The stripes painted around the necks of some examples are probably meant to depict the collar or neckline of the woman's dress rather than any piece of jewelry.

The rather plain costume and hairstyle of the typical hand-drummer figurine constitute a reasonable basis for supposing that these terracottas represent humans and not goddesses, for it is the elaboration of such aspects of adornment that distinguish plastic renderings of deities from those of humans. Furthermore, the almost total absence of adornment suggests that these musicians (like many other figures represented in the small terracottas) are meant to be ordinary people and not members of an elite group, such as royalty or cultic personnel, who were apt to be rendered with some decoration or insignia that would signify their status.

This focus on the simplicity of the terracottas depicting females with frame drums is helpful in understanding some of the confusion that exists in the attempts to identify various other terracottas. A very closely related group of figurines shows a female (or sometimes a male) figure holding a disc-shaped object, often erroneously identified as a "tambourine."[10] However, that object is clutched against the chest or rib cage; it is parallel, rather than perpendicular, to the body. Sometimes the object is decorated with a series of pebblelike impressions, painted dots, or scalloped edges; and the women who hold such discs are themselves adorned, or they are nude though bejeweled. Nothing in the woman's pose or in the object's design suggests that the woman is playing or holding a musical instrument. Still, it is difficult to identify the object in her grasp. Is it a cake or a round loaf of bread?[11] a sun disc?[12] a plate?[13] All of these possibilities have been suggested. In any case, these adorned disc-holding figurines, which perhaps are meant to depict deities, priestesses, or elite women, constitute a separate category of terracottas and are not to be merged with the hand-drummers.[14]

Another closely related group, which also tends to be confused with the group of women hand-drummers,[15] depicts very similar, simple figures holding disc-shaped objects perpendicular to the body. These objects look very much like the frame drums held by the female percussionists in the set of objects under consideration. However, the position of the musician's hands involves a significant difference: instead of one hand holding the disc and the other shown striking it, each hand is held against the side of the disc (see Figure 3-3). These discs, therefore, should be identified as cymbals, which belong to the idiophone category. Since other terracotta figures hold lyres (chordophones) and flutes (aurophones), the basic fourfold repertoire of ancient Near Eastern instruments would be incomplete without the cymbal.

The figures holding discs that are probably cymbals are likewise rendered quite simply but yet are noticeably different in some respects from the frame drummers. They tend to have some sort of cap or hat; they do not have long hair; and some have beards. Almost certainly these terracottas depict male musicians. Yet, much of the archaeological literature, in not noting the position of the hands of these figures, lumps them together with the women hand-drummers, so that it appears that there are terracottas of both men and women playing frame drums. While it has not been possible in preparing this study to examine firsthand all excavated examples, many of which are either unpublished or are published without photographs, removing the largely

Figure 3-3. This terracotta from Cyprus, although similar to Figs. 3-1 and
3-2, is different: it depicts a man holding a disc-shaped object between his
hands. The object, often mistakenly identified as a tambourine or a hand-
drum, is held differently from the latter and hence more likely represents a
pair of cymbals being struck. The musician has no hair but is wearing a headdress, perhaps a stylized wreath. This artifact (no. 74.51.1675) is part of the
Cesnola collection at the Metropolitan Museum of Art in New York and was
acquired in a purchase arranged in 1874–76.

male cymbal players from the corpus underscores the already clear gender pattern of the terracottas: a preponderance of females as hand-drummers. It would perhaps be going too far to state categorically that all figurines with membranophones depict women; but it is certainly legitimate to emphasize the dominance of women in this aspect of musical performance as preserved in the ancient coroplast's art.

A word about provenance as well as date is in order at this point. Although, as indicated above, female figurines in general have been widely found—in both sacred and domestic contexts—at Palestinian sites, the specific type under consideration here is not as ubiquitous at Iron Age sites, dating from the period of ancient Israel, as are the plaques or figures of nude females. Indeed, for the women hand-drummers, it is quite difficult to determine any pattern involving either their place of origin or their date. Many of the known examples have entered museum collections through the antiquities trade and not from legitimate excavation; hence the place where they were actually discovered is often uncertain. Even the excavated examples tend to come from the older field projects—those with less reliable stratigraphy and chronology than more recent ones. Nonetheless, it can be suggested that the Levantine examples of female hand-drummers come mainly from Phoenician or coastal sites (such as Tyre, Achzib, Shiqmona, Kharayeb) and that, in their classic form, they begin some time in the Iron II period (ca. 1000–540 B.C.E.) and continue well into the Hellenistic period (ca. 332–167 B.C.E.).

The paucity of Palestinian examples of these figurines stands in marked contrast to the hundreds that have been recovered from tombs, sanctuaries, and country shrines on the island of Cyprus. Enormous groups of terracottas from sites such as Ayia Irini, Kourion, Idalion, Meniko, and Voni depict both women and men in a variety of costumes and poses and holding a rich array of objects. Apparently part of the island's extensive native artistic tradition,[16] the Cypriot repertoire of terracottas flourished in the Cypro-Archaic period (700–475 B.C.E.), especially in the seventh and sixth centuries.

Despite the vast quantitative difference between the Cypriot terracottas and those found in the Levant, there is reason to believe that many aspects of the Cypriot tradition originated in the east. First, some of the Palestinian examples[17] apparently predate the flouruit of Cypriot production, terracottas being relatively rare in the Cypro-Geometric period (1050–700 B.C.E.). In addition, the use of the mold for parts or all of the terracottas seems to have been introduced to Cyprus, from Syria-

Palestine, by the Phoenicians.[18] The mold, long known in the Near East, had not been part of the age-old Cypriot terracotta industry until after the Phoenicians founded colonies on the island. Also, the appearance of many new types—the erroneously designated female tambourinist being one of the most popular—into the Cypriot repertoire apparently coincided with, and can be attributed to, Phoenician influence.[19] Finally, some specific stylistic features of the terracottas are said to be of "Syrian" or "Egypto-Phoenician" mode.[20]

In short, despite the voluminous quantities of female hand-drummer terracottas from Cyprus, this particular form as well as the technique of manufacture is almost certainly the result of Near Eastern influence via Phoenician colonization. Though it found exceptionally fertile ground in the indigenous coroplastic and religious traditions of Cyprus, the thematic as well as technical inspiration for many of the Cypriot forms apparently came from Syria-Palestine, the land in which the ancient Israelites emerged as a people in the early Iron Age.[21]

Biblical References

The possible Syro-Palestinian origins of the terracotta renderings of women playing the hand-drum is supported in biblical materials that link precisely this instrument with a female musical tradition. Just as virtually all the terracottas of hand-drummers depict females, the biblical references to membranophone playing exhibit a distinct connection with women.[22]

The Hebrew Bible has a rich vocabulary for musical terms. Dozens of different musical instruments are mentioned in the Bible, and these can readily be classified according to the three or four categories of ancient instruments.[23] At least nine kinds of stringed instruments (chordophones) are mentioned; a dozen or so wind instruments (aerophones) appear; and five shaking, scraping, or rattling types (idiophones; this would include cymbals) are mentioned.[24]

What is unexpected in the lexicon of biblical musical instruments is the fact that only one term for membranophones, or drums, is found. The word for drum is the onomatopoeic term *tōp* (pl. *tuppîm*), which is related to other Semitic words for drum (Assyrian *tuppu*, Aramaic *tuppa*, Arabic *duff*; cf. Sumerian *dup* or *tup*) as well as to Greek *typanon* (or, later, *tympanon*) and Latin *tympanum*. English translations of the Bible render the term variously as timbrel, tambourine, tabret, timbre, drum. Although the first four of these words are lexically related to *tōp*, from the perspective of the technical classification of musical instruments, they are not accurate translations of *tōp*.[25]

"Drum" is the best of the English renderings, but "hand-drum" would be preferable, since all sixteen biblical usages of this noun in reference to a musical instrument almost certainly refer to only one kind of membranophone: the small, hand-held frame drum. This is surprising, since other types of instruments are represented in considerable variety in the Bible. In addition, artistic and literary sources from both Egypt and Mesopotamia reveal that the range of drums known in the ancient Near East was considerable.[26] The ancient monuments and texts depict entire families of drums, yet the Bible mentions only one type.

The biblical texts in which "hand-drum" (*tōp*) appears can be divided into two categories.[27] One set, involving eleven passages, mentions *tōp* along with one or more other musical instruments. Most often the hand-drum is paired with the lyre, as in the Book of Genesis when Laban challenges his son-in-law Jacob for having taken his daughters away from their father's household, thereby not allowing him to give them a proper farewell celebration:

> Why did you flee secretly and deceive me and not tell me? I would have sent you away with gladness and songs, with *hand-drum (tōp)* and *lyre*.[28]

Similarly, the association of these two instruments with celebration is found in the words of the prophet Isaiah, who bemoans their absence at the time of God's judgment against sinful Israel:

> The gladness of the *hand-drum* is stilled,
> The noise of the jubilant has ceased,
> The mirth of the *lyre* is stilled.[29]

Although hand-drum and lyre are a prominent pair, the hand-drum is also mentioned with numerous other musical instruments, including in listings of six or seven different instruments. A notable example appears in the Book of Psalms, in a psalm of resounding praise for God:

> Praise Yahweh!
> . . . .
> Praise him with blasts of the *horn*;
> Praise him with *harp* and *lyre*!
> Praise him with *hand-drum* and dance;
> Praise him with *lute* and *pipe*!
> Praise him with clanging *cymbals*![30]

These passages together reflect a performance tradition that, when examined in reference to artifactual evidence from Syria-Palestine, can be called the "Canaanite (or Phoenician) Orchestra."[31] The gender of those playing the hand-drum is not specified in any of these texts. In several of them, the context would seem to indicate male musicians. For example, soon after he is anointed ruler over Israel, King Saul is told to go to a certain Philistine outpost, where he will meet

> a band of prophets coming down from the shrine with *harp, hand-drum, flute,* and *lyre* playing in front of them; they will be in a prophetic frenzy.[32]

Similarly, the entourage of King David included a variety of instrumentalists as well as singers and dancers:

> David and all the house of Israel were dancing before Yahweh with all their might, with songs and *lyre* and *harps* and *hand-drums* and *castanets* and *cymbals.*[33]

If these texts represent groups of male musicians, then the contention[34] that the hand-drum was exclusively a woman's instrument cannot be substantiated.

However, it is clear from artistic depictions of musicians recovered in archaeological excavations in the Near East that women as well as men played all the instruments in these Canaanite or Phoenician ensembles. For example, a bowl (see Figure 3-4) found on Cyprus depicts a group of women musicians, presumably Phoenicians, playing such instruments. Another relevant artifact is an ivory box, probably Phoenician in origin or inspiration, of the Iron II period of Assyria. Carved in relief on this artifact are three female musicians: the first plays the double flute, the second plays the hand-drum, and the third plays a stringed

Figure 3-4. A group of female musicians, commonly called a Phoenician (or Canaanite) Orchestra, as depicted on a silver bowl found on Cyprus and now in the British Museum. From left to right, the musicians are playing a double-flute, a lyre, and either a hand-drum or cymbals. This drawing is adapted from F. Behn, *Musikleben im Altertum und früher Mittelalter* (Stuttgart: Hiersemann, 1954), pl. 33, no. 76.

instrument that is probably a kind of zither.[35] These artistic representations lend support to the possibility that some members of the "Canaanite (or Phoenician) orchestra" could as easily have been women as men.

If there is some ambiguity, especially in light of the archaeological evidence, about the gender of the musicians mentioned in the first set of biblical references, the second set of passages containing the word for hand-drum reveals a distinct musical tradition in which only women are the instrumentalists. These five other uses of *tōp* not only indicate that females are playing the drums but also present these women in a performance context that is distinct from the "Canaanite orchestra" tradition. In these texts, the women playing drums are associated with dances (*mᵉḥolôt*) and also with song (explicitly in four of the passages; implicitly in Judg. 11:34). In each case the context involves celebration of the victory of the Israelite warriors and of God over the enemies. Perhaps the best example is the so-called Song of Miriam, which celebrates the Exodus event—specifically, the triumph of God over the Pharaoh's armies:

> Then Miriam the prophet, Aaron's sister, took a *hand-drum* in her hand; and all the women went out after her with *hand-drums* and *dancing*. And Miriam *sang* unto them:
> > *Sing* to Yahweh, for he has triumphed gloriously; Horse and rider he has cast into the sea.[36]

In this passage and the other related ones, the hand-drum appears with dance and song, and only women are involved. This configuration of features, absent from the first set of biblical references to the hand-drum (*tōp*), is consistent in the second. Furthermore, there are other texts, such as the Song of Deborah in Judges 4, in which music, a woman, and victory appear together and for which the use of a *tōp* can be inferred, given the rhythmic form of Hebrew poetry and song and the close association in folk tradition of both dancing and singing with a percussion instrument to establish the beat.

Taken together, the features of the second set of texts mentioning hand-drums reflect a distinct tradition of women's performance. A group of women are depicted singing, accompanied by drumbeat, with their celebration expressed in movement (dance) as well as in song. Although it is not certain that all the women in these performance groups are doing all three musical acts (singing, dancing, drumbeating), studies of the way traditional songs are composed and performed[37] suggest that the biblical women singers/drummers/dancers were part of a composition-performance tradition in which small groups of performers did in fact sing, dance, and beat the drum, using traditional choruses or refrains and also developing texts in response to a specific occasion.

Both the biblical passages and the Syro-Palestinian terracottas depicting women holding the frame drum reveal a distinct women's performance tradition involving the hand-drum. There are no other ancient textual references to such a women's musical genre, but the distribution of the terracottas would indicate that this genre should not be viewed as an exclusively Israelite phenomenon. Perhaps it can be called a Canaanite women's musical tradition.[38] Such a designation would account for the biblical references, insofar as the Israelites are to some extent the inheritors and transmitters of Canaanite economic, social, and cultural forms.[39] It would also account for the apparent dissemination in the material culture of a female drumming tradition, via the Canaanites or Phoenicians, to Cyprus. A similar tradition may have spread, also via the Canaanites or Phoenicians, to Egypt, where women dominate in depictions of frame-drum players from the New Kingdom onward (see Figure 3-5).[40]

The textual and artifactual materials are compelling in suggesting that this women's drumming and singing (and dancing) musical tradition originated in ancient Syria-Palestine. Yet the evidence is not entirely conclusive because of the Cypriot materials. The extraordinary flourishing of votive terracottas in Cypro-Archaic art, in which female hand-drummers are a popular subject, may indicate a separate, indigenous Cypriot folk music tradition of women performers. In such a scenario, the Phoenician influence would have brought technological and stylistic innovations that capitalized on already existing cultural forms.

Still, the prominence of the drum-dance-song ensemble in ancient Phoenicia, Canaan, and Israel seems clear. Furthermore, the difficulty in proving place of origin, course of development, and direction of dissemination should not detract from the fact that these artifacts and texts together can provide other kinds of information about ancient society. There can be no doubt that a distinctive women's performance tradition existed in the East Mediterranean in antiquity. And for ancient Israel at least, because of the survival of several biblical references to women's musical groups, something of the nature of that performance, and its meaning for the community and for women's lives, can be ascertained.

Women's Performance

Artifacts and texts establish the existence of a women's performance genre of drum-dance-song. In addition, the texts that refer to this genre

Figure 3-5. An Egyptian musical tradition featuring women playing the hand-drum, perhaps developed through Canaanite influence, is depicted on the stele, which is 8 in. high and 14.5 in. wide, of Rameses II (1301–1234 B.C.E.) from Abydos. Beneath a procession of priests and high officials, the lower register shows seven musicians—five female hand-drummers, one female rattle player, and one young, perhaps female, lyre player. These ensembles routinely performed in public at various festivals and celebrations and may also have been used, as in ancient Israel, to greet victorious warriors returning from battle.

contain information that allows for an understanding of its context and thus of the social dynamics involved. Implicit in the biblical passages mentioning women drummers, dancers, and singers are two salient features of the performance act. First, the Israelites expected that, following a military victory, the returning forces would be met by women who had the musical skills to regale them in a specific way. Second, the ensuing performance took place in a public context, before the leaders of Israel (Moses, Jephthah, Saul) and probably some of the returning warriors ready for joyous celebration. Each of these facts about the performance context can tell us something about women's lives if they are considered in light of recent trends in folklore research and in musicology.

Western values have tended to consider women's expressive forms nonlegitimate, or at least less important than men's forms. Virtually all the aesthetic productions in both art and music that have been formally and publicly valued have been works of men; it has been exceedingly difficult for women to achieve public recognition for expressive skills.[41] Thus the investigation of art forms in premodern, preindustrial societies, whether in the West or elsewhere, has all but ignored women's expressive forms. Being less visible, and being considered less legitimate, women's artistic endeavors have been accorded scant attention.

In recent decades, however, research that recognizes the existence and validity of women's experience and investigates aspects of gender both cross-culturally and historically has begun to provide insights into women's performance that had never before been available.[42] Studies of women and music in various cultures are still not plentiful, but some pioneering efforts have appeared.[43] It is becoming increasingly clear that women's performance needs to be examined as such.[44]

At the same time, the character of ethnomusicology, as the systematic study of the total music of the world, has changed from that of a largely descriptive enterprise to one that also examines music as an expression of social values. It is now recognized that music and society are cultural phenomena that are complementary and interdependent, so that investigating musical forms—and especially women's performance genres—should not be distinct from analyzing social structures and values.[45]

These two developments in the academy have led to the recognition that the expressive spheres of women and men are distinct though not necessarily separate or self-contained. Rather, they are two different and equally legitimate halves of music culture.[46] Feminist ethnomusicology, as it moves beyond the purely descriptive, thus investigates the relationship between music behavior and gender behavior. The nature of a society's gender structure impacts upon women's expressive forms, and those forms in turn reflect and symbolize gender structures.[47] That is, a feminist ethnomusicological perspective addresses the question of relationships between music, gender, and social roles and status.

The two features of Israelite female performance mentioned above can now be considered in light of this analytical perspective. The fact that returning warriors and leaders expected the drum-dance-song welcome has as its concomitant that groups of woman performers had to be prepared to respond. Preparedness demands a level of competence that could be achieved only if the women met (sporadically or regularly) to compose and rehearse, even if such preparations were flexible enough to accommodate the element of spontaneity involved in the celebratory response to a particular Israelite victory. In short, the evidence for female percussionists is also testimony to the fact that at least some women had regular contact with their female peers.

Who these women were or whether or not their age or marital status affected their ability to be part of a performance group cannot be ascertained. Yet, the drum-dance-song genre, like the equally significant lament genre associated prominently if not exclusively with women,[48] bespeaks the existence of women's groups. Anthropological research provides significant information about such groups. Women with no access to female groups often have a status little better than servitude, with their lives circumscribed by the parameters set by male authorities. But women who do have social ties with other women—who work with them in groups—enjoy much greater possibilities for enhanced status.[49]

Those possibilities can be realized especially if the women's groups transcend household or domestic life and operate in the public sphere, which clearly was the case for the drum-dance-song ensemble of ancient Israel. The opportunity for the elevation of female status also occurs in women's groups in terms of the internal dynamics of such groups, which typically have their own structures, values, and hierarchies, thus affording prestige to the participants in relation to their competence and accomplishments within the group itself as well as in public activity.

In general, when women group together for whatever purpose, and if they are recognized in this activity—as were the women performers in ancient Israel—the status of women within the society tends to be relatively high.[50] Despite general male domination, at least in public matters, women participating in gender-specific groups are able to exercise control of themselves and their worlds and thus enjoy a sense of power rather than powerlessness.[51] That power may not translate into all social relations, but it is nonetheless real and contributes both to the richness of the cultural expression of the group (performance in this case) and to the sense of worth of the members of that group.

Recognition of the interlocking nature of music, gender, and power can also be the key to understanding other implications of the public context of the drum-dance-song performance genre. Current concepts of performance involve consideration of performance as a two-part entity: it involves an artistic action—the creating or doing of an aesthetic production; and it also involves an artistic event, that is, a complex performance context comprising performer(s), expressive genre, setting, and audience.[52] The audience, no less than the performers, is critical to evaluating the meaning of the expressive act, for performance is in fact a mode of communication as well as an activated instance of an expressive form.

The notion of performance as communication involves an acknowledgment by the audience of skill and competence on the part of those who are performing. The leaders and members of the community of ancient Israel who expected female drum-dance-song ensembles to validate their victories in an artistic form and who watched their performance, were thereby acknowledging the expertise of the women as well as their essential part in concluding the complex series of events that constituted victorious warfare. The women performers would thus have been accorded a high measure of status; for performance has the capacity, at least for the moment of the communicative and professional activity, as well as in the anticipation of the event, to transform social structure.[53]

Women performers could exert this kind of control vis-à-vis the audience not only because of the social function of the performance situation but also by virtue of the intrinsic appeal of expressive events. A successful performance enhances the sense of connection between the audience and the performer, since the expressive act arouses the attention and thus the energy of those who witness it. Because this interaction derives from a communicative flow from performers to audience, a measure of control over the audience, and concomitant prestige, is experienced by the performers. That is, performance entails a general rhetorical power, as ethnomusicologists have demonstrated.[54]

Hence the women musicians of the Israelite drum-dance-song genre would have experienced a significant measure of both control and prestige, of an indeterminate duration, insofar as performance has the possibility to subvert existing hierarchies. Their public moments of power can only have enhanced or intensified the value already accorded to their expressive acts through the interaction of the women with each other within their specialized music groups, however informal such groups may have been.

How often these public moments occurred cannot be estimated. The biblical passages describing them cluster in texts dealing with the premonarchic period, a time when women had considerable social power.[55] However, the virtual absence of references to these ensembles in biblical texts coming from later periods need not be taken as an indication of the disappearance of women's performance groups during the monarchy but rather perhaps only of the increasing androcentrism of the biblical writers. And even if the nonregular performances of drum-dance-song ensembles did diminish over time, especially as the spectacular military victories that occasioned them ceased to occur, there is indisputable evidence that other women's performance groups, such as the women keeners mentioned above and also groups of women temple singers (Ezra 2:41; Neh. 7:44; cf. 1 Chron. 25:5), flourished in the late biblical period. Furthermore, one of the latest biblical books, Ecclesiastes (usually dated to the late third or early second century B.C.E.), contains a reference to "daughters of song" (Eccles. 12:4), a term that probably uses "daughter," just as "son" is used in a significant number of biblical passages,[56] to designate membership in a certain professional group.[57] Thus "daughters of song" means those who belong to a recognized group of singers.[58] Such an organized group probably even had guild status and the public recognition and acceptance accompanying such status.

However, to return to the archaeological data with which we began, the Iron II (monarchic) date of the terracottas of women drummers points to a tradition of women's performance, with the drum as a major component, that continued throughout the Iron Age and beyond. Indeed, in a musical tradition such as that of biblical Israel and of the ancient Near East, in which music was rhythmical rather than melodious or harmonious,[59] the drum provided the rhythm and so was the most important musical instrument. Women as drummers thus played a central role in Israelite musical tradition and probably throughout the East Mediterranean world.

Evidence in artifacts and in texts of women in association with membranophones spans the biblical period. It reveals the prominence of women in performance and thus the existence of ongoing opportunities for female prestige and power. Although most of the biblical corpus is androcentric in its recounting of the largely male public life of ancient Israel, a handful of texts mentioning women as musicians, along with the archaeological remains depicting women percussionists, provide another angle of vision on women's lives in biblical antiquity. It is now clear that women had access to sophisticated cultural forms and to important modes of participation in public life. Multidisciplinary analysis of literary and artistic materials allows us to reclaim these aspects of women's lives and of Israelite musical tradition.

4

Female Musicians
in Pharaonic Egypt

Emily Teeter

Music was an integral part of secular and religious life in ancient Egypt. Musicians appear in scenes of daily life, at banquets and festivals, and in the palace. Since the majority of the ancient Egyptian records have a religious function and are from the temple or funerary context, it is in those realms, rather than from a secular context, that musicians are best documented. This association of music with religion is emphasized by the many scenes in which male and female musicians appear at funerary feasts and processions or at festivals for the king and gods. Music was thought to have the ability to please and placate the gods, and musicians commonly held religious titles. Even the gods could function as musicians. For example, the deity Bes is frequently shown strumming a lute or beating a frame drum,[1] and the god Ihy is shown with a ritual rattle (sistrum). The Seven Hathors, a group of minor deities who appear at the birth of a child, sang to placate the goddess Hathor as they decreed the fate of the newborn.[2] Bands of female as well as male musicians were attached to temples in all periods of Egyptian history.[3]

Female musicians appear in many roles: as singers, as instrumentalists, both as soloists and in orchestras, and more rarely, as directors of music. The role of dancers will also be considered, since they are often portrayed in conjunction with musicians. Musicians are attested not only by representations on temples, tombs, stelae, and other classes of objects, but also through direct and indirect references in biographies, tomb texts, and honorific titles. Since the majority of the depictions of female musicians appear on painted or incised decorated surfaces of temples and tombs, they reflect the ritual function of musicians. However, on certain levels these scenes were meant to portray actions of daily life, and should not, therefore, be considered merely symbolic of the ritual sphere. As Davies has noted, "the distinction between life and life after death tends to vanish, since the dead may repeat as a spirit what he performed as a man."[4] Thus although "secular" musicians can be documented, the vast majority of our sources come from the religious, primarily funerary, context.

Documentation of musicians starts from the earliest periods of Egyptian history and extends into the Roman and Byzantine eras. These comments will be restricted to the pharaonic period, prior to the arrival of Alexander the Great in 332 B.C.E. Perhaps the earliest record of a musician of any gender is a portrayal of female dancers that appears on a fragmentary predynastic vessel. Four human figures, arms raised above their heads, are shown in an attitude which, from later sources, can be identified as a dance done by females to musical accompaniment.[5]

Female Musicians in the Old Kingdom (ca. 2524–2260 B.C.E.)

Male musicians and female dancers are well attested through textual references and portrayals from Dynasty 4 (twenty-sixth century B.C.E.).[6] Although there is a reference to a certain Hemre, a lady who was associated with the performance of music in the palace,[7] and titles refer to an organization of women known as "*mrt* singers of Upper and Lower Egypt" (Dynasty 4, ca. 2550 B.C.E.),[8] representations of female musicians do not become common until Dynasty 5 (ca. 2524–2400 B.C.E.).

In this period, female musicians are shown with a limited variety of musical instruments: the so-called shoulder harp,[9] percussion instruments such as frame drums, clapsticks, and the ritual rattle, or sistrum. Frame drums were made by stretching an animal skin over a wooden frame; clapsticks were sticks held in each hand and clapped together, and the sistrum was a type of rattle consisting of a U-form to which metal rods and small discs were loosely attached so that they jingled when the rattle was shaken. While women are depicted playing only harps and percussion, men are shown playing a much wider range of instruments including single and double flutes (like the Arabic *nay*), an oboe-like instrument (similar to the Arabic *zummara*),[10] as well as a range of percussion instruments. Virtually all musicians are portrayed either accompanying a singer or singing to their own instrument, leading Hickmann to conclude that in ancient Egypt, "Musik ist Gesang,"[11] and hence that the instruments were secondary to the vocal component.[12]

One of the most common roles for female musicians in the Old Kingdom was as harpist,[13] appearing either alone or with a vocalist to entertain the spirit of the deceased. As indicated by the hieroglyphic captions, the musicians may be unrelated to the family and are therefore presumably professionals hired for their services. One such illustration appears in the Dynasty 5 tomb of Nikawre and his wife Ihat at Sakkara (ca. 2505 B.C.E.; Figure 4-1). This stone relief, now in the Egyptian Museum in Cairo, shows a harpist and a female singer.[14] The hieroglyphic captions record the personal name of each woman, yet omit any familial connections, indicating that neither of them is related to the family for whom they perform.

The custom of a female member of the family entertaining the tomb owner is represented in many tombs.[15] One scene, from the tomb of Mereruka at Sakkara (Dynasty 6, ca. 2400 B.C.E.; Figure 4-2), shows Watetkhethor with her harp, seated on a low couch with her husband, Mereruka. Although the explicit reference "his wife" is missing from the caption, enough is preserved of her personal name to confirm their relationship. In other more completely preserved scenes, the harpist may be labeled as wife, daughter, or granddaughter of the deceased.

Figure 4-1. The harpist Heknut accompanying the vocalist Iti. From the false door in the tomb of Nikawre and Ihat from Sakkara (Dynasty 5, ca. 2524– 2400 B.C.E.). Egyptian Museum, Cairo, CG1414.

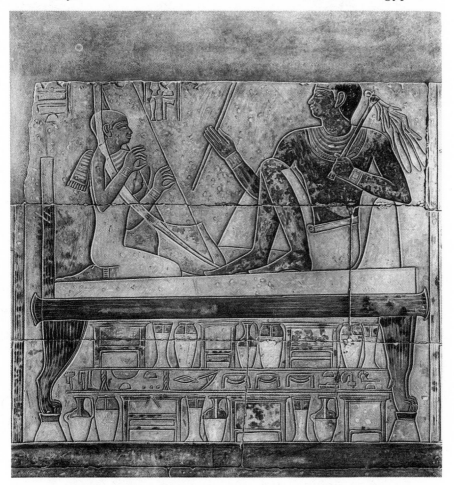

Figure 4-2. Watetkhethor playing the harp for her husband, Mereruka. From the tomb of Mereruka at Sakkara (Dynasty 6, ca. 2400 B.C.E). Courtesy of The Oriental Institute of the University of Chicago.

During the Old Kingdom, musicians are commonly shown in large orchestral scenes complete with dancers and singers. These groupings include both males and females. However, scenes portraying exclusively male orchestras are more numerous than ones showing female instrumentalists or mixed-gender bands. In interpreting the scenes with multiple participants, we must be aware of conventions governing ancient Egyptian art, particularly with regard to the segregation of musical groups by gender. In Old Kingdom orchestral scenes that include dancers and singers, the participants are usually arranged in several registers. Most commonly, the male band sits in one section of the scene, while the female singers and dancers occupy another. This arrangement has led some writers to suggest that men and women musicians were segregated during this period.[16]

The uncertainty in interpreting these sources is due to two differing conventions of Egyptian art for the organization of pictorial representations: objects placed higher in a scene may be spatially behind those in the lower register, or the same arrangement may indicate separate realms of time and space.[17] Although it is difficult to demonstrate a chronological development for the manner in which orchestras were arranged, the earliest scenes portray males and females on separate register lines. Yet, even when shown in separate registers, musicians and dancers may have been considered to perform together, as suggested by a scene from the tomb of princess Mersyankh III at Giza (Dynasty 4, ca. 2580 B.C.E.; Figure 4-3). Here the instrumentalists, who are all male, appear in the uppermost register before an oversize representation of Mersyankh. The band is made up of two harps, an oboe, and a flute. A singer, who perhaps also functions as a director of the music, is seated to the right.[18] The female dancers (seven figures with short, round coiffures, dressed in short kilts with arms upraised) and three women who sing and clap the rhythm appear in the lower register. Not only are the activities of the singers, dancers, and instrumentalists interdependent, with the dancers and singers responding to the music, but all the entertainers are tied together by their relationship to the double-register representation of the tomb owner. The perspective of this type of composition suggests that the dancers are performing in front of the orchestra, dancing in a line for the princess's inspection and enjoyment.

A similar scene appears in the tomb of Debhen at Giza (Dynasty 4, ca. 2548 B.C.E.).[19] In this example, the orchestra is made up of two harps, two oboes, a flute, and two singers. Four female dancers and three singers (and a dwarf!) appear in the lower register. The representation of

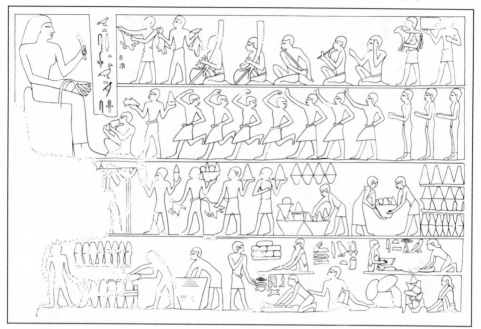

Figure 4-3. Dancers, singers, and musicians entertaining Queen Mersyankh. From the tomb of Queen III Mersyankh at Giza (G 7530-7540) (Dynasty 4, ca. 2580 B.C.E.). Courtesy of the Egyptian Department of the Museum of Fine Arts, Boston.

the tomb owner spans five registers, the upper three of which represent food offerings with no musical content.

More evidence for interdependence between musicians in different registers is found in the tomb of Nenchefka at Sakkara (Dynasty 5, ca. 2400 B.C.E., Figure 4-4).[20] In this scene, however, the male orchestra, including an oboe, flute, and harp, and the female dancers and singers are all shown on registers below the larger representation of the tomb owner. The hieroglyphic captions are more complete in this tomb, and the two women to the right are clearly designated as "singing," as are the four men shown without instruments in the register above them. These identical indications in different registers may suggest that men and women were simultaneously creating music for the tomb owner.

By the end of the Old Kingdom, this integration of male and female musicians is more explicit, with both genders being shown in the same register. One example showing a transition in the representation appears in the Giza tomb of Iymery dating from the end of Dynasty 5 (ca. 2477 B.C.E.).[21] In that scene, a long register portrays four female singers,

Figure 4-4. Relief from the tomb of Nenchefka at Sakkara showing a male orchestra playing for a line of female dancers and singers (Dynasty 5, ca. 2400 B.C.E.). Photograph courtesy of The Oriental Institute of the University of Chicago, used with permission of The Egyptian Museum, Cairo.

nine female dancers, and a male orchestra made up of a flute, an oboe, two harps, and four singers. Another scene in the same tomb shows female dancers and singers with a male harpist and singer, all on the same register.[22]

A relief from the tomb of In-Snefru-Ishtef at Dashur (end of Dynasty 5 to early Dynasty 6, ca. 2400 B.C.E.), portrays another step in the composition and organization of orchestras.[23] Here, the band is composed of a female and male harpist, a male singer, and a male oboe player. This relief may be the earliest example of male and female instrumentalists shown playing together in an ensemble. The female dancers are grouped into a register above the mixed-gender orchestra.

This integration of males and females in orchestras continues in Dynasty 6, as attested by a scene in the tomb of Idu at Giza[24] (Dynasty 6, ca. 2390 B.C.E., Figure 4-5). In the fourth register from the top of this intricate painting, seven musicians are shown: five female harpists, a

Figure 4-5. An orchestra composed of men and women entertaining Idu. From the tomb of Idu at Giza (G7102). Drawing courtesy of the Egyptian Department of the Museum of Fine Arts, Boston.

man playing an oboe, and a male singer-director. Unlike other tombs, where the orchestra is depicted adjacent to the dancers, the musicians are here separated from the dancers by an intervening register that shows men playing board games.[25]

This survey of scenes from the Old Kingdom suggests that male and female musicians were not traditionally separated, but that they performed together. Although it was only toward the later part of this period that artists depicted male and female instrumentalists side by side, their separation by register lines in the earlier paintings may indicate not so much a physical segregation as an artistic convention. There is evidence of gender roles, however. The many representations of musicians playing flutes and oboes consistently show men, suggesting that these instruments were exclusively played by men during the Old Kingdom.

Women are usually depicted with percussion instruments in the Old Kingdom, providing an interesting parallel to the drums played by Israelite women described by Carol Meyers in the preceding essay. But while the frame drum seems to have been the preferred instrument of the Israelites, Egyptian women are shown with a variety of percussion, including the clapstick, the *menat* (a beaded necklace whose strands were shaken), and the sistrum. The last two are associated with rituals of the goddess Hathor, whose epithets include "mistress of the dance" and "mistress of inebriety, of jubilation and of music,"[26] and who is herself associated with music, singing, and festival. Priestesses of Hathor from the Old Kingdom onward through Egyptian history often are shown carrying the sistrum and the *menat*.

In addition to these percussion instruments, there is evidence in the Old Kingdom for professional singers, the best known being Iti (Figure 4-1), who is shown in the tomb of Nikawre and Ihat, her hand to her ear, as she sings. Her other hand is lifted, apparently to conduct the harpist. This pose is still a tradition among vocalists in the modern Near East. Iti is known not only from the representation in the tomb of Nikawre and Ihat, but also from her own tomb and from textual references, prompting Hickmann to suggest that she was the first musician to have "star" status.[27] The vocal arts were central to ancient Egyptian music, and singers might perform with accompaniment as diverse as a single harp or an entire orchestra.[28] Although most of our records of vocalists are from the funerary sphere, a title such as "singer of the great house (palace)" indicates that vocalists were employed for secular occasions.[29]

While a single female singer is commonly shown in conjunction with a harpist, singers in orchestral scenes more commonly appear in pairs and trios, singing and beating the rhythm for dancers (Figures 4-3 through 4-5). The dress of these singers is known from many different contexts, including painted scenes of music making. The costume consists of the typical Old Kingdom tightly fitted sheath dress with broad shoulder straps. This garb is also worn by harp players. The hair is usually worn in a short rounded style. The coiffures of the singers in the tomb of Rashepses (Dynasty 5, ca. 2458 B.C.E.) are exceptions, for they wear their hair long, trailing over their shoulders.[30]

From at least Dynasty 4 on through ancient Egyptian history, professional musicians were grouped into organizations, the best known being the *ḫnr*.[31] The existence of the *ḫnr* is attested by titles appearing as captions over singers and dancers. The *ḫnr* poses an interesting problem in Egyptology. Long viewed as a "harem" in the Oriental sense of the word—lovely ladies secluded for the pleasure of males[32]—this institution has now been identified less romantically as a band of professional singers and dancers.[33] The earlier and erroneous identification was perhaps influenced by the tendency of historians to impose either

Islamic traditions or Victorian conceptions of the Near East upon ancient Egyptian culture.

Ḥnr titles indicate that the organization was associated with particular cultural institutions. Thus the *ḥnr* of the palace is attested by the title *imy-r ḥnrt n nsw*, "overseer of the singers and dancers of the king."[34] The *ḥnr* could be attached to funerary estates (*ḥnr n pr-ḏt*).[35] The *ḥnr* was also attached to temples of the goddesses Bat and Hathor, and the gods Wepwawet (guardian of the necropolis) and Horus Iwnmutef.[36]

Both Fischer and Ward have suggested that the *ḥnr* was always overseen by a woman until at least the First Intermediate Period (post-Old Kingdom, ca. 2200 B.C.E.).[37] Female supervisory titles include *imyt-r ḥnr*, "overseer of the *ḥnr*," and *sḥḏt nt ḥnr*, "inspector of the *ḥnr*."[38] Membership in the *ḥnr* was originally restricted to women, but by the end of the Old Kingdom, males are included among *ḥnr* singers and dancers.[39] By the early Middle Kingdom, even the orthography of the word *ḥnr* was modified to express both male and female determinatives, confirming that both genders were members of this organization.

As indicated by the hieroglyphic captions that accompany representations, the *ḥnr* was composed of singers and dancers. However, the range of events at which their attendance was considered to be appropriate is not clear, for most of our documentation of the *ḥnr* is from paintings and carved reliefs from tomb chapels that show the *ḥnr* entertaining the deceased while he or she is seated at a table of offerings. The *ḥnr* is also shown before the tomb on the day of burial, during celebrations for the deceased, or in funerary processions. By the First Intermediate Period (ca. 2250 B.C.E.), a divine determinative appears in conjunction with the writing *ḥnr*.[40] Such contexts have led to conclusions such as that the *ḥnr* was "the group responsible for the music performed in the context of cult activities."[41] Indeed the *ḥnr* is well attested, especially from Dynasty 5 onward, in association with rituals of the goddess Hathor.[42] Yet the following titles held by *ḥnr* members suggest that the ensemble also had a secular function related to simple entertainment: *imy-r sḥmḥ-ib nb n ḥnw štзw pr-'з*, "overseers of all the entertainment and of the secrets of the palace," *imy-r sḥmḥ-ib nb nfr n nsw*, "overseer of all the fine entertainment of the king,"[43] and *imy-r ḥst pr-'з*, "overseer of the singing in the palace" and an epithet for singers who "daily rejoice the heart of the king with beautiful songs and fulfil every wish of the king by their beautiful singing."[44]

The dancers of the *ḥnr* appear in groups, usually of at least three women. Until the end of the Old Kingdom, the dance performed by the ḫnr appears to be fairly sedate, consisting of raised arm movements. However, by the end of the Old Kingdom, these dances became considerably more vigorous. Such dances appear among the reliefs executed for Lady Watetkhethor in the mastaba tomb of her husband, Mereruka, at Sakkara.[45] There, the dancers assume the postures of acrobats. Balls tied onto the end of their long pigtails accentuate their movements.

Ḫnr dancers are dressed in short, masculine-style kilts, their bare chests crossed by broad bands of fabric.[46] This style of dress sometimes makes it difficult to distinguish males from females in damaged scenes.[47] The majority of dancers dressed in this fashion are identified by the captions as belonging to the ḫnr, so unidentified figures wearing the distinctive dress were probably also members.

Female Musicians in the Middle Kingdom
(Dynasties 11–12, ca. 2134–1784 B.C.E.)

In contrast to the monuments of the Old Kingdom, the relatively small number of tombs and temples of the Middle Kingdom makes it difficult to draw conclusions about musicians in this era. The primary sources for this period are scenes in the decorated tombs at Meir, Beni Hasan, and Deir el Gebrawi, which attest to the continuation of musical traditions of the Old Kingdom, especially the theme of the wife of the deceased playing the harp for her husband,[48] and female choirs who sing to the accompaniment of orchestras.

The Old Kingdom tradition of male and female musicians playing side by side is also preserved in the Middle Kingdom. This sort of composition is documented by an early Middle Kingdom wooden model from Sakkara, now in the Egyptian Museum, Cairo. The little figures comprise a small ensemble made up of two harps, one played by a man, the other by a woman, who are positioned on either side of a settee upon which the deceased and his wife are seated.[49] Three female singers are positioned before the couple, their hands raised as if clapping.

Another example of a mixed-gender ensemble is found in the tomb of Amenemhet at Beni Hasan (ca. 1971 B.C.E.), where a male and female harpist are shown seated side by side.[50] Two similar scenes of male and female harpists playing side by side appear in the Theban tomb of Antefoker (ca. 1971 B.C.E.).[51] The tomb of Khety at Beni Hasan (ca. 1990 B.C.E.) is decorated with a scene of two pairs of musicians seated together: to the left, a male singer and harp player; to the right, a female harpist and singer.[52] The female musicians of the Middle Kingdom in these three scenes are shown wearing the tightly fitted sheath dress with broad shoulder straps, attested for many occupations in the Old Kingdom, including singers and harpists.

In contrast to the preceding and following periods, less documentation survives from the Middle Kingdom. The most significant changes in the role of women are the increasing integration of male and female musicians and the greater variety of instruments played by women in iconographical representations. Scenes of female flautists occur in the tomb of Ukhhotep at Meir and the tomb of Antefoker at Thebes.[53] Written sources also attest to the role of female musicians in the Middle Kingdom. A letter records the payment of a troupe of female musicians who performed in the local temple,[54] indicating that women continued to be professional musicians during this time.

Female Musicians in the New Kingdom (ca. 1570–945 B.C.E.)

The New Kingdom period presents especially rich documentation about ancient Egyptian music through more numerous and better-preserved source material. In addition, the accompanying inscriptional material that captions many of the scenes is more complete, giving a clearer sense of the activity portrayed. These brief inscriptions indicate that most of the scenes of musicians from the New Kingdom have a funerary function. Others are related to Hathoric rituals associated with the revivification of the king.

In this period, the trend seen in the Middle Kingdom of female musicians playing a wider variety of instruments is continued, and the range of instruments played by women does not, with the exception of the trumpet and the rectangular frame drum, differ from that played by male musicians.[55] The many scenes of musicians in action provide information not only about the instruments but also about the way in which they were played.

The instruments played by females in the New Kingdom include various stringed instruments with round or oval sounding boxes (lutes, Figures 4-6 and 4-7), lyres (Figure 4-6), wind instruments including flutes and single or double oboes (Figures 4-6 through 4-9),[56] the shoulder harp (known from the Old Kingdom, Figure 4-8) and a new style of standing harp (Figures 4-6 and 4-7),[57] a rectangular frame drum with concave sides,[58] and a range of percussion instruments including frame drums,[59] clapsticks,[60] and the sistrum.[61] Although the lute and various

Figure 4-6. Female musicians and a young dancer in the tomb of Djserkareso-neb at Thebes (Dynasty 18, ca. 1400 B.C.E.). Courtesy of The Oriental Institute of the University of Chicago. Facsimile painting by Nina M. Davies.

types of harps are played by both men and women, the double oboe and the rectangular frame drum[62] were apparently restricted to female musicians during the New Kingdom.[63] Trumpets, which are attested from the New Kingdom, are played exclusively by men, perhaps due to their association with the military.[64]

The scenes of musicians in the New Kingdom are considerably different from those of the Old and Middle Kingdoms. The previous themes of a single female harpist singing and playing for the tomb owner is almost abandoned, although a single male harpist may appear as an entertainer in a banquet scene or on funerary monuments of the New Kingdom.[65] The single female harpist is replaced by compositions involving groups of women rather than individuals. The Old Kingdom orchestras of seated male and female musicians who played for groups of ḫnr singers and dancers is generally replaced by the very common New Kingdom composition that portrays banquets at which groups of musicians, most commonly women,[66] entertain the tomb owners and groups of guests. In contrast to the Old Kingdom, when instrumentalists did not appear to dance, and dancers were not integrated into the orchestra, the musicians in the later period appear to undulate[67] or stamp to the music,[68] and dancers perform among the groups of musicians.

Figure 4-7. Musicians in the tomb of Nakht at Thebes (Dynasty 18, ca. 1419 B.C.E.). Photograph courtesy of The Oriental Institute of the University of Chicago, with permission of The Metropolitan Museum of Art, New York. Facsimile painting by Lancelot Crane.

Figure 4-8. Orchestra of harp, lute, and double pipe in the tomb of Amenem-het at Thebes (Dynasty 18, ca. 1440 B.C.E.). Courtesy of The Oriental Institute of the University of Chicago. Facsimile painting by Nina M. Davies.

Although the *ḫnr* is still attested in the New Kingdom through honorific titles held by many New Kingdom women, representations of *ḫnr* dancers accompanied by women who clap and sing are rare in the New Kingdom. One relic of this ancient theme can be found in the tomb of Kheruef at Thebes (ca. 1355 B.C.E.), where two women beat round frame drums as three pairs of women clap and sing.[69] Five dancers appear behind them. Their pose, with arms over their heads, and their short kilts and bare chests crossed by the Libyan bands, are direct borrowings from Old Kingdom iconography.[70]

One of the best illustrations of the typical New Kingdom representations of groups of female musicians at a banquet appears in the tomb of Djserkaresoneb at Thebes (ca. 1400 B.C.E.; Figure 4-6). There, the orchestra is composed of four women who play a standing harp, lute, double oboe, and lyre. At least one of the women (the lutenist) appears to be singing in accompaniment to the music. There is marked contrast to the Old Kingdom compositions. Not only is a wider variety of instruments portrayed, but the women are active: the lutenist raises her foot as she lifts her head to sing, and the oboist turns her head toward the lyre player. Also, the orchestra has been joined by a young dancer who performs amid the musicians.

Figure 4-9. Dancers, musicians, and singers in the tomb of Khereuf at Thebes (Dynasty 18, ca. 1349 B.C.E.). Drawing courtesy of The Oriental Institute of the University of Chicago.

This scene illustrates the manner in which female musicians of the New Kingdom were dressed. In contrast to the garb of the musicians of the Old and Middle Kingdoms, which was generally the sheath dress with broad shoulder straps, these women are dressed in various styles expressing the gamut of ancient Egyptian contemporary fashion. The harpist wears a white linen dress with a brightly striped shawl knotted at the waist. The lutenist and the young dancer are nearly nude with the exception of a broad beaded collar, bracelets and armlets, and a girdle slung around their waists. Behind them, the player of the double oboe wears the popular New Kingdom flowing dress made of a nearly transparent fabric. The lyre player wears the traditional form-fitting sheath. She, as well as the harpist, wear cones of scented fat on their heads atop flower circlets. As the party became more lively, the scented fat would melt and perfume their wigs. (Styles of dress and their implications for status will be discussed below.)

A scene from the tomb of Nakht (ca. 1419 B.C.E.; Figure 4-7)[71] is very similar to that in the tomb of Djserkaresoneb. Although the dancer and the lyre player are absent, the standing harp, lute, and double oboe appear in the same order (although in reverse orientation). As in the tomb of Djserkaresoneb, the lutenist wears only a girdle and jewelry, and she exhibits a sense of animation, not unlike a dancer. These similarities may be more a function of the copy books from which the scenes were drawn than any indication that lutenists were more simply clad and more animated than other instrumentalists.[72] A scene in the tomb of Rekhmire at Thebes (ca. 1475 B.C.E.) shows a group of female musicians—a harp player, a lutenist, and a frame drum player—where the garb of the lutenist does not differ from the dress of the other musicians.[73]

A related scene in the tomb of Amenemhet (ca. 1440 B.C.E.; Figure 4-8)[74] that also includes a harp, a lute (here played by a man), and a double oboe suggests that this particular combination of instruments had become a standard for New Kingdom tastes. The harpist in this representation is portrayed with her lips parted, singing. Her activity is narrated by the hieroglyphic caption above her head.

As shown in the scenes from the tomb of Amenemhet as well as other monuments,[75] the tradition of orchestras of mixed gender continued in the New Kingdom, although it was more common to see exclusively female groups (Figures 4-6, 4-7, 4-9).[76] All-female orchestras also appear with regularity on monuments at Tell el Amarna, the capital city of king Akhenaton and his queen Nefertiti (ca. 1320 B.C.E.).[77] The scenes in the tombs at Tell el Amarna indicate that bands of professional musicians were attached to the houses of the wealthy.[78] Groups of female musicians were employed by the palace at Tell el Amarna, as indicated by scenes in the tomb of Meryre.[79] There, the king and queen are entertained by six women, pairs of whom play the harp, the lyre, and the lute. Other groups of male and female musicians are seen positioned before the gateway of the palace.[80] As in the Old Kingdom, the lady of the house is seen in the role of musician, indicating, as stated by Davies that "[music] was a prominent part of the duties or recreations of the women of the house."[81]

In the New Kingdom, we have much more explicit mention of women musicians associated with temples, primarily the cults of Hathor and Amon. The rituals for the goddess Hathor are especially well represented. Some of these rituals are associated with the jubilee festival (*heb sed*) of the king, which was thought to revive the powers of the monarch.[82] Although snippets of such scenes are known from the Old Kingdom (twenty-fifth century B.C.E.),[83] they are best depicted in several New Kingdom tombs and on the *talatat* blocks from the temples of Akhenaton.[84] The musicians of the goddess Hathor at the jubilee are shown playing long oboes (Fig. 4-9) and beating round drums[85] as well as shaking sistra and the beaded *menat* necklace sacred to the goddess Hathor.

The most complete of these rituals appears in the aforementioned tomb of Kheruef (ca. 1349 B.C.E.; Figure 4-9), where the festivities were celebrated by musicians, dancers, singers, mimes, and acrobats. The music and song were thought to be able to "open the doors of heaven so that the god may go forth pure." To this end the crowds were exhorted to "rejoice" through their song, dance and actions. The indication that music was an integral part of the effectiveness of the ritual is made clear by the inscription "Behold him [the king] as he makes for [you] sacred music . . . in order that he may celebrate the jubilee."[86] Although none of the dancers in the Kheruef scenes is specifically called a member of the *ḥnr*, the characteristic dress of the dancers, with short kilts and fabric strips that cross their chests, is taken directly from the ritual enacted some 1500 years earlier.[87]

Another well-documented group of musicians is the chantresses, or temple musicians. Such women are known by two terms, *ḥst* and *šm'yt*. Although the *ḥst* are attested first in the Old Kingdom (twenty-seventh century B.C.E.) and the *šm'yt* are known from the late Middle Kingdom (eighteenth century B.C.E.),[88] our documentation of these institutions becomes most clear in the New Kingdom (sixteenth century B.C.E.). In that period, both groups included a great number of women of privileged backgrounds at Thebes and elsewhere, including queens, princesses, and other members of the royal family.[89] Participation in these musical groups is best documented by the association of either title with personal names on coffins, in tomb biographies, letters and administrative documents. By the New Kingdom, female temple musicians of both classifications were associated with a number of deities including Isis, Mut, Osiris, Montu, and Amon.[90]

The administration and organization of the *šm'yt* is documented more fully than that of the *ḥst*. The women of the *šm'yt* of each temple were divided into four groups called phyles (*s3*), each of whom served on a part-time, rotating basis under the supervision of a woman who bore the title "great one [of the musicians]" (*ḥry s3*).[91] The entire corps of women was overseen by the High Priest of the particular priesthood. The most fully documented of these groups of women was associated with the god Amon at Thebes. They were administered by the High

Priest of Amon who, during the New Kingdom and Third Intermediate Period, was immediately below the vizier in the governmental chain of command.

The importance of the groups of singers (*šmʾyt* and *ḥst*) is reflected by texts that indicate chanting and singing contented and entertained the gods. For example, a text from the time of queen Nefertiti (ca. 1350 B.C.E.) recounts that the queen is one "who pacifies the god [Aton] with a sweet voice and whose two hands carry the sistra."[92] A later text (ca. 1250 B.C.E.) states that a wife of Rameses II "pacifies [the god] Horus with her voice."[93]

The genealogies inscribed on the coffins of many *šmʾyt* as well as *ḥst* indicate that they, like other nonpriestesses, could and did marry and raise families. Indeed the daughters and granddaughters of many temple singers followed, and accompanied, their mothers into the role of temple musician. The tomb of Rekhmire at Thebes records a scene of the arrival home of the male head of the household. Upon his return, he is greeted by eleven of his daughters and granddaughters, all of whom hold the title *šmʾyt n Imn* (temple musician of Amon).[94]

The proliferation of the title "Chantress of Amon" in the New Kingdom and Third Intermediate Period, and the part-time nature of the position, suggests that it was, as were many male priestly roles, a low-level, volunteer, clerical post. Sendrey has indicated that these women were more likely to have been part-time priestesses than professional musicians.[95] Hickmann elaborates upon this idea when he suggests that our appraisal of their musical ability may also be exaggerated by the title: "Very probably it [the music of women designated Chantress of Amon] did not constitute singing in the true sense of the term, but liturgical recitations of a more ritual than musical bearing."[96] Hickmann's suggestion is also supported by the fact that both the *šmʾyt* and *ḥst* are normally associated with the percussion instruments sistrum and *menat*,[97] which may have been more appropriate for chanting of songs and hymns than the stringed or wind instruments that made up orchestral arrangements.

Status of Female Musicians

Although there is no explicit information to shed light upon the status of musicians in ancient Egypt, scholars have made wide-ranging asser-

tions such as the following: "Those who played at the houses of the
rich, as well as the ambulant musicians of the streets, were of the lower
class";[98] "Music was not regarded as an entirely reputable occupa-
tion";[99] "Playing the harp must have been as important to the education
of a young lady of the Old Kingdom as playing the spinet or piano used
to be in our own recent past";[100] and "Musicians had a privileged,
sometimes even an honored position."[101] Perhaps the safest conclusion
is taken by Ellen Hickmann in the *Lexikon der Ägyptologie*, where she
suggests that we cannot be certain of public perceptions of musicians,
but in light of the other changes in the role and involvement of women
in music, their status must have changed over time.[102]

The evidence from the Old Kingdom, the era during which women
were restricted to playing the harp and percussion instruments, provides a fairly clear picture. An important element is that many harp
players were members of the family of the deceased.[103] For example, the
harpist in the tomb of Idu (Figure 4-5, first harpist on the right) is the
daughter of Idu, while in the tomb chapel of Pepi at Meir, the harpist
is the wife of the tomb owner.[104] Moreover, Pepi's wife bears the title
rḫt nsw, "she whom the king knows," a title associated with social
status in the court.[105] In other cases, such as in the tomb of Nikawre
and Ihat (Figure 4-1), and the tombs of In-Snefru-Ishtef[106] and Idu (Figure 4-5), the personal name of each female musician is given. According
to ancient Egyptian sensibilities, this documentation of the personal
name accords them a measure of respect for posterity. The fact that
female musicians in the Old Kingdom are related to the tomb owner,
or are given the honor of their name being preserved, suggests very
strongly, as indicated by Fischer, that the performance of music was an
integral part of polite society.

The location of Old Kingdom tombs of musicians near the royal pyr-
amids at Giza[107] also suggests that musicians were considered to be hon-
orable, for the grant of such a choice spot for a private tomb was a sign
of favor from the king, a reward that would be unexpected if the musical profession were not reputable. Biographies of the Old Kingdom as
well as the later *History* of Herodotus (fifth century B.C.E.) record that
sons and daughters followed their parents into the role of musician.[108]

The situation is not as clear in the Middle Kingdom because of the
expanded role for females in the musical world and the relatively few
sources. A factor that is certainly important, yet oblique, is the appearance of men and women musicians together. A clearer indication of the
status of musicians is preserved in the biography of a Middle Kingdom

official who boasts that he trained ten musicians.[109] So too, private funerary stelae are decorated with scenes of musicians.[110] If music were a dishonorable profession, one would expect that it not be mentioned on monuments intended to commemorate the honor of the deceased eternally.

Papyrus Westcar may also illuminate the status of musicians in this period. The papyrus contains stories written in the late Middle Kingdom (eighteenth century B.C.E.) but set in the pyramid age of the Old Kingdom (ca. 2500 B.C.E.). In one of the tales that deals with the birth of the kings of Dynasty 5, four goddesses, including Isis and Nephthys, sisters of the foremost chthonic god Osiris, transform themselves into a band of musicians (ḫnyt), presumably to avoid drawing attention.[111] This suggests primarily that the role of female musicians in this period was not of ill repute, for it was a role assumed by deities, and secondarily, as suggested by Watterson,[112] that bands of female musicians were a fairly common element in society.

A fact to be taken into account when evaluating the status of musicians in the New Kingdom is that hieroglyphic captions indicate that relatively few of the musicians are related to the tomb owner, suggesting that musicians were increasingly professional. They may have been hired for specific purposes, or they may have been groups who were attached to cult organizations. For example, the dancers in the tomb of Kheruef are described as "women who have been brought from the oasis."[113] In the tomb of Nakhtamun at Thebes, a lyre player appears with a tattoo of the god Bes on her thighs.[114] This marking has been interpreted, perhaps with little basis in fact and with some twentieth-century negative reaction to tattoos, as "The girl is manifestly a professional."[115]

Although there was clearly a growing professionalism among musicians in the New Kingdom, professionalism itself does not indicate that musicians, especially female musicians, were of low social regard. One might argue that the continuing tradition of recording the name of the musicians who appear at banquets suggests that they were considered significant individuals.[116] Other records indicate that having a musician among the members of the family was not a matter of disgrace. Papyrus Anastasi IV of the Late New Kingdom records the disgust of a family at the antics of their son who had achieved the training to enable him to "sing to the pipe, to chant to the w3r-flute, to intone to the lyre, and to sing to the nth [unknown instruments]." Their complaint continues that in spite of that specialized training, he does nothing but drink, molest people, and keep company with harlots.[117] It should be stressed that his musical training was viewed in contrast to his boorish state, and that music was not in any way to blame for his poor conduct.

The groups of female temple musicians (*šm'yt* and *ḥst*) are another indication of the prestige perhaps associated with musical training, or at least that musical training and status were not incompatible. The coffins of many female temple musicians are of superb quality, indicating that the family allocated considerable resources to their funerary equipment.[118] A group of *šm'yt* of the gods Osiris, Isis, Horus, Mut, and Amun were granted unusual honor upon their death, that of being buried at Abydos, the most sacred mortuary site in Egypt.[119] This again is an indication that women who were trained in musical skills were highly regarded by society.

Music was a profession considered prestigious enough to be carried on by several generations, as indicated not only by the scene in the tomb of Rekhmire discussed above,[120] but also by another depiction in the tomb of Amenemhet at Thebes, where a singer is shown with her two daughters, both of whom are also singers.[121] One of the last of the Ptolemaic rulers, Ptolemy XII (80 B.C.E.), bore the nickname "Auletes," the flute player. This suggests that even in that Late Period negative connotations were not associated with music.[122]

Although one might expect that the garb of musicians may provide a clue to status, the association between dress and social standing is not so clear. Female musicians appear in a wide variety of dress, from nearly nude to the Old Kingdom fitted sheath and the New Kingdom diaphanous pleated gown. All of these styles of dress are attested for women in other occupations and situations and they cannot be exclusively associated with music. An exception is the Old Kingdom dress of the *ḫnr* dancers; the short kilt and the Libyan bands across their otherwise bare chests are distinctive of their activity. However, this ritual style does little to illuminate their social reputation.

It is difficult to draw any inferences of status based upon the level of dress or undress of female musicians, for nudity, or near nudity, was an accepted form of fashion for women throughout Egyptian history, and it was not uncommon for adult women to appear with an absolute minimum of clothing. The degree to which the body was clothed often depended upon the activity. Female field workers are often depicted wearing only a beaded girdle around the waist, for more elaborate clothing was a hindrance to movement. This acceptance of revealing the female body was not restricted to the lower class, for among the elite, pleated diaphanous gowns were designed to accentuate the still-visible female form rather than to obscure it. The display of the female body was not obstructed by undergarments, which were virtually unknown in ancient Egypt. Statues and paintings clearly outline the pubic area and navel of gowned women. Formal dresses, especially designed to reveal the breasts, are attested in various forms throughout Egyptian history (Figures 4-2, 4-6, 4-8). Overall, the design and manufacture of female clothing for all classes seems to have been dictated by climate and activity, with the goal of revealing and accentuating the body rather than obscuring it, therefore suggesting that nudity was not associated with social stigma or reduced status.

In spite of the evidence that nudity had little to do with social status,[123] the lack of clothing of female musicians has been interpreted as an indication of lack of status and societal respect, and by extension, a comment upon the disreputable nature of female musicians.[124] However, one cannot make such an association between musicians' dress and status, for there was no single standard garb that might provide a diagnostic marker of status. For example, lute players appeared nearly nude in some circumstances (Figures 4-6, 4-7)[125] and clothed in others.[126] Nudity had a ritual significance as well. The gods Bes and Ihy, who are associated with rebirth, are routinely depicted as being nude. Female musicians and dancers who are represented in the temple of Bes at Edfu are often shown naked.[127]

Conclusions

Women musicians are documented throughout the pharaonic period. In the Old Kingdom (twenty-seventh through twenty-third centuries B.C.E.), they appear as singers, dancers, harp players, and percussionists. The scenes from the mid-Old Kingdom (Dynasty 4 to middle of Dynasty 5) indicate that orchestras of that era were composed exclusively of men. By the later part of Dynasty 5 orchestras were composed of both sexes, and sources from that period onward indicate that there was no tradition or stricture against such groupings.

The relatively few sources from the Middle Kingdom (twentieth through eighteenth centuries B.C.E.) show that women of that period played an expanded repertoire of instruments, including the oboe and flute. By the New Kingdom (fifteenth through eleventh centuries B.C.E.), women are shown with virtually all of the instruments played by men, with the exception of the trumpet, which was associated exclusively with the military. New Kingdom scenes suggest that all-female orchestras were favored over mixed-gender and exclusively male orchestras.

There is no evidence that female musicians in ancient Egypt were considered to be of disreputable character. Domestic scenes represent family members as musicians, and distinction is given to these women as well as to some professional musicians by immortalizing their personal names in the hieroglyphic captions that accompany the vignettes. The indication of status that is associated with female musicians is also indicated by the presence of many women of the upper classes and the royal family who served as musicians in temples as well as in the royal residence.

5

Private Speech, Public Pain:
The Power of Women's Laments
in Ancient Greek Poetry and Tragedy

Nancy Sultan

Women's discourse in Greek society has been traditionally controlled and restricted by strict sociocultural codes. Barred from participating in the exclusively male public political scene, women have developed another mode of expressing their concerns and opinions about the world around them—through performance of ritual laments. In these songs of mourning women are empowered through their pain to address publicly issues of social importance; the most successful performers skillfully weave sometimes abrasive, often persuasive, and always highly charged juridical and political language into their lament. Women use this medium of public mourning as a protected vehicle through which they pronounce moral judgments with political immunity, much like the professional male praise-poet, who uses his craft to direct strong but subtle criticism toward the individual whom he is praising.[1]

Owing to a lack of evidence, we know very little about the sound of ancient Greek music. Studying ancient Greek ritual laments as *songs* is tricky because we lack musical notation and possess no clear understanding of an ancient lament's melodic composition; we must rely on the context and form of the text and its meter, which, thankfully, we do know something about.[2] Meter in tragedy distinguishes the speech of an actor from the song and dance of the chorus, and we know from ancient scholars, poets, and playwrights that each meter, together with the rhythm and melody of musical accompaniment, evokes a different emotional expression in song and dance.

In ancient Greek culture, and indeed in many parts of Greece today, ritual laments are best described as performed speech-acts.[3] The words of the laments in song mixed with cries and shrieks must not be perceived simply as sounds, but as actions displayed before witnesses in an open strategy of what Nadia Seremetakis calls "truth-claiming."[4] The laments are directed toward the doomed, dying, or dead individual, or structured as a dialogue between the dead and the living; by extension, the lament effects emotional responses in the listeners and forces them to react, thereby reinforcing values of truth, social justice, and natural law.

Professional male poets and playwrights of ancient Greece, recognizing the expressive power of women's ritual laments, often exploit them in critical narrative moments. I focus here on the narrative context of women's lamentation in archaic Greek epic and tragedy, considering (1) how women use the techniques of "witnessing" and "truth claiming" to defy or condemn male social attitudes and institutions, (2) how women use expressions of *pónos* (pain) to control their own discourse, and (3) how the use of woman's ritual lament as a narrative maneuver in Greek poetry and tragedy effects changes in the male participants.

Background: Categories of Laments

Margaret Alexiou's 1974 book on Greek women's ritual lament paved the way for a host of other analyses of women's voices in Greek life and literature, both ancient and modern.[5] Her comparative approach shows that the most ancient ritualistic aspects of women's laments can still be found in modern Greek practice and that there is continuity on the levels of form, content, and style from antiquity through the Byzantine Period into modern times.

The two most common words for "ritual lament" in ancient use, *thrênos* and *góos*, are a bit difficult to differentiate. Both are from an Indo-European root meaning "a shrill cry,"[6] and both contain intense emotions associated with mourning—grief, anger, blame, and so on—as well as words of praise for the deceased. From their earliest vocalizations as loud cries and screams, they developed into songs with music, and eventually, as the narrative structure took on a life of its own in the hands of writers, the musicality was lost. Alexiou argues that in Homer, where the word *thrênos* appears only twice, it is meant to be a composed dirge performed by (1) the Muses for the dead Achilles (*Odyssey* 24.61), and (2) male professional mourners at Hektor's funeral (*Iliad* 24.721); the *góos*, a much more frequent term, refers to the improvised, context-specific weeping performed by kinspeople and close friends of the deceased.[7] The *góos* in Homer seems to work both as the expression of general grief at the loss of a loved one and as a stylized ritual lament performed specifically by women.

Alexiou sees these *góoi* as inarticulate wails and shrieks uttered as an antiphonal response to the more thoroughly composed *thrênos*; we have no text of the supposedly polished *thrênoi*, however, while the verses of the kinswomen's *góoi*—Thetis's (*Iliad* 18.52 ff.) and those of the three women closest to Hektor—his wife, mother, and sister-in-law at his bier (*Iliad* 24.723 ff.), are fully and eloquently narrated. Homer presents us with three sets of mourners at Hektor's bier: (1) professional singers (*aoidoi*), who may be playing songs that are full of mourning (*stonóessan*) on their instruments, but are not actually singing,[8] (2) kinswomen Andromakhe, Hecuba, and Helen, who sing solos (*góoi*), and (3) a group of related and nonrelated women (*stenákhonto gunaîkes*) who wail in refrain. We must agree with Alexiou that these *góoi*, at any rate, are *songs*, but as we will see, they are also a *voice*.[9]

In Athenian tragedy of the classical period *thrênos* and *góos* as terms were often conflated, and later Greek scholars used the term *thrênos* more than *góos* to denote a sung lament that contained praise. The *thrênos* was introduced by a new term specific to tragedy, the *kommós*, a word that is derived from the Greek verb *koptô*, "to beat the breast in lamentation,"[10] a common image exploited in tragedy as the most visually compelling exhibition of physical and psychological pain. Aristotle (*Poetics* 12.1452b) defines the *kommós* as an antiphonal song of lament between an actor and the female chorus, such as this one, from the final scene of Euripides' *Trojan Women*, in the aftermath of Troy's demise at the hands of the Greeks (1302–9):

> HECUBA (soloist): *iô!* Earth that nourished my children!
> WOMEN: *eh! eh!*
>
> HECUBA: Oh, children, hear! Attend to your mother's voice!
> WOMEN: You call to the dead in your lament!
>
> HECUBA: Setting my old body on the ground, I beat the earth
>   with my two hands.
> WOMEN: We kneel on the earth in succession, weeping for
>   our own wretched husbands below.

In exchanges like this, which occur with extraordinary frequency in Greek tragedy, women mourn the death of an entire city through the public expression of their own personal losses. Each action is echoed with a counteraction; the women complete each other's thoughts. Their lament is not simply a description of war's destruction, it *is* that destruction. The sound of their wailing voices, their bodies falling and beating the ground, are reenactments of war's battlefronts.

Voice of the Female Sex

In his *Life of Solon* (21.90.4) Plutarch (first century C.E.) tells us that the Athenian lawgiver Solon forbade women's performance of "composed dirges" (*thrênein pepoiêména*). Plato (*Rep.* 3.395 d–e) states that lamentation is "weak and feminine"; he is adamantly opposed to the irrational expression of grief. In his *Laws* (12.960a) he remarks that "ideal lawgivers" would prohibit public outcries at funeral processions. These decrees by men suggest highly that the women's laments contained language that was perceived as politically threatening, especially to the patriarchal democratic institutions of Athens.

Roger Just correctly interprets the lawgivers' objections to laments: "Women's lamentations cause disruptions and pose a threat to the good order—indeed to the very survival—of society by their introduction of the unrestrained, the emotional, the illogical."[11] He uses as an example a scene from Aeschylus' *Seven Against Thebes* (181–95), when the besieged Theban general Eteokles tries to silence the laments sung by a chorus of young women by charging that their behavior is antithetical to what is *sophrones*, "right minded" (186); he aggressively turns their fear of enslavement inside out: "You yourselves are the ones who enslave me and the entire city" (254). Eteocles wishes that the women could "suffer in silence" (250, 252, 262), and expresses utter exasperation at their display of emotion (256–59):

> ET. Oh Zeus! what a race of women you gave us!
> CH. A wretched one, like men whose city has been sacked!
> ET. You will speak ill-omens embracing the god's images?
> CH. Fear has seized my tongue with a weak spirit!

If we look closely at this exchange, we must notice several points. First, Aeschylus' audience knows that, according to tradition, Thebes was indeed sacked, Eteocles was killed, and the Theban women were taken as slaves. Second, Eteocles, as a warrior-hero, must believe that mortal men, not gods, are in control of their fate. Yet the women's laments indicate otherwise; alternating prayers with moans and cries, holding their hands up to heaven in a ritual posture of supplication and mourning as they move in dance across the stage, their song openly expresses what the hero-warrior has been trained not to express—fear and appre-hension—those sentiments that are natural in war but that weaken the morale of the fighting men (181–86):

> I ask you, insufferable creatures,
> is this protection and safety for the city or
> courage for this beleaguered army here,
> for you, falling before the wooden images of the city's gods
> to shout and howl . . . ?

Although men's discourse projects women's laments as illogical, the opposite, of course, is true; it is the truth that war is an evil waste that men cannot afford to hear or be generally willing to allow themselves to act upon.[12] As the warriors continue to equip for battle, women try to prepare themselves to face the inevitable funerals and the pain of their own lives, as they continue afterward. For ancient Greek society, war was a seasonally recurring crisis, an evil very close at hand, not as it is for us North Americans living in the twentieth century—remote, abnormal, difficult to understand.[13] In ancient Greek society, women generally did not go into battle; left behind each year during war sea-son, they must have felt themselves to be prisoners of war, helpless to change the repetitive cycle of devastation to family and property but resigned to it. Witness the bitter truth exclaimed in Hecuba's lament over the body of Hektor (*Iliad* 24.754–56):

> But you, when Achilles had seized your *psukhê* [soul] with the
>   fine-edged bronze,
> he hauled many times around his companion's tomb,
> Patroklos' whom you killed; but even so, did not restore his
>   life.

Women's pónos/Men's pónos

One way of investigating the reasons why the male-dominated political structure was so wary of women's performed laments is to explore the engendered discourse of *pónos* (pain) in Greece. In Hesiod (*Theogony* 226–32), whose poetry is blatantly misogynist,[14] *Pónos* was born from *Eris*, that divine force that instills manly competition, and is grouped together with battles (*Mákhas*) and fights (*Husmínas*). There is no room in Hesiod for women's pain, but ironically, *pónos* did not exist for *men* before *women* were invented (Hesiod *Works and Days* 92). Again, in Homer's *Iliad*, a poem of Achilles' wrath and its destruction,

96

pónos is the physical exertion of battle (e.g., 6.77; 10.164; 16.568; 21.525) and the quintessential metaphor for war itself (6.525).

In the *Odyssey*, which is not about war but the coming home from war, *pónos* is used most frequently as the ritual of preparing communal meals (e.g., *pénonto daîta*, "they prepared their dinner": 2.322; 4.531; 4.624; 4.683; 14.251; 22.199; 24.412). Here we are a bit closer to the ideas of social cohesiveness that women's expressions of *pónos* intend. The theme of fasting while mourning is most strikingly illustrated in the myth of Demeter: when the goddess is in mourning over her lost daughter Kore, not only does she refuse food herself, but as she is in charge of the world's agriculture, everyone is deprived of sustenance. There is a modern saying among the Maniats that illustrates this power of *pónos* over the body: *kállio ekhô moirologó pará na pháô kai na pió*, "I would rather lament than eat or drink."[15] Another common saying of grieving people is *den katevaínei kátô to phaï*, "food will not go down."

Although the act of mourning is seen to consume to the point of blocking out bodily needs, at crisis moments in Homer male heroes consider it "inhuman"[16] to put sorrow above the stomach's needs. Odysseus says that eating helps one forget *pénthos* (220–21). Achilles agrees, and tells Priam that they must eat despite their states of mourning (24.601–20). To keep in mind the practical necessity of satisfying bodily needs (i.e., hunger) is to shut out overpowering *pónos*.

The strict laws in antiquity that limited and manipulated women's public voice were primarily due to the widespread belief in Greek (and Roman) politics that women were not in control of their discourse because they were ruled by emotion.[17] Women were excluded from public politics, justifiably, according to men, because their mental and physical health depended on their reproductive health, and their sexuality was regarded as a pollution.[18] A social barometer of a woman's honor (or shame), even today in Greece, is her sexual behavior.

In both ancient and modern Greek daily life, political banishment is compensated for, in a very important way, by women's dominance over family and religious life; they are empowered with maintaining the spiritual health of their communities.[19] Their duties include all human rites of passage, mediation between one stage and the next, from entrance to exit. If a young person dies before marriage, women dress the corpse in wedding attire and marry the youth "to the black earth," effectively thwarting Death's attempt to deny this important transition.[20] In Greek poetry and tragedy, women who mock their role of mediator come to a bad end. Clytemnestra murders her husband and then refuses to "close his eyes and mouth in death," the proper rituals that prepare the body for burial. For this neglect she wins an everlasting song of loathing (*Odyssey* 11.424–26). Hecuba stabs out Polymestor's eyes, a stark contrast to the gentle ritual of closing the lids in death; she is changed into a dog (Euripides *Hecuba* 1045 ff.).

In preparing a corpse for burial, women make close contact with a ritual artifact, a polluting entity:[21] *It is precisely through their connection with pollution that women define social order.* Patriarchal systems are stubborn to concede this fact, and a great tension is created between the sexes, each side trying to assert the validity of its own truth claims. It is important to note that participation in Athenian State Theater is a ritual of initiation reserved for male adults and, through the chorus, young up-and-coming male citizens in the democratic city; the impersonation of female characters (leading women, captive women, female Furies, etc.) by male actors and chorus boys gives them a unique opportunity to experience firsthand those female powers that are beyond men's control.[22] In Greek tragedy, it has been quite clearly shown by Froma Zeitlin that the male characters' dramatic plans succeed though their association with women. She observes that "women's plots are generally more successful than men's," citing as an example Orestes' need for help from Electra and the female chorus in order to achieve his goal.[23]

So, men need exposure to the woman's experience if they are to fully understand and realize their own potential and their own operative emotions. Since real women are denied an independent public voice, they exert power through manipulative techniques: through family, especially male kin,[24] and through the power of ritual lamentation performed with riotous group support. Tragedians have made good use of women's primary role in funeral rituals, arranging turns of plot that fall on a false burial rite intended to facilitate, for example, an escape (as in Euripides *Helen* 1049 ff.) or a long-awaited reunion (such as Sophocles *Electra* 42 ff.).

The expression of *pónos* can be viewed as a discursive tool in the male-female conflict of power and influence within the ancient Greek sociopolitical structure. Just as there is male honor in fighting wars, competing in athletics, and performing tasks requiring enormous physical strength in order to win personal glory, women find their honor in patiently enduring suffering, hardships, and loss. A bard's song of the hero-warrior's praise can turn into a lament when perceived by a woman: Penelope begs Phemios to stop singing a song about the glory of Odysseus, for it "causes her unforgettable sorrow" and makes her long for "his dear head" (*Odyssey* 1.343–44). The head, of course, is caressed by the wife in love, and in death—it is cradled in her hands during ritual lamentation (for example, *Iliad* 18.71). The Greek word *pónos* applies both to the male "pain" of physical exertion and the "pain" felt and performed by women in their songs of lamentation. For men, *pónos* embodies an agonizing personal struggle to achieve victory; for women, it involves the struggle to resolve personal and social conflicts back at home.

Far from being detached from pain (*pónos*), women's laments *must* be outward expressions of it. Euripides, in his *Trojan Women*, creates a scene in which both male and female *pónoi* are highlighted simultaneously in a lament, an intensely dramatic moment that must stand as one of the best examples of this playwright's genius. Hecuba, who is described by the chorus of captive women as the most full of *pónos* (722, *poluponotátên*) among mortals, laments the death of her grandson Astyanax, whom the Achaeans hurled from the walls during the sack of Troy. He was the child of her favorite son, Hektor, who is also dead. Now Astyanax lies limp inside Hektor's shield, in which he will be buried. Her long lament over his body, spoken with antiphonal response sung by the chorus, uses the image of the shield to punctuate both her *pónos* and Hektor's.

She begins by chiding the Achaeans for their irrational fear (*mê diekselthôn lógô*) that caused them to murder a child. In a tearful address to the child, she chides him for dying before her, for robbing her of the right to be buried by him—this reversal of nature caused by war; she then sheds harsh blame on the Achaeans for this crime of fear:[25]

> What then would the poet write on your tomb?
> "This child the Argives once murdered because they were
>   afraid?"
> An inscription of shame for Greece!
>
> (1188–91)

Hecuba then addresses the image of war's destruction directly (1196–99), focusing on the impression of the child's body lying motionless in the shield—a *pónos* for her and the boy's mother Andromakhe—and the sweat stains on the shield's rim, a visible symbol of Hektor's *pónos* in battle, his physical triumphs. Only the women's *pónos* is alive, however, for the dead feel nothing; this is womankind's strongest claim, that their *pónos* endures. They set themselves apart as the ones who bear the burden of pain—not even the divine have *pónos*,[26] yet the religious rituals for the dead and the living are conducted and controlled on a daily basis by women.

As caretakers for the dead, women find both *timê* (honor) (Aeschylus *Suppliants* 116) and cathartic joy (Euripides *Trojan Women* 608–9) in lamentation. We find Sophocles' Deianeira in the *Trachiniae* caught in a cycle of unending *pónos*: "one night brings *pónos* and the next night dispels it by receiving *pónos* in its place."[27] Helen, in Euripides' play of the same title (329), is helped by the chorus of captive women because "it is right for a woman to share *pónos* (*sumponein*) with another woman." Women claim to possess such *pónos* that they cannot easily satisfy their desire to express it in the form of sung lamentation (*góos*), as Euripides' chorus of Argive maidens pronounce in their song of lament for their dead sons (*Supp.* 79–84):

> An insatiable delight for *góos* comes to me
> Suffering much *pónos*, as from a steep rock
> the running drop flows
> of eternal, never-ceasing *góos*.
> The *pónos* for dead children
> that's the woman's concern,
> born to suffer in *góos*, eh, eh. . . .

While *pónos* is a spiritual and physical motivating force for women's laments, men cannot easily sustain the *pónos* of ritual mourning. Homeric poetry is full of examples. In *Odyssey* 4.103, Menelaos admits that a man "may quickly have one's fill of gloomy lamentation [*góos*]"; even Achilles tires of lamenting Patroklos, and tells Agamemnon, "even of mourning [*góos*] there can be enough" (*Iliad* 23.157). Odysseus tells Penelope that "it is not good to grieve [*penthêmenai*] always without end" (19.120). In a typical display of male bravado, Hektor (*Iliad* 6.450–65) admits to his wife, Andromakhe, that he would rather be praised as a dead hero than be alive to witness his wife's enslavement after he falls in battle. Like most heroes of Greek myth, Hektor earns his valor at the expense of his wife, who must live on only as a reference to the great hero to whom she was once wedded. This is precisely Cassandra's complaint in her cynical lament in *Trojan Women* (353 ff.), where she declares that she will not live on as a trophy of Agamemnon's victory at Troy, but will kill him and her own death will follow.

Tragedy, too, displays male insecurity and discomfort in the face of emotion. Both Euripides and Sophocles characterize Theseus, the protoking of Athens, as a powerful political figure who displays a strong discomfort in the face of women's public mourning. In Sophocles' *Oedipus Coloneus* (1751–53) Theseus implores Antigone and Ismene to "cease the dirge" over their father, but they continue nonetheless; in Euripides' *Suppliants*, Theseus is moved by the women's laments but not like his mother, whom he bids to stop weeping because she has no binding *reason* to lament their cause—she "has no kinship ties to these people" (286–91). We have already seen the reaction of Eteocles to the women's mourning in Aeschylus' *Seven Against Thebes*.

I can find no instance in ancient Greek poetry or tragedy when comments such as these are made by a woman. Always the ritual of lamentation is stopped by men. The outlawing of women's laments in fifth- and fourth-century Greece gave rise to men's "funeral orations"—*élegoi, epitáphios lógos,* and *epikédeion,* which were contrived by male literary society. These orations were devoid of explosive emotion and made use of controlled, subdued language, but expanded on and emphasized the elements of praise found in laments; they functioned in the male social and political sphere in a way very different from the oldest manifestations of the ritual laments.[28]

Women's Control of Discourse

In her book on the current social practices of the Maniat people in the southern Peloponnese, Nadia Seremetakis writes: "Truth claiming through the force of emotion and shared moral inference often occurs when the subject is in conflict with the social order. It is in this type of situation that the validation of truth claims turns to media outside the official jural forms. In Inner Mani, death rituals, in the past and present, have been a performative arena, demarcated by gender, where pain (*pónos*) figures prominently as an orchestrating and prescriptive communicative paradigm. In these rites, the vocalization and physical display of pains construct an affective enclave of women where alternative codifications of their relation to the social order achieve a formal status as biographical testimony and oral history."[29]

We see this clearly in Greek tragedy, perhaps most strikingly in the plays of Euripides, whose highly charged, emotional music made him famous. In his *Trojan Women* (110–11) Hecuba, lying on the ground, ponders aloud her entitlement as a bereaved mother and recent widow to vocalize her pain: "Should I be silent, or not be silent? Should I lament [*thrênêsai*]?" Hecuba invites the women to join her mourning (143–45), to double her discourse. Silence is tabooed. For the women there is a strength in numbers, and a power through the acoustics of death embodied in lamentation that give validity to their discourse. In *Odyssey* 24.48 ff., the cry (*boê*) of the Muses' *thrênos* for Achilles' death makes soldiers tremble.

Besides sonics and physical gestures (dressing the body, holding the corpse's head) women's tears in weeping are exceptional in their sheer magnitude; they are one of the primary manifestations of emotional display. To "weep like a woman" means to "melt down" (*têkô*). This verb is synonymous with the modern *leiônô*, an expressive metaphor for the burning pain of crying and tears "which liquefies the self" in women's laments.[30] Helen "melts down" with tears (*Iliad* 3.176), as do Polyxena and her mother Hecuba (Euripides, *Hecuba* 433–34). In *Odyssey* 19, *têkô* appears no less than five times as a metaphor for the inner pain of Penelope's tears flowing for Odysseus (19.204, 205, 206, 207, 208), and he urges her to stop "melting" her heart with lamentation for him in 19.264. Odysseus himself comes to a point in his life when he "melts down" and sheds tears "like a woman" (*Odyssey* 8.522–23), upon hearing the bard sing of his atrocities at Troy. Here is a critical juncture for this character, for at this moment he is metaphorically transformed into a woman who is violently beaten with spear butts as she laments over the body of her dead husband. Odysseus is lost in a woman's *pónos* (529) until his male companions rally to remove him from this state of mind.

Consider also the scene in *Iliad* 18.22–51, when Achilles first hears of the death of his companion Patroklos. As he falls to the ground and begins a ritual of lamentation (defiling his body), he is immediately joined by the wailing captive women, and when he himself cries out, his mother Thetis hears him (37) and immediately responds. She leads all her female kin in lamentation not for Patroklos, but for her *own* son Achilles, who is fated to die later (50–51). When she bids the chorus of Nereids to "hear her" (*klute*) she is asking them to bear witness to her pain, through which her pronouncements are disseminated to the rest of society.[31] Thetis tells the women that she will go "to look on [her] dear son, and *listen to the pain* [*penthos*] that comes to him" (63–64). Though Patroklos and Achilles die, there are witnesses to their death, female representatives for the pain, who avert a taboo of silent death.[32]

Seremetakis discusses what she sees as "gender dichotomies of the lament session—in which women are vocal and emotionally demonstrative in public and the men are silent, inhibited, and spatially segregated." She hastens to point out that "the men are not ignored by the women mourners during the ceremony, nor are they oblivious to what is happening within the circle of mourners; they function like a silent chorus."[33] This describes the very scene in *Iliad* 24, when Hektor's body is laid out. Men are present and feel *penthos,* "sorrow," (709), but the actual lament is performed by alternating female soloists, as we have already seen. Men are not expected to, nor do they sing laments in the presence of others like the women.

Performance Categories

Classicist Charles Segal and musicologist Susan Auerbach have both described Greek women's laments as "non-music."[34] They do not mean to suggest that laments are not *song,* but that they lack *musicality.* In his discussion of song in Greek tragedy, Segal refers to Hecuba's tears in Euripides' *Trojan Woman* as "negated music." In a medium in which a singing and dancing chorus plays the crucial role of mediation between the action of the story and the audience, Segal points out that women's laments in tragedy are described as "undanced (*akhoros*) and unlyred (*alyros*)" (343–45); at the same time, however, he states:

> By absorbing the cries of grief into the lyricism of choral lament, the tragic poet is able to identify the emotional experience of suffering with the musical and rhythmic impulse that lies at the very origins of the work. This transformation of cries of woe into song constitutes at least part of the creative power of the poet-maker and of his divinity, the Muse.[35]

Greek laments are both elaborate and intricate, employing many different techniques; they are comparable to the modern Greek laments described by Holst-Warhaft and Seremetakis, who observe that in the Maniat tradition mourning women use solo-chorus interplay, solo improvisation and antiphony, stylized sobbing, pitch alteration, and other musical techniques in combination with physical gestures to create spatial and acoustic dynamics.[36] The importance of gesture in lamentation performance is certainly vivid in Hektor's laying out in *Iliad* 24, and can be seen on many depictions of ancient Greek women's ritual mourning in the plastic arts.

Figure 5-1 shows typical postures of mourning Greek women as they stand around a dead man's bier. The women raise their white arms over their heads, tear their hair, cover their heads with their hands. A woman stands at the corpse's head, caressing it. Notice the absence of men at the bier. In Figure 5-3, a woman tears her hair in grief over the body of a dead hero who lies naked near his heaped-up armor, which

Figure 5-1. Ritual lamentation performed by women at the hero's bier. Attic black figure vase painting, ca. 500 B.C.E. Courtesy of The Metropolitan Museum of Art, Purchase, Funds from Various Donors, 1927 (27.228).

has been stripped from him. Figures 5-2 and 5-4 illustrate how Greek women's physical postures and ritual gestures of grief have continued into modern times. In Greece today, many bereaved women wear black for life, making them conspicuous signifiers of grief in everyday life.

Euripides, in his musical tragedy *Helen,* transforms the harshness of a formal *góos* (164 ff.) into a soothing song. In this lyrical lament over her role in the carnage at Troy and the loss of lives in a preventable war, Helen wishes that the Sirens could accompany her mourning with the Libyan harp, with the syrinx, with lyres, and with tears of their own to match hers "suffering for suffering, care for care, antiphonal chorus to my lament." Her call for witnesses appears less anxious than Hecuba's or Thetis's; she seems to be caught up in the lyrical beauty of her song and treats this lament almost as if it were not a lament at all.

When the chorus of captive Greek women enter with a song in response to Helen's lament, they delyricise the performance, heightening its sense of urgency and tension; they call her sounds a "confused noise" (*hómadon*), and an "unlyred elegy" (*alyron elegon*), a sharp voice of pain such as a fleeing nymph would make when seized in the woods by Pan (186 ff.). The reference to Pan here is significant because it reflects back to Helen's lament in the previous lines. According to myth, a nymph fleeing from the desires of Pan was transformed into a bed of reeds, which Pan then cut and fashioned into the pipes, the *syringas* that Helen wishes could accompany her sorrowful song; built into the music of the pipes is the cry of the assaulted nymph.

This image of the captured nymph who becomes the instrument of

Figure 5-2. Women lamenting at a gravesite, Olymbos, Karpathos, 1966. Photograph by Constantine Manos/Magnum.

Pan's play epitomizes both Helen's own position as "captive" (the very meaning of her name, line 1674), and that of the chorus, who are spoils of war, forced out of their homes to bed men who killed their husbands, sons, and brothers. That is, they are performing *moirologia*—laments—that "speak their fate."[37] The chorus's striking imagery inspires the self-conscious Helen to a greater outpouring of emotion in her next strophe addressed directly to the chorus, where she reveals to them the news of Troy's demise and the death of her kin, which Teucer had lately told her:

> *iô, iô* [inarticulate cries]
> Captives of foreign oars,
> Greek maidens,
> some Achaian seaman
> came, he came, bringing for me tears upon tears. . . .
> Ilium overthrown
> belongs now to burning fire,
> on account of me, murderess
> on account of my name, *polúponon.*
>
> (191–99)

The significance of *polúponos* (much-suffering) has been discussed. Helen here is blaming herself for being a captive, which is the same as blaming herself for being a woman. This is not the first time Helen

Figure 5-3. Women mourning over a dead hero-warrior. Attic black figure vase painting, ca. 525 B.C.E.

blames herself, her womanhood, her sexuality, for war's destruction.[38] Her sexuality is blamed for forcing mothers to mourn, and their mourning is equivalent to the mourning of all of Greece (*Helen* 362–70).

Helen's song is subtle, but it speaks out loudly against pervading attitudes toward war. As speech-acts the ritual lament must be interpreted simultaneously as a "voice" and a "song."[39] Notice how Aeschylus' Danaid maidens, who are fleeing a forced marriage to their Egyptian cousins, combine song and speech in their lament (*Suppliants* 112–15):

> I pronounce [*légô*] sufferings such as these, crying out songs,
>   tears flying, shrill, sad,
> *iê, iê,*
> I am famous for crying *iê*!

The maidens have no real rights to refuse the marriage, and they admit that "left alone, women are nothing; no Ares is in them" (748–49); the only personal, independent action they can take in response to and against male aggression is their song and dance of lament, charged speech-acts that compromise the majority of the drama's 1073 lines.

An even more dramatic illustration comes from the traditional connections that women have with birds whose cries are sonically suggestive of lamentation.[40] Bird sonics are perceived as a cross between cries

Figure 5-4. Women mourning during the Turkish invasion of Cyprus, 1974.

and song in Greek poetry and tragedy, and are used by tragedians in moments requiring critical mediation between the living and the dead. In Euripides' *Trojan Women* (145–52), Hecuba leads the chorus in lamentation for the destruction of the city:

> And I, as mother of winged birds, lead forth the cry [*klangan*],
> the song [*molpán*]; not the same song as once long ago, when
> leaning upon Priam's scepter
> my feet led the chorus in the Phrygian beat
> fine-sounding, to the gods.

One myth in particular that is a frequent metaphor for a woman's greatest expression of grief through bird imagery is the shocking Thracian story of Procne (Ovid *Metam.* 6.572 ff.), who kills her son Itys to render her husband sterile (that is, by destroying his male heir) after he rapes her sister Philomela and cuts out her tongue. Both women are transformed into birds: Philomela becomes a swallow, whose voice (*phônê*) is incoherent; Procne is transformed into the mournful nightingale, whose voice is often compared to that of lamenting women.[41] Such a one is Penelope, who is discovered mourning in *Odyssey* 19.518–22:

> As when the daughter of Pandareos [Procne], the greenwood
>   nightingale
> in the newly arrived spring sings her beautiful song
> perched on the sheltered leaves of trees
> varying her cadence continually, she pours out her much
>   trilling voice [*phônê*],
> mourning her dear son Itys.

In Aeschylus' *Suppliants* (58 ff.), the chorus of women sing that anyone who understands the flight and cries of birds (*oiônopólôn*) would know, upon hearing their song, that they lament, for they sound like nightingales (*aêdónês*). Similarly, the women's chorus in Euripides' *Helen* asks for a "nightingale's song of sorrow that is sweetest to join their *thrênos*" (1107 ff.), and Electra, in the play by Sophocles (147–49), responds to the chorus of women urging her to rest from mourning her dead father:

> But as for me, suited to my mind is the distraught bird
> who groans "Itys," always she laments "Itys,"
> a messenger of Zeus.

Electra's goal is to secure divine help in avenging her father's death; in comparing her sorrow to Procne's, she delivers her pain not only in the marked sonics of birdsong, but even more powerfully, she pronounces it as a *messenger* (*angelos*) to Zeus.[42]

Conclusion

When we consider the fate (*moira*) of mortal women featured in Greek poetry and tragedy, we find that most of them succumb to *pónos*, dying either from the weight of their pain (Antikleia, for example), by suicide (like Antigone, Phaedra, Jocasta, Deianira), or at the hand of a male murderer (such as Polyxena, Cassandra, Clytemnestra, Odysseus's serving maids). Are these women as dispensable as they appear? Certainly not. They have been given the public platform that is ritual lamentation, upon which they are empowered to speak and act on matters of personal and civic importance, exclaiming truths that make men nervous, angry, and if they are listening, changed. Tragedians who, for the most part, avoided making overt political statements in their plays could do so subtly through the *kommós*, the antiphonal exchange between chorus and actor.[43] The tragic male actor, impersonating a woman, trains himself to experience her pain, to express suffering *her way*— communally. Whoever plays the role of Andromakhe in her tragedy must feel her pain as she pleads with Menelaus (Euripides *Andromakhe* 390 ff.):

> I slept with my master through force,
> You would kill me, and not him?
> The guilt is his. . . . I saw Hektor dragged. . . .
> I saw Troy in flames. . . .
> I, a slave, dragged by the hair, aboard Argive ships;
> Since I came here to Phthia, as bride
> to my husband's murderer . . .

If this performance is to be convincing, the male player must become Andromakhe and extend her essence to the audience. Pain (*pónos*) must be understood by both player and audience as a legitimate motivating force for the politically marginal woman, which compels her to declare binding truths before witnesses. Mourning women, through their association with death and pollution, define purity and social order; they praise the righteous and highlight the wider concept of justice by indicating and judging the guilty in their laments. It is no wonder, therefore, that female characters in poetry and drama are generally given the best monologues and choral odes, and have a profound effect on the success or failure of a plot.

There is much more to say; we have barely scratched the surface here. With no musical examples save one problematic fragment with musical notation from the *Orestes*,[44] our next step must involve a comparative look at the metrics of women's choral laments in tragedy. There we might find a hint of their musicality, which *must* be there for the dramatic opposition of *unlyred* and *undanced* songs of lamentation to be fully understood.

6

The Traditional Role of Greek Women in Music from Antiquity to the End of the Byzantine Empire

Diane Touliatos

Streams of holy rivers run backward, and universal custom is overturned. Men have deceitful thoughts; no longer are their oaths steadfast. My reputation shall change, my manner of life have good report. Esteem shall come to the female sex. No longer will malicious rumor fasten upon women. The Muses of ancient poets will cease to sing of my unfaithfulness. Apollo, god of song, did not grant us the divine power of the lyre. Otherwise, I would have sung an answer to the male sex.

This text was sung by the female chorus of Euripides' *Medea* in 431 B.C.E. depicting the image of Greek women in Antiquity as perceived by the male gender.[1]

The perception of the role of Greek women throughout history can be traced to Antiquity, when the mythological god Zeus created the first woman, Pandora, making her a subordinate figure. Pandora, comparable to the later Eve, would be a source of evil to men and the box she would open would symbolize the carnal knowledge of women. And yet, in spite of woman's subordinate role in society, the Greeks were the first known culture to consider and question women's roles in society. In the case of music, one only has to look at Plato's *Republic*, where a distinction was made in music for the sexes: for men, music was to be noble and manly, but for women, only modest, submissive songs were acceptable.[2]

Greek society tended not to acknowledge women. Women who did become known were usually on the lowest level of society, such as notorious prostitutes, or on the highest level, women who played a role in politics and history, such as the Hellenistic queens and heroines or the famous women of the Imperial court of Byzantium. Consequently, few names of Greek women in music have been immortalized. But Greek women have always been active participants in the musical life of their society. Many visual representations preserved from Antiquity depict Greek women in musical activity, such as performing on the aulos (shrill pipes)³ or dancing in seminude bodies⁴ in the traditional Greek round dances.

An early example of a Greek woman chanter in Antiquity is the oracle of Apollo at Delphi. The god Apollo spoke through the medium of a prophetess named Pythia, who was allowed into the temple. Questions were put to her by a male and her responses were chanted in sounds patterned in hexameters, which were sung in a state of frenzy and subject to various interpretations by the male priests. Pythia's role was nothing more than that of a courier. An explanation for the choice of a female prophet may be that Delphi was formerly the site of a female chthonic cult.⁵

The Archaic Age (ca. 550–ca. 405 B.C.E) of Greek Antiquity gives us some of the names of famous women lyric poets and musicians. All the lyric poetesses of Archaic Greece were educated women from the upper class and, interestingly, none came from Athens.⁶ One such lyric poetess is Telesilla of Argos of the fifth century B.C.E., who came from an aristocratic family. Her name has been preserved in history, not because of her monodic compositions but because of her heroic actions. In his treatise on the bravery of women, Plutarch documents that Telesilla of Argos had been encouraged to compose lyric poetry because of her weak constitution. However, when the Argine army had suffered a severe setback against an attack from the Spartan army, it was Telesilla who organized the women of Argos to arm themselves and successfully defend their city against the Spartans.⁷ After this crisis, Telesilla and the women of Argos resumed their conventional roles, but because of her actions a statue of Telesilla was erected in her honor in Argos.⁸

The most famous woman of all Greek lyric poetesses and musicians is Sappho of Lesbos, who was born into an aristocratic family ca. 612 B.C.E. on the island of Lesbos. Sappho was greatly admired during her life by fellow poets, such as Alcaeus, her male contemporary, and by a following of students. During her mature life, Sappho was known for leading a cult of aristocratic young girls of Mitylene (chief city of Lesbos) in study and in worship involving a performance of ritual and music to Aphrodite, the Muses, and the Graces.⁹ Sappho's compositions were composed for this cult. Her versatile poetry is personal, sometimes biographical, and even political. She used new poetic structures and meters in setting to music the Aeolic dialect of Lesbos. This new form of lyric monody contains a specific structure of stanza that has since been called a Sapphic stanza. Although Sappho never wrote erotic lyric monody to men, much of her poetry consists of passionate love poems addressed to women, including references to the sexual activities of women. Fragments of her surviving poetry give evidence for the erotic and sexual behavior among the women in her cult. One of Sappho's preserved fragments of lyric monody clearly mentions the first five letters of *olisbos*, a leather phallus.[10] Sappho was married and had a daughter, yet such fragments of verse give credence to the homosexual reputation of the Lesbian women of her cult. Like many aristocratic Greek males, Sappho was probably bisexual.

Besides her lyric monody, Sappho was also known for composing choral compositions. Far fewer fragments have been preserved of this type, including choral wedding songs (*epithalamia*) that were performed antiphonally between divided choirs of girls and young men.[11]

Sappho's lyric monody and choral compositions were intended to be sung to music that she presumably composed. Although none of her music has survived, there is no doubt that she accompanied herself on a musical instrument while singing her poetry. The performance practice of Antiquity dictated that the recitation of lyric poetry be simultaneously accompanied by instrumental improvisation. The instrument most often associated with Sappho is the barbiton,[12] a harplike instrument with greater string length than the kithara. The lower pitches produced by the barbiton provided an appropriate accompaniment for the Aeolic dialect. In her poetry, however, Sappho mentions other types of string instruments: the *pektis*, a harplike Lydian instrument, and the *chelys*, the correct Greek name for lyre or kithara.[13] These references substantiate Sappho's intention that a string instrument accompany the singing of her lyric monody.

Other Greek women contributed to lyric poetry: Erinna, Nossis, Anyte, and Corinna. Similarly to Sappho, the late third-century B.C.E. poetess Corinna of Boeotia was known to have written her lyric poetry to the white-robed Boeotian women.[14] There were also songs in Greek Antiquity performed by choirs of maidens and women. These choral songs were probably very diverse, encompassing the folksongs of spinners and weavers, the ritual laments sung by women, and works for professional performance by women's choirs at festivals. There was also a type of maiden-song known as Partheneia, which was a choral hymn sung by virgins to the accompaniment of the flute.[15] The Classical scholar Sarah Pomeroy states that in these all-girl choirs, *Hagesichora*, lesbian relationships flourished and were perhaps even encouraged in Lesbos and Sparta.[16]

Other prominent female figures in the music of ancient Greece were the *hetairai*, or "companions to men." The *hetairai* were the highest class of prostitutes in ancient Greece. Different from the common courtesans, the *hetairai* were physically beautiful, had acquired some intellectual training, and possessed artistic talents such as singing and playing musical instruments. Some of these *hetairai* were as educated as or more educated than their upper-class male clients. The *hetairai* were known to have been active participants in the intellectual, artistic, and musical life of the period. Because of their diverse artistic talents and musical contributions, *hetairai* were in great demand as entertainers and companions to Greek men at parties, more so than were legitimate wives and respectable women. *Hetairai* also provided the main musical entertainment at the *symposia*—dinner parties featuring the consumption of wine, which originated during the Hellenistic period of ancient Greece (ca. fourth century–ca. 30 B.C.E.) and continued through Byzantine times.[17] Since *hetairai* were courtesans, they never achieved esteem or respectability for their musical abilities.

In the Hellenistic period of ancient Greece, women began to achieve social, economic, and educational reforms so that even respectable women were allowed the advantages of acquiring some education, thus opening to them professions outside of the home. Aristotle had advocated that female children be taught the four subjects: reading, writing, gymnastics, and *mousikê* (music). He included under the heading *mousikê* not only the playing of musical instruments and singing, but also poetry, and possibly dance in the case of girls, since there is much iconographical evidence in vase paintings of girls dancing.[18] These reforms did not necessarily elevate women in the eyes of male Greek society, but they enabled women to pursue their interests without losing respectability. Women newly educated in the arts became the main competitors to the *hetairai*, resulting in two categories of female musicians during the Hellenistic period: respectable women pursuing professional concert careers and unrespectable *hetairai*, prostitutes who used music to entertain and seduce their lovers. References to female musicians by both Plato and Aristotle substantiate this division. Plato in *Protagoras* and Aristotle in *Athenian Politics* distinguish between respectable fe-

male musicians and harp-girls and flute-girls, who were not respectable.[19]

Respectable women who pursued music as a professional career had
probably been trained to play the lyre or aulos from childhood, either
in a school or under private tutelage in their homes. There is documentary evidence that professional female musicians of this sort received
monetary compensation. A respectable woman was distinguished from
hetairai by the occasional citation of her name and by the obligatory
citation of her patronymic and city of origin. In some instances performances were commemorated or honored with inscriptions. One such
case is Polygnota, a daughter of Socrates, a Theban, who in 186 B.C.E.
was paid five hundred drachmas for her kithara playing and recitations
at Delphi.[20] Her performance was cited in a decree. Another respectable
professional Greek female musician known for performing in theaters
and festivals was the daughter of Aristocrates of Cyme, who gave a
concert at Delphi in the middle of the second century B.C.E.[21]

The participation of respectable women performing musical instruments was short-lived; the beginnings of Christianity brought great
change to Greek culture and to the role of Greek women. In the period
of early Christianity, when men dominated all aspects of religious, political, and social philosophies, Greek-Byzantine women were considered to be intellectually and spiritually inferior to men. No longer bearing the stigma of Pandora, the Byzantine woman was now viewed as a
descendant of Eve, the cause of woman's dishonor and bondage to
whom every evil of mankind was attributed.

With the conversion of Emperor Constantine to Christianity in the
year 312 C.E., two broad categories of music began to prevail within the
Byzantine Empire: secular music and liturgical music. Byzantium's liturgical music was monophonic, sung by voices without instrumental
accompaniment in the cathedrals and monasteries of the Empire.[22] The
secular music encompassed many subcategories of music outside of the
liturgical rites of Byzantium—from folk and epic songs to sophisticated
court music for the festivities of the Imperial palace.[23] Although it was
not intended as strictly instrumental music, medieval Byzantine secular
music more than likely included an instrumental accompaniment. The
sacred music of the Byzantine Empire has been preserved in thousands
of musical manuscripts, notated by the literate scribes who were usually
clergy and monks of monasteries. Secular music also existed in the Empire in great abundance, but the educated scribes of music were usually

men of the habit who did not consider secular music worthy of notation.[24] As a result, far fewer examples of secular music have survived.

It can only be surmised that the involvement of Byzantine women in
music was minimal during the early centuries of the Empire. Because
of its association with prostitution, performance on musical instruments was forbidden to young, unmarried women in the early period
of Christianity. This attitude was obviously transmitted from the former role of the *hetairai* in Antiquity. Furthermore, women of all ages
were forbidden to participate in any type of liturgical choir singing.
(This attitude had been voiced by the apostle Paul to the Corinthian
Greeks in I Corinthians 14:34–35.) Contrary to the position held by the
early church, documentation proves that women did participate in con-
gregational singing between the second and fourth centuries in such
locales as Samosata, Syria, Jerusalem, and Edessa; this trend probably
reached Byzantium as well.[25]

Roles for Byzantine women in the early church were limited to
wealthier women who were contributors of philanthropic works and potential martyrs; most Byzantine female saints came from wealthy backgrounds.[26] The offices of the church were exclusively dominated by the
male hierarchy, although until the sixth century women could serve as
deaconesses, which involved recitations of Scripture.[27] A Byzantine
woman of lesser means even encountered difficulties entering a convent, since these places were usually reserved for unmarried wealthy
women with substantial dowries and land. (A stipulation for entrance
was that all or most prior wealth be donated to the nunnery.)

Next to nothing is known about the role of women in liturgical music
during the early centuries of the Empire. Very little liturgical music has
survived from the early centuries and even this is preserved only in
adiastematic ecphonetic notation, which includes indications to guide
the recitation of liturgical texts but the exact musical significance of
which is unknown. It is not until the late eleventh through thirteenth
centuries that medieval diastematic neumatic notation was developed
for Byzantine music. This type of intervallic notation places neumes
horizontally on a folio over the Greek text and can be transcribed into
modern notation with accuracy.

Most of our information on secular music in the early centuries of
the Empire comes from the admonishments of the Church Fathers. In
Byzantium we know that there was music for the accompaniment of
theatrical performances and other public shows, ballets, and pantomimes in which women participated alongside men in song, dance, and

instrumental performance. These activities are documented in chronicles by the Church Fathers who regarded them with contempt for all profane music. In his *Homily,* St. John Chrysostom, a deacon and later priest at Antioch (381–98 C.E.), refers to the theater as the "theater of the devil" (*tou diavolou to teatron*).[28] Other Church Fathers who condemned secular music and its participants are Tertullian, Cyprian, Clement of Alexandria, Gregory Nazianzen, Basil the Great, Ambrose, Augustine, and Jerome.

The pantomimes were a popular form of entertainment for secular activities in the Empire. Both male and female mimic dancers (*tragodos*[m] and *tragode*[f]) performed to music.[29] Although these dancers were greatly admired and held in celebrity status by the public, the church regarded them on the same low social level as actors; consequently, they were not allowed to participate in the sacraments of the church. Generally, actors, dancers, and musicians, regardless of sex, were considered to be on the same social level as prostitutes because of the sexual promiscuity that characterized their lives.[30]

Another Byzantine practice was the performance of musicians during banquets of the Imperial court. These banquets with musical entertainments were called *symposia* or *sympotika,* and they continued the tradition of Antiquity. Musicians entertained with singing and performances on wind and string instruments.[31] As in Antiquity, the instrumentalists who performed during the *symposia* of the third and fourth centuries C.E. were female musicians referred to by the Church Fathers as prostitutes.

The purpose of the *symposium* transcended culinary matters and focused on intellectual and ritualistic communication. The entertainment consisted of female musicians and dancers. Condemnations of *symposia* by the Church Fathers make clear that actors were also present, although they did not necessarily participate in the program; it seems that their presence was sought to provide brilliance and celebrity status to the *symposium.*

In his *Expositio in Psalmum 41,* St. John Chrysostom discusses the evils of *symposia:* "Those inviting mimes and dancers and prostitutes [musicians] to the symposia introduce demons and invite the devil there, and fill their houses with wars [since this leads to jealousy and adultery and many other ills]."[32] He further refers to the music of the *symposia* as pornographic songs (*asmata pornika*) where demons are celebrated, for songs accompanied by the lyre are songs to the demons (*daimonon asmata*).[33] The practice of *symposia* was also condemned by

Clement of Alexandria and Basil of Caesarea. Basil especially condemned the practice of performing on the lyre, because it supposedly increased the drunkenness brought on by wine and led to the ritualization of orgies.[34] Following changes in the status of women in Byzantine society, male musicians performed at the *symposia* of the fourteenth and fifteenth centuries.

The Byzantine Empire existed for more than a thousand years, from its beginnings in the fourth century until its fall in 1453. Throughout this time, there were constraints on the participation of women in all aspects of life. Some of these constraints were legal edicts, while others were implied.[35] From the ninth century until the end of the Empire, the Byzantines were unusually conservative in aspects of relations concerning women, leading to the seclusion, or at the very least segregation, of women from men. For example, women of the Imperial court were known to be housed in private quarters of the palace away from the men; urban women who attended the large cathedrals of Constantinople were seated on the left side of the cathedral (facing the altar) to separate them from the men seated on the right side. It is from these centuries of constraint that very few names of Byzantine women composers-musicians have survived.

The Byzantine woman composer-musician is much harder to discover than is her Western counterpart. In the area of secular music very little has survived and hence no names of women composers have been given. Manuscript sources of liturgical music have survived in great number, but anonymity was so honored in Byzantium that composers' names were often omitted, especially in early sources. For female composers, anonymity was perhaps observed in later periods as well, since they probably wished to be measured by the merit of their music and not by their gender. The absence of compositions attributed to or signed by women might also result from the reticence of Greek scribes. Throughout the Eastern and Western medieval periods, Greek scribes rarely included names or information about themselves.[36] In Byzantium the women composers' names that have survived were associated exclusively with liturgical chant. These women were all literate and of middle- to upper-class social status. With the exception of one they were all nuns: Martha, mother of Symeon the Stylite; Theodosia; Thekla; Kassia; Kouvouklisena; and Palaeologina. The one for whom we have no knowledge is referred to as the daughter of Ioannes Kladas.

Of these women whose names are documented in sources as composers of Byzantine chant, only the music of Kassia and the daughter of

Ioannes Kladas is preserved in manuscripts. Since music by only these two of the women hymnographers survives, one might ask whether the other women wrote music as well as the texts for their liturgical poems. Most of these female hymnographers were nuns who wrote their liturgical compositions for use in their nunneries. It is believed that these liturgical compositions were chanted, since liturgical rites were sung throughout in medieval Byzantium. Male Byzantine hymnographers such as Romanos Melodos and John of Damascus traditionally wrote both words and music.[37] However, whether women composed their own music or employed contrafacta is a point for debate.

The surviving information concerning the other female composers is easily summarized. Martha was the mother of Symeon the Stylite, a Byzantine saint. Little is known about her: she lived toward the end of the ninth century and was the abbess of a nunnery at Argos.[38] It is assumed that most of her musical works were composed for the nuns of her convent.

Theodosia, a devout abbess of a convent near the Imperial city of Constantinople, also lived during the ninth century.[39] She is known for her composition of Kanons, a poetical form comprising nine odes and found in the Byzantine Morning Office known as Orthros.[40]

Another ninth-century composer is Thekla, who was also probably an abbess of a convent near Constantinople.[41] Thekla has been described as "a self-confident woman, proud not only of herself, but also of her sex."[42] Her only surviving hymn is a Kanon in honor of the *Theotokos* (the Byzantine attribution for the Virgin Mary). Since this composition praises the Virgin Mary, it has also been called an *encomium*, or "hymn of praise." In the millennium years of existence of the Empire, this Kanon is the only preserved hymn to the *Theotokos* by a woman. An examination of Thekla's literary skills in this complex Kanon attests to the fact that she was educated in literature as well as in Scriptures. In the several themes presented in the Kanon, the most significant is Thekla's premise that the *Theotokos* has emancipated Byzantine women from the guilt of Eve and has given women respect and honor in the Byzantine church. In addition to lauding the *Theotokos*, the woman most revered in Byzantium, Thekla shows her feminist traits by praising female martyrs, saints, and consecrated virgins of the Eastern Orthodox Church.

The hymnographers Martha, Thekla, and Theodosia have been overshadowed by the fame of their contemporary, Kassia, who is the most prominent woman composer in the history of Byzantine music. Unlike the other three writers, much is known about Kassia, whose father held a very high rank in the Imperial court.⁴³ Kassia is known by the various forms of her name found in manuscripts and service books: Kasia, Kassia, Eikasia, Ikasia, and Kassiane.⁴⁴ A gifted composer and poetess of sacred and secular verse, Kassia (born ca. 810 C.E.) is a historical figure whose name is documented in several instances in the chronicles of the Byzantine Empire. She was an extremely well educated woman who was trained not only in Scriptures but in secular literature and poetry; her exceptional talents are praised in the writings of St. Theodore the Studite. From his correspondence it is known that Kassia participated in riots against the iconoclasts (those against icons) and was persecuted for her actions.⁴⁵ She is most often mentioned in history because of her participation in the brideshow of Emperor Theophilos. Because of her extraordinary beauty and intelligence, Kassia was brought to the brideshow of Theophilos, who would select his bride-to-be in the Classical manner with a token of a golden apple. Legend has it that before presenting the golden apple, Theophilos tested the intelligence and wit of the candidates. The story is best related by the historian Edward Gibbon:

> With a golden apple in his hand he [Theophilos] slowly walked between two lines of contending beauties; his eye was detained by the charms of Icasia [Kassia], and, in the awkwardness of a first declaration, the prince could only observe that in this world, women had been the occasion of much evil [in reference to Eve, God's first created woman]: "and surely, Sir," she [Kassia] pertly replied, "they have likewise been the occasion of much good" [in reference to the Virgin Mary]. This affectation of unseasonable wit displeased the imperial lover; he turned aside in disgust; Icasia concealed her mortification in a convent, and the modest silence of Theodora was rewarded with the golden apple.⁴⁶

To Theophilos, Kassia's defense of women demonstrated a lack of modesty and a quickness of wit superior to his own. She had captured Theophilos's mind and heart, but her bold answer lost for her the opportunity to become empress. Following this incident Kassia vowed to become a nun, fulfilling her vow after 843 C.E., when she founded a convent in her name in the western part of Constantinople. As the abbess of this convent, Kassia wrote sacred and secular compositions until her death sometime in the second half of the ninth century.

Kassia's secular poetry clearly reveals her perception of the Byzantine woman. Her poetic references to women are usually derogatory and caustic. For Kassia, the Byzantine woman is a *kakon* (a bad entity), even if she is beautiful. If she happens to be ugly, then her fate is far worse.[47] Kassia's writings cast a bitterness on all women because of their gender and because of the misogynist attitude that is fundamental to Byzantine thinking.

Kassia's musical compositions (along with incipits, modes, and occasions of performance) include forty-nine liturgical works, of which twenty-three are unquestionably by her with the remainder of doubtful authorship.[48] She is also known for having written music to the poetry and prose of other Byzantine hymnographers, such as Byzantios, Georgios, Kyprianos, and Marcos Monachos.

Most of Kassia's music falls in the category of *sticheron*, a lengthy verse chanted in various parts of the Byzantine Morning (Orthros) and Evening (Vespers) Office. A *Sticheron Idiomelon* has its own melody composed specifically for a verse, as opposed to a melody that is shared by other *stichera*. A *Sticheron Doxastikon* is one that glorifies or commemorates a saint or martyr.[49] Nearly every medieval *sticherarion* manuscript contains Kassia's works. She is the only medieval woman hymnographer whose musical works are represented in the present-day Eastern Orthodox Church.

Kassia's music is interesting textually and musically. She is known for her metrical rhyming schemes, the wittiness of her texts and use of puns, and the parallelism of textual and musical themes. A popular *sticheron* by Kassia is *Augustus, the Monarch*, in which the structure of melody follows one of the patterns for the sequence form: aabbccd. Because of the structure found in this *sticheron*, some scholars assume that the sequence was brought from Byzantium to the West.[50] Although this is difficult to prove, at the very least it can be stated that the medieval sequence was not only a Western form.

Kassia's most famous musical composition is her troparion *The Fallen Woman (Kyrie, e en pollais amartiais)* sung in the Morning Office of Holy Wednesday. This troparion, based on the sinful woman described by St. Luke (7:36–50), is considered to be autobiographical in part.[51] Emperor Theophilos later regretted his decision not to choose Kassia as his bride, and he attempted to meet her to express his sorrow and love. Although Kassia avoided him, in her heart she felt she had returned his love and had become a *porne*, a fallen woman.[52] Within a century of her death, Kassia's music, poetry, and romantic-tragic story had been immortalized, making her music among the most popular to be arranged by Greek composers through to the present day.

A later Byzantine woman musician is Kouvouklisena, a thirteenth-century precentor identified in Lavra MS Gamma 71, a manuscript in the largest monastery of Mount Athos.[53] The citation in the manuscript pertains to the date of her death. More important, it identifies her as a *domestikena*, or chantress and leader of a woman's choir. Although there were other female singers of chant, the acknowledgment of her musical role by a Greek male scribe from a monastery indicates her extraordinary vocal abilities and importance for the period. There is no clear indication that Kouvouklisena was a composer, but since many leading male precentors of the period were composers or at least arrangers of traditional chant, she also probably composed and improvised.

A Byzantine woman composer for whom we have a single musical reference is identified only as "the daughter of Ioannes Kladas." The sole musical composition and inscription in reference to this composer appears in Athens MS 2406, folio 258v. The composer is identified by the patronymic and the relationship of the composer to the patriarch of the family, following the ancient Greek tradition of identifying respectable women. The inscription reads, "It is said that this [composition] is [written] by the daughter of Ioannes Kladas."[54] It is interesting that in the single reference to this female composer no given or Christian name is indicated. In instances where male members of a family are cited, a given name is usually included in addition to a family relationship. From this reference, it appears that the daughter of Ioannes Kladas was probably known as a singer and composer.[55] Her fame, however, is not as great as that of her father, who was a leading composer of Byzantine chant of the late fourteenth century as well as "The *Lampadarios*" or *maistor* of the Hagia Sophia of Constantinople.[56]

Based on the known lifespan of Ioannes Kladas, the composition by his daughter would have originated during the late fourteenth or early fifteenth century. The composition is included in a section of the manuscript that contains a collection of compositions by Ioannes Kladas— possibly suggesting a dual authorship between father and daughter or a master-apprentice relationship. The selection attributed to the daughter is a simple antiphon from the *octoechos* and appears in the section of chants in Mode IV Authentic.[57]

A later Byzantine woman hymnographer who might have lived in the fifteenth century is identified as Palaeologina.[58] This hymnographer was obviously a well-educated, aristocratic woman from the Imperial family and dynasty Palaeologus that ruled from 1259 to 1453. Palaeologina is thought to have been a nun in one of the convents of Constantinople.[59] It was for the convent that she composed Kanons, for which only the texts have survived.

From Antiquity through the end of the Byzantine Empire, women were considered to be subordinate figures and were viewed as descendants of Pandora and later Eve, symbolic of the evil attributed to the female. This misogyny was based on a patriarchal structure that permeated every aspect of culture, within which respectable women were identified only by their patronymic. As might be expected, the women documented in music from both epochs were aristocratic and well educated, such as Sappho of Lesbos, Telesilla of Argos, and their Byzantine successors Kassia, Thekla, and Theodosia. The main differentiating factor between the two eras was the development of the Christian culture of medieval Byzantium from the pagan society of Antiquity.

In the Hellenistic period of Antiquity, the female musicians providing musical entertainment at *symposia* were the *hetairai*, highly intellectual courtesans. This tradition continued from Antiquity into the early centuries of the Byzantine Empire, when women continued to participate in secular entertainments by performing on musical instruments but were consequently condemned by the Church Fathers as prostitutes. Such condemnation prevailed until the decline of the Empire, stifling the participation of decent, respectable women in secular music. With no other outlet for musical participation, female composers and performers turned to sacred music and created new works for the nunneries of Byzantium; these convents served as cultural retreats for those aristocratic, wealthy, and educated women who did not marry. It was for the convents of Byzantium that the few known women composers and hymnographers wrote their compositions, to be chanted in liturgical services by their female peers. Some of these, such as Kouvouklisena, possessed outstanding vocal abilities that were admired by their male counterparts—an extraordinary measure of success. There is no doubt that the convents were centers for much musical activity and productivity by Byzantine women. However, few of the *typika* from nunneries have survived; more importantly, misogyny taints much of the documentation of Byzantine women's participation in music. Women were measured by the standard Byzantine phrase: *"Ismen de pantos kefalin tes gynaikos ton andra"* (Women are always under the head of the man).[60]

7

Feminized Devotion, Musical Nuns, and the "New-Style" Lombard Motet of the 1640s

Robert Kendrick

One of the most remarkable aspects of "early modern Catholicism" is the continued survival of late-medieval spirituality in the works of sixteenth- and seventeenth-century mystics.[1] Certainly the renowned women mystics of the post-Tridentine Church were an essential part of this phenomenon, along with the continuation (often in other guises) of devotional themes that had been associated with specifically female piety in the later Middle Ages. In this essay, I will outline one such case in early seventeenth-century Italy: the ways in which a gender-specific "female spirituality" was justified philsophically, expressed aesthetically, and enacted ritually, as seen (and heard) in one repertory associated with the most famous musicians of Seicento Lombardy, the numerous nuns (up to 75 percent of patrician daughters in Milan) who inhabited the female monasteries of the region.[2]

Most studies of post-Tridentine spirituality have focused on the great figures of Spanish and (later) French mysticism.[3] Yet Italian devotional life also experienced a major surge in the early Seicento.[4] Many of its representatives were nuns: Maria Maddalena de'Pazzi of Florence, Caterina Vannini of Siena, Giovanna Maria Bonomo of Bassano, and the Sicilian Isabella Tomasi.[5] The peninsula continued to produce holy women, female followers of semisuspect charismatic movements, and visionary nuns throughout the century.[6] In the Italian Church after the Council of Trent, these figures continued the late-medieval traditions of "living female saints," locally venerated *beate*, court prophetesses, and "irregular" communities of observant women that have been described by Gabriella Zarri.[7]

Even more important than their biological sex was these mystics' re-formulation of the kind of feminized devotional themes that have been brilliantly outlined by Caroline Bynum.[8] These include an emphasis on the suffering Body of Christ as food, recreated in Passion meditations and reenacted in Eucharistic devotion; the central role of Marian intercession, somewhat more prominent after Trent than before; and the reworkings of cults of female saints, most notably Mary Magdalen, but also Cecilia and lesser-known figures.

In Milan, a center whose rigidity and conservatism have been exaggerated in all but the most recent literature, these kinds of devotion flourished,[9] due in part to the opportunities for religious women's self-expression afforded by the remarkable pastoral philosophy and practice of Archbishop Federigo Borromeo (1564–1631; in office 1595–1631). Borromeo was passionately interested in female mystics (such as the reformed courtesan Vannini) throughout the peninsula, recording their lives and visions, traveling to visit and support them, and positing them (along with Mary Magdalen) as models for the roughly three thousand nuns in his own diocese, the largest of Catholic Europe.[10] His intense correspondence with numerous nuns in his charge, including women at the Umiliate house of S. Caterina in Brera and the Benedictine foundation of S. Maria del Lentasio, testifies to his personal interest in their interior lives, and includes some detailed descriptions on the part of his cloistered correspondents of their own spiritual progress.[11]

The philosophical basis for Borromeo's policy was formed by his gender-specific epistemology. In his guide for the pastoral "care" of female mystics, *De ecstaticis mulieribus et illusis* ("On Ecstatic and Delusional Women," Milan, 1616), Borromeo outlined his idea that the natural (Aristotelian) constitutions of men and women were different, and that consequentially women were by nature more open to true and false mystical experience than were men.[12] This essentialist idea, apparently original, had obvious influence when held by one of the most important prelates and patrons of the Seicento.[13]

What is the relation of all this to music? Very recent archival and stylistic studies of documents and musical repertory hitherto little known have highlighted the centrality of female monastic music in certain cities of the Cinquecento and Seicento.[14] Indeed, the episcopal interpretation and implementation of the Tridentine-era monastic enclosure (It. *clausura*) that was forced on all female (and only female) religious orders (except the Ursulines) seem actually to have promoted the spread of such musical life, both by their practical ineffectiveness in many cities and by their channeling of nuns' previously public role into not-so-cloistered monastic institutions for which music making was an acceptable if contested artistic outlet. In this transformation, music functioned as the literal and symbolic projection of nuns' voices into the world of the urban patriciate whence they had come.[15]

Certainly the Milanese and Lombard evidence would seem to bear out this idea. Significant traces of the cultivation of polyphony (nun composers, famed singers, *maestre di canto figurato*, and *madri concertatrici*) can be documented for some 70 percent of the female houses in the Lombard capital, with a significant spread outward from the most patrician foundations toward the less-prestigious houses, an expansion noticeable by the mid-Seicento. At several monasteries, including the Benedictine house of Santa Radegonda and the Augustinians of Santa Marta, there were two competing ensembles (singers and instrumentalists) in the same foundation; these musicians attracted local and foreign visitors to the monastic church on a regular basis.[16] In the (Spanish-ruled) State of Milan as a whole, similar evidence appears for the following dioceses: Novara, Vercelli, Como, Pavia, Cremona, and Lodi. On the Venetian *terrafirma*, nun musicians are found in Bergamo, Brescia, Verona, Padua, Vicenza, and in Venice itself.[17]

In their efforts to create and maintain musical traditions, efforts that included (at some houses) semilicit lessons from and even possible musical collaboration with outside (male) musicians, nuns could rely on the backing of their patrician families. In Milan, less expected but equally as helpful was the support of Federigo Borromeo for nuns' musical self-expression, at least within limits that did not violate the norms of *clausura*.[18] Borromeo sent music and instruments to his monasticized charges, and encouraged their music making within cloistered walls, including the use of the still-suspect violin family in informal paraliturgical celebrations. The prelate's writings specifically linked the musical activity of certain famous (and "certified") mystics, such as his protégée Caterina Vannini, to these women's visionary experiences:

> A woman of holy life . . . once was forced by the pleas of her companions to give them some sign and example of Heaven's harmony. . . . She took a lute in her hands, and touching some of its strings played a song so sublime . . . that similar melodic graces and progressions of consonances had never been heard. Now this woman continued to sing and play only a short time before achieving rapture.[19]

In this kind of atmosphere, it is no surprise that individual nuns connected their music to their deeply felt interior lives and spiritual states.

One of Federigo's correspondents, Suor Ippolita Confaloniera of the Umiliate house of S. Caterina in Brera, linked her musical activity to her devotional life in such words as the following:

> One past Sunday, after supper, many of my fellow [nuns] were walking for *ricreatione* . . . and since I was there I began to sing; and I sang a motet from memory . . . and while I sang, I felt my heart inflame, so much so that it seemed on the outside as if it were a little crazy.[20]

The ritual aspects of nuns' performances should also be noted here. In Federigo Borromeo's view, nuns represented "the most select portion of the flock of Christ," a special status of holy virgins consecrated to God. Their monasteries were characterized by several features that reinforced this idea, most notably the physical separation by means of a wall in the primary space for musical performance, the monastic church. The ritual space of female monastic choirs, thus distanced from the outside world, provided an earthly prefiguration of the heavenly Jerusalem in the eyes (and ears) of the prelate and many of his lay contemporaries.[21] Nuns' music making anticipated the celestial harmonies of the angelic choirs awaiting the saved individual soul. The association of transcendence and rapture with music in the monasteries seems to be more characteristic of the female houses than of the male foundations; music in the latter received cursory mention, if at all, without the "heavenly" references omnipresent in both episcopal and patrician descriptions of musical nuns.

Polyphonic psalms, Mass Propers, and motets clearly played an important role in formulating devotional themes in the interior life of Lombard nuns. In order to focus on one case study of the role of music in expressing themes in spirituality, it seems best to turn to one repertory at one specific juncture: the marked changes in the central north Italian motet that took place beginning around 1640 (here called, for convenience's sake, the "new Lombard style"). This period was marked by a flurry of activity in public ritual life in the city and in charismatic movements, not all of which were greeted enthusiastically by the church hierarchy.[22] For instance, the "Pelegian" heresy, led by the Brescian G. F. Casolo, flourished in a number of places in and around Milan during this decade until its repression at the hands of the strict Archbishop Alfonso Litta (in office 1652–79); its following was overwhelmingly female.[23] Other kinds of "false" or "failed" female saints were to be found in Milan, coexisting with the tradition of "certified" visionaries whom Federigo Borromeo had supported a generation before.[24] New kinds of affective spiritual literature circulated in the female monasteries and more generally in the households of the city's patriciate, a fact also noted by Archibishop Litta's curia.[25]

Several studies have noted the ritualization of public life in early modern Milan; in the city, important political and religious events (the distinction is neither firm nor heuristically helpful) were commemorated by processions, litanies, feasts, spectacles, and public liturgy.[26] Specific kinds of Eucharistic and Marian devotion—most notably the Forty Hours' Devotion (which originated in Milan) and the pilgrimages to Marian shrines like the Sacro Monte above Varese—flourished. The unsettling effects of the 1629–31 plague and the ongoing wars in Italy also seem to have encouraged this turn toward the social cement of ritual on one hand and the cultivation of an internally focused spirituality on the other.

It is in this turbulent atmosphere of the 1640s that a new kind of motet style appeared, introduced by composers active in Lombardy and Emilia. Central to the diffusion of this style was the *maestro* in Novara (twenty-five miles west of Milan), Gasparo Casati (ca. 1610–ca. 1641). Other composers in this stylistic current include the *maestro* at S. Maria presso S. Celso in Milan, Francesco (della) Porta, the peripatetic Franciscan Orazio Tarditi (working at a variety of posts in Emilia), and, last but by no means least, one of the musical nuns whose activities were outlined above, Chiara Margarita Cozzolani (1602–ca. 1677) at Santa Radegonda. To judge by the reprints and piratings, both Venetian and transalpine, of these composers' collections, the style was immediately and immensely popular with a wide range of audiences.[27]

What are the characteristics of the new style? It is best to begin with the kinds of texts increasingly set by these composers. The small-scale concertato motet in the Lombardy of the 1620s had still largely relied on the kinds of texts popular since the late Cinquecento: items from the breviary (not necessarily to be performed in their liturgically correct place), psalm or Gospel verses, and (most vitally, especially in Milan) centonized passages from the Song of Songs, particularly those citations that fit best into the second great tradition of canticle exegesis in Western Christianity, the "tropological" approach, which interpreted the spousal love of the Old Testament book as symbolic of the relation between Christ and the individual Christian soul. Since the twelfth century, this explanation had also been specifically applied to female monastic vocation.[28]

The Lombard motet of the 1640s made a radical break from biblical or liturgical texts. In their place, apparently newly written (and anonymous) texts appeared increasingly, often written in metrically Italian poetic stanzas or in a sort of prose poetry. The themes of this repertory are also markedly different, with almost equal emphasis on the Body of Christ (in all its forms, especially the Eucharist, but also the Incarnation and Passion) and on Marian intercession. But what is most striking about the literary language of these texts is their concentration on the physical details of such intercession, their employment of highly personalized and affective imagery, and their overwhelming parallelism of syntactic and rhetorical construction—all points that, in the context of the flourishing of female spirituality characteristic of the time, can only recall some of the major themes in late-medieval devotion that Bynum has argued were most fully expressed by female mystics.

Several quotes from the motet texts of Casati, Porta, and Cozzolani provide a sample of the literary style:[29]

> Oh how sweet you are, good Jesus,
> oh how joyful to those who love you,
> Inflame me with your love
> that I may seek you for all eternity.[30]

> O sweetest Jesus,
> O holiest Mary,
> hear the voice of one who cries out to you;
> miserable, I seek refuge in you
> that I may feed from your wound
> that I may suck from your milk. . . .[31]

> O sweet Jesus, you are the source of goodness
> and the source of love
> and in you is the source of life,
> O sweet Jesus.
> Let my soul then drink from you only,
> let it plead to you only,
> let it cry to you day and night.[32]

This theological and literary distance from the concerto of the 1620s was matched by a marked break in musical style.[33] The pace of declamation was speeded up, relatively quick antiphonal motives become omnipresent, sequences and quasi ostinatos extended the length and complexity of musical phrases and periods, and bass lines become more active, while rhetorical emphasis was provided primarily by textural and harmonic means such as homophonic writing in parallel thirds, and the almost syntactic use of irregularly prepared (major and minor) seventh chords. In their approach to texts, the concertos of the 1640s were also characterized by their composers' willingness to change and even to invert the traditions of how a particular text or topic was set.[34]

Many of these pieces are immediately attractive; the regularity of the new poetic forms in the literary texts is matched by the melodiousness of the style. When this approach was applied to the standard liturgical texts (the Ordinary of the Mass and Vespers psalms), the result was a "tuneful" (*arioso*) setting, found in the works of Casati and Cozzolani, which made prominent use of concertato solos and duets, internal refrains, and rhetorical perorations.

What is the relationship between this style and the music sung and played in the female monasteries of Lombardy? First, because of the dispersal of monastic libraries and service books during the Josephine and Napoleonic suppressions of the late Settecento, almost no music belonging to female houses has survived.[35] However, the printed editions that *can* be documented as having been owned by nuns, at least in Milan and Como, fit squarely into the new Lombard style and its imitations; these editions include motet books of another Casati (Girolamo, called Filago), Tarditi, Federico Pedroni, and others.[36]

Second, we should consider the kind of social circle within which this music first circulated. In Milan, the new style was cultivated by composers working in the parishes or monasteries—in essence, figures in the orbit of the urban patrician families who supported female monastic houses. The most famous performers from this class were precisely nuns, whose institutions (and their singers) had survived the plague and famine years of 1629–31 better than the rest of the city. Indeed, most nuns received their outside musical training from figures associated not with the Duomo but with the other institutions of Milan.[37] The increasingly "feminized" nature of the mid-century concerto repertory of urban parishes and monasteries is evident not only from the devotional themes expressed therein but also from the activity of cloistered female patricians as its primary performers. Indeed, it may be precisely to the new style that the increasingly conservative composer and organist at the Duomo, Michelangelo Grancini, would intend a slighting (and gendered) reference in a dedication to Archibishop Cesare Monti, dating from 1645.[38]

The final point of connection between nuns' music (or at least one nun's music) and the new style is this: Cozzolani's *Concerti sacri*, op. 2 (1642; this is her first book to have survived), represents the first employment of the new style by a composer working in the city of Milan proper. In light of the nominal *clausura* affecting Santa Radegonda, this is remarkable.[39] In order to trace the musical expression of one theme in spirituality traditionally associated with specifically female devotion, I should like to consider two of the "free-texted" concertos cast in the new Lombard style and included in her last book, the *Salmi à otto* of 1650.

Both these pieces concern a topic of great importance in late-medieval devotion, the so-called Double Intercession of Jesus and Mary on behalf of sinful humanity, a concept that viewed Christ and his mother as partners in pleading for iniquitous mortals before God the Father. This theme had been submerged to some extent in the Tridentine era, only to re-emerge in the motet repertory (although it is not widely found in the religious literature or pictorial iconography of mid-century). The first of these motets, *Tu dulcis, o bone Jesu* (scored for two altos, two tenors, and continuo), assigns praise of Jesus' and Mary's benignity and intercession to each of the two vocal types, respectively (Example 1). Cozzolani rounds off the concluding tutti section of the motet by a peroration in four-part invertible counterpoint that sets a typically hymn-like stanza imploring Mary to invoke her Son:

> You, sacred Mother,
> holy Mother,
> merciful Mother,
> our path in this world,
> achieve favor,
> obtain grace,
> so that Jesus your Son
> may grant us his glory.[40]

The other motet on this theme in the 1650 book, *O quam bonus es*, is a somewhat different piece. First, it is almost the only "free" (non-liturgical or non-Scriptural) text in the Milanese repertory of the decade to have been set independently by two different composers; Francesco della Porta had published a version two years before Cozzolani's setting in this *Motetti à 2–5*, op. 3.[41] Second, the text's extended and extremely graphic imagery focuses not on the generalized aspects of the Double Intercession but on the highly specific function of Jesus and Mary as food for the individual Christian soul: Christ's blood shed on the Cross and Mary's milk that fed her Son (and by extension, all Christians). A passage from the text, whose speaker is presumably the individual Christian, gives some idea of the striking literary imagery and language:

Example 1. Cozzolani, *Tu dulcis, o bone Jesu* (1650), opening.

Example 1 (*continued*)

ri- a,

a- vis, o al- ma Ma- ri- a,

Oh how good you are, how soft
how joyful, my Jesus:
Oh how kind you are, how sweet
how delightful, O Mary;

Loving, sighing,
having, tasting you.

Oh happy, blessed me:
here I feed from his wound,
here I suck from her breast,
I do not know where to turn next.

Life in his wound,
salvation in her breast.[42]

His blood strengthens me,
her milk purifies me,
his blood refreshes me,
her milk revives me,
his blood intoxicates me,
her milk gladdens me.[43]

The image of Christ offering the wound in his side while Mary offers her breast had received several treatments in both northern and southern European painting around 1500, while the general idea seems to have survived in some areas, such as Naples, into the Cinquecento.[44] In later medieval iconography, the idea was often associated with the so-called Fountain of Salvation, fed by Christ's blood and Mary's milk.

Bynum has documented the ways in which this *topos*, with its combination of Eucharistic, Passion, Marian, and nutritional references, was central to the view of Jesus and Mary as food in the later Middle Ages.[45] Both men and women experienced this dual nourishment, in which Christ's wounds are equated with a mother's milk. The difference between men's and women's accounts lay not so much in the symbolic content of the vision as in the ways in which female mystics sought the *imitatio* of Christ's corporal feeding through their own bodily behavior.[46]

There are few pictorial representations of this theme in Seicento Milanese painting.[47] But one altarpiece by Melchiorre Gherardini, created around 1640 for the Marian shrine of S. Maria presso S. Celso (where Porta was organist and *maestro* after 1642), makes the explicit link between nuns' piety and the physical nourishment provided by the bleeding Christ (Figure 7-1). In this picture the most famous female monastic saint of early modern Italy, the Dominican tertiary Catherine of Siena, nurses from Christ's wounds as part of her mystic vision. The parallels with the text set by Porta and Cozzolani are striking.

Cozzolani's motet is among the most remarkable pieces in the mid-century Milanese repertory. It is certainly one of the longest concertos, running 285 bars and employing a plethora of melodic ideas, along with the quick declamation typical of the new style. Like Porta's version, it is cast in the preferred scoring of the new Lombard style: the high-voice duet (here, as normally, two sopranos), a layout whose accessibility to female monastic singers should not be underestimated.[48] The piece begins with a long, harmonically closed melodic period for canto I answered (in the manner of another popular genre, the musical dialogue) by canto II. From the opening onward, several sets of parallelisms (illustrated in Example 2) determine the text and its setting: the apportioning of the meditation on Christ's blood to the first soprano and on Mary's milk to the second; the ecstatic cataloguing of the virtues of these fluids, set by short antiphonal exchanges between the voices; and the balanced placement of sections around an internal refrain (o me felicem, o me beatum/quo me vertam nescio).[49] The summation of this opening section (in rhetorical terms, the end of the exordium) is marked by the homophonic declamation and dissonance of mm. 113–17, which combine both Jesus' wound and Mary's breast in a single melodic gesture.

There is another structure present in the piece as well, the meditative process of alternation between Jesus' and Mary's bodies on one hand and their effect on the individual Christian on the other. This effect is encapsulated in the constant oscillation between the two pitch centers of the piece, B^b and G (also notable on the phrase level in Example 2). This back-and-forth movement is broken by a series of tonally stable sections (on either pitch), and it is worthwhile to recall that standard devotional manuals on the Passion, including at least one written by a

Figure 7-1. Melchiorre Gherardini, *St. Catherine of Si-ena Kissing the Wounds in Christ's Side* (ca. 1640).
Milan, Church of S. Maria presso S. Celso. Photograph
courtesy of Ministero dei Beni Culturali e Ambientali,
Sopraintendenza di Brera, and Istituto per la Storia
dell'Arte Lombarda.

Example 2. Cozzolani, *O quam bonus es* (1650), mm. 80–118.

Example 2 (*continued*)

Robert Kendrick

Example 2 (*continued*)

Benedictine nun and mystic, recommend that meditation on the various aspects of Christ's suffering be broken by pauses for reflection and summation.[50]

O quam bonus moves towards a concluding triple-time ostinato in an *alla zoppa* ("limping," or syncopated) rhythmic pattern, followed by an *adagio* homophonic period; the two sections link Christ's and Mary's nourishment to joy and laughter, and then to Christian life and death (O potus, o cibus / o risus, o gaudium / o felix vita, beata mors).[51] The juxtaposition of the imagery may seem unusual. However, Federigo Borromeo's philosophy of Christian optimism provides one explanation.[52] In his *I tre piaceri della cristiana* (The Three Pleasures of the Christian Mind, Milan, 1625), a treatise apparently intended for nuns, the prelate had discussed the "celestial laughter" experienced by his beloved female mystics, modern and medieval, as the highest form of Divine revelation.[53] This explication is followed in Book IV of the treatise by a chapter on the idea of "most joyful death," viewed as a gateway to eternal life and as the culmination of the Christian's "happy life."[54]

Hence, Cozzolani's motet should be seen (and heard) as a sort of epitome of one nun's view of Christian life: a view in which the traditionally female or feminized expression of Eucharistic devotion was combined with new emphasis on Marian intercession. Its musical setting provides a statement of this kind of spirituality in the one form of public self-expression possible for Milanese nuns after Trent. And its musical substance reflects one woman's reworking and extension of the style that her own works, and possibly the performances of her house's ensembles, had helped to introduce to Milan. Finally, *O quam bonus* highlights the remarkable survival of medieval spirituality in the genres and styles associated with the performances of women religious in the seventeenth century.

8

Symbols, Performers, and Sponsors:
Female Musical Creators
in the Late Middle Ages

Kimberly Marshall

[Christine de Pisan:] "But please enlighten me again, whether it has ever pleased this God, who has bestowed so many favors on women, to honor the feminine sex with the privilege of the virtue of high understanding and great learning, and whether women ever have a clever enough mind for this. I wish very much to know this because men maintain that the mind of women can learn only a little."

She [Reason] answered, "My daughter, since I told you before, you know quite well that the opposite of their opinion is true, and to show you this even more clearly, I will give you proof through examples. I tell you again— and don't doubt the contrary—if it were customary to send daughters to school like sons, and if they were then taught the natural sciences, they would learn as thoroughly and understand the subtleties of all the arts and sciences as well as sons."[1]

Reason's reassuring words to Christine de Pisan suggest that short-comings in women's understanding of the arts and sciences during the early fifteenth century resulted from a lack of schooling. Education was especially vital for the musician of Christine's day, when the development of polyphonic writing had begun to undermine the prestige of monophonic song, a musical form in which women had always been active. "Only in the fourteenth century, when secular music became generally polyphonic, did women's opportunity to compose fall far be-hind men's, because women lacked access to musical training in eccle-siastical schools and universities."[2] The results of women's "falling be-hind" became increasingly significant as the centuries passed. The accelerating specialization of Western music broke many of the tradi-tional links between women and music. Its complexity required notation, sometimes separating the composer from those who performed the score. Music lost its close relationship with domestic life and community ritual, becoming a public entertainment to meet the needs of increasingly larger audiences. This in turn necessitated the organization of public musical establishments and specialized institutions for musical education, to which women were often denied access. These developments placed obstacles in the way of women desirous of pursuing an advanced musical education or career. Already by the early fifteenth century, women were being conditioned to accept traditional roles, as illustrated in another dialogue between Christine de Pisan and Reason:

> [Christine] "My lady, since they [women] have minds skilled in conceptualizing and learning, just like men, why don't women learn more?"
>
> She [Reason] replied, "Because, my daughter, the public does not require them to get involved in the affairs which men are commissioned to execute. . . . It is enough for women to perform the usual duties to which they are ordained."[3]

These "usual duties" were those of keeping a house and mothering children; they did not include developing specialized musical skills. Women's strong links with music through spiritual ritual and domestic entertainment were gradually broken in Europe as the Church exercised its control of the former and the growing professionalism of musical performance undermined the latter.[4] "Mulier in ecclesia taceat" took on renewed significance in the fourteenth century, as Churchmen inveighed against the vices of the women who were leading caroles throughout Europe.[5] The teaching of polyphonic music took place largely in the ecclesiastical schools and choirs, which reduced women's access to instruction in contrapuntal composition. Similarly, there was no place for women in the University, whose liberal arts curriculum dealt less with polyphonic practice than with Boethian theory, but whose degrees were necessary for admission into the profession.[6]

It is easy to explain the scarcity of musical works by women as a result of the educational and social obstacles confronting female musicians. But some women clearly managed to overcome these obstacles, and their creativity remains largely unacknowledged because of the way modern scholarship has interpreted surviving evidence about them. Iconographical sources depicting allegorical women musicians have been viewed as "symbolic" without recognizing the close link between symbolism and real-life women. Archival and literary accounts of women singing and playing instruments have been considered merely to document "performers," sometimes in contexts where the performer most likely invented her own music. Many women involved in the genesis of musical composition either through financial patronage or personal influence have been classified as "sponsors" and thereby denied credit as active participants in the creative process. In this article I will re-evaluate some late-medieval evidence for women making music to show how they have been "cut out of the picture" of music history by redefining them as accessories to the act of creation.[7] We shall see that the barriers to a musical education did not deter some medieval women, although their musical activity remains largely unacknowledged by modern scholars.

The Symbols

Many depictions of women making music have survived from the Middle Ages. Yet despite convincing elements of realism in some of these pictures, most have been interpreted to be merely symbolic rather than to document real-life female musicians. The significance of women playing musical instruments is overlooked as scholars debate issues of chronology and iconography. I propose to re-investigate some of these depictions to see if they might provide evidence for medieval women as performers and teachers of polyphonic music.

Concurrent with women's falling behind in musical education in the thirteenth and fourteenth centuries, there appear several female personifications of music: the Classical liberal art, Musica, is depicted as a woman with various musical instruments in medieval art through the fifteenth century; a fourteenth-century literary narrative describes an allegorical female associated with divine music; and toward the end of the fifteenth century, a quasi-mythological Cecilia is introduced as the patron saint of music. Although these figures of musical women are clearly meant to be symbols, the instruments with which they are shown reflect a shift in emphasis from monophonic to polyphonic music. This coincides with evidence for the development of polyphony during the thirteenth century, suggesting a layer of meaning behind the myth of the female musical persona.

In the same way that the Muses of Classical myth portrayed inspirational forces directing the artist or scholar, the very arts and sciences themselves were personified as women. Female images with special attributes denoted the Classical liberal arts, and this tradition was continued in the Middle Ages to depict the disciplines of the seven liberal arts.[8] Why were female figures chosen to fulfill these allegorical functions? It is clear that abstract nouns such as Musica and Geometrica are feminine and therefore suggest female personifications.[9] But a deeper motivation is suggested by Joseph Campbell, the noted scholar of mythology: "Woman, in the picture language of mythology, represents the totality of what can be known. The hero is the one who comes to know."[10] According to Campbell's interpretation of myth, the Muses and the Liberal Arts represent areas of knowledge that must be conquered by male heroes.[11]

In a curious reversal of the male insemination of women for procreation, such personifications suggest a female "inspiration" of men for artistic creation. The medieval symbols of music would appear to be deeply rooted in a mythology that attributes the quest for knowledge and artistic creation to men, with women at most serving to inspire male efforts.[12] Depictions of Musica and the Muses are locked into these symbolic stereotypes and might seem to offer few clues about real women musicians.

Yet the iconography of Musica reflects real developments in Western sacred music.[13] Over the course of several centuries, images of the Liberal Arts were produced in media as diverse as stone sculptures decorating Gothic cathedrals and illuminations ornamenting medieval manuscripts. In early depictions, Musica is depicted with three other female figures representing the quadrivium, as in a ninth-century illustration preceding Boethius' "De Arithmetica," where she holds a plucked stringed instrument of the lute family (Figure 8-1).[14] By the twelfth century, when she is sculpted with the other Liberal Arts in the west facade of Chartres Cathedral, Musica holds a psaltery and plays cymbala above her head, while two stringed instruments, perhaps echoing the depiction with lute mentioned above, frame her on either side (Figure 8-2).

Similar instruments are shown in the historiated initial of "Exultate" in the thirteenth-century *St. Louis Psalter*, where a seated Musica holds a psaltery. Four bells hang at either side of her, and a fiddle and a harp appear underneath the bells (Figure 8-3). The presence of these floating stringed instruments is reminiscent of the Chartres sculpture; another similarity between the two depictions is their function as sacred art, in contrast to the earlier illustration in the Bamberg manuscript.

Musica is shown with the monochord in illustrations of the "Meister der Musik." The monochord was an instrument containing a single string that could be stopped at different points along its length in order to calculate melodic intervals and to teach them to singers. Since the

Figure 8-1. Miniature of Musica with the other three arts of the quadrivium. Tours, mid-ninth century. From Boethius, "De Arithmetica," Bamberg, Stadtsbibliothek, MS class. 5, fol. 9v.

Figure 8-2. Sculpture depicting Musica among the liberal arts. Chartres Cathedral, Royal Portal, south door, south side. French, twelfth century. Photograph courtesy of Archive Photographique, Paris, S.P.A.D.E.M.

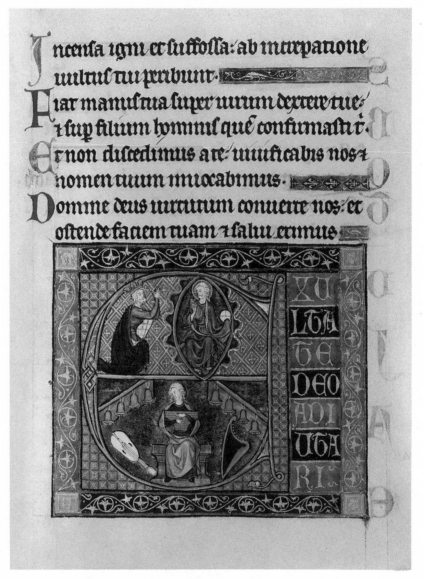

Figure 8-3. Historiated initial, "Exultate deo," from the *St. Louis Psalter*. French, thirteenth century. Paris, Bibliothèque nationale, MS lat. 10525, fol. 175r.

monochord was an important theoretical and pedagogical device, it was a suitable instrument to include in depictions of music's "masters." Except for the allegorical Musica, these masters are exclusively male, such as Saint Gregory, credited with codifying the chant that bears his name, and Pythagoras, attributed with discovering the principles of musical proportion while listening to a blacksmith's hammers. An early example of this iconographical cycle was created in Augsburg ca. 1100,[15] where a seated Musica plays the monochord (Figure 8-4). A thirteenth-century cycle depicts Pythagoras on the same folio as Musica, who carries the symbolic monochord, toward which he seems to point (Figure 8-5).

The cymbala also were used iconographically to represent Pythagorean proportions, as in the Chartres sculpture and the *St. Louis Psalter* (Figure 8-2 and 8-3). The different sizes of a set of bells provide a more explicit visual representation of the proportional correspondence between pitch and size than does a single string. In addition, the cymbala were clearly associated with sacred music, to the point that King David was sometimes substituted for Musica in this iconography.[16]

The close association between Musica and David is reflected in the *St. Louis Psalter,* where they are both depicted within the aforementioned historiated initial decorating Psalm 80, *Exultate deo.* In the upper half of the initial, King David prays before Christ; Musica and her instruments occupy the lower half. The combination of Musica with King David in this psalter decoration suggests the changing status of the liberal arts. Musica, the liberal art of music, is studied in order to gain a greater understanding of the psalmist's worship of God as described in Psalm 80. The presence of Musica in this context reflects the new theological significance given to classical pagan learning. In the thirteenth century, " 'Theology' triumphed over 'Grammar' and the Liberal Arts to such a degree that surviving Greek and Latin literature was transformed into moralized lessons in the service of theology."[17] No longer were the liberal arts to be pursued as ends in themselves; scientific knowledge was to serve theological inquiry, and not the other way round.

At the very time when the scientific aspect of music was subsumed as an element of theological inquiry, the art of polyphony was cultivated to adorn the Christian liturgy. This evolution of sacred vocal music, from monophonic chant to polyphonic organum, is also reflected in the instruments depicted with images of Musica. First she was shown with monophonic instruments such as the monochord and cymbala.

Figure 8-4. Pen and ink drawing of Musica, from a series representing "Meister der Musik," Augsburg, ca. 1100. Wolfenbüttel, Herzog August Bibliothek, MS Gud. lat. 8° 334, fol. 2v.

Figure 8-5. Pen and ink drawing of Musica with Pythagoras, from a series representing "Meister der Musik," Cistercian Abbey of Aldersback, Salzburg, thirteenth century. Johannes of Afflighem, *De Musica*, Munich, Bayerische Staatsbibliothek, MS 2599, fol. 103r.

During the thirteenth century, her iconography was further diversified to include the organ, which was capable of executing polyphony. In a miniature decorating the anonymous *Roman des sept sages de Rome*, Musica plays four cymbala with two mallets; instead of the usual entourage of stringed instruments surrounding her, a small organ is shown (Figure 8-6).

As with the cymbala discussed above, the lengths of the organ pipes are meant to represent the proportional sizes and pitches of Pythagorean music theory. "There is little need to offer any elaborate explanation of the choice of organ for Lady Music, since the organ was the instrument traditionally associated with music in medieval images, and especially those aspects of music that concern measurement."[18] More important to the organ than its association with Pythagorean measurements, however, was its ability to realize polyphony, the new art that was developed with great vigor during the thirteenth and fourteenth centuries. The introduction of a key action to move sliders, documented on Western organs as early as the eleventh century, enabled one person to execute two or more lines of music simultaneously.[19] The organ was the instrument ideally suited to the performance of polyphonic composition, and it consequently was featured with Musica increasingly often in late-medieval iconography. The measurement symbolized by the organ was twofold: the proportional sizes of Pythagorean intervals and the vertical ordering of pitches to create polyphony.

Although they may be seen as mere symbols, the organs shown in depictions of Musica sometimes included details taken from real instruments. One such detail is the presence of labels above keys, as shown in a thirteenth-century French manuscript where Musica plays an organ whose keyboard compass is labeled with letters, starting with A (Figure 8-7). This is reminiscent of earlier manuscript representations of organs, such as that in the *Harding Bible*, dated 1109, where organ sliders are identified by the letters of the diatonic alphabet.[20] The inclusion of alphabetical labels in these depictions reflects the construction of actual instruments, for the earliest surviving organ fragments from the fourteenth century still bear the remains of parchment strips on which were written the letters of the keyboard compass.[21] The presence of this detail in the Musica miniature of Figure 8-7 suggests that its artist was incorporating aspects of real organs into the depiction.

Even more important to our discussion is the possibility that miniatures of Musica with realistic instruments depict real female music instructors. In his discussion of a thirteenth-century French depiction of

Figure 8-6. Miniature showing Musica with cymbala and organ. French, thirteenth century. *Le roman des sept sages de Rome*, Paris, Bibliothèque nationale, MS fr. 19166, fol. 2r.

Figure 8-7. Miniature showing Musica with an organ. French, thirteenth century. Vrigiet de Solas, *Verger de Consolation,* Paris, Bibliothèque nationale, MS fr. 9220, fol. 16r.

Musica (Florence, Biblioteca Medicea Laurenziana, Plut. 29 I), Seebass concludes that the female figure "has taken on the features of a real music teacher." He hypothesizes that the teaching of the liberal arts by female preceptors may have been known to the illuminator who painted the representation of Musica in this manuscript.[22] Seebass' argument that the iconography of Musica sometimes depicts real teachers can be extended to include female instrumentalists, as we shall see in the next section on performers.

From the fourteenth century onward, the use of the organ to depict polyphonic practice may seem to be undermined by the increasing frequency of portative organs in the iconography. In an illumination from a fourteenth-century manuscript now in the National Library in Naples

(MS V.A. 14, f. 47v), Musica plays a portable organ in the center of a folio, surrounded by musicians playing other instruments. The famous painting of the Liberal Arts and Sciences in the Spanish Chapel of Santa Maria del Fiore in Florence also shows Musica playing a portable organ.[23] Such instruments were very limited in the execution of polyphony, since their keyboards were played with one hand only while the other pumped the bellows. But these small organs may have been depicted to symbolize larger ones, especially in manuscript illuminations where space was limited.[24] The same use of portable organs is found in miniatures depicting King David, such as a miniature in a fifteenth-century French Book-of-Hours (Paris, Musée du Petit Palais MS 35, f. 93), where David plays his harp before a table on which sits a portable organ.[25]

The musical iconography of King David had a long history similar to that of Musica in many ways. In the earliest surviving manuscript illuminations of the Psalmist, he is shown with a stringed instrument, the *cithara*, depicted as various types of lyre, and intended to represent the enigmatic *kinnor* of the Biblical text. The *cithara* was an instrument associated with Antiquity; it was depicted in many shapes and sizes by medieval artists, undoubtedly because they had no contemporary models upon which to base their drawings. Eventually, illuminators settled on a stringed instrument taken from the medieval instrumentarium, and the harp became the instrument of King David, as seen in the *Exultate* initial of the *St. Louis Psalter* (Figure 8-3). In an evolution remarkably similar to that of the Musica depictions, David was also shown with cymbala and, by the thirteenth century, with the organ. The instrument legitimated by the Church was anachronistically thrust upon the Psalmist to denote him as the ancestor of liturgical music.[26] David was considered to have unveiled the mysteries of musical science in order to glorify God, and he thus provided a perfect model for the theologically based humanism of the thirteenth century. According to Seebass, King David, "unlike the other musical personifications, contains within himself both liturgical and theoretical connotations."[27]

Yet, as we have already seen, Musica, too, developed into a musical personification with both liturgical and theoretical aspects. Indeed, it would appear that by the fifteenth century, these aspects were indistinguishable in the iconography. The depiction of an organ and stringed instruments provided a standardized background for the representation of all musicians, whether they sang in church or played at court, whether they were performers or theorists. In a rare depiction of a historical female musician, even the pagan Sappho is depicted with the harp, psaltery, and organ of the medieval instrumentarium (Figure 8-8).

It is interesting to note the similar iconographies adopted by medieval artists to depict allegorical figures like Musica and historical figures like Sappho and King David. During the fourteenth and fifteenth centuries, all are shown with late-medieval instruments, sometimes represented with great accuracy. Although such pictorial sources have been the subject of many studies attempting to glean information about performance practice, the issue of gender has been largely ignored. Despite the large quantity of illustrations that show women playing the organ, they are invariably used to document a performing tradition that is essentially male. This approach to interpreting the iconography is typified by the following conclusion: "Lady Music plays the organ in the later *trecento* pictures because it is one of the oldest instruments, because the measurement of its pipes was the subject of intensive investigation in the middle ages, perhaps, too, because expert and famous musicians of the fourteenth century, *men* like Francesco Landini, learned in music as well as the other arts, had mastered the technique of performing upon it" (emphasis mine).[28] As we shall see, some expert, if not famous, musicians of the fourteenth century were women. Their contributions to medieval music may be documented in the many surviving portrayals of Musica.

Musica was not the only female musician to appear within the pages of medieval manuscripts. A rich cycle of illuminated copies of Deguileville's *Pèlerinage de la Vie Humaine*, written ca. 1330 and revised by the author fifty years later, depicts an allegorical female figure with the tools of the musical trade. This woman is introduced in the text as Latria (Latin for *worship*), and she is responsible for awakening the King (God) with a horn and for entertaining him with music on the organ and psaltery (Figure 8-9).[29] Latria clearly symbolizes liturgical music in Deguileville's account, and her performance on organ and psaltery brings to mind the representations of Musica and King David discussed above. In all of these, the science of music, along with its spiritual connotations of celestial harmony and divine proportion, is symbolized by a combination of stringed instruments and organ.

But while images of King David denoted a historical person, a man who lived, labored, and loved, Musica and Latria did not denote famous women. Rather, they were vague portrayals of the science of music or the religious function of music, in many ways serving as female coun-

Figure 8-8. Miniature of Sappho. French, ca. 1470.
Bocaccio, *Des cleres et nobles femmes,* New York
Public Library, Spencer MS 33, fol. 24r.

Figure 8-9. Miniature showing the Pilgrim's encounter with Latria and her musical instruments. English version, ca. 1440. Guillaume de Deguileville, *Pèlerinage de la Vie Humaine*, London, British Library, MS Cotton Tiberius VII (5), fol. 104v.

terparts to the iconography of King David. They evolved as empty allegories for changing musical technology, without reference to a female role in forging musical development. It is striking that medieval depictions of music show real men and allegorical women.[30] The standard female counterparts to David, Tubal, Pythagoras, and St. Gregory are Musica and the Muses, not Miriam or Sappho. This is clearly shown in the iconography of the Chartres sculpture, where figures denoting real men accompany the female personas of the Liberal Arts; underneath Musica is a male figure that represents either Tubal or Pythagoras (see Figure 8-2).[31]

In the late fifteenth century a female persona, rather than a real-life model, was introduced as the patron saint of music. Although there is little evidence that she actually existed, Saint Cecilia begins to appear in the art and literature of the late fifteenth century, either carrying or playing an organ, often of the portable variety, as in earlier personifications of music such as Musica and Latria. Cecilia's association with music is only beginning to be understood. A fascinating new theory suggests that her link to the musical art derives from the Scriptural lesson that is read during the stational liturgy at S. Cecilia in Trastevere: "Hear our prayer, and look kindly on the people you claim as your own; turn our mourning into joy, so that we may live and praise your name, O Lord; and do not close the mouths of those who sing your praises" (Esther 13:17).[32] This text is a plea from Esther that her people's mourning be turned into joy and that this transformation be expressed through music, by singing praises to God. These words from Cecilia's stational liturgy linked her to the concept of music expressing joy, and she became another female symbol of music, bearing as her attribute the organ found in earlier iconographical traditions.

Like Musica and Latria, Cecilia may have been a mythical creation. Although her betrothed, Valerian, and his brother Tibertius were documented as Christian martyrs, there is no mention of her until ca. 500 C.E.[33] Her stational liturgy, held on the Wednesday after the second Sunday of Lent, originated at the shrine of a Roman goddess, the Bona Dea, who cured eye disease under the names Oclata (the Good-Goddess-with-the-Eye) and Restitutrix or Restituta (the Restorer).[34] Cecilia may be no more than a fanciful creation adapted from pagan myth to correspond to a Christian context. Ironically, her introduction as the patron saint of music in the fifteenth century heralds the devaluation of women's musical activity in the Western world.

The Performers

Do these abstractions of women musicians compensate for a dearth of real-life examples? Or is it a subtle method of idealizing the female, of distancing women from the creation of music while making them the inspiration for men's compositions? If the world of courtly love is "a fantasy created to compensate women for their declining influence in the real world,"[35] might the musical personas of Musica and Saint Cecilia be no more than fantasies to compensate women for their diminished roles in creating music?

No one seems to question that women were active as musical performers during the late Middle Ages. Making music was an important aspect of gentility, as recorded in many thirteenth-century romances, where women pass the time embroidering, playing board games, and singing, with or without instrumental accompaniment. In *La clef d'amors*, young girls are advised to sing and to play instruments,[36] and such advice seems to have been heeded, judging from accounts in the many romances where women provided musical entertainment. Music was an ornament with which women decorated court life. They were expected to perform publicly as singers and dancers; young women were responsible for leading the dancing and singing of caroles, "the most conspicuous of all court festivities."[37]

Yet despite this documented musical activity, it is still tacitly assumed that when women sang even simple monophonic songs they were performing notated works by others. This assumption is clear in a recent interpretation of an account from *L'Histoire de Guillaume le Maréchal*.[38] The narrative reports that in 1219 William Marshall was on his deathbed and summoned his daughters to sing for him. Significantly, the daughters sang individually, first Maheut, then Joane, who was reluctant to sing at such a sad occasion. But desirous of pleasing her father, the skilled Joane finally complied with his request, singing a stanza of a *rotruenge*, a poem documented in the troubadour and trouvère repertory. No more information is given in the account. A leading modern scholar has the following to ask about this tantalizing reference to a woman creating music in the early thirteenth century:

> [T]here can be little doubt that the author of William Marshall's biography has carried us directly to the realm of trouvère monody as we know it from the surviving chansonniers. How did William Marshall's daughters gain access to such pieces? Did they own written copies of them, and was there already a written tradition of trouvère monody c. 1220? These are wide-ranging and controversial questions which cannot be treated here in anything like the fashion they deserve.[39]

Perhaps other questions, even more wide-ranging and controversial, also need to be asked. Might Joane have sung a *rotruenge* of her own invention, without the need for "access to such pieces" or "written copies" by others? Might the "written tradition of trouvère monody" have included melodies conceived by other women? Might some of the "women's songs" attributed to male composers have been conceived by women and notated by men? There is much documentation for women singing monophonic songs in late-medieval literature, and correspondingly little reason to believe that singers were dependent on written copies of compositions by other people. Perhaps the opposite was true, and some of the music notated by the trouvères preserved for posterity a corpus of songs by women that were transmitted orally. Although this is speculation, it seems a plausible explanation of the link between narrative accounts of women singing and the function of written compositions during this early period.

Given the reluctance to acknowledge possible female creativity in the realm of monophonic song, it is hardly surprising that polyphony has been considered the major stumbling block to composition by late-medieval women. But the argument that women disappeared from the compositional limelight because of the rigid demands of polyphonic writing does not explain why the absence of a single musical composition attributed to a woman between ca. 1300 and 1566 was followed by a wealth of published collections of polyphonic music by women after that date.[40] Did women suddenly gain access to a better musical education during the sixteenth century? Perhaps the inexplicability of such a musical void resides less in the inability of late-medieval women to create music than in our assumptions when interpreting the data. In the same way that pictures of Musica and Saint Cecilia are now relegated to the status of symbolism, late-medieval accounts of female musical creators are interpreted to provide information about performers or sponsors, those who *inspire* compositions by men.

There is no dearth of sources documenting the participation of women in the performance of many types of polyphony, both sacred and secular, vocal and instrumental. As early as 1935, Yvonne Rokseth published an article documenting the musical roles of late-medieval women, including the performance of polyphony when it became popular in the fourteenth century.[41] Her purpose was to provide a summary of references to women musicians before the fifteenth century, in most cases leaving the reader to draw conclusions from the evidence presented. Although most of Rokseth's references have been amplified by later scholars, some have remained in relative obscurity, including a payment in the accounts of the hôtel d'Artois for All Saints' Day of the year 1320 to "Jehanne, qui jeue des orgues" (Joan, who plays the organ).[42] Unlike the case of the earlier Joan who sang a song for her father, there is no surviving notated repertoire to suggest that Jehanne played works by other "composers." One therefore feels comfortable in assuming that she created her own music for the organ. The reference predates the earliest surviving keyboard music by thirty to forty years and is the earliest medieval reference to a female organist of which I am aware.[43] Although it is dangerous to rely too heavily on such an isolated source, one is tempted to see Jehanne as a real-life counterpart to symbolic figures like Musica and Latria. The chronology coincides nicely as well: the documentation for a real woman organist comes after the general shift from monochord or cymbala to organ in some depictions of Musica during the thirteenth century, and just before Deguileville's allegorical organist Latria.

The lack of written instrumental music from the fourteenth century helps us to remember that during this early time instrumentalists did not rely on notation in musical performance; they either improvised or learned from memory the music they performed. The few scores that have survived probably served more as a reference in the preparation of a performance or in the dissemination of a style than as *aide-memoires* to a verbatim rendition of the notated music. Although more keyboard music survives from the next century, the use of a notated score had probably changed very little, to judge from the information contained in fifteenth-century German pedagogical treatises. Both Conrad Paumann's *Fundamentum organisandi* and an anonymous Latin treatise on composition and improvisation[44] provide methods for creating a free upper voice and a countertenor based upon a slow-moving tenor part. In the anonymous work, the author includes a sample composition to demonstrate the practical application of the rules discussed in prose. The methods in these two sources were intended to help organists improvise or compose a two- or three-part piece based upon any given melody and thus to arrange diverse vocal forms for instrumental performance, sometimes utilizing only the tenor of the original model. Not surprisingly, the keyboard pieces attributed to Paumann in the *Buxheimer Orgelbuch* follow the basic principles elucidated in his *Fundamentum*, also included in the manuscript.[45] That many unattributed works in the same volume adhere to the same style suggests that organists other than Paumann were able to create music using the formulae he codified.

Given the small amount of surviving organ music from the fifteenth century compared with the great amount of documented activity by organists, it is plausible to suggest that the organist's art was still based largely on improvisation or the memorization of previously conceived music. With this in mind, let us assess the information contained in a reference to the fourteen-year-old Bianca de' Medici, who entertained the entourage of Pope Pius when it stopped in Florence in early 1460 on the way back from the Council of Mantua.[46] The Apostolic Protonotary Teodoro da Montefeltro described two occasions on which Bianca performed on the organ. The first gives little clue as to her repertoire, although it is explicit about aspects of the performance:

> Then he [Cardinal of Rohan] took them into a hall and had Bianca play the organ; she plays it very well with fine phrases and proportion and impressive rhythm.

Bianca's talents were later solicited by Rodrigo Borgia, the Vice-Chancellor:

And when she arrived, he touched her hand. . . . Then Bianca tuned the pipes of the organ. . . . Once the organ was tuned [Bianca's] sister, who is about eleven years old, began to pump the bellows of the organ, and not knowing what would please Monsignor [Borgia], I [Montefeltro] had [Bianca] perform two songs for him: "Fortuna" and "Duogl'angoseus" and then she did another, highly unusual one.

Later the same evening, Bianca played again:

When the dance was finished, everyone ate something and then Bianca played an angelic song on the organ, then she sang a canzonetta [a light, secular vocal genre] with her sister, and then in addition, another young girl began one that says "Moun cuer chiantes ioussement."[47]

Thanks to these remarkably explicit accounts by Montefeltro, we can gain insight into the sort of music that was being performed by female aristocrats in the mid-fifteenth century. All three of the pieces given a title in Montefeltro's letters can be identified. "Deuil engoisseux" and "Mon cuer chante joyeusement" are chansons by Gilles Binchois, and "Fortuna" may refer to Johannes Bedyngham's "Fortune, helas."[48] Since both "Fortuna" and "Duogl'angoseus" were performed on the organ, someone had arranged the original vocal pieces for instrumental performance.[49]

Might the anonymous intabulator have been Bianca herself? We know from the German didactic sources discussed above that organists learned rules of improvisation and composition in order to create purely instrumental music based on vocal models. Similar techniques of adding a florid upper voice to a known melody in slower note values are documented in the music of the *Faenza Codex*, a manuscript of polyphonic Italian instrumental music from the early fifteenth century.[50] This music is our only guide to the intabulator's art in Italy; thus, although not a note survives of the music Landini played on the organ,[51] instrumental versions of his vocal pieces have been preserved by the intabulator of the *Faenza Codex*. This ingenious musician remains anonymous because the pieces are identified solely by the titles of the vocal models, without any mention of either the original composer or the person who arranged them for instrumental performance.[52] The same holds true for the later *Buxheimer Orgelbuch*, where many compositions that are only loosely based upon a preexisting melodic line are unattributed.[53] Was the work of the intabulator considered to be so banal that it warranted no mention? Or might we surmise that no attribution was necessary because the manuscripts containing such pieces were compiled by individual instrumentalists for their personal use?[54]

I cannot prove that Bianca de' Medici composed the music she performed before the papal visitors to Florence in 1460. Although Montefeltro's reference to a "highly unusual" piece could lead to tantalizing speculation about the young virtuoso's original style, it cannot singlehandedly support a claim to her authorship. Similarly, the lack of precise titles for the "angelic song" and the *canzonetta* that Bianca sang with her sister does not necessarily indicate that they were composed by the performers, although it does suggest that they were not part of the standard French courtly tradition that Montefeltro documents so well.[55] As for the songs "Fortuna" and "Duogl'angosseus," both are intabulated in the *Buxheimer Orgelbuch*. To assume that Bianca had access to such a score in the preparation of her performances, however, seems as unfounded as the suggestion criticized above that the thirteenth-century Joane had access to the notated music of the trouvères, from which she learned the *rotruenge* that she sang at her father's deathbed.

In the realm of late-medieval instrumental music, little distinction can be made between the performer and the composer, and thus references to female organists during the fourteenth and fifteenth centuries imply that women were creating polyphony, as suggested by the symbolic representations of Musica. The significance of evidence for the creative activity of musical women may be overlooked because it is couched in allegorical terms or because it describes performances rather than notated musical works. In the same way that modern scholars prefer details of a real person's life over aspects of a symbolic portrayal, they pay more attention to music preserved in a score than to other, often more plentiful, types of documentation. Yet it is anachronistic to imagine that late-medieval performers were dependent on composers to mastermind their efforts. The modern bias toward written compositions is a hindrance in the study of much medieval music, which was never codified in notation and was freely adapted to different media and contexts by the performers. It is futile to examine this repertoire according to a modern paradigm of literacy: "the model of the composer producing finished works that circulate in stable form through closed written channels in scores that are blueprints for performers, who must be able to read them in order to produce performances that are essentially identical from one time to the next."[56]

Even today, there are significant musical movements that do not adhere to this paradigm. One wonders how twenty-fifth century musicologists will reconcile the performer/composer dichotomy in their assessments of jazz. Like all innovative styles, jazz opened new horizons for the formation of musical sound, breaking the bonds of notation and the composer/performer hierarchy. As explained by one jazz musician: "To us the two things are one, a guy composed *as* he played, the creating and performing took place at the same time—and we kept thinking what a drag it must be for any musician with spirit to have to sit in on a symphonic assembly-line."[57] If enough sound recordings survive, jazz artists might be recognized by posterity for their important contributions; if the musical sounds are preserved, they can be transferred into written notation and analyzed as compositions according to the "paradigm of literacy."[58] But this approach to scholarship, which relies solely on notated compositions, is not adequate for the study of predominant aspects of medieval musical culture.

In my emphasis on unwritten traditions, I do not mean to suggest that late-medieval women were musically illiterate. There is much evidence that women in courtly circles and in convents were well versed in both literature and music,[59] and this makes all the more surprising the dearth of notated music attributed to them. One would expect to find compositions by the noblewomen who influenced the works of famous composers, since they would have had some access to education in polyphonic music.[60] Yet because of their social standing, these women would have been the least likely to claim authorship for their work. As Howard Mayer Brown notes:

> [I]f some noble Italian women of the late fifteenth century did write music, modesty and a sense of decorum would most likely have prevented them from admitting it. While the ideal courtier was encouraged to become a skillful singer and performer on several instruments—and apparently was even expected to improvise his part on occasion—he should not seem to take an overweening pride in his accomplishments, lest someone suppose music his principal profession.[61]

Such an aristocratic detachment from professionalism, in conjunction with the unnecessary presence of attributions in manuscripts for personal use as discussed earlier, might explain the apparent absence of female composers before 1566, when changing social conditions fostered the rise of professional women musicians.[62]

There is a great deal of information about Italian female composers that confirms for the late sixteenth and early seventeenth centuries two hypotheses I have put forward in relation to the creativity of late-medieval women. First, female singers sometimes composed the pieces they sang. The singer Laura Bovia was described by a contemporary as "most skilled in composing"; three other singers, Vittoria Achilei and Settimia and Francesca Caccini, are credited with composing the *ottave* which they performed in the *Mascherata di ninfe di Senna,* produced in Florence in 1611.[63] In a letter of 1616, Monteverdi suggests that the Basile sisters composed as well as sang their parts in a Mantuan entertainment; this is confirmed in a letter of 1620, where the acclaimed singer Adriana Basile refers to one of her own compositions.[64] Because such works were composed by the performers, they may never have been written down for wider dissemination. The only surviving traces of these compositions are contained in contemporary descriptions of the singers and their performances, as is the case for the earlier repertoire discussed above.

The second hypothesis that is echoed by later documentation is the link between composing and playing the organ. Several Italian sources describe women as both organists and creators of music. Spaccini's chronicle of life in Modena describes the young nun Faustina Borghi as being "exceedingly virtuoso in counterpoint . . . [and] in playing the cornetto and organ."[65] Two other nuns were similarly described in the early seventeenth century as being composers of music and famous organists.[66] In 1660, the nun Maria Cattarina Calegri was "acclaimed as a heavenly singer, a composer of angelic harmonies, and in organ playing a divine Euterpe."[67] Although these references are much later than the late-medieval examples of women organists, they suggest a tradition of composition and improvisation at the organ that is clearly documented for men as early as the fifteenth century. There is no reason to doubt that women partook of this tradition; the later references to "composer" organists were written during a time when women were acknowledged as composers and were publishing their works.

The advent of professional singers and music printing is largely responsible for the preservation of music attributed to Italian women in the late sixteenth and seventeenth centuries. Works that were published had a better chance of survival. Without music printing, many creations of female composers would have been lost to posterity; as it is, most of Francesca Caccini's music was never printed and was subsequently lost, while there is currently no trace of even the published works of Maria Cattarina Calegri.[68]

These factors help us to understand the dearth of written music attributed to women before 1550. Before the opening of professional avenues to women in the second half of the sixteenth century, female musical creators would most likely have been of the nobility or of the cloth and thus would have had little incentive to establish themselves as composers in a professional sense, with works attributed to them. The music of many courtiers and clerics, both male and female, has been preserved without attribution. The pieces that have survived offer a severely limited perspective on medieval musical creation, given the frequency of lost works from even later times and the fact that much music was never written down at all.

The Sponsors

Beyond the question of women composers lies an awareness of the influence women exerted on the development and dissemination of musical art. Here there is an important parallel with literature: just as women were actively involved in performing music and in sponsoring composers, their reading tastes affected the production of books. In a fascinating article on medieval women book owners, Susan Groag Bell dispels the myth of the book as a possession of the cloister or of the male head of household.[69] She presents compelling evidence for a large increase in the number of laywomen book owners in the fourteenth century and a dramatic surge in that number by the fifteenth century. Women were influential in determining the iconography that decorated their books, and this resulted in many portraits of reading women, including numerous paintings and sculptures of the Annunciation where Mary is shown reading. In the same way that medieval depictions of Musica reflect the activities of real female musicians, "artists' insistence on portraying the most significant medieval female ideal, the Virgin Mary, as a constant reader was surely based on the reality of their patrons' lives."[70]

Because laywomen after 1300 often lacked proficiency in Latin, they were responsible for commissioning works in the vernacular, and since women were forced by late-medieval marriage customs to move from their homes to those of their husbands, they often effected cultural change by distributing books over a broad geographic area. Despite this documented influence on book content and women's active role in the dissemination of ideas, "the authors of the most widely used recent Western civilization textbook, who are aware of the literacy of medieval laywomen, see those women as literary subject matter rather than as creators or users of books."[71]

Many of the same points can be made about female influence in the creation of music. The musical interests of women determined the content of music books that were prepared for them, and women who traveled to the courts of their husbands effected important cultural exchange through the music they brought with them. The musical editor of the *Mellon Chansonnier* concludes his study with the hypothesis that the volume was prepared as a gift to Beatrice of Aragon before her marriage in 1476 to Matthias Corvinus, King of Hungary, "in order that her arrival in a strange and distant land might be softened to some extent by a 'Fair Welcome' from a familiar repertory of the music in which she took such a delight."[72] A later example of musical transmission occurred when Marguerite of Austria brought a chanson album (now Brussels, Bibliothèque Royale MS 11239, olim 832) from the ducal library of Savoy to the Netherlands in 1507. Picker believes that this collection "may have served as a model for the larger and later MS 228, which certainly was written for her in the Netherlands."[73] It is clear that MS 228 was compiled under Marguerite's direction, and several scholars acknowledge her authorship of some of its poems.[74] In 1495, she received instruction in "many instruments of music" from Govard Nepoti, the court organist; her skills in both vocal and instrumental music were praised by the court poet, Jehan Lemaire.[75] Marguerite's extensive musical interests and training led Picker to speculate that she might occasionally have composed music, "as a natural extension of poetic composition."[76] It is interesting that Marguerite's authorship of poems was acknowledged by literary scholars as early as 1809, while the possibility that she composed music has only recently been considered.

Many accounts of women's involvement in musical projects need to be reevaluated, remembering that the creator was not always the one who notated. Some reports of female patronage suggest the potential for active musical creativity, although such potential is rarely acknowledged by scholars of music. As early as the twelfth century, the Anglo-Norman poet Gaimar reports that Adeliza of Louvain "made a great book" of the life of King Henry I, with the first stanza (vers) notated for singing.[77] Although the text is not explicit concerning the composer of the notated song, it does not exclude the possibility that Adeliza might herself have devised the melody she had notated into the book. Not surprisingly, a recent interpretation seems oblivious to this, although the author stresses Adeliza's initiative in having the book made.[78]

If female aristocrats are ignored as possible creators of monophony, much more so have later "patrons" such as Marie of Burgundy, Marguerite of Austria, Anne of Brittany, Isabella d'Este, and Beatrice of Aragon been overlooked as creators of polyphony. These noblewomen wrote poetry, played musical instruments, and displayed a keen understanding of polyphony, if we are to judge by the numerous important collections of polyphonic music dedicated to them. As in the case of women book owners, these sponsors helped to mold the artistic product: Isabella d'Este and Lucrezia Borgia played dynamic roles in the development of the frottola (see William Prizer's essay in this book), while Beatrice of Aragon and Marguerite of Austria were actively involved in musical production and dissemination.

I stress the "dynamic" and "active" aspects of these women to avoid viewing their patronage as merely financial or otherwise detached from the musical process. Just as the Muses came to personify the artistic motivation of the poet, and Musica to represent the theoretical laws followed by the composer, female aristocrats could be viewed as passive personas who served only to inspire male creativity. But women were often acutely knowledgeable about the music they sponsored, a point amply demonstrated in Paula Higgins's article in this volume.

The influence of late-medieval women on musical creation is undeniably hidden behind the symbols, the performers, and the sponsors. These medieval records of music must be reinterpreted to reveal the active participation of women, in the same way that anagrams have been unraveled to suggest that women were the anonymous authors of song texts.[79] One such anagram reveals the name of a real woman, Péronne d'Armentières, as the character "Toute Belle" in Machaut's *Livre du Voir-Dit*. Although some writers have questioned the existence of "Toute Belle," Higgins suggests that the key issue is not her reality, but rather her portrayal as an intelligent and gifted female musician (see p. 183 below). This is perhaps the most persuasive evidence to demonstrate that late-medieval women possessed the skills and initiative to understand the intricacies of polyphonic composition. Péronne's correspondence with Machaut might even be viewed as a clever strategy to acquire the musical education that was denied to her by both the Church and the University. In the same way that female writers are known to have taken advantage of their subordinate roles to gain power within the male hierarchy,[80] Péronne perhaps exploited her female role as an elderly man's object of courtly love in order to learn from him the secrets of polyphonic writing. This would explain why she so avidly solicited Machaut's music, suggesting that he continue to send her songs even after she ended their romantic association.[81]

Machaut's positive portrayal of "Toute Belle" in the *Livre du Voir-Dit* distinguishes him from the men described by Christine de Pisan a century later, who "maintain that the mind of women can learn only a little." If a female disciple inspired this much respect from the greatest composer of the fourteenth century, she certainly deserves as much from the twentieth-century musicologist. May we continue to search behind the allegories and anagrams to uncover those of the feminine sex with "the virtue of high understanding and great learning."

9

The "Other Minervas":
Creative Women at the Court
of Margaret of Scotland

Paula Higgins

Et m'esbahis que mot ne son
N'as fait de la belle Jamette,
Niepce de Pierre de Nesson:
Ele vault qu'en rench on la mette,
Car n'est rien dont ne s'entremette,
Et l'appell'on l'aultre Minerve.

(And I am astonished that you have not mentioned a word about
the lovely Jamette, niece of Pierre de Nesson; she deserves to be
recognized—nothing prevents it—and called the other Minerva)
Martin le Franc, *Le Champion des Dames*, ca. 1440

Thus the indignant Adversaire, one of the interlocutors of Martin le
Franc's *Le Champion des Dames*, admonishes Franc-Vouloir, the enthusiastic panegyrist of Christine de Pisan, for neglecting to mention
the evidently considerable creative accomplishments of one Jamette de
Nesson, whose claim to literary immortality otherwise rests on a lone
surviving rondeau.[1] Judging from the ardent defender's juxtaposition of
her with the renowned Christine, de Nesson's reputation and presumably her creative production must have been far more substantial than
the single attributed poem would lead us to believe.[2]

Le Franc's gratuitous biographical tidbit identifying the virtually unknown woman as the niece of the poet Pierre de Nesson enabled the
early twentieth-century literary historian Antoine Thomas to clarify
further details of Jamette de Nesson's life. Her marriage to Merlin de
Cordebeuf, an *escuyer de l'escuierie du roy* in the households of
Charles VII and Louis XI, provides concrete evidence linking her to the

inner sanctum of the French royal court.[3] The survival of her poem in
two poetry manuscripts emanating from French court circles[4] signals
her contact with the literary coterie of the dauphine Margaret of Scotland, which, despite its frequent superficial treatment, has never attracted serious scholarly attention. In the discussion that follows I shall
briefly highlight the cultural and historical contexts surrounding this
little-known medieval princess, and use them to explore a broader spectrum of possibilities than has existed heretofore of the ways in which
other female magnates and their ladies-in-waiting participated in the
literary and musical culture of the late Middle Ages.

Certain events in the short life of the Scottish princess Margaret Stuart
(1424–45) may well have spawned many a fairy tale. Eldest daughter of
King James I of Scotland and Queen Joan Beaufort, she went to France
at age twelve to wed the reluctant young dauphin Louis in extravagant
nuptial festivities held at Tours in 1436. Many anecdotes blending myth
and reality surround this mysterious princess, dubbed "the melancholy
dauphine" by her biographer, and whose dying words were "Fy, fy de
la vie de ce monde! Ne m'en parlez plus!"[5]
   The most celebrated tale about her, though probably apocryphal, is
especially appropriate in light of what follows here. As the story goes,
the dauphine came upon the poet Alain Chartier sleeping on a bench,
and bent over and kissed him on the mouth. When her alarmed companion exclaimed, "My Lady, I am astonished that you have kissed
such an ugly man!" she replied, "I have not kissed the man, but rather
the precious mouth which has been the source of so many good and
virtuous words."[6] Though frequently recounted, undoubtedly for its
amusing, anecdotal charm, the story has been dismissed by all modern
scholars as being totally without foundation, since Alain Chartier was
dead by the time Margaret came to France in 1436. Although Chartier
did in fact visit the Scottish court in Edinburgh in 1428 as a member of
the diplomatic embassy sent to negotiate the marriage of Margaret and
Louis, it is further presumed that Margaret, who was four years old at
the time, would have been too young to appreciate Chartier's talents.
And yet, there is a ring of childlike innocence to the incident; one could,
in fact, easily imagine both words and actions being more typical of a
four-year-old girl than a mature woman. Whatever unusual precocity
it would seem to imply would probably not have been incongruous with
the likely sophistication of a privileged noble child reared in the flourishing literary, artistic, and musical climate of James I's court.[7] More

importantly, whether apocryphal or not, the anecdote, which seems to have originated in the mid-seventeenth century, illustrates the extent to which folklore about the dauphine's literary interests must have survived in the popular memory at least two centuries beyond her own lifetime.

Much has also been written about Louis's reluctance to marry the Scottish princess, who had been chosen for him by his father, Charles VII, as part of a politically strategic alliance with James I of Scotland. The reasons for his evidently intense dislike of her are not clear, since contemporary chroniclers described the princess as "beautiful, well-formed, and endowed with every positive attribute that a noble and high-born lady could have" and as an "extremely beautiful and wise lady."[8] But there is no basis for the often repeated and somewhat misogynous testimony of the sixteenth-century English chronicler Richard Grafton, who claimed that her poor hygiene and bad breath drove Louis away: "The lady Margaret maryed to the Dolphin, was of such nasty complexion and evill savored breath, that he abhorred her company as a cleane creature doth a caryon."[9]

The principal cause for concern at the French royal court was her apparent inability to produce an heir, which doctors variously attributed to a lack of sleep, to drinking too much vinegar, eating sour apples, and wearing her belts either too tight or too loose.[10] These nuggets of medieval medical lore concerning the causes of female infertility bear striking similarity to the nineteenth-century "cult of female invalidism," whereby "tight-lacing, fasting, vinegar-drinking, and similar cosmetic or dietary excesses were all parts of a physical regimen that helped women either to feign morbid weakness or actually to 'decline' into real illness."[11] The even more bizarre medieval analogues for such behavior are the subject of Carolyn Walker Bynum's compelling study, *Holy Feast, Holy Fast*. Taking as her point of departure the centrality of food and food imagery to women's lives, Bynum argues that the various food practices of medieval women

> frequently enabled them to determine the shape of their lives—to reject unwanted marriages, to substitute religious activities for more menial duties within the family, to redirect the use of fathers' or husbands' resources, to change or convert family members, to criticize powerful secular or religious authorities, and to claim for themselves teaching, counseling, and reforming roles for which the religious tradition provided, at best, ambivalent support.[12]

If the rumors about the dauphine's curious gastronomic habits had basis in fact, and if Louis's animosity toward her was as great as certain chroniclers would have us believe, her case would provide yet another example of a medieval woman who resorted to excessive food practices as a means of exerting external control over otherwise unalterable situations in her private life.

Whatever its etiology, the dauphine's sterility had even more sinister implications for courtly scandalmongers who recognized tight lacing, vinegar drinking, and eating sour apples as methods of birth control.[13] This interpretation would seem to explain the insinuations of the self-serving courtier Jamet de Tillay, *bailli de Vermandois*, who claimed to have discovered Jean d'Estouteville, seigneur de Blainville and Torcy, and another unidentified gentleman in a compromising position in the dauphine's darkened chambers late one night, together with her ladies-in-waiting.[14] Tillay then proceeded to broadcast the "great lewdness" of the situation and to decry the dauphine's behavior as "more fitting of a whore than of a great lady."[15] Tillay's suspicions were perhaps excessively heightened by the highly charged sexual climate of the French royal court, where Charles VII was alleged to have routinely availed himself of the ladies-in-waiting of both the dauphine and the queen, who included his most celebrated mistress, Agnes Sorel.[16] Eight months later, when the twenty-one-year-old princess fell ill and eventually died on 16 August 1445 at Châlons-sur-Marne, the official cause was given as pneumonia. Rumors at court, however, suggested that her already debilitated state of health had been exacerbated by the insinuations of infidelity perpetrated by the courtier Jamet de Tillay.[17]

The troubled Charles VII ordered two legal inquests into the cause of her death at which many ladies and gentlemen of the court were required to testify.[18] The sworn depositions of Jamet de Tillay unwittingly provide an exceptionally rare glimpse into the private circle of a late-medieval princess who, in this case, seems to have had a passion for writing poetry shared and encouraged by her ladies-in-waiting. Unlike those who attributed the rapid decline in the dauphine's physical condition to her deep chagrin over Tillay's defamatory statements, Tillay himself blamed the dauphine's illness on her female attendants, who, he claimed, kept her up all night writing rondeaux and ballades:

> [T]he said Nicole asked him [Jamet de Tillay] what was wrong with her, and what caused her illness and [Tillay] answered that the doctors said she had much rancor in her heart, which was harmful to her and exacerbated by lack of sleep; and then the said Nicole replied that the doctors had told him the same thing, and also added: "If only she had not had that woman [in her service]!" "Who?" said [Tillay]. Nicole answered, "Marguerite de Salignac."

And Tillay retorted: "Nor Prégente, nor Jeanne Filloque!" Asked why he said such things, he answered that he had heard that they were the ones who kept her up too late writing rondeaux and ballades.[19]

When interrogated further as to what he had told King Charles VII about his daughter-in-law's death, Tillay gave the following testimony:

> [A]nd the king asked him if she were pregnant, and [Tillay] answered no, as the doctors had said. And the king asked him what caused her illness; and [Tillay] said that it came from a lack of sleep, as the doctors had said, and that she frequently stayed up so late that it was often dawn before she went to bed; and sometimes my lord the dauphin had been asleep for some time before she joined him, and often she was so busy writing rondeaux that she sometimes wrote a dozen in a day, which was not good for her. And when the king asked if that could give her headaches, my lord the treasurer, Maistre Jehan Bureau who was present, said, "Yes, if she does it too much; but these [i.e., writing poetry] are pleasurable things."[20]

Any allusion to the creative process in the late Middle Ages is unusual enough, but this one is unmatched as sworn legal testimony to the literary creativity of late-medieval women. And it is transparently clear from Tillay's lengthy version of events that he strongly disapproved of their activities. Writing poetry was not only detaining the dauphine from the conjugal bed, it was contributing to her moral depravity, and, worst of all, it "was not good for her"—it was making her sick. Tillay's testimony, a compendium of the negative attitudes toward creativity directed at women writers, artists, and composers from the beginning of recorded history,[21] echoed in part that of the doctor who had performed the autopsy. Stopping short of linking the dauphine's illness directly to her creative endeavors, the doctor nevertheless diagnosed her lung disease as having been caused by her habit of staying up too late, which weakened her brain, and thereby rendered it more vulnerable to a cold, which then turned into an infection and eventually traveled to her lung, causing its ulceration.[22] Similar examples of women whose creative activities were thought to have had pathological consequences, particularly insanity, generally come from later historical periods.[23] But an interpretation of the doctor's report as implicitly associating the dauphine's passion for writing poetry with the cerebral origin of her lung disease finds striking corroboration in Erasmus of Rotterdam's colloquy "The Abbot and the Learned Woman," in which the ignorant Abbot Antronius, parroting popular wisdom, warns his erudite interlocutor Magdalia that "books destroy women's brains."[24]

Tillay accused three women of aiding and abetting the dauphine in

her literary pursuits: Marguerite de Salignac, Prégente de Melun, and
Jeanne Filleul, all three of whom were ladies-in-waiting of the dauphine
and of Queen Marie d'Anjou.[25] And lest the credibility of Tillay's generally mendacious testimony be justifiably challenged as a desperation
tactic concocted to get himself off the hook, it is fortunate that external
evidence corroborates the literary activities of all three women. Concerning Marguerite de Salignac, the first of the ladies mentioned, the
poetry anthology *Le Jardin de Plaisance* transmits a poem, apparently
an encomium of Margaret of Scotland, concealing an acrostic on Salignac's name.[26] Prégente de Melun, another of the ladies mentioned by
Tillay, had borrowed a copy of *Clériadus* from Marie of Cleves, duchess
of Orléans, who had to send one of her servants to the French court to
retrieve it from her.[27] The book in question undoubtedly refers to the
courtly narrative *Clériadus et Méliadice*, recently discussed by Christopher Page as a rich source of information concerning late-medieval
musical performance practices.[28] This not only provides further concrete
evidence of literary exchanges between the French royal court and that
of Orléans, but also seems to hint at the existence of a kind of literary
subculture among the women of the two courts.[29] A bergerette ascribed
to Jeanne Filleul, the third lady-in-waiting mentioned by Tillay, survives in the poetry collection Paris, Bibliothèque nationale, fonds français 9223 (hereafter Paris 9223).[30] This manuscript preserves dozens of
poems by other of the dauphine's courtiers (including her nocturnal
companion the Seigneur de Torcy),[31] several poems set to music by fifteenth-century composers,[32] and an otherwise unknown rondeau attributed to another fifteenth-century composer, Antoine Busnoys.[33] Another of the dauphine's ladies, the fifteen-year-old Annette de Cuise,
though not among the guilty parties cited by Tillay, seems to have been
the custodian of several of the dauphine's books and papers, including
"un livre qui parle d'amours" and another of "chansons et ballades."[34]
Annette de Cuise, and her sister Jeanne, a lady-in-waiting to Queen
Marie d'Anjou, were siblings of Antoine de Cuise, whose name is attached to some dozen rondeaux in Paris 9223, including a text set to
music by the fifteenth-century composer Guillaume Dufay.[35] Still another *damoiselle* of the dauphine, one Jacqueline de Hacqueville, may
well be identical with a woman whose name appears in no fewer than
four texts of chansons by Antoine Busnoys, and who may have authored one of the texts in question as well as the text (and possibly the
music) of the anonymous rondeau *Pour les biens* preserved in the chansonnier Nivelle de La Chaussée.[36]

Paris 9223 and another closely related poetry anthology, Paris 15771 (Bibliothèque nationale, nouvelles acquisitions françaises 15771) are unusual among late-medieval poetry sources in bearing author attributions, and even more rare in transmitting the names of five women poets: the dauphine's lady-in-waiting Jeanne Filleul,[37] Madame d'Orléans (Marie of Cleves, wife of Charles d'Orléans),[38] Mademoiselle de Beau Chastel,[39] Jamette de Nesson,[40] and Queen Marie d'Anjou.[41] With the exception of Marie of Cleves, only a single poem by each of them has survived. But at least Jamette de Nesson, Martin le Franc's "other Minerva," must have written a good deal more, if his testimony is to be believed. What are we then to make of the sole bergerette attributed in the same manuscripts to Jeanne Filleul? Should we assume that she exhausted her imagination in writing it? Or might her poem, like that of de Nesson, bear accidental witness to the creative productivity of yet another "Minerva" otherwise shrouded in perpetual anonymity? And what of Marguerite de Salignac and Prégente de Melun? How do we weigh the independent evidence of sworn depositions and contemporary documents attesting to the literary creativity of a circle of medieval women against the powerful silence of contemporary authors and the paucity of attributions that seem to deny their very existence?

And what of Margaret of Scotland herself, not a single verse of whose poetry has survived, but who, if we take Tillay at his word, sometimes wrote a dozen poems in a day?[42] To put this remark in perspective, a dozen poems a day would have exceeded the "one hundred verses" Machaut claimed to be capable of writing when he was having a good day.[43] Even accounting for the probability of Tillay's exaggeration, this output is considerable by any standard. Margaret of Scotland might well have been a female analogue of Charles d'Orléans. Surprisingly, though, none of the dozen or so historians and philologists who have touched on her literary activities has ever raised this possibility.[44] While earlier writers regarded the evidence with a combination of fascination and bemusement, recent scholars, particularly those writing since about 1970, have treated it skeptically, and have even felt compelled to speculate about the mediocrity of her lyrical gifts, even though her poetry has not survived. The two most recent histories in English of King Louis XI, for example, both published in the early 1970s, are striking in their similar treatment of the matter:

> Like her father, James I of Scotland, Margaret was enamoured of poetry, though it is doubtful—none of her compositions has survived—that she possessed her father's genius.[45]

and:

> No examples of Margaret's verses survive. . . . [S]he fervently admired Alain
> Chartier and Charles of Orléans. . . . [I]t is improbable, however, that she
> attained the heights of lyrical imagination and delicacy of statement they
> achieved.[46]

In the most recent study of Charles VII, published in 1974, by far the
most accessible and the only one existing in English, any residual evidence of Margaret of Scotland's literary activities all but vanishes in a
cryptically ambiguous sentence: "She died on 16 August, aged twenty-
one, allegedly worn out by her over-fertile poetic imagination."[47]

And lest Margaret of Scotland's literary circle risk dismissal as an
aberration, one might also wonder about that of Marie of Cleves, the
duchess of Orléans, for whom two attributed poems survive and whose
literary interaction with the women of the French court has already
been noted. The autograph signatures of several of her ladies-in-waiting appearing in her personal copy of poems by Alain Chartier attest to
the likelihood of their participation at least as an audience for, and possibly as creators of, courtly poetry.[48] Moreover, the gift to her in 1470
from Regnault le Queux and Robert du Herlin of "certains livres par
eulx fais de ballades et rondeaulx"[49] attests to her independent and ongoing literary interests even after the death in 1465 of her husband, the
poet-prince duke Charles d'Orléans. The literary coterie of Margaret of
Austria, whose activities as a poet are well known, also merits closer
scrutiny, since the names of no fewer than four of her female attendants appear in the margins of some dozen poems in one of her personal poetry albums.[50] The parallel of Margaret of Austria's court with
that of the dauphine Margaret of Scotland is striking in light of the fact
that the former was raised at the French court and imbued with its
literary traditions. Hers may represent yet another circle of courtly
women who emulated and participated in the literary interests of their
lady.

Evidence that women did participate in the writing of courtly poetry,
and probably in greater numbers than has hitherto been supposed, challenges the widespread assumption that, since there were no medieval
women poets of any significance besides Christine de Pisan, the authors
of texts in a woman's voice must, by default, have been men. The coed-
itor of a well-known fifteenth-century music manuscript known as the
Mellon Chansonnier, for example, claimed that the authors of seven
"woman's songs" in that manuscript were probably all men, since

Christine de Pisan "was the only woman poet of the day to make a name for herself."[51] Significantly, the same critical tactic reverberates in the work of Machaut scholars arguing against Toute Belle's authorship of the poems attributed to her in the *Voir-Dit*. If such a woman poet existed, they claim, she "would have been noticed by her contemporaries. But they say nothing of Agnès de Navarre, Péronne d'Armentières, or any other lady poet until Christine de Pisan."[52] Since "her poems are of the same high quality as his," and the style of her lyrics "indistinguishable" from Machaut's, employing "identical rhyme, meter and diction," they cannot possibly be written by her: "[t]he brilliant young poetess existed only in Guillaume de Machaut's imagination. A fictional character, she is not to be identified with Péronne d'Armentières or anyone else who actually lived in the fourteenth century."[53]

The alleged indistinguishability of Toute Belle's putative lyrics from Machaut's notwithstanding, the late Machaut scholar Sarah Jane Williams's more critical examination of the poems found striking divergencies from Machaut's standard procedure at every turn: "Whereas ballades far outnumber rondeaux elsewhere in Machaut's literary and musical repertory, the proportion is reversed in the *Voir Dit*, where rondeaux outnumber ballades thirty to nineteen." Moreover, the first few rondeaux attributed to Toute Belle "are written in forms of the rondeau rarely if ever found in Machaut's work elsewhere." The third rondeau sent by Toute Belle is unique among all Machaut's others in alternating long with short lines; two of the virelais have only a single stanza, instead of three; and her ballade *Regrete la compaignie* and the virelai *Cent mille fois esbahie* both have only two instead of three stanzas, an irregularity commented upon by Machaut in the text.[54] Another study, using a computer-aided linguistic analysis of the poems, demonstrated that there are in fact striking qualitative differences in the vocabularies of the poems attributed to Machaut and Toute Belle respectively.[55] Literary critics challenged this evidence on the grounds that the apparent linguistic discrepancies might have been deliberately contrived by Machaut. This, however, seems to me the strongest evidence in favor of the existence of Toute Belle or a woman like her. Even if Machaut himself wrote the poems, in emulation of the style of a young woman, this would seem implicitly to acknowledge the existence of women poets as well as generally perceived qualitative "differences" in their writing. Insomuch as the issues of essentialism and gendered differences in literary texts are controversial topics of late twentieth-century postmodernist criticism, it would be interesting indeed if Machaut and his contemporaries took such distinctions for granted some six hundred years ago.

The critical argument *ex vacuo* that unquestioningly accepts the non-existence of other creative medieval women underscores how powerfully "a discourse of the exceptional woman," as I have called it, in literature, art, and music functions not as the signifier of a more widespread creativity among women than has been generally thought, but rather as further proof of women's creative sterility. Evidence revealing that some half-dozen women in a single French court of the 1440s, including the "other Minerva" explicitly compared to Christine de Pisan by Martin le Franc, wrote poetry that survives in the same manuscripts which preserve many texts set to music seems legitimate enough reason to reconsider the notion that Christine de Pisan was the only late-medieval woman poet of consequence. This is not to accord these women the presumably "professional" status Christine de Pisan enjoyed (although one should probably wonder about "the other Minerva," Jamette de Nesson). But even if their literary activities were those of courtly amateurs, this provides, at the very least, further valuable information about women's literacy in the late Middle Ages. Apart from the difficulty of defining *professional* and *amateur* in a period when such distinctions in the literary and musical culture may have been more apparent than real, Howard Mayer Brown has recently provided further evidence that courtly amateurs—men and women alike—regularly performed secular music at court.[56]

Regrettably, the undoubtedly substantial poetic legacy of Margaret of Scotland disappeared among her papers, of which Louis XI ordered the destruction shortly after her death in 1445.[57] But there is little question that some of her works, those of her ladies, and others by the handful of women poets acknowledged in the manuscripts discussed here also survive among the anonymous texts transmitted in other poetry collections of the fifteenth century.[58] In light of repeated claims by literary critics that poems in a woman's voice were all written by men, it is curious that the few anthologies that do give authors' names fail to corroborate this assertion. None of the 188 poems ascribed to male authors in Paris 9223, and none of the 86 poems attributed to men in Paris 15771, is written in a woman's voice. Of the five poems attributed to women in the same sources, three are in a woman's voice, and two are in a neutral voice. Another woman's poem in Paris 9223 bears no author's name. On the basis of this admittedly limited, but at least consis-

tent, statistical evidence, it seems plausible to suppose that when writing individual lyric poems in the *formes fixes*, men and women tended
to use the gendered voice of their own sex. That is, of course, unless
they adopted the gender-masking alternative of the neutral voice, an
option that would for obvious reasons have been particularly attractive
to women poets. Many women, such as the sixteenth-century Lyon-
naise poet Pernette Du Guillet, for example, wrote in a neutral voice so
that their poems, taken out of context, might be assumed to have been
written and experienced by a male persona.[59] In fact, if we add to the
poems by the five women mentioned here a second poem attributed to
Marie of Cleves,[60] an interesting statistic emerges: of six poems attributed to women, three are in a woman's voice and three are in a neutral
voice. Therefore, it is not out of the realm of possibility that poems by
women survive among the many courtly texts in a neutral voice. In
other words, while songs in a woman's voice do form a relatively small
percentage of fifteenth-century poetry anthologies,[61] there is no reason
to assume that women who did write poetry would have necessarily
confined themselves to the woman's voice. For that matter, if male
poets could ventriloquize a woman's voice, what would theoretically
prevent any woman poet from ventriloquizing a male voice, as did some
of the *trobairitz* (women troubadours) and Christine de Pisan herself in
several of her *débats* between male and female interlocutors?

The complex theoretical issue of gendered voices becomes an especially relevant one for music historians because at least one influential
authority on medieval performance practice, again writing in the early
1970s, claimed that "medieval music-making was an all-male affair"
since songs are "almost invariably written from the man's point of
view."[62] Based on an assumption about the nonexistence of women in
medieval musical culture, this misguided notion is contradicted by the
significant numbers of women musicians known to have performed
publicly, at least in the secular sphere, before medieval and renaissance
princes of both sexes.[63] Evidence accumulated in the past twenty years
of the active participation by women in the vocal performance of secular
music of the Middle Ages has had little more than abstract intellectual
implications for the late twentieth-century performance practice industry, judging from the virtual hegemony of all-male vocal groups that
still tends to reflect this mistaken perception of medieval musical culture.

Since the boundaries between poet and composer were still extremely
fluid in the late Middle Ages, the disparity between the testimony of

contemporary documents and paucity of attributions takes on even more dramatic proportions if we juxtapose it with the perplexing absence of a single musical composition attributed to a woman between ca. 1300 and 1566, followed by a proliferation of publications of polyphonic music by women from 1566 on.[64] Can these really be the fruits of a musical creativity sprung forth fully formed from a musical void? Several musicologists have tried to rationalize the apparent absence of polyphonic compositions by women from the fourteenth to sixteenth centuries. Maria Coldwell attributed the phenomenon to political considerations, specifically that "when Salic law prohibited the passage of the French crown through women, women were no longer able to compete as composers with men," a reductive argument that clearly begs many questions.[65] Howard Mayer Brown, on the other hand, blamed the exclusion of women from cathedral schools.[66] Curiously, though, precisely the same obstacles existed for women composers from the mid-sixteenth century on and they somehow managed to circumvent them. Brown is much closer to the mark, I think, when he suggests that perhaps women were composing music but could not admit to doing so.[67] The more fundamental question we need to raise is this: since there is abundant evidence that women in convents and monasteries, as well as aristocratic women, did compose music up to ca. 1300 and from 1566 on, often against considerable odds, what would have stopped them from doing so during the intervening two hundred and fifty years? Given the large number of anonymous works in musical manuscripts from the fourteenth to the sixteenth centuries, it would not be at all surprising if latent works by women were among them.

We need to gain deeper insight into the role of women as active agents in the creation and propagation of musical culture in the late Middle Ages. There is little question that further investigation of the daily musical activities in female convents, monasteries, and *béguinages*; studies of the musical manuscripts produced therein; inventories of women's libraries, particularly of manuscripts of music and music theory; and a closer scrutiny of archival records, both municipal and courtly documents (especially those of female magnates), will shed important light on issues relating to the creation and diffusion of music by late-medieval women.

Anne Bagnall Yardley's study of music in medieval English nunneries provides an excellent point of departure for further studies of music making in individual convents.[68] Despite her unduly modest claim to the contrary, Yardley's study shows more than ample cause for a major revision in the common understanding of sacred music in the Middle Ages.[69] In the context of a larger study, Reinhard Strohm draws attention to the musical activities of the Rich Clares and the *béguines* of Bruges as music teachers, music scribes, performers, and possible conduits of polyphonic music, subjects that merit fuller exploration.[70]

Identification of individual music manuscripts produced in or destined for female monasteries and convents will also shed some sorely needed light on the thoroughly unexplored subject of women's musical literacy and creativity in the late Middle Ages. Yardley's working list of sacred polyphony surviving in manuscripts emanating from medieval nunneries offers a solid foundation for the pursuit of further studies in this area.[71]

One manuscript from late fourteenth-century Florence that deserves investigation is the anonymous *Notitia del valore delle note del canto misurato*, written in Tuscan dialect. One of the rare music treatises of the Middle Ages not written in Latin, the manuscript emanates from a Florentine convent of nuns, thereby explaining its use of the vernacular. Apart from its manifest interest as an instruction manual about polyphonic music for the use of late-medieval nuns, it is also extraordinary among theoretical treatises of the period in using unusual musical vocabulary, curious notation, and unorthodox designations of the rhythmic modes, most of which are apparently without theoretical precedent.[72]

Indeed, the number of late-medieval music manuscripts destined for women speaks strongly in favor of a much higher level of musical literacy than has generally been presumed. The best-known examples include the fifteenth-century songbook known as the Mellon Chansonnier and the manuscript in Naples preserving six anonymous *L'Homme armé* Masses, both gifts to Beatrice of Aragon, queen of Hungary; the manuscripts Brussels, Bibliothèque royale 228 and 11239, chanson albums made for Margaret of Austria, regent of the Netherlands, and the famous *basse danse* manuscript, Brussels, Bibliothèque royale, MS 9085, which she owned; and Paris 1596, owned by Margaret of Orléans, niece of Louis XII. Other manuscripts, such as the Wolfenbüttel and Laborde chansonniers, each of which opens with the devotional song-motet *Ave regina* by Walter Frye, could signal the destination of both manuscripts for female aristocratic patrons. Similarly, the Pixérécourt chansonnier (Paris 15123), bearing a blank shield whose shape identifies its owner as a woman,[73] also opens with a Marian song-motet, *O pulcherrima mulierum*. The textual allusions to the Virgin Mary as celestial queen in these salutory pieces could well signal their destination for terrestrial female patrons.[74]

Although music historiography has tended to valorize the musical patronage of male magnates such as the dukes of Burgundy and the kings of France, many important patrons of late-medieval music—and of secular music in particular—were, in fact, women. Like their better-known fathers and husbands who have been the subjects of more focused music historical attention, they too employed some of the best-known male composers and musicians at their courts. Many of them also wrote poetry, played musical instruments, and possibly composed music as well, but their roles in the history of music have tended to be seen as that of passive promoters of the work of gifted men and as musical dilettantes only superficially knowledgeable of the music and musicians they patronized. For example, Beatrice of Aragon, mentioned earlier, married to King Matthias Corvinus of Hungary, was not only the destinée of two of the more important music manuscripts of the fifteenth century mentioned above, but also the dedicatee of no fewer than three of the twelve Latin treatises by the leading music theorist of the late Middle Ages, Johannes Tinctoris.[75] Surely this signals her far greater interest in and understanding of polyphonic music than her generally accorded status as patron of music and musicians would suggest.

Moreover, although some attention has been paid to the chamber valets of male magnates as significant contributors to the cultural life at court, little has been done to scrutinize the contributions of ladies-in-waiting—the female counterparts to the chamber valets and the women with whom female magnates shared a great deal of their daily lives—to the musical culture of the court.[76] Aristocratic women patrons not only supported the literary and musical careers of the male and female troubadours (*trobairitz*) and trouvères, but also served as the principal audience for the massive production of secular poetry and music of the twelfth and thirteenth centuries.[77] And it is precisely from female courtly circles that the professional female virtuoso singer emerged in Italy during the second half of the sixteenth century.[78] The renowned singing ladies at the court of Ferrara appeared officially on the court books not as musicians but as "ladies-in-waiting" to the duchess, a function that scarcely hints at the significance of their vital musical role at court.[79] Similarly, the late-Renaissance painter Sofonisba Anguissola was employed as a lady-in-waiting to the queen of Spain.[80] So it would seem likely that, just as male composers and artists of the late Middle

Ages served secular princes under the rubric *varlets de chambre*,[81] ladies-in-waiting may have performed analogous roles in the households of female princes.

Finally, evidence from literary sources and the much-debated issue of the truth or fiction of characters like Toute Belle from Machaut's *Voir-Dit* assume a greater importance for the music historian than for the literary critic, whose concern is limited to the text itself. According to Machaut, Toute Belle was a gifted young woman from a noble family and "the best singer born in a hundred years," who allegedly sought him out for his music.[82] And she is sufficiently literate musically to read and perform Machaut's compositions, many of which he claims to have written at her behest. While Machaut does underscore Toute Belle's exceptionality as a singer ("la mieulx chantans qui fust née depuis cent ans"), he fails to note anything at all unusual about a matter of much greater import: she is sufficiently fluent in the reading of polyphonic music that she instantly recognizes his attempt to pass off a reworking of an old piece of music under the guise of a new work.[83] If this woman were a product of Machaut's imagination, we need at the very least to ask why it is that he portrays her as being so gifted at music and poetry and, moreover, why he so readily and unabashedly acknowledges that she has the stuff to beat him at his own game. Because the identity of the woman has recently been viewed as a tangential and indeed irrelevant issue,[84] literary critics and music historians alike seem to have overlooked the fact that, in its portrayal of Toute Belle as a strong, independent, assertive, exceptionally literate, and musically gifted woman, the *Voir-Dit* is something of a feminist text.[85] Therefore, unless we must now count Machaut among the prototypical authors of feminist fiction, I think we have to assume that whether Toute Belle was Péronne d'Armentières or someone else, she must have had some basis in the poet's reality. The literary evidence would concord nicely with the numerous courtly documents from the period alluding to performances by female vocalists and serve in turn to reinforce the notion that these women were indeed capable of performing polyphonic art music, a point about which some music historians remain peculiarly skeptical. Perhaps the fictive Toute Belle was based on a lady-in-waiting at one of the many courts at which Machaut served during his lifetime. This would explain not only her seemingly itinerant existence, but especially her interests in literature and music; for it is undoubtedly in an aristocratic setting that she would have heard the music and poetry of Machaut that prompted her to seek him out in the first place.

In conclusion, this study has attempted to shed light on the creative activities of the circle of Margaret of Scotland and her ladies-in-waiting, and to reassess in a more critical way their implications for a broader view of the roles, often hidden from traditional historical scrutiny, played by "other Minervas" in the history of music and literature. It has drawn attention to what I have dubbed the "discourse of the exceptional woman" that has tended in the past to dismiss evidence of female musical and literary creativity as extraordinary, abnormal, and even amusing, rather than as possibly indicative of a larger trend of serious creative accomplishment. It has also highlighted discursive strategies that run like threads through earlier treatments of the present subject matter. These strategies include a growing tendency in scholarship around 1970 to call into question the very existence of creative women because of incorrect assumptions about medieval texts; to presume the mediocrity of creative works by medieval women like Margaret of Scotland whose works have apparently not survived; and implicitly to exclude women from twentieth-century performances of late-medieval music, based on unfounded assumptions about their nonexistence in the music making of the Middle Ages. Coinciding with a period of intense international feminist activism that launched most American and continental women's studies programs, these phenomena are reminiscent of the flood of articles and books on the absence of great women composers that appeared in the 1890s and early 1900s, precisely at a time when women were having a substantial impact in the field of music publishing.[86] And lest we be tempted to consider these phenomena as isolated, bygone, purely coincidental, or unrelated trends, Christine Battersby has astutely observed in her recent study of female creativity that "at the historical moment that second-wave feminism has brought to the surface a rich hidden history of female authors and artists, the very concepts of 'individuality' and 'authorship' have come under attack by an elite group of critics who draw on recent French theories of writing and language."[87] Battersby's observations about women in the histories of art and literature might be usefully appropriated for the history of creative women in music as well: "Women do not simply lie outside [music historical traditions]; they structure the spaces that lie between the bold lines picked out by previous generations of [musicologists and music critics]."[88] Like other fields of the humanities, but to a somewhat lesser extent, music history has benefited from a period of sustained effort by feminist music historians and critics, but unlike art history and literature, it has only just begun to explore the "spaces" structured by musical women. Music historians need now to "adopt the switch in perspective that allows us to appreciate the artistic achievements of many more women in the past" and focus on the creative activities of musical women, not only those from the Middle Ages, but those from all periods of musical history. And in doing so, we would do well to heed Battersby's cautionary advice and resist "postmodernist attacks on the notion of authorship, historical continuity and tradition [that] deflect us from this task."[89]

10

Renaissance Women as Patrons of Music: The North-Italian Courts

William F. Prizer

During the last twenty years, a number of Renaissance scholars have analyzed the musical life of north-Italian courts and cities and have defined the patterns of patronage there. Thanks to their studies, we now know the basic chronology of the development: beginning in the early fifteenth century, more and more rulers began to see music as an aural and visual symbol of their power and standing. We also better understand the systems of supporting music: the rulers expanded small, pre-existing groups of musicians and created new ones, establishing four basic units for the performance of secular and sacred music. These were (1) the singers and players of *bas* instruments for secular vocal music; (2) the pifferi, the shawms and trombones for processions and the dance; (3) the corps of trumpeters also responsible for processions as well as for fanfares and signal calls in battle; and (4) the chapel, the choir of singers of sacred music. To these should also be added the *tamborino*, the player of three-holed pipe and tabor who, like the pifferi, provided dance music, and an organist, attached to the chapel.[1]

In northern Italy, the first to grasp these possibilities seems to have been Pandolfo III Malatesta (1370–1427), signore of Fano, Brescia, and Bergamo, and Leonello d'Este (r. 1441–50) at Ferrara, who established the first court chapels for the performance of sacred music. It is likely, however, that these experiments were in some senses isolated phenomena; the true beginning of the trend is to be found after 1470 in the massive recruitments and elaborate plans of Ercole I d'Este (r. 1471–1505) and Galeazzo Maria Sforza (r. 1466–76) at Milan.[2]

If we now have a basic grasp of how the lords of northern Italy developed and used these groups of musicians, we yet lack an understanding of women as patrons of music. Did they have their own musicians as members of their personal courts, and if so what kinds of music and musicians did they patronize? Alternatively, is it possible that they simply used musicians from the standing bodies of court musicians as the need and wish arose?

It would certainly seem natural for noblewomen to be involved with music at court, since both dance and music were traditional components of their education. Already Francesco da Barberino (1264–1348), in his *Del reggimento e costumi di donna*, included these elements as integral parts of a woman's education. According to Francesco, the girl who was born to the nobility is expected to be able to dance "honestly, not like a court jester," because if she should fall and show a portion of her leg, it would be disgraceful.[3] At the same time the girl should be taught music, and should be able both to sing and to play instruments. The music suitable for her is of a particular kind, however: vocal music and the music of *bas* instruments, which Francesco calls "canto basso chiamato 'camerale.'" It is not clear here if Francesco is actually using "basso" as the technical equivalent of *bas*, but the types of music to be performed by the student are precisely that. She may sing "an honest canzonetta" in a low voice, and should play only quiet instruments; Francesco lists psaltery, viola, harp (which he says is particularly fitting for a great lady), or another "seemly, attractive instrument."[4] By the late fifteenth century, lute and keyboard instruments were also a part of the pantheon of acceptable instruments.

As new documents are unearthed, it is becoming increasingly clear that most elite women of the fifteenth century had a musical education something like that prescribed by Barberino. In Florence, Lucrezia Tornabuoni (d. 1482), wife of Piero de' Medici, sang, and her daughters Bianca and Nannina sang and played the organ.[5] In Milan, Valentina Visconti, daughter of Giangaleazzo Visconti, played harp and lute; Beatrice di Tenda (d. 1418), wife of Filippo Maria Visconti, and Ippolita Sforza (d. 1488), sister of Galeazzo Maria Sforza, also played lute.[6] In Ferrara, Parisina Malatesta (d. 1425), wife of Niccolò III d'Este, Isotta d'Este (d. 1456), Niccolò's daughter, and Eleonora d'Aragona (d. 1493), wife of Ercole d'Este, played harp.[7]

This list could be expanded, but its point is clear: music of some kind was a normal part of the noblewoman's education. What of her patronage of musicians? This question is difficult to answer, since the documentation is extremely slim. Nonetheless, some tentative answers can be attempted. It is clear that noblewomen at court maintained their own households of servants and had a budget for this purpose: Christine de Pisan (ca. 1364–ca. 1431), for example, offers them advice on the wise governance and constitution of their courts.[8] Too, Eleonora d'Aragona in Ferrara had a court of fifty-one retainers in 1476, in addition to her ladies-in-waiting; these included administrators, chamberlains, tailors, a chaplain, and so forth. For this staff she received 700 *lire marchesane* a month. At the rate of 3.1 lire to the ducat, this translates to a budget of slightly more than 2,700 ducats a year.[9]

Lacking from her staff, however, is a self-contained corps of musicians. In fact, fifteenth-century noblewomen do not seem to have supported independent musical ensembles within their own households, at least in Italy. Nonetheless, there is some evidence that they did keep pipe-and-tabor players and dancing masters and that they may have had one or two musicians in their own employ. This is clearest in the case of Eleonora herself, whose personal court did include a certain Nardo tamborino, a player of the pipe and tabor.[10] Furthermore, Lorenzo Lavagnolo seems to have served women in Mantua and Milan as dancing teacher. At Mantua he is recorded as a familiar of Marchesa Margherita von Wittelsbach, wife of Federico I Gonzaga, in her will; after her death in 1479, he went to Milan, where he worked for Bona of Savoy (d. 1503). Also mentioned in Margherita's will is a player of the lira da braccio, Giovanni Pietro dalla Viola.[11]

There are exceptions to this pattern outside Italy. Iolanda of Savoy kept both secular singers and a self-standing chapel of boys and men for the performance of sacred music at least from late 1471 to 1473.[12] Iolanda, however, ruled the duchy as regent for her son Louis during this period, and it seems likely that this is the key to her support of music on a wide scale: as ruler, she supported exactly the same kinds of music that other rulers around her supported. Furthermore, Anne of Brittany kept her own musical establishment, including a chapel of singers; she, however, reigned as queen of France, and it is possible that this office itself required a woman to maintain a chapel.[13]

Nonetheless, the general situation in Italy, at least on the basis of the available documentation, points toward the lack of musicians in noblewomen's own households. This condition began to change in the late fifteenth century with a new generation of women coming to maturity and marrying: Beatrice d'Este (1475–97), wife of Ludovico Sforza in Milan; Elisabetta Gonzaga (1471–1526), wife of Guidobaldo di Montefelto in Urbino; Lucrezia Borgia (1480–1519), wife of Alfonso I d'Este in Ferrara; and Isabella d'Este (1474–1539), wife of Francesco II Gonzaga in Mantua. For the first two of these, there is not yet enough documentation to support definitive findings.[14] For the last two, however, there is fairly abundant material on which to base a study: Isabella d'Este's voluminous correspondence survives virtually intact, and Lucrezia Borgia's Ferrarese pay records, although not complete, survive in sufficient number to allow some assessment of her patronage. For Lucrezia, the correspondence between Ferrara and Mantua is also of prime importance, and this is conserved along with Isabella's *copialettere* in the State Archives of Mantua. There exists, therefore, enough information to measure the roles of two of the great noblewomen of the Renaissance, and, since a direct comparison of styles of patronage is allowed, it is an added benefit that these two women were contemporaries, knew each other well, and were related by marriage. The primary purposes of this study, then, are to examine the musical households of Isabella and Lucrezia and to weigh their importance as patrons, by extension defining the position women enjoyed as patrons of music during the Italian Renaissance.

Although Isabella and Lucrezia were both noblewomen and lived at neighboring courts, their backgrounds and personalities offer strong elements of contrast. Isabella was the legitimate daughter of Ercole I d'Este, duke of Ferrara, and a representative of one of the oldest and most stable *signorie* in Italy. She was raised at her father's court with at least a partly humanistic education, having begun the study of Latin by the age of six.[15] She came to Mantua as the wife of Marchese Francesco Gonzaga (1460–1519) in 1490 and remained there as marchesa of the city and its territory for forty-nine years. She was undoubtedly the outstanding woman of her age and was not only a great patron of the arts, but was also a gifted administrator.[16]

Lucrezia, on the other hand, came from a family of more recent origins. She was born the illegitimate daughter of the Spanish Cardinal Rodrigo Borgia and Vanozza Catenei. Her father's rise to the papacy as Alexander VI (r. 1492–1503) made her the pawn of the Borgia plans for dynastic conquest and her family's search for exactly the kind of lasting status that Isabella's family already enjoyed. She was married first, in a blatantly political move, to Giovanni Sforza, papal vicar of Pesaro. After Alexander managed to have this marriage declared void, she was married again, this time to advance the Borgia plans in Naples, to Alfonso d'Aragona, duke of Bisceglie. This marriage, too, was terminated when

Lucrezia's brother Cesare had Alfonso assassinated in 1500.[17] In 1502, she married Alfonso I d'Este of Ferrara.

History has not dealt kindly with Lucrezia. She was first, thanks to anti-Borgia propaganda, viewed as a mad seductress and poisoner who was a wholehearted participant in the Borgia political game. Gregorovius, attempting to see her more impartially, painted her as almost two different people: she was first the wild enchantress of the Vatican, and then, after her marriage to Alfonso d'Este, the honored and pious duchess of Ferrara.[18] Maria Bellonci changed this picture of Lucrezia in her penetrating biography of 1939, in which she is viewed as more the pawn of Borgia politics than an active participant in them.[19]

From the correspondence between Mantua and Ferrara, Lucrezia's chief interests seem to include *feste* and the dance. This was clearly the case in her earlier period,[20] and remains true in Ferrara as well. The letters from Ferrara are full of descriptions of Lucrezia's banquets and dances, both during carnival and in other seasons. Typical, although unusually detailed, is a letter to Isabella from the Ferrarese chancellor Bernardino de' Prosperi describing a banquet given for Lucrezia in 1513 by Antonio de' Costabili: as the guests entered Costabili's house, they were welcomed by the bagpipes ("pive") of Alfonso d'Este; at the beginning of the dinner, Alfonso's singers sang psalms "in voce bassa"; and during the meal itself, the guests were entertained by lutes, viols, and cornets.[21]

Towards the end of Lucrezia's life, this pleasure in the secular was tempered with a real interest in the church. She took periodic retreats to the Franciscan convent of Ferrara and died in 1519 a tertiary of the order. Although she was far from the mental equal of Isabella, she shared certain intellectual concerns with her, notably a delight in the poetry of Petrarch and his imitators and in musical settings of his verse. Like Isabella, too, she was an amateur musician and poet.[22] Although these abilities are not well documented, they are included in an adulatory Latin poem addressed to her by Pietro Bembo (1470–1547), "Tempore, quo primam miscens fluvialibus undis." Bembo resided in Ferrara for long periods in the first decade of the sixteenth century and carried on a heated if platonic flirtation with the Borgia princess.[23]

> If you recite a poem in Italian,
> You seem a girl born in Italy.
> Or if you take a pen to compose verses and poetry,
> They are worthy of having been written by the nine Muses.
> Or if you touch the harp[24] or lute with your ivory hand,

Conjuring up again in a different way those Theban modes,
The nearby waves of the Po shiver, taken by your songs.
If you choose to indulge in the dance,
And with your foot spring agilely to its rhythm,
Then I fear that one of the gods, seeing you,
Would take you passionately[25] from your castle,
Making of you, O sublime one,
The goddess of a new star.[26]

Lucrezia Borgia came to Ferrara from Rome in January 1502 to marry Alfonso d'Este, first son of Duke Ercole d'Este and himself the future duke of Ferrara and Modena. This was a coup of unparalleled success for the Borgia, for the Estensi were the oldest and most stable of the papal vicars. Ercole, for his part, achieved thereby a certain guarantee that his duchy would be excluded from the ravages of Cesare Borgia throughout the Romagna.

The basic story of the wedding celebration in Ferrara is reported by Bellonci and is familiar to historians of the Renaissance.[27] Although he originally had wanted only a small celebration, Ercole eventually presented five classical comedies and gave seemingly innumerable banquets and dances. The festivities lasted from 1 February, the date of Lucrezia's arrival, until Ash Wednesday, 9 February. Already before her arrival Ercole had placed triumphal arches across her path throughout Ferrarese territory,[28] and Alfonso had given a banquet at which Ercole's singers performed.[29]

It was at this wedding that Lucrezia first met Isabella, and a pattern of rivalry between the two was established that was to encompass competition in the arts, clothing styles, jewelry, and even intellect in general. At one point it included a flirtatious but probably platonic affair between Lucrezia and Isabella's husband, Francesco.[30] This rivalry began before Lucrezia had even arrived in Ferrara. Isabella, not willing to brook a challenge as "la prima donna del mondo" in her native city, prepared carefully for the wedding. She wrote to her agents, requiring gold chains, cloth, and other items, and enlisted Il Prete, servant of Niccolò da Correggio, as a spy in the Ferrarese wedding party that was to go to Rome to accompany the new duchess on her journey. Il Prete reports on Lucrezia's wardrobe, her dazzling abilities at the dance, and on the lady herself, who he claims is a "lady with intelligence, astute; it's necessary to be on your toes [when you are with her]."[31] De' Prosperi writes Isabella on 3 October 1501, describing Lucrezia's jewels and saying, "Your Ladyship must now employ your abilities so that you can show whose daughter you are, and, if you do not have as many jewels, that yours are no less well set than those of the others."[32] For Lucrezia's part, it was later reported that she had pawned her jewelry and had asked for Cardinal Ippolito I d'Este's revenues from the diocese of Ferrara for an entire year because she had spent so much to outshine Isabella during the 1502 celebrations.[33]

During the wedding itself, there was continued rivalry, paticularly on the part of Isabella. Already on 1 February, the marchesa of Crotone, an exile living at the Mantuan court, reported to Francesco Gonzaga that Lucrezia "is not very pretty but has a pleasing aspect. . . . We will bring home the prize for beauty with my Madama [Isabella], your consort."[34] Isabella herself wrote home to Francesco complaining about Lucrezia's habits and caused a scene in one of the comedies of Plautus given by Ercole for the wedding celebrations. On the last day of the celebrations, she wrote to her husband, saying, "I am sure that you have received greater pleasure from my letters than I have from these celebrations, because I have never stayed anywhere with greater annoyance than here."[35] Alessandro de Baesio also reports on 6 February that "up till now the bride has not been friendly with our Lady; they have not yet eaten together."[36]

From the very first, music took a central part in Isabella's designs: she was confident enough of her abilities that she was certain she could outshine Lucrezia at least in this one area.[37] On 12 January she wrote Lorenzo da Pavia, requiring him to put two of her lutes in order; one of these was the *vihuela de mano* Lorenzo had made for her several years before:

> Lorenzo. . . . We are sending you two of our lutes, one of which is the one of ebony, that are splintered and broken in the bowl, as you will see. We ask you to repair them immediately and bring them with you if you come to Ferrara for these wedding celebrations, and [if] not, to send them with a trustworthy person.[38]

The material she ordered for dresses also played a part in her musical preparations. On the day Lucrezia and her cortège entered Ferrara, Isabella, as if to announce her musical superiority at the very outset, was wearing a gown embroidered with her own personal musical device. The marchesa of Crotone reported to Francesco Gonzaga from Ferrara that "the marchesa, your wife, accompanied by several ladies, went to the house of the Administrator of the Gabelles to see the bride pass. She was attired in a lovely gown embroidered with that invention of mensuration signs and rests";[39] Marin Sanudo, the indefatigable Venetian chronicler, also reported that Isabella first received Lucrezia "dressed in a gown embroidered with musical rests."[40]

Finally, on 5 February, the one evening in which Lucrezia stayed in to wash her hair, Isabella gave a banquet for an impressive list of luminaries: the French ambassador, Ferrante and Giulio d'Este, Elisabetta Gonzaga, Laura Bentivoglio, Niccolò da Correggio, and four of the major Spanish dignitaries. Here Isabella had Marchetto Cara sing.[41] She herself also performed, although in her letter to her husband she modestly insisted that she was forced to do so: "After dinner, we danced the hat dance. When this was done, so many requests and demands were made of me that I had to demonstrate my singing to the lute."[42] The marchesa of Crotone was more specific in her comments; according to her, "after dinner, her Excellency the Marchesa, because of the requests of these Lords, sang two sonnets and a *capitolo*, and they were as delighted as it is possible to be."[43]

The rivalry continued after Isabella's return to Mantua and was surely fueled by a letter from an unnamed Roman academy to Isabella comparing unfavorably her behavior to that of Lucrezia during the festivities. The original of this letter is understandably missing, but the humanist Mario Equicola reported the contents to Margherita Cantelma, his patroness at the time:

> The content and tenor of the said letter is that it lists all the vices and failings of the women of Lombardy at the wedding in Ferrara and says, among the other [women], that the Marchesa [Isabella] was not well dressed, that she put on airs during the celebrations, and many other things, that she wanted to appear a boy [instead of a girl]. . . . The Marchesa is livid with anger.[44]

The two women did spend time together during Isabella's many trips to Ferrara, but they apparently were never friendly with one another. On her side, Isabella mocked Lucrezia's lack of intelligence and was infuriated by the duchess's imitation of her dress as well as her artistic patronage. On 6 July 1509, for example, Tolomeo Spagnolo reports that "today my most illustrious Madame [Isabella] made great fun of the Duchess of Ferrara, who, to demonstrate that she is chaste and faithful to her husband, has Pietro Giorgio da Lampugnano sleep in her antechamber."[45]

This rivalry also must have been felt among the two women's retainers, for Lucrezia's court contained several of Isabella's former employees. Paramount among these was the frottolist, singer, and lutenist Bartolomeo Tromboncino, recently in Isabella's employ, but from 1505 a member of Lucrezia's court. On 6 June of this year de' Prosperi reports to Isabella:

> It appears that the Duke [Alfonso d'Este] wants Madonna Elysabeth and all the foreigners who are in the household of his wife [Lucrezia] to leave, even the Neapolitans and Samaritana romana, so that all are in the condition that your Ladyship can imagine. . . . They say also that Madonna Beatrice [de' Contrari] is to serve the aforementioned Madonna [Lucrezia], and that Tromboncino and Ser [Antonio] Tebaldeo are also to be included, but we shall know everything shortly.[46]

With Lucrezia, Tromboncino was a part of a nucleus of musicians responsible for the entertainment of Lucrezia herself and of the guests at her frequent *feste*. Although he was her highest-paid musician at 465 *lire marchesane* (150 ducats) annually, he was by no means her only one. In January 1506, the first date for which there are payment records,[47] he was one of four performers. Also listed are Dionisio de Mantova, called "Papino," Niccolò da Padova, and Ricciardetto Tamborino, a pipe-and-tabor player and instructor of Lucrezia's favorite pastime, the dance. In November of the same year these musicians were joined by another singer, Paolo Poccino.[48] It is symptomatic of the rivalry between Isabella and Lucrezia that Papino was Mantuan, that Poccino had been in Mantuan services at least until 1505, and that Ricciardetto had refreshed Isabella's knowledge of French dances for the 1502 wedding.[49] Of her five musicians, only Niccolò da Padova had been with Lucrezia for a lengthy period: he had journeyed to Ferrara with her for her wedding in January 1502 and may have served on her staff in Rome even earlier.[50] As Lewis Lockwood has discovered, Niccolò remained with Lucrezia until at least 1511, when he was included in a list of benefices as "Messer Nicolò, Cantore de la Duchessa."[51]

Although the personnel of Lucrezia's court fluctuated slightly, from 1506 through 1508 her musicians remained basically the same: Tromboncino, Ricciardetto, Poccino, Papino, and Niccolò da Padova.[52] In September 1507, however, a woman singer is added: Dalida de' Putti, musician and future mistress of Cardinal Ippolito d'Este.[53] Lucrezia had reduced drastically the number of her musicians by 1517, the next year for which there is a register of payments: of the six musicians with her in 1508, only Papino da Mantova remained; he was still there in 1519, the year of Lucrezia's death, as the sole musician in her employ.[54]

Lucrezia seems to have decreased the size of her staff in 1510 or 1511 because of financial problems in the duchy. The years 1511 and 1512 were difficult ones at the court of Ferrara: Duke Alfonso d'Este was at war with Pope Julius II and was hard pressed to keep up payments to his soldiers, much less to his musicians. In fact, he released nearly all his musicians in late 1510, sending the majority to Mantua.[55] Moreover, several of Lucrezia's musicians had definitely left her services during this period. Niccolò da Padova seems to have been released about this time, for in April 1512 Lucrezia, apparently ignorant of his whereabouts, asked Francesco Gonzaga to aid "Niccolò cantor."[56] Francesco replied that he was unable to find Niccolò among the many formerly Ferrarese singers in his employ.[57] Dalida de' Putti also changed employers during this period; in 1512 she first appears in the Ferrarese household of Lucrezia's brother-in-law Ippolito d'Este.[58]

In November 1511 Bartolomeo Tromboncino, too, joined Ippolito's court. He is not listed in the pay registers among the "bocche," that is, with the regular musicians and servants to whom Ippolito gave monthly expenses for food and wine, but is included as an extra-ordinary musician in the *Bolletta dei salariati*, again with a higher salary than any other musician.[59] Bartolomeo remained with Ippolito in this capacity through June 1512, after which he again disappears from the pay records.[60]

There is, however, a Mantuan document indicating that Tromboncino was still in Ferrara the next year. In January 1513 Francesco Gonzaga gave him permission to travel through the Mantuan territory to return to Ferrara with two carts of wine.[61] If Bartolomeo was in Ferrara during 1513, he must have been once again with Lucrezia, for he had left Ippolito by June 1512 and does not appear on the payrolls of anyone in the Este family afterward. By 1513, with the death of Julius II, the tense political situation had eased somewhat, and Lucrezia could have afforded to rehire the frottolist. Ippolito, as an ecclesiastic and one of the wealthiest cardinals in Italy, was not severely affected by this situation and was able to keep his court intact throughout the difficult period. It is possible, therefore, that Ippolito took over Tromboncino's salary for Lucrezia and returned him to her as soon as she was able to resume paying him. This hypothesis is strengthened by two circumstances. First, Bartolomeo's salary of 38 lire and 15 soldi per month was exactly the same with both Ippolito and Lucrezia.[62] Second, in 1518 Lucrezia ordered the Ferrarese ambassador in Venice to request Tromboncino to return to Ferrara from that city. The letter containing this order also implies that the musician had recently moved there, had rented a house, and was teaching gentlewomen lute and singing. The most likely explanation for this letter is that Tromboncino had recently left Lucrezia's services and that she was requesting his return.[63]

Among Lucrezia's musicians, none received anything approaching Tromboncino's annual salary of 465 lire. The next best paid, Ricciardetto, received 148 *lire marchesane* and 16 soldi annually, and Niccolò da Padova, Papino, Poccino, and Dalida de' Putti each received only 96 lire per year.[64] Tromboncino, with over three times the salary of even Ricciardetto, must have been viewed as a particular prize. His privileged position was surely the direct result of his fecundity as a frottolist, as well as, perhaps, of his particular skill as a composer and performer. Certainly Tromboncino was not the only composer on Lucrezia's staff, for at least another two of her six musicians were frottolists: Niccolò da Padova was the author of seventeen pieces in Petrucci's books of the genre, and Papino is listed as a composer in Petrucci's lost tenth book of frottole.[65]

These musicians gave Lucrezia a small but diverse group: she had three frottolists as well as singers of secular music and string players for the performance of the pieces produced by Tromboncino, Niccolò, and Papino. Bartolomeo was clearly a lutenist of some renown, for he is praised for his ability on the instrument in a premature epitaph by Hieronimo Cassio.[66] Poccino, too, was a lutenist: in 1505, the year before the musician's entry into Lucrezia's services, an unnamed writer sent Isabella a *"frotolina,"* telling her to have Poccino set it to the lute.[67] Niccolò da Padova and perhaps Papino must have been lutenist-singers, too, and the female singer Dalida is praised as a singer alongside Tromboncino in Oriolo's *Monteparnasso*.[68] In 1508 de' Prosperi reports an ensemble of Ferrarese singers and string players that must have consisted of just these musicians. During carnival, Ippolito d'Este presented an eclogue by Ercole Pio that compared the virtues of Lucrezia, Isabella, and Elisabetta Gonzaga. In this play a group of shepherds appeared on stage: "Then Dalida, who was dressed, like the others, as a shepherd, began to sing with three companions, among whom was Tromboncino."[69]

Like Eleonora d'Este before her, therefore, Lucrezia had her own small court and a budget assigned her to pay for it. In fact, this budget was a matter of some controversy between Lucrezia and her father-in-law, Ercole d'Este. Lucrezia and her father, Pope Alexander VI, wanted her to have a budget of 12,000 ducats annually for a court of 118 to 120 servants,[70] but Ercole and Lucrezia finally compromised on a budget of 6,000 ducats plus the expenses for feeding her employees;[71] even so, this was over twice the amount of approximately 2,700 ducats Eleonora had received for her court. In December 1506, for example, Lucrezia had 66 servants (plus an indeterminate number of servants in the stables), rather than the 118 she had wanted; these included cooks, tailors, meat carvers, a chaplain, and so forth.[72]

Of these servants, the best paid was Antonio Tebaldeo, who joined Lucrezia's court in 1505, at the same time as Tromboncino.[73] Tebaldeo, a poet, humanist, and priest, worked in Lucrezia's chancery and may have been responsible for much of the poetry set by her frottolists.[74] He was paid the astounding sum of 620 lire annually for this service, 155 lire more than Tromboncino, and exactly the salary Ercole d'Este had paid Josquin Desprez.[75] Next after Tromboncino in annual salary was the court painter Michele Costa, who received 31 lire a month, or 372 lire annually.[76] Lucrezia compensated the majority of her retainers more modestly: she paid her chief cook and her chaplain, for example, 48 lire a year, her tailor, 144 lire, and her doctor, 240 lire.

Lucrezia maintained, therefore, a complete, self-contained court including all the main elements of her husband's court, with the sole exception of military retainers. Unlike Eleonora d'Este and others from the previous generation of Italian noblewomen, she also maintained a self-sufficient corps of musicians. From her pay registers, in fact, one can infer the kinds of music that she, and perhaps other noblewomen of the Renaissance, patronized. Two facts are immediately apparent. First, with frottolists, singers, string players, and a dance instructor, Lucrezia was well furnished with the requisites for secular vocal music designed for court entertainment, as well as for the frottola's devotional equivalent, the lauda. Second, her musical staff was much more limited than her husband's, for she employed neither singers of sacred music nor players of loud instruments: trumpets, shawms, and trombones. Although a case might be made that she had no need of these musicians, since her husband employed them, the same point could be made concerning singers and string players, which she did have in her service. Rather, it seems that the absence of these musicians must have something to do with the proprieties of the era, in which noblewomen were expected to have in their households neither loud instruments, the rightful attributes of the warlike prince, nor a personal chapel.[77] The latter was by far the most costly undertaking in the patronage of music, equaling roughly the cost of all the other groups combined, and it seems logical that each court would maintain only one such ensemble, associated with the ruler himself.[78]

Without doubt, Lucrezia, with her love for dances and *feste*, occasionally needed loud instruments, and these she borrowed from Alfonso or Ippolito. In March 1506, for example, she paid Nicola Piva and his companions for having played at a *festa* that she gave during carnival. Nicola, although a Ferrarese figure, was not Lucrezia's musician.[79] At the end of the same year, she gave presents to Vincenzo Tamborino, servant of Ippolito, and to the trumpets and pifferi of Alfonso, presumably for having played for her during 1506.[80] On the basis of Lucrezia's staff, therefore, it would appear that noblewomen kept musicians for the softer types of court music alone, that is, for secular and devotional vocal music and perhaps for instrumental music played by ensembles of strings. This can be confirmed by examining the kinds of music patronized by Lucrezia's sister-in-law Isabella d'Este.

Without the presence of pay records for the Mantuan court in general, the size and nature of Isabella's particular court is difficult to assess. Nevertheless, that she maintained her own household is demonstrated in several documents, the most important of which are a pair of letters of 1502 between Isabella and her father. Ercole d'Este, outraged at the sum Lucrezia wanted for her court, wrote his daughter on 16 May, asking her for the size of her budget.

> We wish to know how much you are given annually by your husband the Marchese. We therefore ask you to write us immediately, detailing clearly your budget, including the living and eating expenses for you and your servants and everything else, so that we are completely clear as to the quantity and quality of your funds, and so that we know your total budget and how you receive it, and for this reason we are sending this special rider.[81]

Isabella responded to Ercole two days later, answering with some pride in her financial acumen:

> When I came here to this most illustrious house, I was given a budget of six thousand ducats a year in cash for dressing myself and my ladies . . . and to pay the salaries of all my servants and ladies. . . . Beyond this, [my husband's] court gave me the expenses for about one hundred mouths. Afterwards, in order to be freer in increasing or decreasing the size of my court and to be free of the expense, my illustrious consort on the advice of his factors assigned me two thousand ducats for the expenses of feeding my servants, including thus the expenses for my companions.[82] [The money] was assigned to me in the following fashion: six thousand ducats come from the taxes on the mill-stone, one thousand from excise duties, and the other one thousand from the income derived from the village of Palidano, the total coming to eight thousand ducats. It is true that, through my own industry, my income from the said court [Palidano] has increased by one thousand

ducats, and from this income I have acquired the court of Castiglione Mantovano and Bondenazo, so that at present I have an income of around ten thousand, five hundred ducats; but I now have about fifty servants more than I originally had.[83]

Isabella therefore received from Francesco a budget of eight thousand ducats, two thousand ducats greater than that of Lucrezia. Isabella, however, was required to pay the living expenses of her servants and Lucrezia was not, so the actual budgets of the two noblewomen were roughly equal. It is true that Isabella managed to increase her funds, but she had a court of about 150, much larger than that of Lucrezia.[84]

The marchesa's household also included musicians, whom she had in her personal service rather than simply using those attached to Francesco's court. This was already the case shortly after her marriage, for in March 1490 she wrote to her husband:

> Creaco and his companion, [both] singers, have asked me to have your Excellency tell them what they are to do, because they say that you told them to remain here and that they are staying in the hostel. For this reason I ask your Lordship to advise me whether you want to keep them in your services or give them to me or whatever else is your wish so that I can tell them what they are to do.[85]

The singers must have stayed with Isabella, for she asked the Council of Verona several months later to help "Creaco, our singer" with a suit pending there.[86] This is a particularly early indication that Isabella had her own musicians, but it is by no means unique. Through a study of her correspondence, it can be shown that she employed singers and string players, as well as players of keyboard instruments and pipe and tabor.

One of the most important of these musicians who served on Isabella's staff was Bartolomeo Tromboncino. I now believe that, until his departure in about 1505, Tromboncino served as Isabella d'Este's personal musician and that, during this time, Marchetto Cara, the other great frottolist at Mantua, served principally Francesco Gonzaga, Isabella's husband.[87] The most obvious proof of this statement is contained in the few extant financial records, that is, the mandates and decrees ordering payment for special services or exemptions from payment due. All such monetary transactions for Tromboncino come from Isabella and her secretary Benedetto Capilupi.[88] In strong contrast, all those for Cara originate from Francesco and his secretary Antimaco.[89] Documents not concerned with payment also support this separation. Isabella treats Tromboncino as an employee, interceding on his behalf after he killed

his wife, writing to Francesco to beg his forgiveness.[90] Further, she requires Tromboncino to do tasks typical of a musical retainer. When
poets send Isabella their verse to be set it is unfailingly to Tromboncino
whom she turns for the settings, not to Cara,[91] and in 1498 she writes
to her brother Ippolito:

> Your most reverend Lordship wrote me the other day asking that I have your
> old songs recopied. Thus, I have done it and send them to you, even though
> they are not copied as you asked, that is, in a small book, but, in order to
> not delay any longer I wanted to send them as they are. I shall now have
> Tromboncino recopy them and shall send them to you [again].[92]

With Cara, on the other hand, there is a certain distance in these
early years of Isabella's reign. There are few letters concerning Cara in
her correspondence before 1505, and these often relate him to Francesco. In August 1495, for example, she writes to her husband at For-
novo, sending Cara to him and apologizing for not having returned him
sooner.[93] Finally, there is a group of letters of 1499 concerning a trip to
Casale Monferrato by Tromboncino and other musicians that makes explicit this particular division of musicians. Isabella's brother Giulio
writes her on 8 May, sending songs and asking her to have Cara put
them into better form. Isabella answers on 14 May, thanking Giulio for
the pieces, and, without mentioning Cara at all, says that she would
have given them to Tromboncino, if he had not already left for Casale.[94]
On 7 June Marchese Guglielmo Paleologo of Casale writes Isabella, not
Francesco, apologizing for not having sent her singers back to her:

> The singers of your Ladyship who are here having asked permission to re-
> turn to you, we were not able to allow this because we are in the process of
> having performed a comedy, in which it is necessary that these [singers] take
> part in order to sing some verses that were composed for them. We ask your
> Ladyship to be pleased to accept their explanation when they arrive, because
> we have kept them here to do this.[95]

One of these singers must have been Tromboncino, who had gone there
by the middle of May.

Taken together, these documents indicate clearly that Tromboncino
was Isabella's musician and that Cara was Francesco's. Such a situation
helps to explain Tromboncino's early concern with higher-quality text
forms, for it was Isabella and not Francesco who continually corre-
sponded with poets, asking for their latest products, and who wanted
musical elaborations of Petrarch. Conversely, the situation helps explain Cara's disregard of these forms early in his career, and his tre-

mendous importance for them in later years; after Tromboncino's departure, Isabella obviously shared Cara with Francesco.

By using the same types of evidence, other musicians who were members of the Marchesa's personal household can be named.[96] On 10 December 1490, for example, Isabella, returning from Ferrara, wrote to her husband:

This evening I arrived here [in Sermide] safe and sound. Tomorrow I shall be in Sacchetta and the next day in Mantua, as your Excellency knows from another of my [letters]. Having had Maestro Johannes Martini come to Mantua the other day to teach me singing, as your Excellency knows, I have taken great pleasure in this, since it appears to me a most laudable virtue. Now, to continue [my studies], I am bringing him back with me. But because he cannot remain there long, he brought with him a young Frenchman who has a good technique of singing and who would be good for the task because he is alone. If your Excellency approves, I should like to take him to stay with me. For this reason, I ask you to inform me of your wish [in this matter].[97]

This young Frenchman whom Isabella hired must have been Charles (Colinet?) de Lannoy, who deserted her court in 1491 to go to Florence, taking with him her singing method.[98] Another well-known musician, the lutenist and viol player Giovanni Angelo Testagrossa, was a member of Isabella's personal court from at least 1495 to about 1503, when he served as her lute teacher, and again intermittently thereafter.[99] Isabella's court also included a keyboard player named Alessandro and an unnamed pipe-and-tabor player.[100]

Whatever the exact makeup of Isabella's musical household, it contained all the basic elements of Lucrezia's: frottolists, singers, string players, and a pipe-and-tabor player. Unlike Lucrezia, she employed a keyboard player, most probably because she herself played these instruments.[101] Indeed, this may be the key to the entire picture of Isabella's patronage of music, for her patronage was a single-minded one, concentrating on a single type of music: the frottola. There is no trace in her correspondence of interest in sacred music with Latin texts, wind music, the French chanson, or anything other than secular and devotional vocal music with texts in the Italian vernacular.

This narrow focus of Isabella's patronage was the result of several factors, among them the proprieties of the era limiting the kinds of music suitable for a noblewoman's attention. The one that stands out most strongly, however, is that she was interested in patronizing only that music which she herself could perform. It is clear, for example, that

Isabella did not speak or understand French, and therefore was not interested in the chanson.[102] It is also clear that she did sing and play lute, viol, *lira da braccio*, and keyboard instruments, but did not play or appreciate winds.[103]

With slight differences, this is also the kind of music patronized by Lucrezia Borgia in Ferrara. Indeed, the musical forces of the two noblewomen were quite similar and conform to the prescriptions of Francesco da Barberino for music suitable for a lady: *bas* chamber music and music for the dance. This similarity, then, can provide a clue to the kinds of music supported by the new generation of noblewomen in Italy in the years around 1500: they seem to have patronized exclusively secular and devotional music and to have employed composers, solo singers, and players of string instruments to provide for their needs. Too, given the importance of the dance to women, they employed dancing masters and *tamborini*. Because of the social connotations of loud instruments, they left the patronage of pifferi to their husbands. Neither did they support the expensive chapels of singers for the performance of sacred music: this too, at least in Italy, seems to have been the exclusive province of the ruler himself. On the other hand, their establishments of musicians specializing in secular vocal music and string music were strong ones, as strong as those of their husbands, and their importance as supporters of secular and devotional music must be viewed as equal to that of their male counterparts.

Appendix: Documents[104]

Document 1: Letter of Bernardino de' Prosperi to Isabella d'Este, 4 June 1505 (ASMN B. 1240, fol. 298).

Illustrissima Madama. . . . El pare che la voluntà del Signore nostro sia che Madonna Elysabeth et tute l'altri forasteri et forastere che sono in casa de la Illustrissima Signora sua consorte se partino et le napoletane et anche Samaritana romana, donde tuti et tute stano come può pensare la Signoria Vostra. . . . Se dice anche che Madonna Beatrice ne va a stare cum la prefata Signora et che Tromboncino et Ser Thebaldeo sono nel numero de quelli che hano ad essere cossì, ma il tuto vederemo presto. . . . Ferrariae, quarto Junij 1505.

Document 2: Excerpts from the Court of Lucrezia Borgia in December 1506 (ASMO LASP L. 1130, fols. 92v–94).

Al Nome de Idio M.D.VI
Zobia a dì XXXI de dexenbre

[3.] Maestro Lodogivo Bonazolo medigo per havere servito mixj dodexe in ragione de L. 20 dato el mexe—L. 240.

[4.] Messer Antonio Tibaldeo per havere servito mixj dodexe in ragione de L. 51 [S.] 13 [d.] 4 dato el mexe—L. 620.

[*9.] Dionixe de Mantoa dito Papino per havere servito mixe dodexe in ragione de L. 8 dato el mexe—L. 96.

[*13.] Messer Niccolò de Padova cantore per havere servito mixj dodexe in ragione de L. 8 dato el mexe—L. 96.

[*16.] Trombonzino cantore per havere servito mixj dodexe in ragione de L. 38 [S.] 15 dato el mexe—L. 465.

[*17.] Rizardettj Tanborino per havere servito mixj dodexe in ragione de L. 12 [S. 8] dato el mexe—L. 148 [S.] 16.

[23.] Zoanne de Formento sopra chuogo per havere servito mixj dodexe in ragione de L. 4 dato el mexe—L. 48.

[40.] Don Rainaldo Capelano per havere servito mixj dodexe in ragione de L. 4 el mexe—L. 48.

[48.] Maestro Anzelino sarto per havere servito mixj dodexe in ragione de L. 12 dato el mexe—L. 144.

[53.] Maestro Michel Costa depintore per havere servito mixj sette e mezo in ragione de L. 31 dato el mexe—L. 236 [S.] 5.

[*66.] Pozino Cantore per havere servito mixj duj che comenzò a dì primo de novembre in ragione de L. 8 dato el mexe—L. 16.

Document 3: Letter of Ercole d'Este to Isabella d'Este, 16 May 1502 (ASMN B. 1188).

Dux Ferrariae et cetera. Illustrissime et Excellentissime Domine filie nostre dilectissime, Domine Isabelle Marchionisse Mantuae et cetera, salutem. Desideramo de intendere quanta sia la provisione che singulo anno vi è data da lo Illustrissimo Signore Marchese vostro consorte, et però pregamo la Signoria Vostra che subito per una sua lettera ni voglia chiaramente significare quanta è dicta sua provisione, computate le spese del vivere et dil vestire per lei et per la famiglia sua et ogni altra cosa, per forma che restiamo ben chiari de la quantità et qualitade de dicta sua provisione, et che etiam sapiamo se de tuta la provisione gli è provisto a dinari contanti o come, et per questa causa spaciamo questo cavallaro a posta. Et il tuto ni serà gratissimo. Et bene valete. Belriguardi, XVI May 1502.

Document 4: Letter of Isabella d'Este to Ercole d'Este, 18 May 1502 (ASMN B. 2993, L. 13, fols. 71v–72v).

Illustrissimo Signore mio patre observandissimo. Quando io venni a principio in questa illustrissima casa, mi fu deputato de provisione sei mille ducati d'oro l'anno per il mio vestere et de le mie donne . . . et dare la provisione a tutti li servitori et donne . . . et ultra di questo la corte mi faceva le spese a circa cento bocche. Doppo, per essere in magior libertà de acrescere et sminuire la familia a mio modo, condescendendoli etiam voluntariamente lo Illustrissimo Signor mio consorte a persuasione di suoj factori per levarsi in tutto il peso dalle spalle,

mi furono deputati dua millia ducati per le spese, includendoli etiam le spese
de li compagni, li quali me furono assignati in questo modo: li sei mille de la
provisione sopra il datio de la macina, mille de le spese sopra una gabella, et
per li altri mille mi fu data la corte et possessione de Letpaledano, sì che in
tutto ascendino a la summa de octo mille ducati. L'è vero che poi, per industria
mia et di mei, la intrata de dicta corte è acresciuta circa altri mille ducati, et ho
de li avanzi acquistata la corte de Castiono Mantuano et dil Bondenazo, per
forma che al presente mi ritrovo havere de entrata circa dece millia et cinquecento ducati l'anno, ma ho etiam forsi cinquanta bocche più che non mi furono
deputate. . . . Mantuae, XVIII Maij MDII.

Document 5: Letter of Isabella d'Este to Francesco Gonzaga, 15 March 1490
(ASMN B. 2904, L. 136, fol. 10).

Illustrissimo Domino Nostro

Illustrissimo Signor mio. Creaco e lo conpagno, cantarini, me hanno pregata
voglia intendere da la Excellentia Vostra quello che hanno a fare, perché dicono
essa haverli facto restare qua et che sono suso l'hostaria. Sì che prego Vostra
Signoria me avisi se la li vole tenerli a li servitij suoi o darli a me o qual altra
sia la intentione sua atiò possa responderli quanto habiano a fare. . . . Mantuae,
XV Martij 1490.

Document 6: Letter of Isabella d'Este to Ippolito d'Este, 14 December 1498
(ASMO, Estero, Cartegio di Principe e Signorie, Italia, B. 1196, [Mantova, B.
16]).

Reverendissimo et Illustrissimo Monsignor mio. La Signoria Vostra Reverendissima me scrisse l'altro dì che gli facesse refare li soi canti[105] vechi. Cossì ho
facto e mandoli, benché non siano stati notati come havea ordinato in uno libretto picolo. M[a] per non differir più, ho pur voluto mandarli a questo modo.
Farò mo notarne al Trombonzino de novi et mandarogeli, et alla Signoria Vostra Reverendissima me racommando. Mantue, XIIIJ Decembris 1498.

Document 7: Letter of Marchese Guglielmo Paleologo of Casale Monferrato to
Isabella d'Este, 7 June 1499 (ASMN B. 740).

Illustrissima et Excellentissima Domina tanquam Soror honorandissima. Ha-
vendoni li cantori de la Signoria Vostra, chi sono qua, ricerchato licentia per
ritornarsene da lei, non gli l'havemo possuta concedere per essere in atto de
fare recitare una comedia a la quale è bisogno ch'epsi li intervengano per cantare alchuni versi se sono compositi a tale proposito. Pregamo la Signoria Vostra vogla admettere la loro excusatione quando sarano lì, per haverli noi rette-
nuti per fare questo effecto, et così a la Signoria Vostra se offerimo et
racommandiamo. Datum Casali, die VIJ Junij 1499.

Document 8: Letter of Isabella d'Este to Francesco Gonzaga, 10 December 1490
(ASMN B. 2106).

Illustrissimo Signor mio. Questa sera sun gionta qua sana e salva. Domane sero
a Sachetta e l'altro a Mantua, secundo che per un'altra mia haverà inteso la

Excellentia Vostra. Havendo facto venire l'altro zorno a Mantua Maestro Zoan Martino per imparare a cantare, como scià la Signoria Vostra, ne ho preso grande piacere, parendome virtute molto laudabile. Cussì adesso, per sequitare, lo reconduco meco. Ma perché lui non poteria restarli troppo, ha condutto seco uno zovene franzoso, qual ha bona rasone de canto et se ne haveria bon constructo perché è solo. Quando Vostra Excellentia se contentasse, io lo tuoria volunteri a stare meco: però la prego se digni farme intendere la volunta sua, et a la bona gratia de Vostra Signoria me raccomando sempre. Sermedi, X Decembris 1490.

11

"Thinking from Women's Lives":
Francesca Caccini after 1627

Suzanne G. Cusick

For more than a century scholars have understood the late career of singer, teacher, and composer Francesca Caccini through the prism of Alessandro Ademollo's *La bell'Adriana*, published in 1888. Citing as his source a contemporary *ricordo* (memoir), Ademollo concluded his brief account of Caccini's life with this footnote:

> In 1626, her husband died; she remarried a Lucchese, leaving the service of these Highnesses (Tuscany) and died of cancer of the mouth. Excellent in singing, playing and composing.[1]

This end to Caccini's story has been repeated by Masera,[2] Silbert,[3] Raney,[4] Bowers,[5] and various bio-bibliographical sources, including *The New Grove Dictionary*. Only Tim Carter's 1979 dissertation adds to the story: he documents what seems to have been Caccini's last court payment in May 1627, and one apparent return to Florence in February 1635, when she was involved in a court entertainment authored by Michelangelo Buonarotti the younger.[6]

The latter fact hints at a professional life for Caccini after her departure from Medici service and presumed second marriage. Yet most scholars have inferred from Ademollo's footnote that Caccini in effect retired in 1627 (at the age of forty) at the time of her remarriage to the Lucchese and died soon after. No events of either personal or artistic significance are assumed to have intervened between her presumed retirement and her death.

Thinking about Music History "from Women's Lives"

The inference of Caccini's quick and permanent retirement following her first husband's death has long troubled me, for like all readers of history I read stories from the past through the prism of my own life. Like Caccini, I have been a lifelong musician, one whose training began in early childhood and whose youth included public performance by age thirteen. That history has so imprinted the notion "musician" on my self-concept that I have found it impossible to purge, even in longish periods of nonmusical employment. And I was not nearly so immersed in the profession as was Caccini between the ages of thirteen and forty: I did not compose a successful stage work at age nineteen,[7] nor a steady series of them thereafter; I did not enjoy an international reputation as a *virtuosa* and a national one as a teacher and director of chamber singing. How much more deeply imprinted must Caccini's self-concept as a musician have been than my own? How much more inextricable from her identity?

How, I have wondered, could it have felt to turn her back completely and finally on all she had ever been, to become (as the historiography has suggested) a private person, a seventeenth-century housewife, with the aura of virtual imprisonment in the home that historical role implied? Did she choose the renunciation?

If Caccini did choose to renounce her professional life, I have reasoned, that decision might suggest her professional life had not been chosen freely. If her known musical career—so brilliant for a woman of her time—had been *for her* twenty-seven years of forced labor, then her life has a different meaning from what is usually assigned to it by women musicians who seek role models from the past. For there is a plot usually assigned to the Caccini narrative in discussions of women-in-music: best articulated by Bowers, it is that of an extraordinary talent empowered and enabled to flourish by the professional acceptance and musical traditions of her predecessors in *concerti delle donne*. The evidence of her own surviving letters depicts Caccini as a shrewd woman who made the most of every opportunity before her.

But if Caccini renounced her professional life, then the plot of her narrative might be instead a plot of forced musical labor, labor so unloved that it was fled as soon as widowhood provided the opportunity for escape into a "normal," nonprofessional female life. This is a plot I have not wanted to see, because Caccini's rejection of the professional for the purely personal would amount to a rejection of my life as well as hers. I have come to think it was a plot that other scholars interested in Caccini have intuited as well, one they have not wished to see either. They chose to accept Ademollo's claims as probably true but not to investigate their truthfulness, perhaps for the same reason that scholars studying women composers' music have mostly shied away from critical, evaluative studies of that music: we have been nearly paralyzed by an inchoate fear that both the constricting life plots and the negative critical judgments we have defensively attributed to misogyny would prove to be true.

Daughter of a different time, I have responded through my fear with both anger and intellectual doubts about the implied story of the Ademollo tradition. For a decade I thought it was suspiciously like poetic justice for a singer to die of cancer of the mouth. For nearly that long, I thought that perhaps Caccini's retirement was in effect forced either by a change in Florentine attitudes toward women singers or by her own reputedly difficult personality: Ademollo also tells us, after all, that she was *"fiera ed irrequieta,"* proud and restless. But since I began critical, evaluative work on Caccini's *La Liberazione di Ruggiero*, I have become convinced that the Ademollo tradition of Caccini's 1627 retirement had to be wrong: the composer of the protofeminist *La Liberazione*, I have felt, would never have renounced her own professional life. I have been determined to discover what really happened to Caccini after she seemed to vanish from the musico-historical record in May 1627. I have sought confirmation (or refutation) of Ademollo's "facts" and I have sought evidence for a different story from the one his choice of "facts" implies.

My thinking about the supposed end of Caccini's professional life is offered here as a concrete, even mundane example of the feminist theoretical approach American epistemologist Sandra Harding describes as "thinking from women's lives."[8] Thinking from women's lives—from my own life to Caccini's, from hers to her stepmother's, and back again—has enabled me to read with different eyes the sources others have read before me, to ask different questions of traditional archival sources, and thus to find some of the answers I sought about Francesca Caccini's last years.

I have deliberately chosen, as well, to pollute with the textual presence of "I" what might have been a thoroughly objective text describing archival discoveries. My motivations and my agenda as a woman, musician, and feminist are central and necessary to the framing of questions that led to these discoveries. I want to acknowledge the position from which another decade of Caccini's life became visible again, in part as an example of what difference gender and subjectivity can make in the apparently objective business of combing archives for documents. I want to acknowledge my agenda, too, as a way of focusing critical attention on Ademollo's footnote, indeed on his whole telling of Francesca Caccini's story.

Caccini appears in Ademollo's book as a textual diversion in a chapter devoted to one phase of *virtuosa* Adriana Basile's much more conventional life, her brief 1610 stay in Florence en route to taking a position in Mantua. First mentioned immediately after a description of Florentine singer Vittoria Archilei as a "good-natured and very tranquil *virtuosa . . .* content to let others live in peace," Caccini is described as quite the opposite, as *"fiera ed irrequieta."*⁹ In the next nine pages, Caccini is called *"fiera ed irrequieta"* four times; six of the nine pages describe in loving detail the feud she is alleged to have had with Andrea Salvadori, a feud Ademollo calls a black spot on Caccini's reputation. As Ademollo retells the story, Caccini began the feud by publicly ridiculing Salvadori's sexual adventures with women singers at court. Salvadori retaliated by refusing to write the libretto of *La Liberazione di Ruggiero,* "forcing her [Caccini] to marry her notes to the unworthy words of Bali Saracinelli."¹⁰ Caccini's revenge was to persuade the Medici women to cancel an opera by Salvadori on the story of Iole—a woman who was carried off by Hercules and whose collusion with his wife, the former woman warrior (and bird) Deianira, ended in Hercules' death and Deianira's suicide. Caccini's story ends, in Ademollo's telling, with the long-delayed publication of Salvadori's *Iole lusinghiera* "40 years after it had served so well the proud and restless Cecchina's desire for vengeance."¹¹

The footnote describing the death of Caccini's husband, her departure from Medici service, and her death—from cancer of the organ that had brought her fame, professional success, and power—follows immediately. Its function for those who know the story of Iole and Deianira is to echo that story, subtly casting Caccini as the man-killing, self-killing Deianira. Thus, Caccini is moved out of the actual narrative, replaced by anecdote, myth, and Salvadori's implicit vindication by publication. Her real life (if we are to believe Ademollo's source) serves as a footnote to Ademollo's use of her as an icon of an inappropriate woman musician. Caccini is but a rhetorical foil for his subject, the beautiful and socially compliant Adriana Basile. But the footnote's resonance instills just the fear, defensiveness, and paralysis in ambitious women to which I alluded earlier: we feel (as we are meant to) pain and powerlessness at the silencing of Caccini by Ademollo's narrative.

Ademollo, too, had an agenda in telling the story of Francesca Caccini, the only composer among the many *virtuose* whose lives are traced in his book. His agenda was, I think, to make Caccini herself the "black spot" of his text, a cautionary tale about women who go too far. My response, laden with anger, has been to look for and to identify the source of Ademollo's footnote.

The sources for almost everything Ademollo says about Francesca Caccini are acknowledged, although he falsely attributes his telling of the Salvadori feud to librarian Antonio Magliabecchi when he almost certainly used the memoir of Andrea Cavalcante now in the Biblioteca Riccardiana.[12] As it happens, Ademollo seems to have used a single source for the two footnotes attributed to *"un ricordo contemporaneo,"* a source that seems to provide fairly accurate and quite personal information. What was this source?

Ademollo's source was a collection of horoscopes compiled in the Medici court circle sometime in the first third of the seventeenth century, all six volumes of which are now in the Biblioteca nazionale in Florence.[13] Volume 5, entitled "Le Doti" (The Gifted), includes the annotated charts of dozens of poets, painters, and scientists and those of five musicians: Francesco Rasi, Nannicino Fiorentino, Monsu Balard, Giovanni Battista Signorini, and Francesca Signorini, detta la Cecchina.

Caccini's chart is reproduced as Figure 11-1. Comparison of the annotations to Ademollo's footnote reveals that Ademollo did little more than add the appropriate tense of the verb *to be* to create a prose of complete sentences, a prose he could plausibly quote as if it were from a contemporary *ricordo*. Is this a credible source?

Verbal annotations to a horoscope might indeed be useful to scholars, providing hints toward new insights about a subject. But it is hard to believe that statements from a horoscope, uncorroborated by any other source, could have stood as biographical facts for over a hundred years. At least two problems casting doubt on these "facts" should have occurred to the scholars whom I believe to have seen this source. First, it seems only logical that additions written on a horoscope may in some way reflect the astrological predictions of the chart itself. Indeed, the annotations to Francesco Rasi's chart are clearly marked with astrologers' notes connecting the "facts" of his life to the conjunction or opposition of certain planets. Similarly, the "facts" of Francesca Caccini's chart may be merely the implications of her stars.

If, that is, these were her stars. For the second problem casting doubt on these "facts" is that this is not Francesca Caccini's chart at all. It is the chart of someone born 18 September 1588; according to records at the cathedral archive in Florence, Francesca Caccini was born and bap-

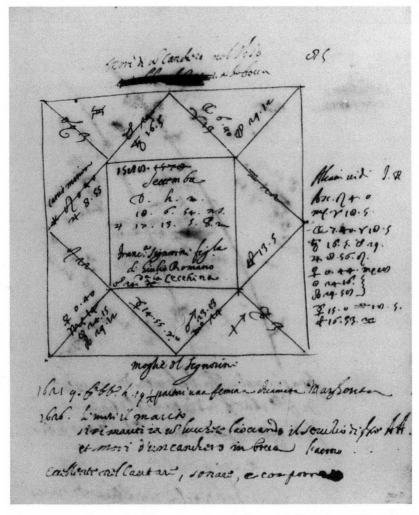

Figure 11-1. Horoscope of Francesca Caccini Signorini, Florence, Biblioteca nazionale, MS II.105 (*Oroscopi diversi*), fol. 85r.

tized exactly a year earlier, on 18 September 1587.[14] Ademollo (and others) obviously failed to check the horoscope's date, even though on the very next page the astrologer noted a similar error in the chart of Caccini's daughter, Margherita Signorini. If the most easily checked "fact" in this document—Caccini's date of birth—is wrong, how credible are the other "facts"?

What did actually happen to Francesca Caccini? Her story—as I've begun to discover it from documents in Lucca and Florence—is much more interesting than the summary bad end Ademollo and his followers have allowed her, raising new questions about the musical lives of both cities and about the relation between gender and class in a seventeenth-century musician's life. Further, these documents both affirm the facts and refute the implied plot of the Ademollo tradition.

"Nel 1626 li morì il marito" (In 1626, her husband died)

Ademollo's first fact is irrefutably true. Giovanni Battista Signorini, a court singer and instrumentalist whom Caccini had married in November 1607, was buried in the common tomb of the confraternity of the Holy Rosary in Santa Maria Novella on 30 December 1626.[15] From the will he had made seven days earlier with notary Paolo Lapi,[16] we know that the Signorini had lived on via Valfonda since April 1610, when Signorini used Caccini's 1,000-lire dowry and other money she provided him to purchase two adjacent houses.[17] Acknowledging that her money had also paid for various improvements to the property over the years, Signorini left both houses to Caccini as the restitution of her dowry that was customary upon a husband's death.[18]

Signorini went on to acknowledge that throughout their marriage his wife had contributed more than half the cash income of their household, using it to furnish and adorn the home and sharing it generously with his family. Furthermore, the house was filled with jewels and gifts she had received as favors from various princes and dignitaries. In fact, he said, save for the clothes on his back, a few lire in his pockets, and the bed that he had bought at the time of their marriage, everything in the house was rightfully hers. Thus, he used the power of his will and testament to deed the wealth Caccini had herself provided into her name. Additionally, Signorini named Caccini guardian of their daughter, Margherita, and asked that she teach her "the sciences and arts that she herself knows."[19]

We know from Caccini's 1627 letters to Michelangelo Buonarotti that

Caccini entered widowhood eager to undertake the legal requirements of guardianship so as to expedite litigation with an otherwise unidentified Marzichi.[20] Assuming no relatives challenged Signorini's will, she also entered widowhood with real and personal property that could be used to endow a second marriage after the legal period of mourning, a year and a day, had passed.

"Si rimaritò in un lucchese" (She remarried a Lucchese)

The notion that Caccini remarried may have been the main obstacle preventing scholars from trying to trace her later life, for it might have been expected that she would have changed her surname: during her first marriage she had chosen to sign her name as Francesca Signorini, even though under Roman law (and in Medici court documents) she remained Francesca di Giulio Caccini. Without knowing her second husband's name, a search for the remarried Francesca Caccini would have required determined alertness to all the "Signora Francesca" references in Lucchese or Florentine documents that might identify the woman as a musician. Such alertness led me to find five letters from "Signora Francesca Raffaelli" to Francesca Caccini's longtime collaborator Michelangelo Buonarotti the younger, all of them letters referring to music, and all of them showing quirks of handwriting and diction startlingly like the letters of Francesca Signorini to Buonarotti twenty years earlier.[21] Armed with a new surname, I traced Francesca Raffaelli through Medici payroll records and Lucchese marriage records until I was certain that she was indeed Francesca Caccini.

Caccini had wasted no time in agreeing to a second marriage, and it was indeed to a Lucchese. By July 1627, two months after she drew what seems like severance pay from the Medici paymaster, the Florentine lawyer Oratio Tuccarelli, in Lucca on official business for the Tuscan government, wrote to his supervisor Dimurgo Lambardi:

> My tardiness in writing you has been caused by my desire to tell you something substantial about S.ra Cecchina, who is as if married to S.re Tomaso Raffaelli. . . . [He] is about 56, lives from the income of his lands, a musician more than anything else. He has a regal villa at Monte s.quilici a mile outside the city, where there are many most beautiful gentlemen's villas, and many intellectual gatherings. And I hear that the wedding will be in a few weeks.[22]

On 13 August, Tuccarelli had no new details but this ironic comment:

It is believed that the two sirens will certainly be joined by the coming September, and because the gentleman is esteemed as quite trained in this profession . . . Lucca is to be transformed into a new Parnassus.[23]

By 15 September, Tuccarelli reported:

The friend who is keeping me advised of S.ra Francesca's affairs has told me that she has sent many things to the house of the S.r bridegroom and that this month will not pass without their having had the wedding, and I believe him without a doubt because I saw the groom today, who seemed to me a Ganymede if quite grey-haired, but very well-groomed and gracious.[24]

Francesca Caccini did, then, "remarry a Lucchese"—a man who lived off his rents, who, like Signorini, was much her elder and a musician, a man with a well-groomed, gracious manner who struck the Florentine lawyer as like the stereotypical younger (often effeminate) partner in a male homosexual couple, despite his greying hair.[25] What did this marriage mean to her life? Did it, as the Ademollo tradition suggests, constitute a professional retirement?

At this stage, I can only suggest some of the answers, drawing on dowry taxes, Raffaelli's will and related documents, and fragments of information about Raffaelli and his circle gleaned from local histories and genealogies of prominent Lucchese. This much is factually clear: Raffaelli paid tax on Francesca Caccini's dowry, valued at 1600 lire, on 3 January 1628, a week after the earliest possible date for their marriage to be concluded legally. When Raffaelli made his will in February 1630, they had an eighteen-month-old son, also named Tomaso. By June 1630 Caccini was once again the widowed guardian of her children and executrix of her husband's estate. But this time her husband had considerably more to leave in her care than their conjugal bed.

Tomaso Raffaelli was a member of Lucca's landed nobility, one of the principal heirs to a network of farms, vineyards, olive groves, and mills near the mountain villages of Fondagno, Partigliano, and Gello in the *vicaria* of Pescaglia.[26] His family had immigrated to Lucca from Mantua in the 1440s and had become prosperous enough to be included in the republic's ruling oligarchy by the mid-sixteenth century.[27] Tomaso himself had served in Lucca's legislature,[28] and had administered both the Fondagno properties and the villa at Monsanquilici since his father's death in 1608.[29] His immediate neighbors in Monsanquilici—his economic and political peers—included some of Lucca's most powerful silk merchants and bankers: the Buonvisi, the Burlamacchi, and the Orsucci.[30] A bachelor for most of his life, Raffaelli had married once before, for notarial indices record his receipt of a 2,000 lire dowry from

Flaminia di Giovanni Fondaro in 1625.[31] The son he evidently produced with Francesca Caccini by August or September 1628 was, however, his only heir.[32]

There is reason to suppose that Raffaelli married both times out of anxiety to produce an heir, responding to an atmosphere of extreme pronatalist pressure within Lucca's oligarchical class in the mid- and late 1620s that has been documented by historian Rita Mazzei.[33] She cites in particular the so-called Libbro d'Oro of January 1628, intended to define in perpetuity the families who could wield political power. All these families (104, including the Raffaelli) were urged to ensure their families' reproduction as a means of ensuring the long-term political stability of their Republic.[34] Tomaso Raffaelli, it seems, did his citizenly duty by marrying a newly available widow and producing an heir in the minimal amount of time.

But why would a fifty-six-year-old member of the landed nobility, a possible homosexual, marry a forty-year-old widow from the artisan class, a woman who in twenty years of previous married life had managed to bear only one child? Why, that is, if his principal aim was to produce an heir?

The answer, I think, lies in the world hinted at by Tuccarelli's ironic comment about the union of sirens transforming Lucca into a new Parnassus. For Tomaso Raffaelli was a musician and a prominent patron of various musical and poetic academies.[35] His youthful home had been one of the meeting sites for the academy organized by Orazio Lucchesini and his talented wife, Laura Guidiccione (the poet of Emilio de' Cavalieri's musical entertainments *La disperatione di Fileno*, *Il Satiro*, and *Il giuoco della Cieca*).[36] When that group dissolved in 1605, Raffaelli created a new musical academy that flourished from 1606 until at least 1620. In the 1620s, if not before, Raffaelli was a leading member of the Accademia degli Oscuri, a group that, despite its name, was the most prominent force in Lucca's cultural and social life, its membership virtually identical with the ruling class defined by the Libbro d'Oro. Further, a letter from Adriano Banchieri to Raffaelli, published in the *Lettere Armoniche*, identifies Raffaelli as a collector of musical instruments.

This same letter mentions in passing that Banchieri has heard in Bologna of Vincenzo Buonvisi's "acquisition" for his household of Francesca Caccini, "sweetest of players and singers."[37] Had Caccini, then, somehow entered the service of her husband's neighbor and friend? Was her marriage to Raffaelli, like her first marriage to Signorini, a means of preserving the proprieties surrounding a woman's chastity when she was employed as a musical servant? Who was Vincenzo Buonvisi, and what was his relationship with Tomaso Raffaelli and with musical life in Lucca?

In the 1620s, the Buonvisi family were the richest investment bankers in Europe. Vincenzo had been a special ambassador to Florence several times, including during the visit of Prince Ladislao of Poland; indeed, it was he who had reported back to Lucca about the performance of Caccini's *La Liberazione*.[38] He could well have hired Caccini away from the Medici, but initially it seems unlikely he would have arranged her marriage to his own social peer, as the usual practice was to marry a woman musical servant to a musical, military, or literary manservant. The idea that Caccini would have married one patron of music in Lucca while entering the service of another, a man whose villa adjoined her husband's in the district of Monsanquilici, contradicts all our assumptions about the behavior of ruling-class people and artisan-class musicians. Yet I think the contradiction can be resolved by considering how Caccini may have served these men's joint interests in the artistic productions of their Accademia degli Oscuri.

Founded in the 1560s by, among others, Buonvisi's father and uncles, the Oscuri was primarily a debating club for most of its history. By tradition it is believed to have met in the Buonvisi palace at Monsanquilici, the very home occupied by Vincenzo in the 1620s; and it is believed that its intermittent amateur theatrical productions for carnival were staged in the Buonvisi's city palace on what is now the via del Fosso.[39]

In December 1627 the Oscuri resolved that their carnival entertainment for the winter of 1628 would be the production of a spoken comedy with two intermedii "in musica"—the group's first theatrical venture since carnival 1612. By 10 January 1628, according to the academy's minute book, they had chosen the subject of the comedy, raised 417 lire from the membership for production costs, commissioned sets from the Lucchese architect Mutio Oddi, and appointed a six-person committee "to see to the composition and setting in music" of the intermedii. The chair of this committee was to be Tomaso Raffaelli, who had one week earlier finalized his marriage to Francesca Caccini.

Astonishingly, in only two days Raffaelli's committee returned to the group with a report detailing the need for a budget of at least 200 lire for the salaries and transportation costs of singers who would have to be brought from Florence and Pisa. Lucca's ambassador to Florence, Filippo Mei, was to negotiate with Archduchess Maria Maddalena for the services of two soprani, Domenichino and Tatini, while the committee itself would ask Antonio Brunelli of Pisa to sing and to recommend an excellent bass.[40] By 24 January a resolution of the Oscuri praised Rafaelli's group for the speed and excellence with which they had completed all arrangements for the music, including securing another 100 lire for the singers' costumes.

The Oscuri's minute book provides a wealth of further details about preparations that need not concern us. Suffice it to say that the entertainment itself was a spectacular success both with the Lucchese audience and with the foreign dignitaries who had been invited. So thrilled were the Oscuri that they contracted to publish the intermedii with their music (a publication that, if it ever emerged, now seems lost) and resolved to make such entertainments a standard feature of future carnivals. Indeed, before the minutes break off in mid-January 1629, they record preliminary preparations for the 1629 season, which was to have less lavish sets but no less lavish music.

Can it be an accident that this highly auspicious resurgence of music theater in Lucca coincided with the arrival of one of Florence's most experienced intermedio performers and composers—indeed, with her arrival in the very household charged with "seeing to the composition"? Can it be an accident that Banchieri had heard that composer's name in association with the man in whose private theater these intermedii were most likely performed?

It seems to me far more likely that Caccini's arrival in Lucca should be seen as one of the preparations for Lucca's 1628 season. Her marriage to Raffaelli was probably even more like a contract for services than were most seventeenth-century unions—and her services were not primarily (possibly not at all) reproductive. She provided Raffaelli and his circle with twenty years' performing, teaching, and composing experience—a classic if extreme case of the "intangible dowry" notion (the substitution of a woman's practical skills for a cash dowry) that had, in fact, helped supply Caccini with artisan-class music pupils in Florence.[41] Very likely, too, she provided the actual music for the intermedii both in 1628 and in the less well documented 1629 season. Her providing of legitimacy to Tomaso Raffaelli's heir was undoubtedly part of the deal, although actually bearing the child may not have been.[42] In return, Raffaelli provided her with lodging, food, clothing (just as the Medici had, although indirectly) and, in lieu of salary, with a social status far higher than any she had ever known. As the wife of an aristocrat, however, she could not be acknowledged publicly as having done the work of an artisan—singing, teaching, composing. Thus, the name of the much-praised composer of the 1628 intermedii is conspicuously absent from the otherwise obsessively detailed account in the Oscuri's minute book.

Remarriage to a Lucchese, then, probably did not signal Caccini's retirement from musical work. Rather, it signaled a retirement from *publicly acknowledged* musical work, a return to the very situation in which she had begun her career as a composer, when as an unmarried girl in her father Giulio Caccini's house she fulfilled his commission for music to Michelangelo Buonarotti's *La Stiava*.[43]

Raffaelli's death in the spring of 1630 transformed Caccini's situation yet again, for his will conferred on her both the status and the responsibilities of the landed aristocracy for the rest of her life.[44] Raffaelli named Caccini executrix and heir for life of his entire estate, provided she not remarry and provided she educate and raise the young Tomaso Raffaelli in ways appropriate to his social status. Further, Raffaelli left Caccini outright his shares in the Barsotti silk-exporting business. To ensure Caccini's dominion over his property, Raffaelli stipulated that she be required to file no papers with the government, that there be no inventory of his estate, and that anyone in his family who tried to contest his will be automatically disinherited.

Because Raffaelli's will waives all requirements for an inventory, there is no complete description of the estate entrusted to Caccini's management. On 4 June 1630, however, she executed eight contracts with the *fattori* (overseers) of various properties. From these contracts it is clear that Caccini had inherited "for life" at least the following: the villa at Monsanquilici; a palazzo at Fondagno; twenty-two wood lots producing chestnut flour as a cash crop for sale in Lucca's markets; ten vineyards; seven olive groves; nine fields producing grain for sale in Lucca's markets; and shares ranging from one-sixth to one-half ownership of four mills in Fondagno or Gello. Her contracts with the *fattori* call for the annual production of specific quantities of cash crops as well as for proportional shares of each property's oil, wine, firewood, and garden production. Thus, Caccini's private household requirements would have been more than met, and she would have had considerable cash income, the size of that income dependent on the variable market prices of grain and flour. Further, she would not have needed to be resident at Lucca to manage the estate.

I have as yet found no other documents pertinent to Caccini's life at Lucca. When her documentary trail surfaces again, she is in Florence in December 1634.

"Lasciando il servizio di queste Altezze" (Leaving the service of these Highnesses)

Caccini's presence in Florence (more precisely, in the Medici's suburban villa of Castello) in February 1635 has been known since Carter's dissertation cited the mention of her contribution to a court birthday celebration in an exchange of letters between Michelangelo Buonarotti and Ugo Cacciotti.[45] It would be easy to suppose that this was only a visit to Florence, possibly associated with her stepmother's final illness, especially as it is her sister Settimia Caccini, not Francesca, whom we know to have been at least intermittently on the court payroll from the 1630s until her death in 1661.[46] No trace of Francesca has been found by scholars seeking to document Medici musical life by traditional systematic reading of extant pay records.

Yet the earliest of five letters from Francesca Raffaelli preserved in the Buonarotti archive at the Biblioteca Laurenziana, dated 14 December 1634, seems to suggest she had already resettled not only in Florence but also into a court-related life.[47] In that letter, Francesca asks Buonarotti to send her some *canzonette spirituali* to use with her daughter; she has heard that he has such things from S.ra Emilia, probably her former pupil Emilia Grazii, who was still on the Medici payroll[48] and who is known to have sung *canzonette spirituali* for the princesses Anna de' Medici and Vittoria della Rovere at their lodging in the convent of La Crocetta.[49] Was Caccini somehow associated with La Crocetta? Had she, like many another widow, "retired" from the world into a fashionable convent? Or had she somehow slipped back into the Medici service the astrologer (and Ademollo) believed her to have left?

How could more traces of her be found? "Thinking from women's lives" enabled me to create a hypothesis that ultimately led to my discovery of Caccini under both her own and her second husband's name in Medici payroll records and letters. The lives I thought from were those of Caccini's mother, Lucia, and stepmother, Margherita.

Shortly after his accession as Grand Duke of Tuscany in 1588 and after his wedding to Christine de Lorraine, Ferdinand I de' Medici had reorganized the music at court. Among those who lost paid positions was Caccini's mother, Lucia, her firing being part of the replacement of

Florence's *concerto delle donne* by a sopranist *concerto dei castrati*.[50] Lucia continued to sing at court occasionally, as did Giulio Caccini's pupil Margherita della Scala, who became his second wife in 1590. Listed on the Medici payroll as a lady-in-waiting rather than as a musician, Margherita formed part of the unofficial *concerto delle donne* re-instituted by Maria de' Medici and Leonora Orsini almost immediately after Ferdinand's dissolution of the official one.[51]

Did Francesca similarly switch payrolls some forty-five years later? Was she paid not as a servant of the grand duke—part of the public musical life of the court—but as a servant or lady-in-waiting in one of the Medici women's households? It seemed both logical and likely; but it seemed, too, that surely someone must have looked for her there. Apparently no one had, for Caccini is easily found in the payroll records both of the dowager Granduchess Christine de Lorraine for 1635 and 1636 and of the new Granduchess Vittoria della Rovere for 1635 and 1636. Indeed, Caccini's payment history for the mid-1630s survives in great detail.

On 3 April 1635 the dowager Granduchess Christine ordered her new paymaster Vincenzo Vespucci to continue the payments previously made by Lorenzo Veneri to Francesca Caccini. Therefore, she may have returned well before December 1634. Therefore, too, scholars need not have known Caccini's second married name to have found her, for the pay order uses her legal birth name. Caccini was to be paid 18 lire per month, of which 6 lire were understood to be for her daughter, Margherita (who was then thirteen, the age her mother had been when she began to sing at court). Additionally, she was to receive 45 lire per year as *pigione* (housing allowance).[52] From September 1635 through all of 1636, however, Caccini's monthly 18 lire and her housing allowance were paid—to Francesca Raffaelli—by the newly formed household of Vittoria della Rovere. In fact, on Christmas Day 1635, Caccini received her entire 1636 salary in advance, the loan guaranteed by another singer, S.ra Selvaggia Guasconi Medici.[53] The two granduchesses' households must have been at least partly interchangeable, however, for after Christine's death in December 1636, Francesca Raffaelli appears on a list of the elder woman's servants who were to be paid six months' salary and housing allowance in advance.[54] Along with Ferdinando Saracinelli, Ugo Cacciotti, Vincenzo Vespucci, and Christine's physicians and chaplains, Francesca Caccini Raffaelli also appears on a list of persons whose continued salary payments were to be discussed with the grand duke—suggesting that they might not be retained.[55] Caccini would seem to have survived the staff cut, if any, for in November 1637 Florentine wool merchant Francesco Forti signed a receipt for her housing allowance for the coming six months.[56]

What did Caccini do for her salary? In April 1635, according to a letter from Cacciotti to retired diplomat Orso d'Elci, she and her daughter restored to its former excellence the traditional singing of the offices for Holy Week.[57] Margherita, at least, sang for the feast of S. Giovanni that year, for in June the paymaster was ordered to give her 24 lire to spend on clothing for that day. Described as a girl who learned exquisitely, Margherita studied guitar and harp with Costanza de Ponte, a *virtuosa* in the service of Camilla Orsini ne'Borghese, who was lent to the Medici for six months along with her husband, Luigi Rossi.[58] Mother and daughter apparently sang to Granduchess Christine often in her last months, their music soothing her deathwatch as Francesca's had that of Duke Cosimo II years earlier.[59] And Francesca probably taught music to the two princesses Anna de' Medici and Vittoria della Rovere, perhaps providing music for the private performances of *commedie* in which they participated while living in the convent of La Crocetta.[60]

Caccini seems to have taught in convents, as well, for in a letter of May 1636 Caccini reported to Buonarotti that certain nuns had been asking her for new *canzonette spirituali*.[61] Two other letters asked for charity toward certain needy widows, one associated with the convent known as Le Convertite, the other with La Crocetta. Caccini sweetened her request for Buonarotti's aid with the astonishing news that she had already extracted donations to these widows from the princesses.[62]

That a certain cheekiness might be detected in the idea of Caccini soliciting contributions from the adolescent Medici princesses is borne out by two documents from early 1637. In late January, at the very time that Caccini's own longterm employment was to be reevaluated by the grand duke, she took what might have been the most prideful (if not "restless") stance of her career. According to notes of the ducal secretary Ugo Cacciotti, Ferdinand II had specifically asked that fifteen-year-old Margherita Signorini sing (*"canti et recitare in comedia"*) during the festivities for his wedding (scheduled for July 1637). Evidently Margherita had agreed, but Francesca refused her permission. On behalf of Ferdinand, Cacciotti asked Prince Gian Carlo to intercede. Caccini turned the prince down as well, citing the potential damage to her daughter's prospects for a good marriage or convent placement, as well as to both of her children's reputations, should she sing *"in scena."*[63]

Both Caccini's reasons for denying Margherita permission to sing, and the place her own name occupies in the surviving payroll records of the Medici women's courts, reflect the change in her social position wrought by her marriage to Tomaso Raffaelli. In the payroll listings she is described as a *musica*, but listed with the ladies-in-waiting rather than with the artisan-class service providers. Indeed, her salary (although somewhat less than it had been in the 1620s) is commensurate with those of the ladies-in-waiting—that is, with the salaries of women whose social position and inherited wealth obviated any notion of wages based on need, workload, or quality of service. The women among whom Christine's and Vittoria's paymasters listed Francesca Caccini Raffaelli were not, conceptually, receiving salaries at all: they were receiving honoraria and tips. Thus Caccini Raffaelli, although providing services recognized in her description as a *musica*, was not a salaried servant. Nor did she need to be, as her private income from Raffaelli's Lucchese land holdings would have at least equaled her "salary" in even the hardest years of the 1630s. Listed among the ladies-in-waiting, while described as a *musica*, Francesca Caccini in the 1630s lived somewhere between two class positions—in a sense, between two worlds.

In her refusal to allow Margherita to sing, I think Caccini rhetorically chose one of those worlds over the other in an effort to determine her daughter's real (not rhetorical) future while fulfilling the status-conscious requirements of Raffaelli's will. Thus, the fifty-year-old Francesca Raffaelli was able to demonstrate an independent attitude toward the Medici family because she had acquired through marriage that which no man of the artisan class could acquire through work—upward social mobility such that she could insist upon being treated as a lady rather than as a servant. It was a privilege she hoped to leave to her only daughter. Caccini's gender worked for her, then, as an instrument to escape the servility that had plagued her father's world. In a way quite different from what I think Ademollo's source intended, she had indeed "left the service of their Highnesses" when she "remarried a Lucchese."

"Et morì di cancro in bocca" (And died of cancer of the mouth)

Did Caccini die of cancer of the mouth? At this writing, I do not know when, much less how, Francesca Caccini died. I remain in doubt about this "fact," my doubt grounded in two kinds of reading, one paleographic and one historicist.

The astrological chart from which Ademollo gleaned his other "facts," reproduced as Figure 11-1, actually lists two causes for Francesca Caccini's death. At the top of the page, someone had written the words *"morì di un canchro nel Viso"* (died of a cancer in the face). Just below that, someone else wrote, *"mirabile nel Canto nella Bocca"* (miraculous in singing in the mouth); then *"mirabile nel Canto"* was crossed out, leaving *"nella Bocca"* as a floating signifier. Below the chart are the annotations Ademollo used for his other "facts." Here, the referent for *"nella bocca"* appears unambiguous—it is cancer, not singing, that was in her mouth. But here, too, the handwriting is different, as is the ink. Can the lower annotations have included a hasty transcription of the upper ones? Can the lower annotator have interpreted the upper one to mean that such a woman ought to die of an excess of her own nature? Can Ademollo have transcribed the lower annotator's cause of death uncritically because it matched his unspoken assumption that there was something monstrous and unnatural about a woman who was so miraculous in singing?

The notion that Caccini's miraculous singing was unnatural in a negative way is consonant with the poetic tropes used to both praise and *not* praise her in her lifetime. For the poems praising Caccini typically do not use the usual imagery of sirens, muses, angelic voices, and seductive sorceresses familiar to readers of the poems addressed to *virtuose* from Livia d'Arco to Adriana Basile.[64] Instead of focusing on the effects of disembodied sounds, poems praising Caccini typically focus on her body—on her hands and her mouth—as acting to produce prodigies of nature. At least one sequence of poems written to commemorate her performances for the Accademia degli Umoristi in Rome in 1623 specifically links these prodigious effects to the trope of Orphic power. Caccini is described as a kind of anti-Orpheus: whereas Orpheus's song calmed the seas, Caccini's is wittily credited with having caused a flood of the Tiber. That is, to the poet (Adriana Basile's brother, writing under the pseudonym G. F. Materdona) the prodigies of Caccini's body produced excesses of nature, not a controlling of nature. While I doubt that the annotator of Ademollo's *ricordo* knew these poems, he surely participated in the discursive world that produced them. Thus, it may have seemed "natural" and logical that Francesca Caccini, *"mirabile nel canto,"* should have died from an excess of her own prodigy-producing nature.

The astrologer's "facts" taken up by Ademollo for his story turn out to be at once true and not true, being, as facts always are, only the bare bones of a story. But where "facts" have been partially true, the inferences by which the Ademollo tradition has fleshed them into a story seem to have been wrong. Francesca Caccini did not slouch off the stage of Florentine musical life amid a storm of controversy born of her "proud and restless" nature. Nor did she retire by age fifty, renouncing a lifetime that seems to us to have included remarkable musical achievements. Rather, her musical talents and skills allowed her to remarry distinctly above her station, acquiring by her marriage new professional opportunities, considerable wealth, and a social position that allowed her to exert a measure of control over her household's artistic production. However she may have died, Caccini's own story seems not to have ended as Ademollo's story about her did, in a rapid succession of vengeance, bereavement, exile, and self-murder.

Instead, Francesca Caccini's story can be read as that of a woman musician who acquired what her musician father had longed for, the social power of the aristocracy. Francesca achieved what Giulio never could because gender made her class position contingent on marriage, enabling her to use exceptional training and talent as an intangible dowry rather than as merely a service to be exchanged for cash. Further, Caccini's story can be read as that of a woman musician whose later years were increasingly spent in a woman-dominated musical world—teaching, coaching, and probably composing for women in convents and at court who seem to have had an active musical life heretofore unknown to and completely unexplored by music historians.

As Caccini's story after 1627 proves not to have been a dead end for her, neither is it a dead end for scholars who pursue it. For Caccini's story points directly to two other musico-historical stories that remain untold. Her apparent professional activity in Lucca in the late 1620s suggests two stories—one about the musical and theatrical relations between Lucca and other Tuscan cities and one about music and civic life in that republic before the opening of Lucca's first opera theater in the 1640s. Both are stories with absolutely no secondary literature. And her involvement with the musical life of Florentine convents in the 1630s points up our startling lack of information about that aspect of Florentine musical life. Thinking about Caccini's story "from women's lives," then, changes both her story and the stories we are able to discern in the world she knew, Italy in the early Baroque.

In his widely read essay "Rethinking Intellectual History," Dominic La Capra cautions that we should read every historical document and every part of the historiographical tradition as literature, not "fact."[65] Read as literature, every document has an ideological agenda, an "angle."

From the angle that most likely was Ademollo's worldview, Francesca Caccini might as well have been dead when, instead, she returned to a gynecentric Florentine musical world in the 1630s. For such a world was not the real world in the ideology of "separate spheres," which was the commonsensical view of gender in Ademollo's time. That ideology has been shifting for a generation in our time toward a view of gender in which a gynecentric world can be just as real as any other. Once that shift of angle occurs, once we think of women as having lives beyond the marriage plot (lives from which we might think and act independently), both "facts" and a story about Caccini that have lain beneath our noses for centuries suddenly move into the reality we call history. New questions about the aging Caccini's activities and the still barely visible world in which early modern women made music for themselves leap forward, begging for answers. We are likely to understand the whole fabric of seventeenth-century musical life better when we incorporate in our view a multiplicity of angles, including those that come of "thinking from women's lives."

Notes

Notes to the Introduction

1. For a description of the types of research involved in subjects that have suffered scholarly neglect, see G. Lerner, *The Majority Finds Its Past: Placing Women in History* (New York: Oxford University Press, 1979), p. 166.

2. J. Bowers and J. Tick, eds., *Women Making Music: The Western Art Tradition, 1150–1950* (Urbana and Chicago: University of Illinois Press, 1986), p. 3.

3. I have chosen to use the term *sponsor* rather than *patron* to avoid any sexist overtones and to suggest a larger spectrum of support than that afforded by financial patronage. Female aristocrats also provided collegial advice and friendly encouragement to the musicians they sponsored.

4. B. Nettl, *The Study of Ethnomusicology: Twenty-Nine Issues and Concepts* (Urbana: University of Illinois Press, 1983), p. 334.

5. E. Hallett Carr, *What is History?* (New York: Knopf, 1963), p. 26.

6. Bowers and Tick (1986), p. 4.

7. These four articles are as follows: A. Bagnall Yardley, " 'Ful weel she soong the service dyvyne': The Cloistered Musician in the Middle Ages"; M. V. Coldwell, "*Jougleresses* and *Trobairitz*: Secular Musicians in Medieval France"; H. Mayer Brown, "Women Singers and Women's Songs in Fifteenth-Century Italy"; and A. Newcomb, "Courtesans, Muses, or Musicians? Professional Women Musicians in Sixteenth-Century Italy," in Bowers and Tick (1986), pp. 15–115.

8. This aspect of the study was inspired by E. Koskoff's *Women and Music in Cross-Cultural Perspective* (Urbana and Chicago: University of Illinois Press, 1989).

9. Hesiod, *Theogony* 56 ff. The *Theogony* in *Hesiod: The Homeric Hymns and Homerica*, English trans. Hugh G. Evelyn-White (Cambridge, Mass.: Harvard University Press, 1914; rpt., 1954), p. 83.

10. T. Seebass provides a reproduction of the introductory illustration to a Pontifical produced in Rheims at the end of the twelfth century, where five of the nine Muses are depicted with musical instruments. *Musikdarstellung und Psalterillustration im früheren Mittelalter* (Bern: Francke, 1973), II, Plate 82.

11. Meyers's article is one of two that were not written especially for this

collection. Her research was previously published in the *Biblical Archaeologist;* William Prizer's article on the patronage of Isabella d'Este and Lucrezia Borgia has already appeared in *Journal of the American Musicological Society.*

12. E. Wood, "Women in Music," *Signs* 6/2 (Winter 1980): 295.

13. Koskoff (1989), p. 15.

14. Milan Kundera, *The Book of Laughter and Forgetting,* trans. Michael Henry Heim (New York: Penguin, 1987), pp. 91–92.

15. Letter from Abraham Mendelssohn to his daughter Fanny, Paris, 16 July 1820, in Sebastian Hensel, *The Mendelssohn Family (1792–1847),* trans. Carl Klingemann, 2 vols. (New York: Harper, 1881), I, p. 82.

16. Judith killed herself one winter night. As Woolf speculates, "Any woman born with a great gift in the sixteenth century would certainly have gone crazed, shot herself, or ended her days in some lonely cottage outside the village, half witch, half wizard, feared and mocked at." Virginia Woolf, *A Room of One's Own* (New York: Harcourt Brace, 1929), p. 53.

Notes to Chapter 1

1. J. von Sturmer, "Aboriginal Singing and Notions of Power," in *Songs of Aboriginal Australia,* ed. M. C. Ross, T. Donaldson, and S. A. Wild, Oceania Monograph 32 (Sydney: University of Sydney, 1987), p. 74.

2. Ibid.

3. G. Béhague, ed., *Performance Practice: Ethnomusicological Perspectives* (Westport, Conn.: Greenwood, 1984), p. 10.

4. D. Bell, "Aboriginal Women and Land: Learning from the Northern Territory Experience," paper read at the Workshop on Aboriginal Land Rights, University of Western Australia, December 14–16, 1983, p. 6.

5. C. Goddard, *A Learner's Guide to Yankunytjatjara* (Alice Springs: Institute for Aboriginal Development, 1981), p. iii.

6. N. B. Tindale, *Aboriginal Tribes of Australia: Their Terrain, Environmental Controls, Distribution, Limits, and Proper Names* (Berkeley: University of California Press, 1974).

7. A. Hamilton, "Descended from Father, Belonging to Country: Rights to Land in the Australian Western Desert," in *Politics and History in Band Societies,* ed. E. Leacock and R. Lee (Cambridge: Cambridge University Press, 1982), p. 98.

8. P. Brock, ed., "Introduction," in *Women, Rites and Sites: Aboriginal Women's Cultural Knowledge* (Sydney: Allen and Unwin, 1989), p. xix.

9. Béhague (1984), p. 9.

10. My experiences are detailed in H. Payne, "Singing a Sister's Sites: Women's Land Rites in the Australian Musgrave Ranges" (Ph.D. diss., University of Queensland, 1988), pp. 56–70.

11. For details of women's ritual training, see ibid., pp. 71–93; and H. Payne, "Rites for Sites or Sites for Rites? The Dynamics of Women's Cultural Life in the Musgraves," in P. Brock (1989), pp. 53–55. In Aboriginal thought, the powers of production and reproduction are not held to reside in the "real" world of material reality, but in the "religious" realm (which is, to them, no opposi-

tion at all). Ritual enactments that release ancestral powers are considered to be a necessary and vital part of life, and they are equated by Pitjantjatjara speakers with the "work" and "business" activities of Europeans.

12. See Payne (1989), p. 42.

13. H. Payne, "Residency and Ritual Rights," in *Problems and Solutions: Occasional Essays in Musicology Presented to Alice J. Moyle*, ed. J. C. Kassler and J. Stubington (Sydney: Hale and Iremonger, 1984), pp. 264–78.

14. A. Hamilton, "Timeless Transformation: Women, Men and History in the Australian Western desert" (Ph.D. diss., University of Sydney, 1979), p. 69.

15. H. Payne, "Matriarchs of Myth," in *Feminist Companion to Mythology*, ed. C. Larrington (London: Harper Collins, 1992), pp. 268–69.

16. Payne (1984), p. 271.

17. T. G. H. Strehlow, *Songs of Central Australia* (Sydney: Angus and Robertson, 1971), p. 354.

18. Ibid., p. 110.

19. Ibid., p. 381.

20. Payne (1992), pp. 269–70.

21. Ibid., p. 270.

22. D. Bell, "In the Tracks of the Munga Munga" (typescript, 1982), p. 14.

23. Strehlow (1971), p. 336.

24. N. Wallace, "Change in Spiritual and Ritual Life in Pitjantjatjara (Bidjandjadjara) Society, 1966 to 1973," in *Aborigines and Change: Australia in the 1970s*, ed. R. M. Berndt (Canberra: Australian Institute of Aboriginal Studies, 1977), pp. 74–89.

25. For an account of how the lack of vehicular transport affected Pukatja women's claims to sites west of the Musgrave Ranges, see Payne (1984), p. 273.

26. S. A. Wild, *Walbiri Music and Dance in Their Social and Cultural Nexus* (Ph.D. diss., Indiana University, 1975), p. 68.

27. Hamilton (1979), p. 270. This division reflects the moiety division operative in this region. See I. M. White, "Generation Moieties in Australia: Structural, Social and Ritual Implications," *Oceania* 52 (1981): 6–27.

28. von Sturmer (1987), p. 71.

29. C. J. Ellis, *Aboriginal Music: Education for Living* (St. Lucia: University of Queensland Press, 1985), p. 92.

30. Ibid., pp. 108–9.

31. Ibid., p. 123; P. Pritam, "Aspects of Musical Structure in Australian Aboriginal Songs of the South-West of the Western Desert," *Studies in Music* 14 (1980): 21.

32. I. M. White, personal communication to the author, 1986. A senior Pitjantjatjara-speaking woman living at Yalata told this information to White.

33. See von Sturmer (1987), p. 71.

34. See C. J. Ellis, "The Role of the Ethnomusicologist in the Study of Andagarinja Women's Ceremonies," *Miscellanea Musicologica: Adelaide Studies in Musicology* 5 (1970): 197–98. Ellis includes photographs of women residing to the east of the region of my focus. These women are painted all over, and Ellis notes that the painting took much longer to prepare than did the actual enactment of the item presented by the painted women.

35. N. D. Munn, "Totemic Designs and Group Continuity in Walbiri Cosmology," in *Aborigines Now: New Perspective in the Study of Aboriginal Communities*, ed. M. Reay (Sydney: Angus and Robertson, 1964), p. 90.

36. See Hamilton (1979), p. 238.

37. D. Bell, "The Alyawarra and Kaititja Land Claim [of the Central Land Council]: A Statement, October 5, 1978, and a Second Statement, October 16, 1978" (typescript, Australian Institute of Aboriginal Studies Library, Canberra), p. 13.

38. R. Buckley, C. J. Ellis, L. A. Hercus, L. Fenny, and I. M. White, "Group Project on Andagarinja Women" (typescript, University of Adelaide Library; vol. 1, 1967; vol. 2, 1968), p. 117.

39. Ibid., p. 72.

40. Ibid.

41. I. M. White, "Sexual Conquest and Submission in the Myths of Central Australia," in *Australian Aboriginal Mythology*, ed. L. R. Hiatt (Canberra: Australian Institute of Aboriginal Studies, 1975), p. 133.

42. Bell refers to a different process among Walbiri-speaking women living northeast of the area discussed in this article. She states that Walbiri-speaking women transfer the powers they have absorbed back into the sacred boards used during the enactment. These boards are then carefully protected by the women until next needed for a performance. See D. Bell, *Daughters of the Dreaming* (Melbourne: McPhee Gribble; Sydney: Allen and Unwin, 1983), p. 128.

43. von Sturmer (1987), p. 74.

44. Hamilton (1979), p. 238.

45. D. Bell, "The Pawurrinji Puzzle: A Report to Central Land Council on the Country of Pawurrinji" (typescript, 1979), p. 22.

46. Personal communication to the author by Pitjantjatjara-speakers, 1989.

47. Personal communication to the author by Pitjantjatjara-speakers, 1978.

48. von Sturmer (1987), p. 73.

49. Ibid.

50. Ibid.

51. For a more detailed explanation, see Payne (1988), pp. 79–93.

52. von Sturmer (1987), p. 72.

53. White (1975), p. 133.

54. Strehlow (1971), p. 380.

55. White, personal communication to the author, 1978.

56. See Bell, *Daughters of the Dreaming* (1983), p. 51.

57. I describe specific examples of the interplay between public performance and land ownership claims in Payne (1984), pp. 272–77, and in Payne (1989), pp. 46–47.

Notes to Chapter 2

I wish to thank the Asian Cultural Council in New York City for its generous support of my research in Central Java in 1990–91. Also, I thank New York University for its current support of my dissertation write-up and the Music Department at the University of Sydney for providing both an office and a supportive atmosphere in which to work. Among the many people with whom I have had conversations about this essay and other aspects of my research, I would especially like to thank Tony Day, Kay Shelemay, Stanley Boorman, Ellen Koskoff, Marc Perlman, and Ray Weiss.

1. S. Weiss, unpublished fieldnotes, 2 July 1991.

2. P. Sanday, "Introduction" in *Beyond the Second Sex, New Directions in the Anthropology of Gender*, ed. P. R. Sanday and R. G. Goodenough (Philadelphia: University of Pennsylvania Press, 1990), pp. 5–6.

3. Ibid., pp. 9–10.

4. A. Schlegel, "Gender Meanings: General and Specific," in Sanday and Goodenough (1990), pp. 37–38.

5. A. Meigs, "Multiple Gender Ideologies and Statuses," in Sanday and Goodenough (1990), p. 102.

6. This summary of male philosophy has been culled from the writings of several authors including W. Keeler, *Javanese Shadow Plays, Javanese Selves* (Princeton: Princeton University Press, 1987); and J. T. Siegel, *Solo in the New Order: Language and Hierarchy in an Indonesian City* (Princeton: Princeton University Press, 1986).

7. It should be noted that the ability to control one's language and physical behavior is proof of one's potency only if everyone else cooperates. Central Javanese men are dependent on the predictability of social interaction for the chance to display their potency. If all persons play by the rules, comporting themselves in a refined manner and maintaining their own and others' reputations as powerful and refined persons, no one will suffer the embarrassment of being in an uncontrollable situation that threatens this guise.

8. W. Keeler, *Symbolic Dimensions of the Javanese House*, Center of Southeast Asian Studies Working Paper 29 (Clayton, Australia: Monash University, 1983), p. 5; and Siegel (1986), pp. 187–202.

9. This point is made by Shelly Errington in her introductory essay to *Power and Difference: Gender in Island Southeast Asia*, ed. J. M. Atkinson and S. Errington (Stanford, Calif.: Stanford University Press, 1990). See also Siegel (1986), pp. 187–88.

10. I have highlighted the aspects of this story that suit my purpose of showing the importance placed on the male notions of proper respect and behavior as a formula for order and control. However, this anecdote also points out that concepts of power and the order of authority are in the process of changing as there is a shift from local to state sources of power. In a more traditional Java, a word from the *dhalang*, as the local spiritually powerful person, would have stopped the unpleasant encounter. As it was, the village head to whom I was supposed to have reported was a transfer from a distant area. Having no immediate reason to heed the wishes of the *dhalang's* family, the village head continued to hassle me while the representative of the *dhalang's* family could only sit and nod in benign agreement with everyone.

11. For some interesting comments on Dewi Sri, see R. E. Jordaan, "The Mystery of Nyai Lara Kidul, the Javanese Goddess of the Southern Ocean," *Archipel* 28 (1984): 99–117; and Jordaan, "Skin Disease, Female Ancestry, and Crops," in *Indonesian Women in Focus: Past and Present Notions*, ed. E.

Locher-Scholten and A. Niehof (Dordrecht, Holland, and Providence, N.J.: Foris Publications, 1987), pp. 120–34.

12. P. Carey and V. Houben, "Spirited Sri Kandhis and Sly Sumbadras: The Social, Political, and Economic Role of Women at the Central Javanese Courts in the 18th and Early 19th Centuries," in Locher-Scholten and Niehof (1987), p. 15.

13. Ibid., pp. 15–16.

14. Solo is another name for the city of Surakarta, which has come to be considered the center of high culture and the arts in Central Java. While there are many who would disagree, this is certainly the opinion, stated or not, of most of the artists in the area.

15. These stories are compiled from written notes of an unrecorded session on 5 April 1991.

16. It has been brought to my attention by Marc Perlman that this reasoning is actually an insidious verification of the Central Javanese perception of women's lesser abilities in language usage, since it is in improvisation of story and thought that the *dhalang*'s abilities are displayed. I agree but point out that the representation of Nyai Panjang Mas is as a preserver and bearer of culture. From this perspective, the fact that she has brought back new verisons of *lakon* only enhances her importance.

17. The *Serat Sastramiruda*, a manuscript in Javanese script found in the Radyapustaka Museum in Surakarta, is a treatise on *wayang* in the form of a dialogue between a teacher and a student. Indonesian and Javanese edition translated and prepared by Kamajaya and Sudibjo Z. Hadisutjipto for the Proyek Penerbitan Buku Sastra Indonesia dan Daerah (Jakarta: Departemen Pendidikan dan Kebudayaan, 1981).

18. Whether Bagong was a clown figure used in East Java or one invented by Nyai Panjang Mas is not clear either from the *Serat Sastramiruda* or from the tale as told by Bapak Naryacarita.

19. S. Weiss, unrecorded interview with Naryacarita, 5 April 1991.

20. Jordaan (1984), pp. 99–117.

21. S. Weiss, recorded interview with Kris Sukardi, 29 May 1991.

22. Ibid.

23. Keeler (1983), p. 108.

24. S. Weiss, unrecorded conversation with Sudarsana, 14 May 1991.

25. S. Weiss, recorded interview with Mara of Boyolali, 7 April 1991.

26. *Ayak-ayakan* forms can fit functionally into either of these first two types of *gendhing*, but they are structurally like the second.

27. A *wayang* performance is divided into three unequal parts, each of which is associated with a particular mode or *pathet* in the *slendro* scale. The first section is associated with *pathet nem* and generally is the longest section, running from the beginning of the performance (9:00 P.M. or so) until sometime after 12:30 A.M. The second section is associated with *pathet sanga* and the hours of 12:30 A.M. to 3:30 A.M. The last section is associated with *pathet manyura* and lasts from the end of *pathet sanga* until the end of the performance just before dawn.

28. S. Weiss, unrecorded conversation with Gandasaruya, 12 March 1991.

29. S. Weiss, fieldnotes, 2 July 1991.

30. "Kalau perempuan main *gender,* bunganya banyak. Kalau laki-laki, nggak ada bunga-bunga, isinya nggak ada"; S. Weiss, recorded interview with Pringga, 29 May 1991.

31. It should be noted that, although this was frequently mentioned as one of the main differences between male and female style, it is rare for any *gender* player, male or female, to reach an arrival tone with both hands at the same time. This generalization, made with apparent disregard for what actually happens, results from a desire to link male and female styles of *gender* performance with culturally defined male and female attributes: male = order and restraint, female = disorder and ebullience.

32. "Bedanya, gaya laki, bisa pakai notasi. Kalau perempuan ndak bisa. Kalau perempuan, lagaknya kenes-kenes. Laki-laki, ndak isa"; S. Weiss, recorded interview with Gandasaruya, 14 March 1991.

33. "Kalau penggender perempuan itu, tekun, tahu, semangat, nggender terus. Kalau laki-laki, nah, berhenti makan, rokok. Kalau laki-laki, dalangnya ndak senang, grimingannya yang khusus ndak ada"; S. Weiss, informal conversation with Kris Sukardi, 29 May 1991.

34. Most of the female *gender* players with whom I worked insisted on the fact that I recognize that they were unschooled, that their knowledge and ability were obtained entirely through their ears and their feelings, and that this was something that was to be highly valued. There is still a certain amount of condescension from skilled village musicians who live *wayang* toward the graduates of the government music conservatories who are called experts on *wayang* after a brief four-year study period. This healthy skepticism is rapidly dying out as more young musicians from the villages go to the conservatories seeking both legitimation as musicians and better-paying jobs with the government.

35. S. Weiss, unrecorded conversation with Bapak Kestik, 9 July 1991. There is no Indonesian translation for this comment, for it was communicated during a *wayang* and reconstructed later from my fieldnotes.

36. The notation insists on a one-to-one or one-to-two rhythmic relationship between the left and right hands. It is rare that any performer, male or female, will play in this manner, known as *kembang tiba,* for more than a few consecutive *cengkok.* The cipher notation system for Javanese music and the theorization of the *pathet* system were invented in the courts in the late nineteenth century to control and bring order to the plethora of *gendhing* (musical pieces) in the court repertoire.

37. For more information about the nature and history of the role of *pasinden* and a different opinion on the power (*kesektan*) of the *pasinden,* see R. Anderson Sutton, "Identity and Individuality in an Ensemble Tradition: The Female Vocalist in Java," *Women and Music in Cross-Cultural Perspective,* ed. E. Koskoff (New York: Greenwood Press, 1987), pp. 111–30.

38. Another fact emphasizing the contrast between perceptions of the *pasindhen* and those of the *gender* player is the difference in their earnings. Even a mediocre *pasindhen* will receive an exorbitant 15,000–40,000 rupiah (U.S. $7–$20) for an evening's performance. The female *gender* player is paid as any

other musician in the ensemble, indicating her role as an equal, and so receives 2000–5000 rupiah (U.S. $1–$2.50). As with high-class prostitutes, the *pasin-dhen* is an object of lust. When men lust after her they must pay, and thus they demonstrate their power through largess; see Keeler (1983). It is nothing to them if they throw money away for their own pleasure; they clearly have more than enough.

Notes to Chapter 3

A slightly different version of this paper appeared in *Biblical Archaeologist* 54, no. 4 (1991).

1. In 1943 James Pritchard published a corpus of all terracottas, 294 in number, of nude female figurines that had appeared in the literature up until that time. Pritchard's work, *Palestinian Figurines in Relation to Certain Goddesses Known Through Literature*, American Oriental Series 24 (New Haven: American Oriental Society, 1943), provided a collection more than twice as large as the previously published catalogue (which contains 124 examples), that of E. Pilz, "Die weiblichen Gottheiten Kanaans," *Zeitschrift des Deutschen Paläs-tina-Vereins* 47 (1924). The flourishing of archaeological work in Syria-Palestine since World War II means that the number of known terracottas has grown far beyond what is accessible in these catalogues. Furthermore, nude female figurines are not the only terracotta representations of females; many others, such as some considered here, are depicted with clothing.

2. Pritchard (1943) himself is wisely cautious in his study of the figurines and cites numerous examples of the propensity of archaeologists to associate many of the terracottas of females with one or another of the goddesses (especially Asherah, Ashtart/Ishtar, and Anat) known from Canaanite mythological texts. In more recent years, the feminist spiritualist movement has seized upon the existence of female figures discovered in archaeological research as evidence of widespread goddess worship that supposedly existed on a popular level but that was ultimately suppressed by patriarchal political religious authorities. The work of M. Gimbutas (e.g., *The Language of the Goddess* [San Francisco: Harper and Row, 1989] and *The Gods and Goddesses of Old Europe: Myths and Cult Images* [Berkeley: University of California Press, 1982]) has provided the material for many works of pop anthropology that herald contemporary goddess worship as the reclaiming of an ancient tradition of the exclusive power of female deities. Such assertions about primeval female hegemony in the divine and human realms are problematic, as pointed out by, among others, S. R. Binford, "Myths and Matriarchies," *Human Behavior* 8 (1979): 63–66; J. Bamberger, "The Myth of Matriarchy: Why Men Rule in Primitive Society," in *Women, Culture, and Society*, ed. M. Z. Rosaldo and L. Lamphere (Stanford: Stanford University Press, 1974), pp. 268–80; and C. Meyers, "Why a Female Hegemony?" *Biblical Archaeologist* 54 (1991): 121.

3. For a brief account, with bibliography, of Israelite music, see E. Werner, "Music" and "Musical Instruments," in *Interpreter's Dictionary of the Bible* (4 vols. plus supplementary vol.; Nashville: Abingdon Press, 1962 and 1979), III, 457–69, 469–76. See also Werner's entry "Jewish Music, Liturgical" in *The*

New Grove Dictionary of Music and Musicians, ed. S. Sadie (London: Macmillan, 1980), VII, 616–34. More extensive treatments can be found in P. Gradenwitz, *The Music of Israel* (New York: W. W. Norton, 1949), and A. Sendrey, *Music in Ancient Israel* (New York: Philosophical Library, 1969).

4. See, for example, the female figure playing a lyre in J. L. Myres, *Handbook of the Cesnola Collection of Antiquities from Cyprus* (New York: Metropolitan Museum of Art, 1914), p. 351, no. 2166, and in C. Meerschaert, "Les Musiciens dans la coroplastie chypriote de l'époque archaïque," in *Cypriot Terracottas*, Proceedings of the First International Conference of Cypriot Studies (Brussels-Liège-Amsterdam, 29 May–1 June 1989), ed. F. Vandenabeele and R. Laffineur (Brussels-Liège: A. G. Leventis Foundation, 1991), p. 187 and pl. XLIV: b, c.

5. The exact position of the hands of the figure holding these discs is critical in assessing the nature of the instrument involved, as will become clear below.

6. See M. Gorali, *Music in Ancient Israel* (Haifa: Haifa Music Museum, 1977).

7. See C. Sachs, *The History of Musical Instruments* (New York: W. W. Norton, 1940), pp. 31–33, and Sendrey (1969), p. 262.

8. See Sendrey (1969), p. 373.

9. E.g., D. Hillers, "The Goddess with the Tambourine," *Concordia Theological Monthly* 41 (1970): 606–19. Most of the works dealing with Cypriot examples call them "tambourinists."

10. Ibid. See also A. Chambon, *Tell el Far'ah I. L'Age du Fer*, Mémoire 31 (Paris: Éditions Recherches sur les Civilisations), pp. 73–74, 234, and pl. 63:1, 2; cf. Rimmer, *Ancient Musical Instruments of Western Asia in the Department of Western Asiatic Antiquities* (London: British Museum, 1961), p. 23.

11. So P. Lapp, "The 1963 Excavations at Ta'anek," *Bulletin of the American Schools of Oriental Research* 173 (1964): 40, fig. 21.

12. R. Amiran, "A Note on Figurines with 'Discs,'" *Eretz Israel* 8 (1967): 99–100 (Hebrew).

13. E. D. van Buren, *Clay Figurines of Babylonia and Assyria*, Yale Oriental Series 16 (New Haven: Yale University Press, 1930), pp. 89–90.

14. So C. Meyers, "A Terracotta at the Harvard Semitic Museum and Discholding Figures Reconsidered," *Israel Exploration Journal* 37 (1987): 117–19; cf. B. Bayer, *The Material Relics of Music in Ancient Palestine and its Environs* (Tel Aviv: Music Institute, 1963), p. 36.

15. See, for example, the classification of terracottas by V. Karageorghis, "The Terracottas," in *Études Chypriotes IX: L'Amathonte. Tombes 113–367*, ed. V. Karageorghis and O. Picaret (Nicosia: Service des Antiquités de Chypre, École Française d'Athènes, and Fondation A. G. Leventis, 1987). Similarly, in his catalogue of the enormous group of terracottas from Cyprus in the Cesnola collection of the Metropolitan Museum of Art (MMA) in New York, Myres (1914), p. 340, presents a group he identifies as males playing various musical instruments, including the "tambourine." The publication does not provide photographs of all the objects. However, through a grant from Duke University's Research Council, I have been able to examine the terracottas in the MMA storerooms. In checking the catalogue references to males playing

"tambourines," I discovered that the hands of those figures have different poses than do the women's hands. Thus, I have concluded that the instrument held by the male figures listed in Myres's catalogue, and perhaps in other such publications, as tambourinists is really a set of cymbals. I am grateful to Dr. Elizabeth Milliker, Research Associate in Greek and Roman Art at the MMA, for facilitating my examination of the Cesnola terracottas.

16. J. B. Connolly, "Standing Before One's God: Votive Sculpture and the Cypriot Religious Tradition," *Biblical Archaeologist* 52 (1989): 210–18.

17. Such as the terracotta from Shiqmona. See J. Elgavish, "Tel Shiqmona," *Encyclopedia of Archaeological Excavations in the Holy Land,* 4 vols. (Jerusalem: Israel Exploration Society and Massada Press), IV, 1102–3.

18. F. Vandenabeele, "Phoenician Influence on the Cypro-Archaic Terracotta Production and Cypriot Influence Abroad," *ACTS of the International Symposium "Cyprus between the Orient and the Occident,"* ed. V. Karageorghis (Nicosia: Department of Antiquities, 1986), pp. 351–60.

19. F. Vandenabeele, "Has Phoenician Influence Modified Cyprist Terracotta Production?" in *Early Society in Cyprus,* ed. E. Peltenburg (Edinburgh: Edinburgh University Press in association with the National Museum of Scotland and the A. G. Leventis Foundation, 1989), pp. 266–71. See also V. Karageorghis (1987), pp. 1–2.

20. J. Karageorghis, *La Grande Déese de Chypre et Son Culte,* Collection de la Maison de l'Orient Méditerranéen Ancien, no. 5, Série Archéologique 4 (Lyons: Maison de l'Orient, 1977), p. 210; cf. Vandenabeele (1989), p. 268.

21. Israel's beginnings are usually dated to the Iron I period, ca. 1200–1000 B.C.E., with the period of Moses and the Exodus being slightly earlier.

22. This connection was first pointed out to me by Eunice Poethig, who graciously shared with me her discussion of this subject in an excursus to "The Women of Israel as Oral Traditioners" (M.Div. thesis, McCormick Theological Seminary, 1975) and who also provided me with a typescript version of her Ph.D. dissertation, "The Victory Song Tradition of the Women of Israel" (Union Theological Seminary, 1985).

23. The fourfold classification system (with a fifth category, electrophone, added in consideration of modern music), based on the mode of tone production, has been suggested by eminent musicologists such as Curt Sachs as a development of the threefold classification system of the nineteenth century, which was based on the external characteristics of instruments (stringed instruments; wind instruments; and percussive, rattling, or shaking instruments). See Sachs (1940).

24. The classification of Israelite instruments is based on Sendrey's analysis (1969), pp. 262–63, except that Sendrey would prefer to combine idiophones and membranophones. To do so, however, violates the distinction in the way tone is produced in those two categories and interferes with recognizing the specialized role of women musicians with respect to membranophones in Israelite performance tradition.

25. See note 8 above.

26. See M. Gorali, "Musical Instruments in Ancient Times," *Ariel* 29 (1971): 70; Sachs (1940), p. 74; and Sendrey (1969), pp. 40, 97.

27. Poethig (1985), pp. 19–30.

28. Gen. 30:27. The translation of this and all other biblical citations is that of the author. Emphasis is also the author's.

29. Isa. 24:8; see also Isa. 30:32.

30. Ps. 150:1–5; note the linking of hand-drum with dance, an association to be explored below. This is the last psalm in the psalter; and with its theme of ringing praise it constitutes a fitting conclusion to this biblical book.

31. Poethig (1985), pp. 23–27. The Phoenicians are a subgroup of the larger geocultural entity known as Canaanites. The Phoenicians emerged in the late second millennium B.C.E. on the Levantine coast and are notable for their sea trade and colonization in the Mediterranean basin. Yet they cannot always be differentiated from Canaanites in their cultural traditions. Thus, the two terms are used more or less synonymously here.

32. 1 Sam. 10:5. The musicians are apparently part of a prophetic guild, professional seers who used certain techniques, such as music and dance, to achieve altered consciousness and thus the ability to receive messages from the deity. These guilds were likely to have been exclusively male. A ceramic cult stand from Tell Ashdod, on the Palestinian coast, depicts musicians, apparently all men, playing the cymbal, the double pipe, the lyre, and perhaps the hand-drum; see M. Dothan, "The Musicians of Ashdod," *Biblical Archaeologist* 40 (1977): 38–39.

33. 2 Sam. 6:5, cf. 1 Chron. 13:8.

34. E. Werner (1980), p. 619.

35. This box was discovered in the southeast palace of Kalat-Nimrud. See R. D. Barnett, "The Nimrud Ivories and the Art of the Phoenicians," *Iraq* 2 (1935): 189, pl. 26.

36. Exod. 15:20–21. See also Judg. 11:34; 1 Sam. 18:6; and Jer. 31:4.

37. E.g., A. B. Lord, *A Singer of Tales* (Cambridge, Mass.: Harvard University Press, 1960); R. Finnegan, *Oral Poetry: Its Nature, Significance, and Social Context* (Cambridge: Cambridge University Press, 1977).

38. Cf. H. L. Ginsberg, "Women Singers and Wailers Among Northern Canaanites," *Bulletin of the American Schools of Oriental Research* 72 (1938): 13–15.

39. See N. K. Gottwald, *Tribes of Yahweh* (Maryknoll, N.Y.: Orbis Books, 1979), pp. 210–19 and passim.

40. So Sachs (1940), p. 97, and Gradenwitz (1949), p. 40.

41. M. Weigle, "Women as Verbal Artists: Reclaiming the Daughters of Enheduanna," *Frontiers* 3 (1978): 2.

42. C. Robertson, "Power and Gender in the Musical Experiences of Women," in *Women and Music in Cross-Cultural Perspective*, ed. E. Koskoff (New York: Greenwood Press, 1987), p. 227.

43. E.g., the volume edited by Koskoff (1987).

44. R. A. Jordan and S. J. Kalcik, "Introduction," in *Women's Folklore, Women's Culture*, ed. Jordan and Kalcik, American Folklore Society New Series, vol. 8 (Philadelphia: University of Pennsylvania Press, 1985), pp. ix–xiv.

45. C. Seeger, *Studies in Musicology 1935–1975* (Berkeley: University of California Press, 1977), pp. 51, 182.

46. E. Koskoff, "An Introduction to Women, Music, and Culture," in Koskoff (1987), p. 1.

47. Ibid., pp. 2–4.

48. Women were the acknowledged "experts" in keening (composing and singing songs to mourn the dead) in ancient Israel as well as in other ancient Near Eastern cultures. See, for example, Jer. 9:17–18 ("call for the mourning women to come; send for the skilled women to come, let them raise a dirge over us at once, so that our eyes may run with tears") and Ezek. 32:16 ("this is a Lamentation; it shall be chanted. The women of the nations will chant it"). For information about women's ritual laments preserved in the writings of Classical authors, see Nancy Sultan's essay in this book.

49. M. Z. Rosaldo, "Women, Culture, and Society: A Theoretical Overview," in Rosaldo and Lamphere (1974), pp. 36–37.

50. P. R. Sanday, "Female Status in the Public Domain," in Rosaldo and Lamphere (1974), pp. 192–93.

51. Jordan and Kalcik (1985), p. xii.

52. See R. Bauman, *Verbal Art as Performance* (Prospect Heights, Ill.: Waveland Press, 1977), p. 4; and Weigle (1978), p. 5.

53. Bauman (1977), pp. 4, 16.

54. E.g., R. D. Abrahams, "Introductory Remarks to a Rhetorical Theory of Folklore," *Journal of American Folklore* 81 (1968): 143–48; cf. T. B. Joseph, "Poetry as a Strategy of Power: The Case of Riffian Berber Women," *Signs* 5 (1980): 418–34.

55. C. Meyers, *Discovering Eve: Ancient Israelite Women in Context* (New York: Oxford University Press, 1988), pp. 173–81.

56. E.g., references to "sons of the prophets" in 1 Kings 20:34; 2 Kings 2:3, 5, 7, 15; 4:1, 38; 5:22; 6:1; 9:1; Amos 7:14.

57. The use of a term denoting a biological relationship in an extended sense to represent other human relationships is common in Hebrew and other Semitic languages. See H. Haag, *"ben,"* in *Theological Dictionary of the Old Testament*, vol. 2, ed. G. J. Botterweck and H. Ringgren, trans. John T. Willis (Grand Rapids: Eerdmans, 1975), pp. 150–53.

58. The similar use of the daughter terminology in reference to associations of women is well attested outside the Hebrew Bible. See the *bnt hll* (translated variously as "daughters of joyful noise," "[female] singers," "artistes," and "female jubilantes") of Ugaritic literature, C. Gordon, *Ugaritic Textbook*, Analecta Orientalia 38 (Rome: Pontifical Biblical Institute, 1965), 2 Aqhat 77: 5–15, 40–50; 132:6.

59. So S. B. Finesinger, "Musical Instruments of the Old Testament," *Hebrew Union College Annual* 3 (1926): 23; and Werner (1979), p. 466.

Notes to Chapter 4

1. H. Hickmann, "Dieux et déesses de la musique," *Cahiers d'Histoire Égyptienne* 6, fasc. 1 (March 1954): 37, fig. 8; R. Anderson, *Musical Instruments*, Catalogue of Egyptian Antiquities in the British Museum 3 (London: British Museum, 1976), fig. 2. The word *tambourine* is consistently used in

Egyptological literature to denote a frame drum without jingles. Since this conflicts with the standard musical definition of a tambourine as having jingles, the term *frame drum* is used throughout this article to denote the instrument called *tambourine* in the Egyptological literature.

2. C. J. Bleeker, *Hathor and Thoth*, Studies in the History of Religions 26 (Leiden: E. J. Brill, 1973), p. 1.

3. Examples of this include the Priestesses of Hathor, the Chantress of Amon in the New Kingdom and onward, and women musicians at the temple doors of el Amarna. Norman de G. Davies, *The Rock Tombs of El Amarna I*, Archaeological Survey of Egypt 13 (London: Egypt Exploration Fund, 1903), p. 29.

4. Norman de G. Davies, *The Tomb of Rekh-mi-Rē at Thebes* (New York: Metropolitan Museum of Art, 1944), p. 59.

5. H. Hickmann, "Quelques considérations sur la danse et la musique de danse dans l'Égypte pharaonique," *Cahiers d'Histoire Égyptienne* 5, fasc. 2–3 (June 1953): fig. 2b.

6. See H. Hickmann, *Orientalische Musik*, Handbuch der Orientalistik, Ergänzungsband 4 (Leiden: E. J. Brill, 1970), p. 144, and Fig. 4–3 of this essay.

7. Hickmann (1970), pp. 143–44.

8. H. Fischer, "Women in the Old Kingdom and the Heracleopolitan Period," in *Women's Earliest Records from Ancient Egypt and Western Asia*, ed. B. S. Lesko, Brown Judaic Studies 166 (Atlanta: Scholars Press, 1989), p. 18.

9. Although there are many examples of men playing harps, women are also frequently shown playing the instrument. These latter cases were either unknown or ignored by Klebs, who writes: "Bei Harfe wird meist von Männer gespeilt, selten von Frauen." L. Klebs, *Die Reliefs des alten Reiches (2980–2475 v. Chr)* (Heidelberg: Carl Winter, 1915), p. 107. For a general discussion of Egyptian harps, see K. Krah, *Die Harfe im pharaonischen Ägypten: Ihre Entwicklung und Funktion* (Göttinger: Edition Re, 1991).

10. Fischer (1989), pp. 15–16. For the difficulty in determining whether wind instruments are flutes or oboes, see Anderson (1976), p. 64. For a summary of the positions of Hickmann and Sachs, see J. Vandier, *Manuel d'Archéologie Égyptienne 4, Bas-Reliefs et Peintures* (Paris: Éditions A. et J. Picard, 1964), pp. 378–79, especially p. 378.

11. Hickmann (1970), p. 146.

12. This continues to be the focus of music through the pharaonic period, as indicated by papyrus Anastasi IV where, in a description of a young man's musical training, the emphasis is upon vocal ability while the instruments are secondary. R. A. Caminos, *Late-Egyptian Miscellanies* (London: Oxford University Press, 1954), p. 182.

13. For a listing of such scenes, see Porter and Moss, *Topographical Bibliography of Ancient Egyptian Hieroglyphic Texts, Reliefs and Paintings* 3/1 (Oxford: Griffith Institute, 1974), p. 357; and idem., 3/2 (Oxford: Griffith Institute, 1981), p. 905. For a general description of such scenes see Vandier (1964), pp. 243–56, 365–90.

14. This scene may be added to the exceptions to the statement "The professional musicians, and the pairs of singers and instrumentalists . . . are virtually always notably men" in Fischer (1989), p. 15.

15. For additional examples of a family member playing the harp for the deceased, see ibid., p. 12, nn. 46–47.

16. Ibid., p. 15, suggests, "Dancers also perform in separate groups of men and women, which perhaps relayed each other." Norman de G. Davies writes, "The entertainment is probably given in the rooms of the harem, and the men are screened off from the females by a draped partition (?)." *The Rock Tombs of Sheikh Saîd*, Archaeological Survey of Egypt 10 (London: Egypt Exploration Fund, 1901), p. 13.

17. H. Schäfer, *Principles of Egyptian Art* (Oxford: Oxford University Press, 1974), pp. 163–66, and, especially, p. 173. Vandier (1964), pp. 410–16, attempts to reconstruct the spatial relationship of individual dancers within the context of a survey of dancing scenes.

18. For a discussion of the musical director, see H. Hickmann, "La chironomie dans l'Égypte pharaonique," *Zeitschrift für ägyptische Sprache und Altertumskunde* 83 (1958): 96–127.

19. C. R. Lepsius, *Denkmäler aus Ägypten und Äthopien* 2 (rpt. Geneva: Éditions de Belles-Lettres, 1972), fig. 36c.

20. H. Hickmann, *Ägypten, Musikgeschichte in Bildern: Musik des Altertums* 2/1 (Leipzig: VEB Deutscher Verlag für Musik, 1961), pl. 4.

21. G 6020, Lepsius (1972), fig. 52; Porter and Moss 3/1 (1974), p. 172 (8). To be published by Kent Weeks in The Boston Museum of Fine Arts *Giza* series.

22. Lepsius (1972), fig. 53a; Porter and Moss 3/1 (1974), pp. 173–74 (13).

23. Porter and Moss 3/2 (1981), p. 891; CG 1778, pictured in H. Hickmann, "Les Harpes de l'Égypte pharaonique: Essai d'une nouvelle classification," *Bulletin de l'Institut d'Égypte* 35 (1954): pl. 2.

24. William K. Simpson, *The Mastabas of Qar and Idu, G 7101 and G 7102*, Giza 2 (Boston: Museum of Fine Arts, 1976), fig. 38.

25. See also a similar scene on the tomb of Seshemnofer in E. Brunner-Traut, *Die altägyptische Grabkammer Seschemnofers III. aus Gîsa* (Vienna: Von Zabern, 1977), pls. 27a and 27b, where two men play harps in the company of six women. For men playing board games near musicians, see Lepsius (1972), fig. 61a. The Tomb of Rashepses is shown in Porter and Moss 3/2 (1981), p. 495 (7–8).

26. Both epithets in reference to Hathor in the Temple at Dendera may be found in C. J. Bleeker (1973), p. 54, n. 5. At Philae, (Ptolemaic-Roman periods) Hathor is addressed as "the lady of the dance, the mistress of the songs and dances accompanied by the lute." F. Daumas, "Les propylées du temple d'Hathor à Philae et le culte de la déesse," *Zeitschrift für ägyptische Sprache und Altertumskunde* 95 (1969): 1.

27. Hickmann (1970), p. 144.

28. This becomes far more frequent in the New Kingdom, especially with the theme of the blind male harpist; see H. Hickmann, "Le Métier de Musicien," in *Cahiers d'Histoire Égyptienne* 6, fasc. 5/6 (December 1954): 299–314.

29. Mert-netcher-nesw of Dynasty 5, Porter and Moss 3/2 (1981), pp. 761–62.

30. Lepsius (1972), fig. 61a; Porter and Moss 3/2 (1981), p. 495 (7–8).

31. One of the earliest examples of the title appears in the tomb of Debhen (contemporary with Menkaure, Dynasty 4, ca. 2548 B.C.E.), where singers are captioned *ḥst in ḥnr*, "singing by the *ḥnr* [members]"; see Lepsius (1972), fig. 35. For the restoration of the label, see E. Brunner-Traut, *Der Tanz im alten Ägypten*, Ägyptologische Forschungen 6 (Vienna: Von Zabern, 1958), p. 84, n. 2. By the following dynasty, *ḥnr* members are frequently designated in tomb scenes: see Ptahhotep in Lepsius (1972), fig. 101b, Iymery in Lepsius (1972), fig. 52, Seschemnofer III in Brunner-Traut (1977), pl. 27b.

32. See, for example, E. Reisner, *Die königliche Harem im alten Ägypten und seine Verwaltung* (Vienna: Verlag Notring, 1972).

33. D. Nord, review of E. Reisner, *Die königliche Harem im alten Ägypten und seine Verwaltung*, in *Journal of Near Eastern Studies* 34 (1975): 142–44; B. Bryan, "The Etymology of *ḥnr*," *Bulletin of the Egyptological Seminar* 4 (1982): 35–54, especially p. 52. For a more recent study, see L. Troy, *Patterns of Queenship in Ancient Egyptian Myth and History*, Boreas 14 (Uppsala: Acta Universitatis Uppsaliensis, 1986), p. 68. Although the author defines the *ḥnr* as a musical troupe, her persistence in using the world "harem" may create mis-interpretations about its function.

34. S. Hassan, *Excavations at Giza, 1930–1931* (Cairo: Government Printing Press, 1936), p. 205, fig. 226.

35. Giza 7211, Kaemankh, Nebkauhor, both listed in Nord, "The Term *ḥnr*: 'Harem' or 'Musical Performers'?" in *Studies in Ancient Egypt, the Aegean, and the Sudan: Essays in Honor of Dows Dunham* (Boston: Museum of Fine Arts, 1981), p. 141, nn. 32–33.

36. H. Fischer, "The Cult and Nome of the Goddess Bat," *Journal of the American Research Center in Egypt* 1 (1962): 8–9, n. 12.

37. Fischer (1989), p. 20; William Ward, "Non-Royal Women and Their Oc-cupations in the Middle Kingdom," in Lesko (1989), pp. 35, 37.

38. Nord (1981), pp. 142–43. These terms are especially prevalent in the tomb of Mehu at Sakkara.

39. Nord (1975), p. 144, notes that the first men to appear as overseers of the *ḥnr* were of "high rank." The dating "at the end of the Sixth Dynasty" is based upon scenes at Deir el Gebrawi, although the caption that refers to *ḥnr* may or may not apply to two separate registers of male and female dancers. Fischer (1989), p. 20, opts for the late First Intermediate Period (ca. 2100 B.C.E.).

40. Nord (1975), p. 145.

41. Troy (1986), p. 68.

42. Edward F. Wente, "Hathor at the Jubilee," *Studies in Honor of John A. Wilson*, Studies in Ancient Oriental Civilization 35 (Chicago: University of Chicago Press, 1969), pp. 83–91; Nord (1975), pp. 141–42.

43. H. G. Fischer, *Varia*, Egyptian Studies 1 (New York: Metropolitan Museum of Art, 1976), p. 71, n. 20.

44. A. Erman, *Life in Ancient Egypt* (rpt., New York: Dover, 1971), p. 250.

45. For a list of dancing scenes in the Old Kingdom, see Porter and Moss 3/1 (1974), p. 357, 12(b); Porter and Moss 3/2 (1981), p. 905, 12(b). The scenes from the tomb chapel at Sakkara are being readied for publication by Ann M. Roth.

46. For this so-called Libyan band see Nord (1975), p. 137, n. 15.

47. See Porter and Moss 3/1 (1974), p. 173 (13) VII where female dancers have been misidentified as males.

48. As in the tomb of Pepi at Meir; see A. M. Blackman, *The Rock Tombs of Meir V*, Archaeological Survey of Egypt 28 (London: Egypt Exploration Society, 1953), p. 58, pls. XLV, LXVI.3. Cairo 20257 is pictured in H. Hickmann, "Le Métier de Musicien" (1954), p. 266, fig. 6b.

49. H. Hickmann (1961), fig. 36.

50. P. Newberry, *Beni Hasan II*, Archaeological Survey of Egypt 2 (London: Egypt Exploration Fund, 1893), pl. XII.

51. Nina Davies, *The Tomb of Antefoker (No. 60)*, Theban Tomb Series 2 (London: Egypt Exploration Society, 1920), pls. XXVII, XXIX.

52. Newberry (1893), pl. XIV.

53. A. Blackman, *The Rock Tombs of Meir VI*, Archaeological Survey of Egypt 29 (London: Egypt Exploration Society, 1953), p. 21, pl. XIX, shows two female flute players in the company of a female harpist. For an example from the Tomb of Antefoker, see Nina Davies (1920), pl. XXIII.

54. E. F. Wente, *Letters from Ancient Egypt*, Society of Biblical Literature Writings from the Ancient World Series 1 (Atlanta: Scholars Press, 1990), p. 77.

55. Watterson, *Women in Ancient Egypt* (New York: Alan Sutton, 1991), p. 53.

56. Note that it is sometimes difficult to distinguish a flute, which is blown from a hole in the side of the instrument, from an oboe or clarinet, both of which are blown from the end.

57. For many other examples, see Norman de G. Davies, *The Rock Tombs of El Amarna VI*, Archaeological Survey of Egypt 18 (London: Egypt Exploration Fund, 1908), pls. XX, XXVIII, where a room in the house is filled with musical instruments, including many types of harps and lyres.

58. Vandier (1964), p. 381; Hickmann (1961), fig. 70. For a surviving example, see H. Hickmann, *Musicologie Pharaonique* (Kehl: Librarie Heitz, 1956), p. 26, fig. 11. Another example is found in the tomb of Rekhmire, as published in Norman de G. Davies (1944), pl. LXVI.

59. Hickmann (1961), fig. 32.

60. Vandier (1964), pl. XXI.

61. The Epigraphic Survey, *The Tomb of Kheruef, Theban Tomb 192*, Oriental Institute Publications 102 (Chicago: University of Chicago Press, 1963), pl. 57.

62. For the restriction of the rectangular frame drum to women, see Watterson (1991), p. 53.

63. For comments about the double oboe, see A. Sendrey, *Music in the Social and Religious Life of Antiquity* (Rutherford, N.J.: Fairleigh Dickinson University Press, 1974), p. 40. However, in the Ptolemaic Period (3d–1st centuries B.C.E.), the double oboe was played by men as indicated by reliefs at Philae. See Hickmann (1961), fig. 13. For the comment that the player of a flute or double pipe at a banquet is "usually female," see Porter and Moss 3/1 (1974), p. 469.

64. The trumpets of Tutankhamun, engraved with representations of gods

for whom divisions of the army were named, are depicted in L. Manniche, *Musical Instruments from the Tomb of Tut'Ankhamūn*, Tut'Ankhamūn's Tomb Series 6 (Oxford: Griffith Institute, 1976), pp. 10–11, pls. X, XI.

65. For a single male harpist in the New Kingdom, see Hickmann (1961), figs. 37, 96 (tomb of Inherkaw, Theban Tomb 359), 117, 120.

66. For an example of male musicians appearing in a group without women, see ibid., fig. 7 (tomb of Benia, Theban Tomb 343).

67. There are many examples, but see Figs. 4–6 and 4–7 in this essay.

68. Annelies and Artur Brack, *Das Garb des Haremheb, Theban Nr. 78*, Archäologische Veröfftlichungen 35 (Mainz: Von Zabern, 1980), pls. 32, 37.

69. *Kheruef* (1963), pl. 59.

70. For comments about the Old Kingdom associations of this scene, see Wente (1969), pp. 85–91.

71. This tomb is published by Norman de G. Davies, *The Tomb of Nakht at Thebes*, Metropolitan Museum of Art Egyptian Expedition 1 (New York: Metropolitan Museum of Art, 1917).

72. The tomb of Amenhotepsise depicts one lutenist who is dressed in girdle and jewelry while others wear white gowns; see Porter and Moss, *Topographical Bibliography of Ancient Egyptian Texts, Reliefs and Paintings* (Oxford: Griffith Institute, 1960), 1/1 (1960), p. 147 (4) 1.

73. Norman de G. Davies (1944), pl. LXVI.

74. The tomb is published by Nina Davies, *The Tomb of Amenemhet (No. 2)*, Theban Tomb Series 1 (London: Egypt Exploration Fund, 1915).

75. See the tomb of Horemheb in Vandier (1964), pl. VII, where two registers of musicians appear, the men in front of the women.

76. Also the tomb of Paser, pictured in Hickmann (1961), fig. 8, and Norman de G. Davies (1944), pl. LXVI.

77. For examples of all-female orchestras, see Norman de G. Davies, *The Rock Tombs of El Amarna II*, Archaeological Survey of Egypt 14 (London: Egypt Exploration Fund, 1903), pl. XXXII; idem (1908), pl. XXVIII.

78. Norman de G. Davies, *Amarna VI* (1908), p. 20.

79. Norman de G. Davies, *Amarna II* (1903), pp. 34, 36, pl. XXXII.

80. Norman de G. Davies, *Amarna I* (1903), pls. VI, IX, XIII.

81. Norman de G. Davies, *Amarna VI* (1908), p. 20.

82. For general information about the jubilee (heb sed) see K. Martin in *Lexikon der Ägyptologie* V: 782–90.

83. Wente (1969), pp. 86–87.

84. Akhenaton Temple Project, University of Toronto *talatat* numbers 12225-10, 468-11, 670-3, 1389-1R, 1515-9, 1519-11; 2733-10, 0202 08608; 2453, 301-6, 2024-11; 245-3, 301-6. These blocks, along with their texts, are to be published by Claude Traunecker.

85. *Kheruef* (1963), pl. 40.

86. Ibid., p. 49, pl. 36.

87. See Wente (1969), pp. 86–91, for additional ways in which the Kheruef scene may be traced to the Old and Middle Kingdom jubilee scenes.

88. The respective duties of the two classes of singer/musicians and how they are differentiated from each other are unclear. See Troy (1986), p. 88, for a discussion of the term $ḥs(y)t$. The title $ḥst$ [of a certain god] continued to be

used in conjunction with personal names on coffins of the Ramesside and Third Intermediate Period (13th–8th centuries B.C.E.), as did the more common title *šm'yt*. For examples of *ḥst n Imn* (singer of Amon), see M. A. Moret, *Sarcophages de l'Époque Bubastite à l'Époque Saite* (Cairo: L'Institut Français d'Archéologie Orientale, 1913), pp. 227, 291, 313–17; and M. H. Gauthier, *Cercueils Anthropoides des Prêtres de Montou* (Cairo: L'Institut Français d'Archéologie Orientale, 1913), pp. 363, 375. Among the earliest *šm'yt* are the chantresses of the god Montu (*Šm'yt n Mntw*); Hickmann, *Metier* (1954), p. 279.

89. Hickmann, *Metier* (1954), p. 279; C. Desroches Noblecourt, *La femme au temps des pharaons* (Paris: Stock, 1986), p. 196; Watterson (1991), p. 40. For the queens and princesses of the New Kingdom and Third Intermediate Period (16th–7th centuries B.C.E.) who held the title *šm'yt* or *ḥst*, see Troy (1986), p. 191.

90. Nina Davies (1915), p. 95, pl. XIX, shows musicians of Amon, musicians of the Great Ennead, and musicians of Hathor. For other groups, see Manniche (1976), p. 124.

91. Sendrey (1974), pp. 39–40; Watterson (1991), p. 43.

92. From the tomb of May at Amarna; Troy (1986), p. 167 (18.41/14).

93. From a statue, "attribution unclear"; ibid., p. 169 (19.5/9).

94. Davies (1944), pls. LXX, LXXI.

95. Sendrey (1974), pp. 39–40.

96. "Très probablement il ne s'agissat pas de chant dans le sens propre du mot, mais de récits liturgiques d'une portée plutôt rituelle que musicale." Hickmann, *Metier* (1954), pp. 278–79.

97. Troy (1986), p. 88, has suggested that there is an association between the words *ḥst* (singer) and *ḥts* (scepter) and by extension with the sistrum carried by many female musicians.

98. J. Gardner Wilkinson, *The Manners and Customs of the Ancient Egyptians*, 3 vols. (London: John Murray, 1878), vol. 1, p. 444.

99. N. Scott, "Daily Life in Ancient Egypt," *Bulletin of the Metropolitan Museum of Art*, New Series, 31/3 (Spring 1973), unpaginated.

100. Fischer (1989), p. 12.

101. Sendrey (1974), p. 32. Sendrey ended this remark with the comment that "many of them were slaves," a conclusion for which there is no basis in fact.

102. *Lexikon der Ägyptologie* IV:231.

103. For a list of such women, see Fischer (1989), p. 12, nn. 46–47. See also Fig. 4-2 of this article (tomb of Mereruka).

104. Blackman (1953), p. 58, pls. XLV, XLVI.3.

105. See Helmut Brunner, " 'Der Bekannte des Königs,' " *Studien zur altägyptischen Kultur* 1 (1974): 55–60; and Rudolph Anthes, "Die zeitliche Ansetzung des Fürster *Nhri* I vom Hasengau," *Zeitschrift für ägyptische Sprach und Altertumskunde* 59 (1924): 103.

106. Porter and Moss 3/2 (1981), p. 891, Hickmann, "Harpes" (1954), pl. II. For other named musicians, both male and female, see *Lexikon der Ägyptologie* IV:231–32.

107. Sendrey (1974), p. 39. See more explicitly the names of these musicians in *Lexikon der Ägyptologie* IV:231–32.

108. Sendrey (1974), p. 40.

109. Tomb of Seba-shesu, in Hickmann (1961), p. 50, and Ernst H. Meyer, ed., *Musik der Urgesellschaft und der frühen Klassengesellschaften* (Leipzig: VEB Deutscher Verlag für Musik, 1977), p. 151.

110. Stelae of Neferhotep, Renseneb, and Sathathor, in Manniche (1976), pp. 122–23.

111. Miriam Lichtheim, *Ancient Egyptian Literature: Volume 1, The Old and Middle Kingdoms* (Berkeley: University of California Press, 1973), p. 220.

112. Watterson (1991), p. 49.

113. *Kheruef* (1963), p. 63, pl. 59.

114. For another example of a lute player with a Bes tattoo on her thigh, see a faience bowl in Leiden, pictured in William H. Peck, *Egyptian Drawings* (New York: E. P. Dutton, 1978), p. 56, pl. XV.

115. Norman de G. Davies, *Seven Private Tombs at Ḳurnah*, Mond Excavations at Thebes II (London: Egypt Exploration Society, 1948), p. 39 and pl. XXVIII. This apparently negative view of women with Bes tattoos and generally of women and eroticism is repeated and expanded upon with little basis throughout Manniche (1976). The negative associations of eroticism do not seem to be appropriate to the Egyptian culture. See her remarks on pp. 108, 110, 112, 116, 118 and the completely unwarranted description of a wooden statue of a woman holding a harp (pl. 18): "The fact that the tip of the harp has been inserted into her vulva is hardly unintentional" (p. 116). It is not at all clear that Manniche's interpretation reflects the original intentions of the artisan who made the statue.

116. For another example of named musicians in the same tomb, see Nina Davies (1915), pl. V.

117. Caminos (1954), p. 182.

118. Among the many examples, see Moret (1913), pp. 226–29 (Amonirdis); pp. 290–98 and pl. 36 (Mrysimn); pp. 313–37 and pl. 38b (Wjaira); Gauthier (1913), pp. 363–75 (Ditankh); pp. 375–81 (Mutshepankh).

119. Manniche (1976), pp. 124–25.

120. Norman de G. Davies (1944), pls. LXX, LXXI.

121. Nina Davies (1915), pl. XL.

122. Regarding the hymn in the tomb of Kheruef wherein the female singers refer to the music that the king makes during the jubilee, see *Kheruef* (1963), p. 49, pl. 36.

123. For the somewhat inexplicable statement that nudity was associated with "Statuslosigkeit," see *Lexikon der Ägyptologie* IV: 292.

124. See, for example, the general comments of Wilkinson and Scott cited in notes 98 and 99 above.

125. See also the tomb of Amenhotepsesi; Nina Davies, *The Tombs of Two Officials of Tuthmosis the Fourth* (nos. 75 and 90), Theban Tomb Series 3 (London: Egypt Exploration Society, 1923), pls. V, XVII.

126. Lute players may be dressed in the same relatively conservative style as other musicians. See examples in Brack (1980), pls. 29, 30a, 37a; Norman de G. Davies (1944), pls. LXII, LXVI; and Manniche (1976), fig. 25 (tomb of Nebamun).

127. Manniche (1976), p. 119.

Notes to Chapter 5

1. For the ancient Greek art of praise poetry see G. Nagy, *The Best of the Achaeans* (Baltimore: Johns Hopkins University Press, 1979), chs. 12–14, and his *Pindar's Homer: The Lyric Possession of an Epic Past* (Baltimore: Johns Hopkins University Press, 1990), ch. 6; B. Gentili, *Poetry and Its Public in Ancient Greece*, trans. A. T. Cole (Baltimore: Johns Hopkins University Press, 1988), ch. 7; R. Martin, "Hesiod, Odysseus, and the Instruction of Princes," *Transactions of the American Philological Association* 114 (1984): 29–48. For comparable African praise poetic traditions, see J. Opland, *Xhosa Oral Poetry: Aspects of a South African Tradition* (Cambridge: Cambridge University Press, 1983); A. Mafeje, "The Role of the Bard in a Contemporary African Community," *Journal of African Languages* 6 (1967): 193–223.

2. See the discussion of form and structure of ritual laments in M. Alexiou, *The Ritual Lament in Greek Tradition* (Cambridge: Cambridge University Press, 1974), ch. 7. For a linguist's comparison of meter and rhythm, song and speech in Greek epic, lyric, and tragedy, see G. Nagy (1990), esp. ch. 1.

3. Where the utterance *is* the deed. See J. L. Austin, *How to Do Things with Words* (Oxford: Oxford University Press, 1962). Swearing an oath with the statement "I do" is one example of a speech-act. For the application of speech-act theory to Homer, see R. Martin, *The Language of Heroes* (Ithaca: Cornell University Press, 1989), pp. 21–22.

4. C. N. Seremetakis, *The Last Word: Women, Death, and Divination in Inner Mani* (Chicago: University of Chicago Press, 1991). Here she states that " 'to suffer for' and 'to come out as a representative for' are narrative devices in laments that fuse jural notions of reciprocity and truth claiming with the emotional nuances of pain" (102). See also G. Holst-Warhaft, *Dangerous Voices: Women's Laments and Greek Literature* (New York: Routledge, 1992), who notes that laments provoke the authority of the state when mourners take sides in local political struggles (114 ff.). See her chapter 3 on the politics of revenge in Inner Mani.

5. Most recently, L. Danforth, *The Death Rituals of Rural Greece* (Princeton: Princeton University Press, 1982); H. Monsacré, *Les Larmes d'Achille* (Paris, 1984); N. Loraux, *Les mères en deuil* (Paris: Seuil, 1990); N. Sultan, "Women in 'Akritic' Song: The Hero's 'Other' Voice," *Journal of Modern Greek Studies* 9 (1991):153–70; Seremetakis (1991); Holst-Warhaft (1992); C. Segal, "Euripides' *Alcestis*: Female Death and Male Tears," *Classical Antiquity* 11 (1992):142–58, and *Euripides and the Poetics of Sorrow* (Durham: Duke University Press, forthcoming).

6. Alexiou (1974), p. 102.

7. Ibid., pp. 12 f; 102 ff.

8. This is the only use of *aoidoi* in this context in Homer, so it is difficult to explain. Charles Segal believes, along with Margaret Alexiou, that the *aoidoi* are actually singing laments and are in charge, but the sense here is too ambiguous. See Segal, "The Gorgon and the Nightingale: The Voice of Female Lament and Pindar's Twelfth *Pythian Ode*" (unpublished draft, courtesy of the author), p. 5, and Alexiou (1974), pp. 103 ff. Traditionally, *aoidoi* are male

singers who sing about the *kleos* (glory) of heroes, an eternal song of praise; they are not lamenters. The accompanying verb *stonóessan* (causing groans) does not necessarily imply that their *singing* caused groans; in modern Greek tradition, men perform an instrumental mimesis of vocal lamentation (on clarino, for example) and do not actually sing laments; since we know that Homer's *aoidoi* played the lyre, perhaps this instrumental mimesis is what we should imagine. Alexiou acknowledges that the *thrênos* and *góos* were frequently performed to a musical accompaniment.

9. The "voice" inherent in women's lamentation can be seen in the modern word for ritual lament, *moirologi*, which means "speaking one's fate." In Greek traditional belief, fate (*moira*) is something from which no one can escape (e.g., *Iliad* 6.486–89), and the Fates (*Moirai*) are personified as three old women weavers who control life's passages through the stages of spinning, measuring, and cutting thread. In myth, characters such as Helen (*Iliad* 3.125–28), Penelope (*Odyssey* 19.510–17), and Philomela (Ovid *Metam.* 6.572 f.) weave words of pain and fate, as they weave cloth. That is, the intricate pattern woven into the cloth is a metonym for the discourse in the polyphonic song of ritual mourning.

10. P. Chantraine, *Dictionnaire étymologique de la Langue Grecque*, vol. 2 (Paris: Editions Klincksieck, 1970), pp. 563–64.

11. See R. Just, *Women in Athenian Law and Life* (London: Routledge, 1989), pp. 198–200.

12. This scenario is repeated in Vergil's *Aeneid* (9.473 ff.), when a beheaded warrior's mother openly laments her pain, anger, and rage that she was robbed of her duty to perform proper rites of preparation for burial:

> Is it thus, Euryalus, that I see you? You, who were so recently the
>   comfort of my old age,
> you could leave me like this, alone, cruel one?
> Nor, before you were sent on such a dangerous mission,
> did I say my last farewell to you!
> Ay! . . . nor did I, your mother, escort you—your corpse,
> or closed your eyes in death, or bathed your wounds. . . .

Hearing this lament, the fighting spirit of the Trojans is crushed—they are disheartened for war and begin to lament themselves—so the woman is quickly and physically removed from the scene.

13. For modern women, especially, war is a complicated dilemma: we join the battle lines and fight alongside men, but there is still the raging debate over the perceived extraordinary dangers women prisoners of war experience (not to mention sexual harassment by comrades-in-arms). In the modern Greek culture of Mani, not only do women place themselves on the front lines in violent clan wars, but they use lamentation as a juridical institution (called the *kláma*) to proclaim and validate their side of the arguments. See Seremetakis (1991), pp. 39–45, 144–53. See also Holst-Warhaft (1992), pp. 155–58, for a brief overview of the feminist perspective on women's attitudes toward war.

14. For Hesiod and the origins of Greek misogyny see E. Cantrella, *Pandora's Daughters* (Baltimore: Johns Hopkins University Press, 1987), pp. 34–35; Just (1989).

15. Holst-Warhaft (1992), p. 94.

16. Odysseus in *Odyssey* 7.216—*kúnteros:* "more like what a dog would do."

17. Just (1989), ch. 6. Michael Herzfeld has observed similar male attitudes in modern Greece; women are considered "incomplete humans because of their stereotyped inability to speak rationally." See his "Silence, Submission, and Subversion: Toward a Poetics of Womanhood," in *Contested Identities: Gender and Kinship in Modern Greece*, ed. D. Loizos and E. Papataxiarchis (Princeton: Princeton University Press, 1991), p. 79.

18. See Just (1989), pp. 214–16; H. Foley, "The Conception of Women in Athenian Drama," in *Reflections of Women in Antiquity*, ed. E. Foley (New York: Gordon and Breach, 1981), pp. 127–68. She notes that the word *hysteria* comes from the ancient belief that women's wombs wandered inside the body and were especially vulnerable to penetration by external evil demons (p. 132).

19. Just (1989), ch. 5; C. Patterson, "Hai Attikai: The Other Athenians," in *Rescuing Creusa: New Methodological Approaches to Women in Antiquity*, ed. M. Skinner (special edition of *Helios* 13 [1987]: 49–67). I believe that it is no etymological accident that the word for the human *psukhé*, "soul, psyche," is a feminine noun. Disembodied after death, she (the soul) travels to the under-world, "fluttering from the limbs, mourning (*goôsa*) her destiny" (*Iliad* 16.856–57).

20. E.g., Astyanax is buried as a groom in Euripides' *Trojan Women* 1218–20; see also L. Danforth (1982), pp. 74 ff.; Alexiou (1974), pp. 120–22. This is still a traditional practice in Greece.

21. See Seremetakis (1991), pp. 102–3, for corpses as pollution in Inner Mani. Also, Shiela Murnaghan mentions the corpse of Patroklos as a ritual artifact in the *Iliad* in "Body and Voice in Greek Tragedy," *Yale Journal of Criticism* 1 (1988): 23–43.

22. F. Zeitlin, pp. 64–76, in "Playing the Other: Theater, Theatricality, and the Feminine in Greek Drama," *Representations* 11 (1985): 63–94.

23. Zeitlin (1985), p. 76.

24. For women's public influence in tragedy see discussions in Foley (1981); M. Lefkowitz, "Influential Women," in *Images of Women in Antiquity*, ed. Cameron and Kuhrt (London: Croom Helm, 1983), pp. 49–64; Zeitlin (1985).

25. Here I am simply augmenting Charles Segal's excellent discussion of this scene in "Song, Ritual, and Commemoration in Early Greek Poetry and Tragedy," *Oral Tradition* 4/3 (1989): 352–53.

26. Cf. *Trojan Women* 606; Aeschylus, *Suppliants* 123–28.

27. See P. Easterling, *Sophocles' Trachiniae* (Cambridge: Cambridge University Press, 1982), p. 77.

28. Alexiou (1974), pp. 14–23; Holst-Warhaft (1992), ch. 4. See Nicole Loraux, *Les mères en deuil* (Paris: Seuil, 1990), pp. 40–45, where she discusses the antagonism between the outlawed laments of kinswomen and the male po-litical *epitaphios logos*. Just (1989), ch. 9, agrees with Alexiou that this law was most likely intended to keep funerals private so as to check potentially explo-sive aristocratic demonstrations under the "protection" of the medium. For modern Greek parallels, see Seremetakis (1991), pp. 169 ff.

29. Seremetakis (1991), p. 5.

30. See Seremetakis (1991), p. 498.

31. See also Euripides's *Helen* (185): the chorus of women *heard* (*ekluon*) her pain, and immediately responded and joined that pain in song. See Seremetakis (1991), pp. 494–95 for "witnessing" in modern Maniat laments.

32. Sophocles must have been aware of the fear of a "silent death" when he created the dramatic scene in the *Trachiniae* during which the dying Herakles discovers that there are no women nearby to facilitate his death. He is forced to become his own mourner.

33. Seremetakis (1991), p. 100.

34. See Segal (1989), 330–59; and S. Auerbach, "From Singing to Lamenting: Women's Musical Role in a Greek Village," in *Women and Music in Cross-Cultural Perspective*, ed. E. Koskoff (New York: Greenwood Press, 1987), pp. 25–44. I disagree with the opinion of Auerbach that laments are "non-music" compared to men's *andrissia*. She believes that while laments have musical form, they do not contain the ornamentation and variety that she finds in men's table songs (p. 27). I have observed Greek Orthodox Easter services where, during the Deposition of the Cross, women burst into extraordinarily creative and highly ornamental songs of lamentation, ones that they have been thinking about and preparing for emotionally in the days leading up to the occasion.

35. Segal (1989), pp. 344, 349.

36. Holst-Warhaft (1992), pp. 48–50; 69 ff.; Seremetakis (1991), esp. ch. 6.

37. See note 9 above.

38. See also *Iliad* 3.125–27; 6.343–49, etc.

39. See Segal (1989), pp. 339, 345, where he discusses the oral poet's special sensitivity to the vocality of laments.

40. Steven Feld, *Sound and Sentiment: Birds, Weeping, Poetics, and Song in Kaluli Expression*, 2d ed. (Philadelphia: University of Pennsylvania Press, 1990), deals with bird sonics and emotion at length. For excellent discussions of bird imagery in laments, see Alexiou (1974), pp. 93–98, 180–86; Danforth (1982), pp. 62–65, 112–15. Lévi Strauss discusses the theme of birds as mediators in *The Savage Mind* (Chicago: University of Chicago Press, 1966), pp. 54–61.

41. In Greek myth, women who are raped are known to give the name of a mourning bird to the child born from that assault, e.g., Halkyonê, *Iliad* 9.561–64.

42. Consider also Halkyonê, Meleager's wife, who uses the medium of lamentation to define justice for her city in *Iliad* 9.161 ff. For more on halcyons, swallows, nightingales, and cuckoos as birds of lament, see Alexiou (1974), p. 97. For an analysis of the greater significance of the story of Meleager and his wife in *Iliad* 9, see Nagy (1979), pp. 110–11.

43. Dare I suggest that the legislation that was enacted to restrict women's public lamentation in Athenian life may have had enough impact on tragedy's effectiveness to contribute to its decline?

44. J. Solomon, "*Orestes* 344–45: Colometry and Music," *Greek, Roman and Byzantine Studies* 18 (1977): 71–83.

Notes to Chapter 6

1. Euripides, *Medea*, 410–29. See S. B. Pomeroy, *Goddesses, Whores, Wives, and Slaves: Women in Classical Antiquity* (New York: Schocken Books, 1975), p. 103.

2. Pomeroy (1975), p. 230.

3. One of the famous representations is Daphne playing an aulos opposite Apollo, who is playing a kithara (lyre).

4. These dancers were surely courtesans.

5. Pomeroy (1975), p. 33.

6. Literary activity among women was not present in Athens. Athenian women-citizens were among the least educated and most submissive. On the other hand, Spartan women-citizens were better nourished and more educated and were allowed to occupy their time with music and gymnastics. Because Spartan women were more educated, they were also more outspoken; and consequently, they were criticized by Plutarch, Aristotle, and Plato. See Pomeroy (1975), pp. 36–39, 56.

7. M. R. Lefkowitz, "Influential Women," in *Images of Women in Antiquity*, ed. A. Cameron and A. Kuhrt (Detroit: Wayne State University Press, 1983), p. 56.

8. Ibid., p. 63, n. 25.

9. U. von Wilamowitz-Moellendorff, *Sappho und Simonides* (Berlin, 1913). Because men had no place in this cult, the scholar Wilamowitz-Moellendorff supports the theory that this was a homosexual cult of women for which Sappho composed her erotic poetry.

10. E. Lobel and D. L. Page, eds., *Poetarum Lesborium Fragmenta*, trans. J. Keller Hallet (Oxford: Clarendon Press, 1955), fragment 99, 5. See also Pomeroy (1975), p. 54.

11. W. Anderson, "Sappho," in *The New Grove Dictionary of Music and Musicians*, 6th ed., ed. Stanley Sadie (London: Macmillan, 1980), XVI, p. 489.

12. Ibid.

13. Ibid.

14. Pomeroy (1975), p. 56.

15. Ibid., p. 55.

16. Ibid.

17. The *symposia* of the Hellenistic period were parties for upper-class men, to which respectable women were never invited. Known for their activities of group sex, the only females present were prostitutes. See Pomeroy (1975), p. 143.

18. S. B. Pomeroy, "Technikai kai Mousikai," *American Journal of Ancient History* II/1 (1977): 53.

19. Ibid., p. 54.

20. L. Robert, "Décrets de Delphes," *Études épigraphiques et philologiques* (Paris: Champion, 1938), pp. 36–38. Also see Pomeroy (1977), p. 54.

21. Robert (1938), pp. 37–38; Pomeroy (1977), p. 54.

22. It was the performance practice of liturgical music to have medieval Byzantine chant sung by two choirs: one that sang the monophonic notated mel-

ody and the other that provided an unwritten, improvisatory drone accompaniment, called the Isokratema.

23. For a detailed study on the genre and performance practice of medieval Byzantine secular music, see D. Touliatos, "Medieval Byzantine Secular Music," in *Dyptichos: Milos Velimirovic 70 Geburtstag* (St. Petersburg: Academy of Sciences, forthcoming).

24. Much of the preserved information on Imperial court practice and secular music comes from Constantine VII, the Porphyrogenitus' *Book of Ceremonies*, documenting practice from 913 to 959, and from *De Officiis* (*The Offices*), documenting fifteenth-century practice. These sources reveal a very cultivated musical society that featured fine orchestras, wind bands, and choral and soloistic singing in theater productions, pantomimes, ballets, banquets, political and pagan festivals, Olympic games, and all Imperial court ceremonies.

25. C. Hannick, "Christian Church, music of the early," in *The New Grove Dictionary of Music and Musicians* (1980), IV, p. 368. For the third century C.E., Thomas Mathiesen cites an educated, aristocratic woman who is a writer of a musical treatise. See his *History of Ancient Music* (forthcoming).

26. J. Herrin, "Women and the Faith in Icons in Early Christianity," in *Culture, Ideology and Politics*, ed. R. Samuel and G. Stedman Jones (London: Routledge and Kegan Paul, 1982), p. 72.

27. J. Herrin (1982), p. 72. See also idem, "Women and the Church in Byzantium," *Bulletin of the British Association of Orientalists* XI (1980): 8–14.

28. E. Wellesz, *A History of Byzantine Music and Hymnography* (Oxford: Clarendon Press, 1961), p. 79, n. 2.

29. See F. Tinnefeld, "Zum profanen Mimos in Byzanz nach dem Verdikt des Trullanums (691)," *Byzantina* 6 (1974): 321–43; W. Puchner, "Byzantinischer Mimos, Pantomimos und Mummenschanz im Spiegel der griechischen Patristik und ekklesiascher Synodalverordnungen," *Maske und Kothurn* 29 (1983): 311–17.

30. A. Karpozilos and A. Kazhdan, "Actor," in *The Oxford Dictionary of Byzantium* (Oxford: Oxford University Press, 1991), I, p. 16.

31. See D. Touliatos, "Medieval Byzantine Secular Music," for the various types of wind and string instruments.

32. John Chrysostom, "Expositio in Psalmos," *Patrologiae Graecae*, LV, ed. J.-P. Migne, col. 157.

33. Ibid.

34. Basil of Caesarea, "Commentarius in Isaiam prophetam," *Patrologiae Graecae*, XXX, col. 372.

35. J. Beaucamp, "La situation juridique de la femme à Byzance," *Cahiers de civilisation médiévale* 20 (1977): 145–76; J. Grosdidier de Matons, "La femme dans l'empire byzantin," in *Histoire mondiale de la femme*, ed. P. Grimal (Paris: Nouvelle Librairie de France, 1974), III: 11–43; A. Laiou, "The Role of Women in Byzantine Society," in *XVI Internationaler Byzantinistenkongress*, Part I/1, pp. 233–60 (*Jahrbuch des Österreichischen Byzantinistik* XXXI/1 [1981]: 233–60).

36. A. Weyl Carr, "Women and Monasticism in Byzantium: Introduction from an Art Historian," *Byzantinische Forschungen* IX (1985): 1–15.

37. Wellesz (1961), pp. 181–82.

38. C. Emereau, "Hymnographi Byzantini," *Echos d'Orient* XXIII (1924): 409.

39. S. Eustratiades, "Poietai kai Hymnographoi tes Orthodoxou Ekklesias," *Nea Sion* 53 (1958): 295–97; E. Follieri, *Initia Hymnorum Ecclesiae Graecae V* (Vatican City: Biblioteca Apostolica, 1966), p. 266; J. Szoverffy, *A Guide to Byzantine Hymnography: A Classified Bibliography of Texts and Studies* (Brookline, Mass., and Leyden: Classical Folia Editions, 1979), II: 48.

40. For a comprehensive analysis of Kanons and their use in Orthros, see D. Touliatos, "The Byzantine Orthros," *Byzantina* IX (1977): 323–83.

41. G. Papadopoulos, *Symvolai eis ten istorian tes par' emin ekklesiastikes mousikes* (Athens: Kousoulinou and Athanasiadou, 1890), p. 253.

42. E. Catafygiotu Topping, "Thekla the Nun: In Praise of Woman," *The Greek Orthodox Theological Review* XXV/4 (1980): 353. This study analyzes the poetic text of the Kanon.

43. For the various musical studies of Kassia and a catalogue of her musical compositions, see D. Touliatos-Banker, "Medieval Women Composers in Byzantium and the West," in *Proceedings of the VIth International Congress of Musicology "Musica Antiqua Europae Orientalis"* (Bydgoszcz, Poland, 1982), pp. 687–712; and idem, "Women Composers of Medieval Byzantine Chant," *College Music Symposium* XXIV/1 (Spring 1984): 62–80. A recording of two of Kassia's musical compositions as transcribed by this author accompanies D. Touliatos-Banker, "Kassia," in *Historical Anthology of Music by Women*, ed. James Briscoe (Bloomington: Indiana University Press, 1987), pp. 1–5. See also D. Touliatos, "Kassia," in *New Grove Dictionary of Women in Music* (London: Macmillan), forthcoming. An anthology of musical transcriptions (by this author) as well as facsimiles of the medieval notation of Kassia's music can be found in D. Touliatos, "Kassia," in *Women Composers: An Historical Anthology*, vol. I, *Composers Born Before 1600*, ed. S. Glickman and M. Schleifer (Boston: G. K. Hall, forthcoming).

44. With the exception of the last name, which is the Greek demotic form of Kassia, the other forms are probably due to scribal error. Cf. K. Krumbacher, "Kasia," *Sitzungsberichte der bayrischen Akademie der Wissenschaften* (1897), pp. 316–17.

45. I. Rochow, *Studien zu der Person, den Werken und dem Nachleben der Dichterin Kassia*, Berliner Byzantinische Arbeiten 38 (Berlin: Akademie-Verlag, 1967), pp. 20–26.

46. E. Gibbon, *The History of the Decline and Fall of the Roman Empire*, with notes by the Rev. H. H. Milman (New York: Hooper, Clarke and Co., 1886), IV: 204. Also see J. B. Bury, *A History of the Eastern Roman Empire from the Fall of Irene to the Accession of Basil I* (New York: Russell & Russell, 1965), pp. 81–83.

47. I. Rochow (1967), p. 61; Karl Krumbacher, *Geschichte der Byzantinischen Literatur* (New York, 1970), II: 715–16.

48. See Touliatos-Banker (1984), pp. 69–71.

49. Kassia's hymns commemorate Holy Saturday, Christmas, Holy Wednesday, Hypapante, St. John Prodromos, the apostles Peter and Paul, and the martyrs Eustratios and Auxentios.

50. G. Reese, *Music in the Middle Ages* (New York: W. W. Norton, 1940), p. 82. Cf. A. Gastoué, "Les types byzantins de la Séquence," *La Tribune de St. Gervais* XXIV (1922): 1–6.

51. An interpretation of the text of this troparion can be found in E. Catafygiotu Topping, "Kassiane the Nun and the Sinful Woman," *The Greek Orthodox Theological Review* XXVI/3 (1981): 201–9.

52. For a musical and textual analysis of this troparion, see D. Touliatos-Banker (1984), pp. 76–80.

53. Lavra MS Gamma 71, fol. 339r; S. Eustratiades, *Catalogos ton Kodikon tes Megistes Lavras* (Paris: Librairie Ancienne Honoré Champion, 1925), p. 42.

54. Athens MS 2406, fol. 258v: "ton se de leg[ete] oti [kallopi]stein tes thegator avtou." The translation is the author's.

55. M. Velimirovic, "Byzantine Composers in MS. Athens 2406," in *Essays Presented to Egon Wellesz*, ed. Jack Westrup (Oxford: Clarendon Press, 1966), p. 12.

56. G. Papadopoulos (1890), pp. 274–75.

57. A musical transcription of this composition can be found in Touliatos-Banker (1984), p. 64, and in Touliatos-Banker (1982), p. 709.

58. H.-G. Beck, *Kirche und Theologische Literatur im Byzantinischen Reich* (Munich, 1977), p. 797; J. Szoverffy (1979), p. 75.

59. Topping (1980), p. 353.

60. The English translation is the author's. See W. Horandner, *Theodoros Prodromos. Historische Gedichte*, no. XX (Vienna, 1974). This theme is also stated in Colossians 3:18.

Notes to Chapter 7

1. I use the term "early modern Catholicism" in preference to the more tendentious and less accurate "Counter-Reformation"; see the essential overviews by John O'Malley, "Was Ignatius Loyola a Church Reformer? How to Look at Early Modern Catholicism," *Catholic Historical Review* 77 (1991): 177–93, and Paolo Prodi, "Contrariforma e/o riforma cattolica: superamento di vecchi dilemmi nei nuovi panorami storiagrafici," *Römische Historische Mitteilungen* 31 (1989): 227–38.

2. For the rate of monasticization, see Dante E. Zanetti, *La demografia del patriziato milanese nei secoli XVII, XVIII, XIX* (Pavia: Università di Pavia, 1972), pp. 52, 59–60, and 81–86. I use the term "female monastery" in preference to "convent" to underline these institutions' subjection to monastic enclosure. Although the figures in Zanetti's study may appear high, archival documents do support the idea that all adult daughters of certain patrician families took the veil; Chiara Margarita Cozzolani's two aunts, older sister, and two nieces, for instance, all became Benedictines at Santa Radegonda. For documentary and stylistic studies of this musical culture, see my "Genres, Generations and Gender: Nuns' Music in Early Modern Milan" (Ph.D. diss., New York University, 1993); all translations and transcriptions in the present article are mine.

3. For a brilliant study of the new topics and methods of post-Tridentine spiritual literature, see Michel de Certeau, *La fable mystique: XVIe–XVIIe siè-*

cles (Paris: Gallimard, 1982; Eng. trans. as *The Mystic Fable* [Chicago: University of Chicago Press, 1992]).

4. For an introduction, see the essays collected in Massimo Petrocchi, *Storia della spiritualità italiana*, vol. 2, *Il Cinquecento e il Seicento* (Rome: Edizioni di Storia e Letteratura, 1978), especially "Dottrine e orientamenti spirituali della scuola lombarda del Cinquecento," pp. 61–110, and "Un Seicento spirituale italiano non formastico," pp. 179–212.

5. On Vannini, see Agostino Saba, *Federico Borromeo ed i mistici del suo tempo* (Florence: Olschki, 1931). For a thorough re-creation in the tradition of "microhistory" of Isabella Tomasi's world, see Sara Cabibbo and Marilena Modica, *La santa dei Tomasi: Storia di Suor Maria Crocefissa (1645–1699)* (Turin: Einaudi, 1989). And for a challenging view of the humanist roots of piety, see Antonio Riccardi, "The Humanist Mysticism of Maria Maddalena de' Pazzi," in *Creative Religious Women in Medieval and Early Modern Italy*, ed. E. Ann Matter and John Coakley (Philadelphia: University of Pennsylvania Press, forthcoming).

6. For the account of one woman who fell afoul of the Venetian Inquisition, see Fulvio Tomizza, *Heavenly Supper: The Story of Maria Janis*, trans. Anne Jacobson Schutte (Chicago: University of Chicago Press, 1991); Schutte's preface is also valuable.

7. See the essays collected in G. Zarri, *Le sante vive: Cultura e religiosità femminile nella prima età moderna* (Turin: Rosenberg & Sellier, 1990); and eadem, "Monasteri femminili e città (secoli XV–XVIII)," in *Storia d'Italia: Annali, 9: La chiesa e il potere temporale*, ed. G. Chittolini and G. Miccoli (Turin: Einaudi, 1986), pp. 357–429. For a study of the variety of female religious communities in Trecento and Quattrocento Rome, see Kathryn Gill, "Penitents, *Pinzochere* and Pious Laywomen: Varieties of Women's Religious Communities in Central Italy, ca. 1300–1520" (Ph.D. diss., Princeton University, 1993).

8. Caroline Walker Bynum, *Holy Feast and Holy Fast: The Meaning of Food to Medieval Religious Women* (Berkeley: University of California Press, 1987), pp. 23–30 and 260–93, and the essays in eadem, *Fragmentation and Redemption: Essays on Gender and the Human Body in Medieval Tradition* (New York: Zone Books, 1991).

9. On the flowering of new kinds of devotion—Eucharistic, Marian, and sanctoral—in the archdiocese, see Danilo Zardin, "L'ultimo periodo spagnolo (1631–1712): Da Cesare Monti a Giuseppe Archinto," in *Diocesi di Milano*, vol. 2 ("Storia religiosa della Lombardia, 10") (Brescia: Editrice La Scuola, 1990), pp. 575–613, especially pp. 592–99.

10. On Borromeo's pastoral philosophy, see the entry by Prodi in the *Dizionario biografico degli italiani*, vol. 13 (Rome: Istituto dell'Enciclopedia Italiana, 1971), pp. 30–39.

11. These letters have been preserved at the Biblioteca Ambrosiana, Milan (henceforth BA); for a selection from the voluminous correspondence, see Carlo Marcora, "Lettere del card. Federico Borromeo alle claustrali," *Memorie storiche della diocesi di Milano* 10 (1964): 177–424.

12. An Italian draft of this work is preserved in BA, G. 26 *inf*.

13. Ironically, this kind of biological essentialism seems far more typical of

male observers' views than of the scattered statements (letters, dedications) of female monastic musicians themselves.

14. See several essays in Craig A. Monson, ed., *The Crannied Wall: Women, Religion and the Arts in Early Modern Europe* (Ann Arbor: University of Michigan Press, 1992), and papers by Monson and the present writer in Matter and Coakley, *Creative Religious Women*. The first archival work on nuns as musicians is owed to Gian Lodovico Masetti Zannini: *Motivi storici dell'educazione femminile (1500–1650)* (Bari: Edizioni Universitarie, 1980), ch. 5; and "Espressioni musicali in monasteri femminili del primo Seicento a Bologna," *Strenna Storica Bolognese* 35 (1985): 193–205; this was followed by Monson's detailed discussion of one source from a Bolognese house, "Elena Malvezzi's Keyboard Manuscript: A New Sixteenth-Century Source," *Early Music History* 9 (1990): 73–128. For a play written by a Tuscan nun, see Beatrice del Sera, *Amor di virtù*, ed. E. Weaver (Ravenna: Longo Editore, 1990); Weaver's introduction and her essays in the above-cited anthologies are key to understanding female monastic theater.

15. It should be noted here that male religious orders in the diocese of Milan were not subjected to the detailed strictures, musical and other, that affected their female counterparts. Compared to the dozens of pages on nuns' music making and its regulation in the Milanese diocesan files (now preserved in the Archivio Storico Diocesano [henceforth ASDM]), only a few scattered notes refer to music in the male monasteries. For detailed documentation of the parallels and differences in Bologna, see Monson's essays cited in note 14 above.

16. For some outsiders' accounts of female monastic singers, see the essays collected in Aldo deMaddalena, ed., *"Millain the Great": Milano nelle brume del Seicento* (Milan: Cariplo, 1989).

17. This evidence is defined as (1) documented polyphony composed by nuns; (2) dedications to individual nuns or entire houses of polyphonic editions by their composers (there are some forty-five such inscriptions to nuns in the diocese of Milan alone between 1592 and 1679); (3) local or Roman curial records of the use of polyphony be female monastic musicians (including the listings of nuns as *maestre del canto figurato* or *madri concertatrici*); and (4) secular records, largely travelers' accounts, urban panegyric literature, bequests of musical instruments, and the like.

18. On Borromeo as musical patron in general and supporter of female monastic music in particular, see my "Four Views of Milanese Nuns' Music" in Matter and Coakley, *Creative Religious Women*.

19. "Una ecstatica di santa vita . . . tal volta era costretta dalle preghiere delle sue compagne . . . a dare ad esse alcun segnale, et alcun esempio, come fosse l'harmonia del Paradiso: Ella . . . prendeva nelle mani un liuto . . . e toccando alcune corde di esso insuonava un canto così delicato, che già già maniere somiglianti di canto, et andamenti simili di consonanze, non si sentivano. Hor questa donna non procedeva innanzi un piccolo spatio di tempo cantando, e suonando ch'essa restava rapita" (from *De ecstaticis mulieribus et illusis*, Book IV; I cite from the vernacular draft in BA, G. 26 *inf.*, fol. 248v–249r). In technical terms, the prelate's use of the words "rapture," "abduction," and "ecstacy" is extremely loose, without the precise connotations attached to each in the Bonaventuran tradition.

20. "E una di queste domeniche dopo cena molte di compagnia così per ri-creatione andavano in cammino . . . e come fui la, cominciai à cantare; e cantai un motetto così a mente . . . e mentre io cantava, mi sentiva ad acender il mio Core, tanto che pareva all'esterieri che fosse una pazarella," undated letter to Borromeo (written in the late 1620s), BA, G. 7 *inf.*, fol. 334r–v.

21. An early biographer of Borromeo, Biagio Guenzati, began the chapter of his work devoted to nuns with these words: "Sì come li sagri chiostri sono tanti Paradisi terrestri" (BA, G. 137 *inf.* fol. 363v.). For references from the diocesan curia to female houses as an earthly prefiguration of the heavenly Jerusalem, see the orders of Antonio Mazenta, vicar of nuns, for the celebration of Christ-mas 1621 in ASDM, sec. XII, vol. 50, fol. 112. Numerous observers of musical nuns, from the Gesuato priest Paolo Morigia in 1595 to the rationalist Protes-tant Charles Burney in 1770, commented on the "heavenly" or "rapturous" effects of their performances.

22. See Zardin (1990), pp. 597–99.

23. Gianvittorio Signorotto, *Inquisitori e mistici nel Seicento italiano: L'er-esia di Santa Pelagia* (Bologna: Il Mulino, 1989), provides an incisive case study of this popular movement that originated in the Brescian valleys, including the women and men who were its followers, its emphasis on interior illumination from direct divine revelation, and its role in the battles between Archbishop Litta and the Milanese patriciate.

24. On this and the new kinds of spiritual literature circulating in post-Bor-romean Milan, see Signorotto, "Gesuiti, carismatici e beate nella Milano del primo Seicento," in *Finzione e santità tra medioevo ed età moderna,* ed. G. Zarri (Turin: Rosenberg & Sellier, 1991), pp. 177–201. For a similar Vene-tian case, see Schutte, ed., *Cecilia Ferrazzi: Autobiografia di una santa mancata* (Bergamo: P. Lubrina, 1990).

25. Several warnings about "unsuitable" spiritual literature are scattered among the curial orders of Litta's tenure, preserved in ASDM, sec. XII, vols. 49 and 52. For the Italian circulation of, and disputes over, the *Mystica ciudad de Dios,* written by the Spanish Franciscan Maria d'Agrada, see Sara Cabibbo, " 'Ignoratio scripturarum, ignoratio Christi est': Tradizione e pratica delle scrit-ture nei testi monastici femminili del XVII secolo," *Rivista storica italiana* 101 (1989): 85–124.

26. On the ritualization of the city, see A. Buretti et al., *La città rituale: La città e lo Stato di Milano nell'età dei Borromeo* (Milan: Franco Angeli Editore, 1982), and the illustrations of festivals and processions in deMaddalena (1989), pp. 153–68. In this sense, the Lombard capital, with its political and religious processions, public liturgy, "angelic" singers in female monasteries, and the like, represents an important exception to the "decline of ritual" that Peter Burke has chronicled in early modern Europe; see Burke, *The Historical An-thropology of Early Modern Italy* (Cambridge: Cambridge University Press, 1987). For the methodological usefulness of ethnological categories in the study of the phenomenon, see idem, "Historians, Anthropologists and Symbols," in *Culture Through Time: Anthropological Approaches,* ed. E. Ohnuki-Tierney (Stanford, Calif.: Stanford University Press, 1990), pp. 268–83.

27. The repertory is found in the following editions: Casati, *Terzo libro de'*

sacri concerti (Venice: Magni [Gardano], 1640, 1642, 1644, 1650); *Il primo libro de' motetti concertati* (Venice: Vincenti, 1643, 1651); *Messa e salmi à 4–5* (Vincenti, 1644); *Sacri concentus à 2* (reprints) (Antwerp: Phalèse, 1644, 1650, 1654, 1668); *Sacri concentus à 3–4* (reprints) (Antwerp: Phalèse, 1644); *Scelta d'ariosi e vaghi motetti* (Vincenti, 1645); *Scelta d'ariosi salmi* (Venice: Gardano, 1645); *Operis primi, pars prior* (reprints) (Phalèse, 1647, 1654, 1662); Cozzolani, *Concerti sacri* [à 2–4], op. 2 (Vincenti, 1642); *Scherzi di sacra melodia* [à 1] (Vincenti, 1648), and *Salmi à otto . . . con motetti, dialoghi . . .* (Vincenti, 1650); Porta, *Motetti à 2–5*, op. 2 (Vincenti, 1645; rpt. Phalèse, 1650); *Motetti à 2–5*, op. 3 (Vincenti, 1648; rpt. Phalèse, 1650); *Motetti à 2–5*, op. 4 (Vincenti, 1651; rpt. Phalèse, 1654); Tarditi, *Concerto decimottavo* (Vincenti, 1641); *Motetti e salmi à 2–3* (Vincenti, 1645); *Concerto vigesimoquinto* (Vincenti, 1647); and *Motetti à 2–3*, op. 31 (Vincenti, 1651). The leading role of Alessandro Vincenti's press in the diffusion of this music is noteworthy.

28. On the traditions of Song of Song exegesis, there is a large literature. Most helpful (and with musical examples) is E. Ann Matter, *The Voice of My Beloved: The Song of Songs in Western Medieval Christianity* (Philadelphia: University of Pennsylvania Press, 1990). The canticle was a key text for nuns, who quoted it frequently to describe their own interior states (for examples, see my "The Traditions of Milanese Convent Music and the Sacred Dialogues of C. M. Cozzolani" in Monson [1992]). On the medieval background to the Song of Songs as a prooftext for female monastic vocation, see John Bugge, *Virginitas: The History of a Medieval Idea* (The Hague: Martinus Nijhoff, 1975), esp. pp. 59–67.

29. Literary authorship in this repertory is difficult to determine. The motet texts did not circulate independently from the music, and there seem to be few textual concordances among settings by different composers (apparently, the only case is *O quam bonus es*, discussed below). Some of the "free" texts rely also on centos of, or allusions to, Song of Songs or Office text passages; Cozzolani's 1642 *O quam suavis est*, for instance, combines the Office antiphon for Corpus Christi with canticle tags and a free, metrically regular hymnlike conclusion. Quite possibly, Benedictines male or female could have supplied the texts for her "free" motets.

30. "O quam suavis es, bone Jesu / o quam jocundus amantibus te, / Tuo amore incende me / ut in aeternum diligam te"; from Casati, *Terzo libro* (1640).

31. "O dulcissime Jesu, / o piissime Maria, / audite vocem deprecantis; / ad vos confugio, miser, / ut pascar a vulnere, / ut lacter ab ubere"; from Porta, *Motetti à 2–5*, op. 2 (1645). The image of parallel feeding from the wounds of Christ and the breast of Mary will recur presently.

32. "O dulcis Jesu, tu es fons bonitatis / fonsque amoris / et apud te est fons vitae / o dulcis Jesu / Bibet ergo in te solo anima mea / ad te solum confugiat / ad te die nocteque clamet"; from Cozzolani, *Concerti sacri*, op. 2 (1642).

33. Jerome Roche, concerned with an earlier generation, has noted the "fragmentary rather than a unifying effect typical of Casati, whose music was also unsettled, even nervous in feeling" (*North Italian Church Music in the Age of Monteverdi* [Oxford: Oxford University Press, 1982], pp. 103–4). *Pace*

Roche and his magisterial overview of the *terra incognita* represented by early Seicento sacred music, a case could well be made that the aesthetics of the new style rest precisely on rhetorical (reiterative and additive) principles, not on any kind of "organic" unity. In this sense, the "new Lombard" motet reflects and parallels the new trends in spirituality.

34. This practice is most evident in such pieces as *Tota pulchra es* from Casati's 1643 *Primo libro*, in which a favorite and personalized canticle text is given an unusual energetic and declamatory setting; and the *Pater noster* from the same collection, which approaches the most "objective" and communal text in Catholic culture in an extravagant and virtuoso soloistic style.

35. This also renders the question of performance practice, especially the execution of lower voices, more difficult, although there seem to be contemporary solutions (including octave transposition) to this problem.

36. The prints include a copy of G. B. Mazzaferrata's *Sacri concerti a voce sola* (Milan: Camagno, 1661) owned by the Benedictine house of S. Maria del Lentasio in Milan; a copy of Girolamo Casati's (known as Filago) motets à 1–3, book 5 (Milan: C. F. Rolla, 1657), and Orazio Tarditi's *Sacri concentus à 2–3*, op. 35 (Venice: Vincenti, 1655), both owned by a Donna Angela Giustina Mugiasca (i.e., a Benedictine nun, for the members of which order the title "Donna" was reserved in Seicento Milan); and the *Motetti ecclesiastici . . . à voce sola* (Milan: Camagno, 1659) by the Monzese Federico Pedroni, owned by an Angelica Maria (i.e., a member of the *Angeliche* order, founded in 1535). The Mazzaferrata, of which only the voice part is preserved in I-Mb, has an inscription reading "Ex libris Monasterij B[eata]e M[aria]e Lauretani Mediolani"; the copies of the Casati and the Tarditi are preserved at I-COd (there is a chance that Angela Mugiasca was actually in a monastery in the diocese of Como); and the copy off the Pedroni is also at I-COd. For these latter two, see Alessandro Picchi, *Archivio Musicale del Duomo di Como: Catalogo delle opere a stampa e manoscritte dei secoli XVI–XVII* (Como: Rotary Club Como Baradello, 1990); my thanks to Prof. Picchi for his kind help. The Pedroni book also has barlines drawn in and a handwritten change (in the script of Angelica Maria) from "Bartholomei" to "Agustini" in a sanctoral motet, suggesting that Augustine's feast day was important at her foundation.

37. For instance, in a later generation, the future *maestra* at Santa Radegonda, Maria Domitilla Ceva (ca. 1640–ca. 1722), would request the Franciscan Antonio Cossandi as a teacher (her father's letter from 1661 is preserved in the Archivio Segreto Vaticano, Sacra Congregazione de' Vescovi e Regolari, sezione monache, 1661, gennaio).

38. "Eminentissimo e Reverendissimo Principe . . . mi goderò almeno d'hauer incontrato il genio di Vostra Eccelenza, la quale havendo effigliata dalla Sua Diocesi quella Musica effeminata, che prima con arie profane turbava l'aria delle Sue Chiese, gusta altretanto di ammettere quell'altra," Grancini, dedication to Archbishop Cesare Monti of his *Musica ecclesiastica da capella* (Milan: Rolla, 1645), p. [2].

39. Another measure of the loose monastic enclosure affecting at least the Benedictines of this house (subject not to the archbishop but to the male branch of their order) is the fact that Cozzolani's 1650 Vespers book represents the

only large-scale (double-choir) application of the features of the *salmo arioso* in all Lombardy.

40. "Tu mater sancta, / tu mater pia, / tu mater clemens, / in hoc mundi via / impetra veniam / obtine gratiam / ut Jesus filius / donet gloriam."

41. Space does not permit an analysis here of Porta's less-sectionalized and less-contrasted approach to this text.

42. "O quam bonus es, o quam suavis / O quam jocundus, mi Jesu / o quam benigna es, o quam dulcis / quam delitiosa, o Maria; / Diligenti, suspiranti, / possidenti, degustanti te. / O me felicem, o me beatum / Hinc pascor a vulnere / hinc lactor ab ubere / quo me vertam nescio. / In vulnere vita / in ubere salus." Porta and Cozzolani set exactly the same text, with the same internal refrains. It should be noted that, unlike later Milanese repertory, the speaker's (singer's) grammatical gender in this and similar pieces is explicitly masculine ("beat*um*"); there would be a complete reversal in this regard by the time of the concertos and solo motets of the 1680s, including but not limited to the solo motets (1684) of another inhabitant of Santa Radegonda, Rosa Giacinta Badalla.

43. "Sanguis me emundat / lac me purificat / sanguis me recreat / lac refocillat / sanguis inebriat / lac me laetificat."

44. Pictorial representations include Niccolò Gerini, *The Intercession of Christ and the Virgin* (now New York, Metropolitan Museum of Art), and Jean Provost, *The Last Judgment* (Bruges, Groeningemuseum), both published, along with a discussion of the topic's popularity in Cinquecento Naples, in Pierroberto Scaramella, *Le Madonne del Purgatorio: Iconografia e religione in Campagnia tra rinascimento e controriforma* (Genoa: Marietti, 1991), pp. 58–59. For other sixteenth- and seventeenth-century examples on both sides of the Alps, see Maj-Brit Wadell, *Fons Pietatis: Eine ikonographische Studie* (Göteborg: n.p., 1969), pp. 55–61, 77–88.

45. Bynum (1987) pp. 272–74 and pls. 28–29.

46. With appropriate caution, one might seek to apply these insights to the differences between Porta's and Cozzolani's settings of *O quam bonus*, which draw on similar sectional structures (ostinato, refrain) but which feature differences in rhetorical emphasis within sections as well as in organizing principles (there is no parallel in Porta's setting to the tonal oscillation of Cozzolani's version, for instance).

47. My thanks to Robert Randolf Coleman and Pamela Jones for their advice on iconography and to Louis Jordan for his help with the holdings of the Biblioteca Ambrosiana. It is possible that this graphic realism and emphasis on the physical aspects of the Double Intercession had received earlier pictorial expression in mid-Cinquecento Lombardy, notably in some altarpieces and devotional works by Moretto da Brescia (1498–1554) (Coleman, personal communications).

48. High-voice duets had been dedicated to nun singers famous and obscure since G. P. Cima's *Concerti ecclesiastici* (1610) and Andrea Cima's *Secondo libro* (1627, the latter with a double inscription to two nuns of one such piece). The difficulty in finding competent choirboys, even for *stile antico*, is a constant lament of Milanese composers throughout the century; in light of the

increasing difficulty of these concertos' vocal lines and the parallel spread of female monastic music, it must be assumed that nuns were among the principal performers of this repertory.

49. A translation of the text in Ex. 2 might run as follows: "O happy, blessed me; here I feed from his wound, here I suck from her breast; I do not know where to turn next. In his wound is life; in her breast, health; in his wound, rest; in her breast, peace; in his wound, nectar; in her breast, honey; in his wound, jubilation; in her breast, joy; in your wound, O Jesus; in your breast, O Virgin. O happy, blessed me."

50. See Giovanna Maria Bonomo's *Confessione di un cristiano al pensiero . . . della Passione* (Bassano, 1659).

51. Porta's version also employs a quasi-ostinato, longer and freer than Cozzolani's, for the setting of "O potus."

52. On this, and for an exploration of the prelate's views on the plastic arts resulting therefrom, see Pamela Jones, *Federico Borromeo's Ambrosiana: Art, Patronage and Reform in Seventeenth-Century Milan* (Cambridge: Cambridge University Press, 1993).

53. I cite from the Latin version of this treatise, *De christianae mentis jocunditate* (Milan, 1632), Book I, ch. 9, "De caelesti Risu": "Narravit mihi ecstatica quaedam grandis natus, et spectata eadem sanctitatis, contigisse sibi, ut inter ecstasim tali quadam iucunditate afficeretur. Dixit ipsa: Domine, nihil aliud a te expeto, quam te ipsum. . . . Neque ultra responsum accepit, sed tanta suivitate risus interioris delibuta est, ut pene moreretur[:] illa longi temporis fuit" (a certain nobleborn woman mystic, certified for her sanctity, told me [the following]: it had happened to her that during an ecstasy she was overcome by such a kind of joyfulness. She said: Lord, I wish nothing from you but you yourself. . . . Nor did she receive a further response, but she was filled with such sweetness of interior laughter as if she were almost dying. That [rapture] was of long duration). This passage is followed by a similar account told of Catherine of Genoa.

54. "De jucundissimo nonnullorum obitu"; a preceding chapter (Book III, ch. 11), "Quibus sit amabile mori," had introduced the topic as the summation of the Christian soul's happiness.

Notes to Chapter 8

1. Christine de Pizan, *The Book of the City of Ladies* (orig. *Le Livre de la Cité des Dames*, Paris, 1405), trans. E. J. Richards (New York: Persea, 1982), p. 63.

2. M. V. Coldwell, "*Jougleresses* and *Trobairitz*: Secular Musicians in Medieval France," in *Women Making Music: The Western Art Tradition, 1150–1950*, ed. Jane Bowers and Judith Tick (Urbana and Chicago: University of Illinois Press, 1986), p. 55.

3. Pizan (1982), pp. 63–64.

4. For a study of the Church's manipulation of two southern beguines during the early fourteenth century, see Jo Ann McNamara, "*De Quibusdam Mulieribus:* Reading Women's History from Hostile Sources," in *Medieval*

Women and the Sources of Medieval History, ed. J. T. Rosenthal (Athens: University of Georgia Press, 1990): 237–58.

5. "Let your women keep silent in the churches, for they are not permitted to speak, but they are to be submissive, as the law also says." This Pauline injunction against women's speaking in church is found in the Book of 1 Corinthians 14:34. Concerning the ecclesiastical condemnation of the carole, see J. Stevens, *Words and Music in the Middle Ages* (Cambridge: Cambridge University Press, 1986), pp. 161–62; also C. Page, *The Owl and the Nightingale* (London: Dent, 1989), pp. 110–29.

6. For evidence to suggest that musical study in Paris was confined to Boethius's *De institutione musica*, see C. Page (1989), pp. 139–42. The professional problems encountered by women who were excluded from university studies are graphically illustrated by the plight of female doctors in fourteenth-century Paris. Eileen Power describes the case of a certain Jacqueline Felicie de Alemania, a noblewoman, presumably of German birth. In 1322, when she was about thirty years old, she was prosecuted by the medical faculty of Paris for disobeying the statute requiring both a faculty's degree and the chancellor's license for anyone who wished to practice medicine in the city and suburbs. Witnesses defended her, and one stated that "he had heard it said by several that she was wiser in the art of surgery and medicine than the greatest master doctor or surgeon in Paris." She made an eloquent defense, speaking of the need for women doctors in general because many women were ashamed to reveal their infirmities to a man. *Chartularium Universitatis Parisiensis*, ed. H. Denifle (Paris: 1889–97), vol. II, pp. 255–67. Jacqueline Felicie's case was not unique, as her indictment also contains an interdiction against other women: Margaret of Ypres, Belota the Jewess, and a certain Johanna, "lay sister." Eileen Power, *Medieval Women*, ed. M. M. Postan (Cambridge: Cambridge University Press, 1975), p. 88. Although it is difficult to imagine that a woman creating music could be as threatening to the status quo as a woman practicing medicine, these cases show how the educational bureaucracy was able to rob women of their traditional roles.

7. Paula Higgins concludes a fascinating article reestablishing the "woman's voice in late-medieval song" with two iconographical examples to demonstrate how women were literally cut out of the picture. See P. Higgins, "Parisian Nobles, a Scottish Princess, and the Woman's Voice in Late Medieval Song," *Early Music History* 10, ed. I. Fenlon (Cambridge: Cambridge University Press, 1991): 195.

8. The seven liberal arts were divided into two groups: the *trivium*, comprising the three subjects grammar, logic, and rhetoric; and the *quadrivium*, including the four subjects arithmetic, astronomy, geometry, and music.

9. For a detailed discussion of the pagan legacy of female abstraction in twelfth-century Christian allegories, see J. M. Ferrante, *Woman as Image in Medieval Literature* (New York: Columbia University Press, 1975; rpt., Durham, N.C.: Labyrinth Press, 1985), pp. 37–64.

10. J. Campbell, *The Hero with a Thousand Faces* (Princeton: Princeton University Press, 1971), p. 116.

11. The similarity between intellectual pursuits and sexual conquest is ex-

pressed in the dual meanings of the Biblical verb *yode'a* (to know), indicating either a state of knowledge or sexual relations with a woman, the ultimate physical "knowing" of a person.

12. As early as 1948, Sophie Drinker includes as one of the social changes affecting women's relationship to music "the limitation of the woman to the position of being the object of men's music, instead of the creator of music of her own." This led to "the exaltation of the woman as the inspirer and sponsor of men's music." Sophie Drinker, *Music and Women: The Story of Women in Their Relation to Music* (Washington, D.C.: Zenger, 1948), p. 211.

13. For a thorough discussion of the Musica iconography and the relationship between its symbolism and real-life elements, see T. Seebass, "Lady Music and her *Protégés* from Musical Allegory to Musicians' Portraits," *Musica Disciplina* 42 (1988): 23–61. See also H. Mayer Brown, "St. Augustine, Lady Music, and the Gittern in Fourteenth-Century Italy," *Musica Disciplina* 38 (1984): 25–65.

14. The pictorial tradition of depicting Musica with a lute continued well into the fourteenth century, concurrently with the developments discussed below. See Mayer Brown (1984).

15. T. Seebass, *Musikdarstellung und Psalterillustration im früheren Mittelalter* (Bern: Francke, 1973), I, p. 94, pl. 79.

16. R. van Marle, *Iconographie de l'art profane au Moyen-Age et à la Renaissance*, vol. II: Allegories et Symboles (The Hague, 1931; rpt., New York: Hacker, 1971), p. 219.

17. J. Adhémar, *Influences antiques* (London: Warburg Institute, 1939), p. 34; paraphrased by G. Foster, *The Iconology of Musical Instruments* (Ph.D. diss., City University of New York, 1977), p. 38. Foster contends that the common thirteenth-century iconography of the *Exultate* initial showing King David playing the bells is a "short form" of the more complete statement found in the *St. Louis Psalter*, where both David and Musica are depicted together. She interprets the Old Testament king as a representation of the old law and the old worship, while Musica represents the harmony of the old and new laws and the Pythagorean harmony of the cosmos. See Foster (1977), p. 28.

18. Mayer Brown (1984), p. 41. Nevertheless, the author overlooks the possibility that "Lady Music" might represent real women organists.

19. The eleventh-century organ keyboard was composed of wooden sliders with perforations corresponding to the number of pipe ranks. These were fitted into channels in the chests; each slider handle was marked with the letter of its position in the scale. The Anonymous of Berne provides for keys that are attached to the sliders: when the key is depressed, the slider is pushed forward to align a hole with the pipe foot, allowing the passage of wind to the pipe. For a transcription of the Latin and an English translation of the relevant passage from the Anonymous of Berne's treatise, see J. Perrot, *L'Orgue: de ses origines hellénistiques à la fin du XIIIe siècle* (Paris, 1965); Eng. trans. N. Deane, *The Organ . . .* (London, 1971), pp. 303, 242–43.

20. For a reproduction of this depiction, see ibid., pl. XXV.

21. For information about the parchment strips on four late fourteenth-century organs from Gotland (Sundre, Norrlanda, Hejnum, and Anga), see M.

Kjersgaard, "Technische Aspekte des Mittelalterlichen Orgelbaus in Schweden," *ISO Information* 27 (July 1987): 13–14.

22. Seebass (1988), p. 30.

23. Both the depiction in the Naples manuscript and that in the Spanish Chapel of Santa Maria Novella are reproduced in Mayer Brown (1984), figs. 14 and 11. A later manuscript illustration by the Paduan school from the beginning of the fifteenth century depicts Musica with positive organ and lute, two instruments associated with intabulations of polyphonic vocal music. See R. van Marle (1971), p. 218, fig. 244. This may be a simplification of an earlier iconography that shows Musica tuning a lute and surrounded by various other instruments, including the organ. See Mayer Brown (1984), figs. 4 and 5.

24. This is discussed at much greater length in my book about the late-medieval organ, *Ars pulsandi organorum: The Organist's Art in Late-Medieval Europe* (forthcoming).

25. This illumination is reproduced in E. Bowles, *La pratique musicale au moyen-âge: Musical Performance in the Late Middle Ages* (Geneva: Minkoff, 1983), p. 106, pl. 73.

26. For a cursory discussion of this development and a reproduction of a historiated initial showing David in the harp-tuning pose as he plays an organ, see pp. 22–24 of my article "From Temple to Theatre: The Use of Musical Instruments in Jewish and Christian Liturgy before the Twelfth Century," *Sydney Organ Journal* 22/6 (December 1991/January 1992): 18–27.

27. Seebass (1973), p. 96.

28. Mayer Brown (1984), p. 41.

29. The text describes her as follows: "Une autre avoit leans encor / Qui en sa main tenoit i cor / Et faisaoit leens i grant son / D'orgues et de psalterion / Si comme fust jouglerresse / Et de gent (une) esbaterresse." The first recension of Deguileville's *Pèlerinage de la Vie Humaine* is published in a modern edition edited by J. J. Stürzinger (London: Roxburghe Club, 1893); the relevant text may be found on p. 396.

30. Ferrante notes that female characters in twelfth-century literature "are not portrayed as 'real people' with human problems; they are symbols, aspects of philosophical and psychological problems that trouble the male world." Ferrante (1985), p. 1.

31. The art historian Emile Mâle suggests that this figure depicts Pythagoras; E. Mâle, *The Gothic Image*, trans. D. Nussey (New York: Harper & Brothers, 1958), p. 88: "The man at Chartres who, pen in hand, reflects as he composes a didactic treatise, bears a closer resemblance to a scholar than to a patriarch of primitive time. He is most probably Pythagoras, and the sculptor at Chartres has followed the tradition of Cassiodorus and Isidore of Seville which attributed to him the discovery of the laws of music." Late-medieval manuscript sources transmit a similar iconography, where underneath Musica is shown a seated male figure hammering on an anvil, clearly labeled as "Jubal" or "Tubal," indicating the Biblical father of musical science. See Mayer Brown (1984), pp. 26, 28 and pls. 1, 4, 5, 6, 7, 8, 11, 12, 13.

32. This text was added to the Book of Esther by the redactors of the Septuagint and thus does not appear in the Hebrew Bible, which ends with Chapter

10. I am grateful to Thomas Connolly of the University of Pennsylvania for sharing with me sections of his monograph on Saint Cecilia, to be published by Toronto University Press in 1993. Connolly's book explores the link between Saint Cecilia and the tradition of "mourning into joy," a centuries-old understanding that the path of spiritual development proceeds in complex ways from mouring to joy, with music viewed as a medium to express these experiences. Connolly attempts to piece together this lost tradition of "mourning into joy" in order better to understand the iconography of the saint, especially the famous painting by Raphael, now in the Pinacoteca in Bologna, where she holds upside down a portable organ from which the pipes are sliding toward the ground. This new research contests the long-held belief that Cecilia's association with music resulted from the omission of the words "in corde suo" (in her heart) from the Vespers antiphon used on her feast day, November 22. The text of the antiphon is taken from her legend, which relates that she sang in her heart to God; it has been posited that when the words "in her heart" were excluded from the antiphon, Cecilia's internal praise was reinterpreted to be a musical performance. (See McKinnon's article on Saint Cecilia in *The New Grove Dictionary*.) Connolly considers the text from Esther that was used for Cecilia's stational liturgy to be far more significant to her eventual association with music. For an earlier account of the saint and her iconography, see Connolly's article "L'iconografia di Santa Cecilia prima di Raffaello," *L'Estasi di Santa Cecilia di Raffaello da Urbino* (Bologna: Edizioni ALFA, 1983), pp. 229–34.

33. A citation of Cecilia's *Passio* appears in a portion of the *Liber Pontificalis* that is known to have been written before 535 C.E., so it is possible to date the *Passio* between 485 and 535. According to Connolly, "the Passio Caeciliae is one of the more stable saints' legends, with comparatively few variants in its tale, none of them of any substance." A later account of the *Passio* was published by A. Bosius, *Historia passionis beatae Caeciliae virginis, Valeriani, Tiburtii et Maximi martyrum, necnon Urbani et Lucii pontificum et martyrum vitae* (Rome, 1600).

34. See Connolly (1983), p. 229.

35. M. V. Coldwell (1986), p. 40.

36. A. Doutrepont, ed. *La clef d'amors* (Halle, 1890; rpt., Geneva: Biblioteca Normannica, 1975), lines 2589 ff.

37. See C. Page (1989), pp. 103–4. For a contemporary account of women's musical participation at court, Page singles out the *Romance of Escanor* "whose author has a highly developed sense of the way in which courtly women could enliven court festivities and even be summoned to do so." H. Michelant, ed., *Der Roman von Escanor* (Tübingen: Litterarischen Verein in Stuttgart, 1886), lines 6163 ff., 6324 ff., 8596 ff.

38. C. Page (1989), pp. 105–7. For a modern edition of the original text, see P. Meyer, ed., *L'Histoire de Guillaume le Maréchal,* 2 vols. (Paris, 1891–1901), lines 18572 ff.

39. Page (1989), pp. 106–7.

40. Higgins (1991), p. 194.

41. Yvonne Rokseth, "Les Femmes Musiciennes du XIIe au XIVe Siècle," *Romania* 61 (1935): 464–80.

42. Ibid., p. 474. Rokseth's source for this information was Jules-Marie Richard, *Une petite-nièce de Saint-Louis: Mahaut, comtesse d'Artois et de Bourgogne (1302–1329)* (Paris: Champion, 1887), p. 110; Richard studied the original archives and found this account in MS A 386, Series A, of the Pas-de-Calais Archives.

43. The earliest documented organist in history was a woman, however. Her name was Thaïs, and she was the wife of the Greek engineer Ctesibios, who is credited with the invention of the hydraulis. See Perrot (1971), pp. 43, 78, 165–66. The earliest surviving keyboard music is generally considered to be the *Robertsbridge Codex*, two folios now in the British Library (Add. MS 28850) containing three estampies (first incomplete), two intabulations of motets from the *Roman de Fauvel*, and what may be a hymn arrangement (incomplete). Although Apel and other scholars have dated this manuscript as early as ca. 1320, the use of the minim, the fully chromatic compass, and the possibility that the manuscript originated with the musical establishment of the French King John II while captive in England, 1357–60, all suggest a date no earlier than the third quarter of the fourteenth century. See E. H. Roesner, *Works of Philippe de Vitry* (Monaco: Editions de l'Oiseau-Lyre, 1984). I am grateful to John Caldwell of the Music Faculty at Oxford University for drawing these points to my attention.

44. There are several versions of this treatise, the most complete of which is found in the *Buxheimer Orgelbuch*, Munich, Bayerische Staatsbibliothek, MS Cim. 352b. This version is published in both modern facsimile: B.A. Wallner, ed., *Das Buxheimer Orgelbuch. Documenta musicologica*, 2/1 (Kassel: Bärenreiter, 1955); and in a modern transcription: B. A. Wallner, ed., *Das Buxheimer Orgelbuch. Das Erbe Deutscher Musik* (Kassel: Bärenreiter, 1958–59), vol. 39, pp. 287–397. The anonymous treatise is contained in Munich MS 7755, transcribed by T. Göllner, *Formen frühen Mehrstimmigkeit in deutschen Handschriften des späten Mittelalters* (Tutzing: Schneider, 1961), pp. 157–79.

45. The *Buxheimer Orgelbuch* is the most important surviving source of fifteenth-century organ music. This voluminous collection of 174 folios was discovered during the nineteenth century in the library of the Carthusian monastery of Buxheim, which is on the River Iller in southern Germany. In 1883, the manuscript was transferred to the Bayerische Staatsbibliothek in Munich, where it still resides as Cim. 352b (formerly Mus. MS 3752). The *Buxheimer Orgelbuch* contains four principal types of composition: intabulations of pre-existing polyphony, settings of pre-existing monophony, freely invented preludes, and collections of short didactic pieces known as *fundamenta*. The vast majority of the pieces belong to the first two categories, 229 of the total 260 items. More than 60 percent (142) of these are clearly based on polyphonic models, including German *lieder*, French *formes fixes*, and Italian *trecento* forms. The remaining pieces are settings of melodies, such as plainsong, solmization syllables, German *lied*, chanson tenors, and *basse danse* tunes. Conrad Paumann's *Fundamentum* elucidates many of the techniques used in compositions based on both polyphonic and monophonic originals.

46. I am grateful to William Prizer for drawing my attention to this account, the details of which are published in his article "Games of Venus: Secular Vocal

Music in the Late Quattrocento and Early Cinquecento," *Journal of Musicology* 9/1 (Winter 1991): 3–56.

47. All of the passages concerning Bianca's performances are taken from ibid., pp. 3–4.

48. Ibid., pp. 5–6.

49. There is some ambiguity about whether Bianca was actually singing the songs as she accompanied herself on the organ, but if this were the case, it would still entail some arrangement of the polyphonic *chansons* for execution by a single voice with instrumental accompaniment. It is difficult to imagine that a literal rendition of the unsung parts on the organ would have excited such lavish praise from Montefeltro of Bianca's outstanding abilities as an organist.

50. For more information on the *Faenza Codex* and arguments suggesting that it may have codified the practice of lute duos during the early fifteenth century, see T. J. McGee, "Instruments and the Faenza Codex," *Early Music* 14/4 (November 1986): 480–90.

51. It is startling to realize that if Landini had confined his efforts to instrumental music, he would probably be unknown today; his present renown as a composer is due to his preserved vocal compositions.

52. This can be seen in the facsimile edition published by A. Carapetyan as *An Early Fifteenth-Century Italian Source of Keyboard Music* (American Institute of Musicology, 1961).

53. The absence of attributions to instrumental pieces continues into the sixteenth century: Andrea Antico's *Frottole da sonare organi* (1517) bear the initials of the composers of the original *frottole* rather than the name of the intabulator; Pierre Attaingnant's collections of intabulated *chansons* and dances (1531) are similarly anonymous.

54. This hypothesis is supported by the appearance of the three manuscript sources containing early keyboard music. None are notated in the neat script with elaborate decoration that was typical of presentation copies. Rather, they seem to have been compilations of both secular and sacred music made by organists for personal use in different contexts, perhaps even to be played on different instruments. Organists today still create their own arrangements of vocal and orchestral models, and where these scores are for personal use, they rarely include any attributions. If a twenty-fifth century musicologist happens to stumble upon any of these twentieth-century "intabulations," she or he will face the same dilemma: the original title and composer might be indicated, but the arranger's name will be absent because she or he was the one who used the manuscript.

55. Prizer suggests that "they might represent three of the standard Italian repertories of the time: the angelic song . . . could have been a lauda; 'canzonetta' was a standard name for the *giustiniane* or *viniziane* that were in vogue at this time; and the other might possibly be an arrangement of one of the Neapolitan works that circulated in Tuscany during the 1460s and 1470s." Prizer (1991), p. 6.

56. L. Treitler, "Oral, Written, and Literate Process in the Transmission of Medieval Music," *Speculum* 56/3 (1981): 473.

57. M. "Mezz" Mezzrow and B. Wolfe, *Really the Blues* (New York: Random House, 1946), pp. 124–25, cited in L. W. Levine, *Highbrow/Lowbrow: The Emergence of Cultural Hierarchy in America* (Cambridge: Harvard University Press, 1988), p. 239.

58. This approach to the study of jazz and other recorded musics is already prevalent. Among others, Lewis Porter's study of John Coltrane's recorded improvisations emphasizes their similarities to written compositions: "Listening to Coltrane's recorded performances, we hear a composer at work, shaping, developing, and connecting musical ideas while attempting, often successfully, to keep the musical whole in perspective." See L. Porter, "John Coltrane's *A Love Supreme:* Jazz Improvisation as Composition," *Journal of the American Musicological Society* 38/3 (Fall 1985): 621.

59. For information about musical education in courtly circles, see Prizer (1991), p. 5, n. 4; and H. Mayer Brown, "Women Singers and Women's Songs in Fifteenth-Century Italy," in Bowers and Tick (1986), pp. 65–66. For a description of the education of nuns, consult A. Bagnall Yardley's article " 'Ful weel she soong the service dyvyne': The Cloistered Musician in the Middle Ages," also in Bowers and Tick (1986).

60. All of the female aristocrats discussed below in the section on sponsors received musical tuition, often from very prominent composers and theorists.

61. H. Mayer Brown (1986), p. 64.

62. For a discussion of the conditions opening the way for professional women performers and composers in sixteenth-century Italy, see A. Newcomb, "Courtesans, Muses, or Musicians? Professional Women Musicians in Sixteenth-Century Italy," in Bowers and Tick (1986), pp. 90–115. In the same volume, Jane Bowers describes the compositional activities of Italian women and explains the positive and negative influences on the development of women composers in late sixteenth- and seventeenth-century Italy; see "The Emergence of Women Composers in Italy, 1566–1700," pp. 116–67.

63. This information is found in Bowers (1986), pp. 120–21, n. 26–27.

64. Ellen Rosand, "Barbara Strozzi, *virtuosissima cantatrice:* The Composer's Voice," *Journal of the American Musicological Society* 31 (1978): 254. Rosand gives additional references to demonstrate that foreign visitors were impressed by the compositional skills of Italian women. She concludes that "seventeenth-century references to compositions by women are considerably better preserved than the works themselves," and suggests that "if such music has not survived, part of the reason must lie in the fact that it was neither printed nor copied in manuscripts. It may have been partly or totally improvised, and thus never committed to paper, even originally."

65. Giovanni Battista Spaccini, *Cronaca modenese (1588–1636),* 2 vols., ed. G. Bertoni, T. Sandonnini, and P. E. Vicini, *Monumenti di storia patria delle provincie modenesi, Serie delle cronache,* 16–17 (Modena: Giovanni Ferraguti, 1911–19), 16, p. 34. I am indebted to Jane Bowers for bringing this and the following two sources to my attention. See her article in Bowers and Tick (1986), p. 120, n. 20.

66. These two women were Cecilia Torniella, a nun in the convent of Giesù in Asti, and Caterina Cellana, a nun in the Ursuline convent in Galliate; refer-

ences to the original sources describing them are found in Bowers (1986), p. 120, n. 22.

67. Ibid., p. 127, n. 59. Note the metaphor "divine Euterpe," which evokes the symbolism of the Muses in describing a real female musician and composer.

68. New information about the life and work of Francesca Caccini is now being uncovered thanks to the efforts of Suzanne Cusick, whose essay ends this volume. Concerning Calegri, see Bowers and Tick (1986), p. 118.

69. S. Groag Bell, "Medieval Women Book Owners: Arbiters of Lay Piety and Ambassadors of Culture," in *Women and Power in the Middle Ages,* ed. M. Erler and M. Kowaleski (Athens: University of Georgia Press, 1988), pp. 149–87.

70. Ibid., p. 173.

71. Ibid., p. 150.

72. *The Mellon Chansonnier,* ed. L. L. Perkins and H. Garey (New Haven: Yale University Press, 1979), 1, p. 32.

73. M. Picker, ed., *The Chanson Albums of Marguerite of Austria: MSS 228 and 11239 of the Bibliothèque Royale de Belgique, Brussels* (Berkeley: University of California Press, 1965), p. 5.

74. C. A. de Laserna-Santander quotes some of the song texts of MS 228, reporting that "many are believed to have been written by the duchess [Marguerite] herself"; *Mémoires historique sur la Bibliothèque dite de Bourgogne, présentement Bibliothèque publique de Bruxelles* (Brussels, 1809), pp. 32–37, 134–45. The literary historian Francisque Thibaut published many poems that he believed to be the work of Marguerite in *Marguerite d'Autriche et Jehan Lemaire de Belges, ou de la littérature et des arts aux Pays-Bas sous Marguerite d'Autriche* (Paris, 1888; rpt. Geneva: Slatkine, 1970), pp. 53–54.

75. For the reference to Marguerite's instruction from Nepotis, see E. Vander Straeten, *La Musique aux Pays-Bas avant le XIXe siècle,* vol. 3 (Brussels, 1867–88), p. 214. Passages extolling Marguerite's talents in Lemaire's writings are cited in Picker (1965), pp. 14–15. Picker's translation of "gens savans, érudites et étendues" as "wise and learned men" overlooks the importance of the female presence at court. As Paula Higgins notes with regard to several eminent patrons of fifteenth-century music, "It is well known that all of these women employed some of the best-known male composers of their day, and it seems unlikely that they would have chosen to surround themselves with women with whom they shared little in common." Higgins (1991), p. 193.

76. Picker (1965), p. 15.

77. G. Gaimar, *L'estoire des Engleis,* ed. A. Bell (Oxford: Blackwell, 1960), line 6486. Bell argues for the authenticity of the epilogue containing this reference and for a dating of 1135–40 in "The Epilogue to Gaimar's 'Estoire des Anglais,' " *Modern Language Review* 25 (1930): 52–59.

78. C. Page (1989), p. 108. For a modern edition of the original text, see Gaimar (1960), lines 6477 ff.

79. Higgins (1991), pp. 173–89, uses the information in anagrams and aspects of poetic style to argue that Jacqueline de Hacqueville was a participant in a musical-literary exchange with Antoine Busnois. On the female fascination with the alphabet and linguistic cryptograms, see S. Gilbert and S. Gubar,

"Ceremonies of the Alphabet: Female Grandmatologies and the Female Autograph," in *The Female Autograph*, ed. D. C. Stanton (New York: New York Literary Forum, 1984), pp. 21–48.

80. See J. Ferrante, "Public Postures and Private Maneuvers: Roles Medieval Women Play," in Erler and Kowaleski (1988), pp. 213–29.

81. Guillaume de Machaut, *Le Livre du Voir-Dit*, ed. P. Paris (Paris: Société des bibliophiles françois, 1875), pp. 47–49.

Notes to Chapter 9

This article has been developed from ideas first set forth in my extended study entitled "Parisian Nobles, A Scottish Princess, and the Woman's Voice in Late Medieval Song," *Early Music History* 10, ed. Iain Fenlon (Cambridge, Eng., 1991): 145–200. I am grateful to Cambridge University Press for permission to reuse portions of this article. Translations from French originals are all mine unless otherwise indicated.

1. *C'est pour me receller les biens*, Paris, Bibliothèque nationale, MS français 9223 (hereafter Paris 9223), fol. 36v; "Jammette de Nesson," in *Rondeaux et autres poésies du quinzième siècle publiés d'après le manuscrit de la Bibliothèque Nationale*, ed. G. Raynaud, Société des anciens textes français 30 (Paris, 1889), p. 59; and Paris, Bibliothèque nationale, MS nouvelles acquisitions françaises 15771 (hereafter Paris 15771), fol. 39r, "Denesson a ja," in *Le Manuscrit B.N. Nouv. Acq. Fr. 15771*, ed. B. Inglis (Paris, 1985), p. 148. The poem survives anonymously in Paris, Bibliothèque nationale, MS fr. 1719 (hereafter Paris 1719), fol. 44r. All manuscripts cited hereafter as "Paris" refer to Paris, Bibliothèque Nationale, fonds français, unless otherwise indicated.

2. A. Thomas, "Jamette de Nesson et Merlin de Cordebeuf," *Romania* 35 (1909): 82.

3. Ibid., pp. 88–91.

4. On the provenance of the manuscripts see Inglis (1985), pp. 15–19, 213–14.

5. P. Champion, *La Dauphine mélancolique* (Paris, 1925). For more information on Margaret of Scotland see L. A. Barbé, *Margaret of Scotland and the Dauphin Louis* (London, 1917), pp. 114–49; R. S. Rait, *Five Stuart Princesses* (Westminster, 1902), pp. 3–46; G. L. E. du Fresne de Beaucourt, *Histoire de Charles VII*, 6 vols. (Paris, 1881–91), IV, pp. 89–111; C. P. Duclos, *Histoire de Louis XI*, 3 vols. (1745–46); A. Vallet de Viriville, *Histoire de Charles VII*, 3 vols. (1863–65), III, pp. 81–90; Le Roux de Lincy, *Les femmes célèbres de l'ancienne France* (Paris, 1848), I, pp. 451–53; M. Thibault, *La Jeunesse de Louis XI* (Paris, 1907), pp. 503–51; H. Menu, "Charles VII et la Dauphine Marguerite d'Écosse à Châlons-sur-Marne (4 mai–18 août 1445)," *Annuaire administratif, statistique, historique et commercial de la Marne* (1895), pp. 555–64; D. B. Wyndham Lewis, *King Spider: Some Aspects of Louis XI of France and His Companions* (New York, 1929), pp. 162–94.

6. The most easily accessible source for the Chartier anecdote is P. Champion, *Histoire poétique du quinzième siècle*, Bibliothèque du XVe siècle 27, 2 vols. (Paris, 1923), I, pp. 131–32, citing J. Bouchet, *Annales d'Aquitaine*.

7. King James I of Scotland (1394–1437), author of *The Kingis Quair* (standard ed., J. Norton-Smith, Oxford, 1971), has had a curious historiography that has either elevated him as a poet to the level of Chaucer or diminished him as Chaucer's second-rate epigone. See W. Scheps and J. A. Looney, *Middle Scots Poets: A Reference Guide to James I of Scotland, Robert Henryson, William Dunbar, and Gavin Douglas* (Boston, 1986). He evidently enjoyed a considerable posthumous reputation as a performer and composer of music as well, according to the testimony of John Fordun, John Major, and Alessandro Tassoni, discussed at length by the anonymous author of a curious late eighteenth-century monograph (also containing an edition of *The Kingis Quair*) entitled *Poetical Remains of James the First, King of Scotland* (Edinburgh, 1783), pp. 5–7, 195–224.

8. "... belle et bien formée, pourvue et ornée de toutes bonnes conditions que noble et haute dame pouvoit avoir," and "excellentement belle et prudente dame"; Beaucourt (1881–91), IV, p. 89, citing Mathieu d'Escouchy, t. I, p. 67 and *La Chronique Antonine*.

9. Beaucourt (1881–91), IV, 90, n. 1, citing *Chronicle at large and meere history of the affayres of Englande* ... (London, 1809), t. I, p. 612.

10. "... ainsi qu'ils parloient de madite dame, ledit M. de Charny dit qu'il avoit entendu qu'elle n'étoit point habile à porter enfans, et si ainsi étoit qu'elle allât de vie à trespassement, il faudra marier monseigneur le Dauphin à une autre qui fût encline à porter enfans; et lors il qui parle [Jamet de Tillay] dit qu'il avoit ouï dire à madame Dubois Menart qu'elle avoit autrefois dit à madite dame qu'elle mangeoit trop de pommes aigres et de vinaigre, et se ceignoit aucunefois trop serrée, aucunefois trop lâche, qui étoit chose qui empêchoit bien à avoir enfans." C. P. Duclos, *Oeuvres complètes de Duclos*, 20 vols. (Paris, 1820), V (Histoire de Louis XI), pp. 51–52.

11. See S. Gilbert and S. Gubar, *The Madwoman in the Attic: The Woman Writer and the Nineteenth-Century Literary Imagination* (New Haven, 1979), p. 25. For a compelling discussion of infirmity and sickness as "physical evidence of mental and physical purity" as well as a provocative analysis of the "cultural apotheosis of the sublime consumptive" in nineteenth-century *fin-de-siècle* art, see B. Dijkstra, *Idols of Perversity: Fantasies of Feminine Evil in Fin-de-Siècle Culture* (Oxford, 1988), pp. 25–36.

12. *Holy Feast and Holy Fast: The Religious Significance of Food to Medieval Women* (Berkeley, 1987), p. 220.

13. See note 10.

14. First deposition of Jamet de Tillay, 1 June 1446: "... dit qu'environ Noel, l'an 1444, un soir environ neuf heures de nuit, autrement du jour ne du temps ne se recorde, le roi étant à Nancy en Lorraine, lui qui parle [Jamet de Tillay] et Messire Regnault de Dresnay, chevalier, allèrent en la chambre de ladite dame, laquelle étoit lors couchée sur sa couche, et plusieurs de ses femmes étoient autour d'elle; aussi y étoit Messire Jean d'Estouteville, seigneur de Blainville, appuyé sur la couche de ladite dame, et un autre qu'il ne connoît; et pour ce que ladite dame étoit en sadite chambre sans ce que les torches fussent allumées, il qui parle dit audit messire Regnault, maître d'hôtel de ladite Dame, que c'étoit grande paillardie à lui et autres officiers de ladite dame, de ce

que lesdites torches étoient encore à allumer, et dit qu'il dit lesdites paroles pour le bien et honneur de ladite dame et de sa maison." *Oeuvres complètes de Duclos,* V, p. 41.

15. ". . . elle a mieux manière d'une paillarde que d'une grande maîtresse." Tillay denied making the statement of which he had been accused by one of the courtiers interrogated. *Oeuvres complètes de Duclos,* V, p. 52.

16. See F. F. Steenackers, *Agnès Sorel et Charles VII: Essai sur l'état politique et moral de la France au XVe siècle* (Paris, 1868), pp. 250–59.

17. Beaucourt (1881–91), IV, pp. 109–10.

18. The depositions from the two inquests are published in Duclos (1745–46) *Histoire de Louis XI* (see note 5 above), which exists in numerous editions. The edition I have used for the present study is *Oeuvres complètes de Duclos,* V (Paris, 1820), pp. 27–56.

19. (Second deposition of Jamet de Tillay, 23 août 1446) " . . . ledit Nicole lui demanda ce qu'elle avoit, et d'où procédoit cette maladie, et il qui parle [Jamet de Tillay] lui répondit que les médecins disoient qu'elle avoit un courroux sur le coeur, qui lui faisoit grand dommage, et aussi que faute de repos lui nuisoit beaucoup; et lors ledit Nicole dit que lesdits médecins lui en avoient autant dit, et aussi dit: Plût à Dieu qu'elle n'eût jamais eu telle femme à elle! Et quelle dit il qui parle? Et lors ledit Nicole lui répondit: Marguerite de Salignac. Et il qui parle, lui dit: Plût à Dieu, ne aussi Prégente, ne Jeanne Filloque [*sic:* Filleul]! Requis pourquoi il dit lesdites paroles, dit pour ce qu'il avoit ouï dire que c'étoient celles qui la faisoient trop veiller à faire rondeaux et balades." *Oeuvres complètes de Duclos,* V, pp. 49–50.

20. ". . . Et lors le roi lui demanda si elle étoit impédumée; et il qui parle répondit que non, comme disoient les médecins. Et le roi lui demanda, d'où procède cette maladie, et il qui parle, lui dit qu'il venoit de faute de repos, comme disoient les médecins, et qu'elle veilloit tant, aucunefois plus, aucunefois moins, que aucunefois il étoit presque soleil levant avant qu'elle s'allât coucher, et que aucunefois monseigneur le Dauphin avoit dormi un somme ou deux avant qu'elle s'allât coucher, et aucunefois s'occupoit à faire rondeaux, tellement qu'elle en faisoit aucunefois douze pour un jour, qui lui étoit chose bien contraire. Et lors le roi demanda si cela faisoit mal à la tête, et monsieur le trésorier maître Jean Bureau, là présent, dit: Oui, qui s'y abuse trop; mais ce sont choses de plaisance." *Oeuvres complètes de Duclos,* V, pp. 50–51.

21. The morals of creative women in music, literature, and art have historically tended to be viewed with suspicion. For examples of the notion that music making, and especially music composition, was dangerous to a woman's chastity, see J. Bowers, "The Emergence of Women Composers in Italy, 1566–1700," in *Women Making Music: The Western Art Tradition, 1150–1950,* ed. J. Bowers and J. Tick (Urbana, 1986), pp. 139–41. In later centuries, women composers like Corona Schröter feared that publication of their music would be perceived almost as an act of promiscuity. See M. Citron, "Women and the Lied, 1775–1850," in Bowers and Tick (1986), p. 230. Many creative women were the targets of innuendo. Sixteenth-century poet Louise Labé, for example, was accused of granting sexual favors to the men of Lyon (A. R. Jones, "City Women and Their Audiences: Louise Labé and Veronica Franco," in *Rewriting*

the Renaissance: The Discourses of Sexual Difference in Early Modern Europe, ed. M. W. Ferguson, M. Quilligan, and N. J. Vickers [Chicago, 1986], pp. 302–3). Seventeenth-century English writer and playwright Aphra Behn was considered a "shady lady" (Gilbert and Gubar [1979], p. 63), and composer and singer Barbara Strozzi (1619–1664?) was reputed to have been a Venetian courtesan (E. Rosand, "The Voice of Barbara Strozzi," in Bowers and Tick [1986], p. 172). Since many creative women clearly did have libertine attitudes toward sexuality, such suspicions were not always without foundation. In fact, given the stigma of impropriety associated with any public acknowledgment by a woman of her creative activities, it is probably no coincidence that women who did publish their work seem to be those least concerned about notions of respectability, or whose respectability was presumably beyond question (nuns). As Rosand (1986, p. 172) and others have pointed out, a long tradition of serious music making by courtesans existed in Venice. Curiously, though, the subject has never been pursued in a scholarly study. The degree of literary cultivation among certain Venetian courtesans must have been high, to judge from Pietro Aretino, who said of one: "She knows by heart all Petrarch and Boccaccio and many beautiful verses of Virgil, Horace, Ovid, and a thousand other authors." Quoted in J. Burckhardt, The Civilization of the Renaissance in Italy (New York, 1958), p. 394, n. 2. With regard to women writers in the nineteenth century, morality and respectability became so closely linked to economic success that they could no longer risk the kind of sexual innuendo surrounding a woman like Aphra Behn. See Gilbert and Gubar (1979), pp. 63–64.

22. Deposition of Guillaume Léotier, in Paris, Bibliothèque nationale, MS Dupuy 762, fol. 51v, quoted in the original French in Beaucourt (1881–91), IV, pp. 106–7, n. 3.

23. See Gilbert and Gubar (1979), pp. 55–56.

24. See The Colloquies of Erasmus, 2 vols., trans. N. Bailey, II (London, 1878), p. 380.

25. Jeanne Filleul and Marguerite de Salignac were damoiselles d'honneur of Marguerite d'Écosse, and Prégente de Melun was damoiselle d'honneur of Marie d'Anjou, Charles VII's queen. See Beaucourt (1881–91), IV, p. 90, n. 4.

26. "Mademoiselle de Selignac," in Le Jardin de plaisance et fleur de rhétorique, ed. E. Droz and A. Piaget, 2 vols. (Paris, 1925), I, p. ci, and II, p. 205.

27. According to Vallet de Viriville (1863), III, pp. 85–86, n. 1: "Le 18 août 1450, Marie de Clèves, duchesse d'Orléans, envoie un messager d'Yèvre-le-Châtel à Corbeil, où était la reine, pour recouvrer des mains de Prégente de Melun, dame de la reine, un roman de chevalerie intitulé Clériadus, que la duchesse avait prêté à Prégente." The now-lost document in question, one of ten items included under no. 852 in the Catalogue des archives de M. Le Baron de Joursanvault, contenant une précieuse collection de manuscrits, chartes et documents originaux (Paris, 1838), p. 145, was subsequently acquired by the Bibliothèque du Louvre, which was destroyed by fire in 1870.

28. See C. Page, "The Performance of Songs in Late Medieval France: A New Source," Early Music 10 (1982): 441–50. Evidence that Marie of Cleves owned a copy of the narrative, which she in turn lent to the female attendants at the French royal court, is interesting in light of Page's observations concern-

ing its "evidence of a French aristocratic and possibly royal provenance" (p. 442), since "the author speaks of the chivalry, the court and the king of France in the most flattering terms" (p. 450). An edition of *Clériadus et Méliadice* has appeared since the publication of Page's article: G. Zink, ed. *Clériadus et Méliadice: Roman en prose du XVe siècle* (Paris and Geneva, 1984).

29. The concept of a separate tradition of women's culture especially among literary women is central to the pioneering work of Gilbert and Gubar (see note 11), as well as that of the literary critic Elaine Showalter, *A Literature of Their Own: British Women Novelists from Brontë to Lessing* (Princeton, 1977).

30. *Helas mon amy sur mon ame*, fol. 46, ed. Raynaud (1889), p. 76. The poem is also published, translated, and discussed in Higgins, "Parisian Nobles, a Scottish Princess, and the Woman's Voice in Late Medieval Song," *Early Music History* 10, ed. Iain Fenlon (Cambridge, Eng., 1991): 182–85.

31. Paris 9223 transmits 34 poems by three male courtiers in the dauphine's circle: Blosseville (29), Tanneguy du Chastel (3), and Jean d'Estouteville, seigneur de Torcy et Blainville (2). Torcy's rondeau *N'ai ge pas esté bien party* follows that of Jeanne Filleul in the same manuscript. For the most recent biographical information on these poets, see Inglis (1985), pp. 19–24 (Blosseville), pp. 35–36 (Tanneguy du Chastel), and pp. 58–60 (Seigneur de Torcy).

32. No fewer than nine texts in Paris 9223 were set to music. See Raynaud (1889), nos. VII, XXIV, XXXI, CVII, CXIII, CXVI, CXX, CLXXXVIII, CXCIV. For sources of the musical settings see Higgins (1991), p. 165, n. 63.

33. Raynaud (1889), no. CLXXXII, p. 153.

34. Deposition of Annette de Guise, Paris, Bibliothèque nationale, MS Dupuy 762, fol. 53: "Interrogée sy elle a aucune chose en garde de madicte dame, dict que non, fors un livre qui parle d'amours, et de chansons et ballades, et aucunes lettres d'estat qui sont en son coffre lequel elle auroye avec le bagaige de la Roine."

35. *Les Douleurs dont me sens tel somme*, Raynaud (1889), no. VII. For the most recent biographical information on Antoine, Jeanne, and Annette de Cuise, see Inglis (1985), pp. 29–33.

36. I have dealt at great length with the musical and literary issues surrounding Jacqueline de Hacqueville in my article "Parisian Nobles," pp. 145–200. I discussed the evidence of intertextuality among the poems attributed to Hacqueville and those by Jeanne Filleul, Jamette de Nesson, and other members of the dauphine's circle on pp. 182–85 of that essay.

37. *Helas mon amy sur mon ame*, Paris 9223, fol. 46, "Jehanne Filleul," in Raynaud (1889), p. 76–77; Paris 15771, fol. 38r, "Jehanne Fillieul," in Inglis (1985), p. 146. The poem also survives anonymously in Berlin, Kupferstichkabinett, Rohan 78.B.17 (hereafter Roh), fol. 178r, in *Die Liederhandschrift des Cardinals de Rohan (XV Jahr.)*, ed. M. Löpelmann, Gesellschaft für romanische Literatur 44 (Göttingen, 1923), p. 343; Paris 1719, fol. 121r; and *Le Jardin de Plaisance*, fol. 81, in Droz and Piaget (1925), no. 212.

38. *En la forest de Longue Actente*, "Madame d'Orléans," Paris 9223, fol. 26v, in Raynaud (1889), p. 43; Paris 15771, fol. 2r, "Madame d'Orléans," in Inglis (1985), p. 73; Paris 1104, fol. 87v, "Madame d'Orléans"; Paris 25458, fol. 415r, "Madame d'Orléans." The poem survives anonymously in Paris 1719,

fol. 4v, 64v, 129r; Roh, fol. 64v; Carpentras, Bibl. mun. fr. 375, fol. 50v; London, British Library, MS Harley 6916, fol. 171v; Paris fr. 1722, fol. 76v.

39. *En ce monde n'a saint ne saincte,* "Madamoiselle de Beau Chastel," Paris 9223, fol. 69, in Raynaud (1889), p. 113. The poem survives anonymously in Roh, fol. 204r, Löpelmann (1923), pp. 408–9.

40. See note 4 above.

41. *Pour tous les maulx d'amours guerir,* Paris 15771, fol. 34, "Recepte de la Raine," in Inglis (1985), p. 137. The poem survives anonymously in Paris 1719, fol. 75r; Roh, fol. 202v; Carpentras, Bibl. mun. MS 375, fols. 55r, 65r; Paris 25458, fol. 441r; Paris 1104, fol. 92v; London, British Library, MS Harley 6916, fol. 181v; and Paris n.a.f. 7559, fol. 68r. The attribution "Recepte de la Raine" in all likelihood refers to Queen Marie d'Anjou. See A. Angremy, "Un nouveau recueil de poésies françaises: Le MS B. N. nouv. acq. fr. 15771," *Romania* 95 (1974): 4. The dauphine's household was incorporated with that of Queen Marie d'Anjou, with whom she traveled constantly. Marie d'Anjou was the sister of Duke René d'Anjou, another of the noble literary amateurs of his day. Champion published the poem as a work of Charles d'Orléans because it appears in his autograph manuscript without an attribution. The existence of several other poetic "recipes" "for curing the ills of love" by other poets suggests that it was among those themes developed at the Orléans court, such as "je meurs de soif auprès de la fontaine." B. Inglis (1985), p. 206, has suggested the possibility that "La Raine" could also refer to Jeanne de Laval, "reine de Sicile," second wife of René d'Anjou. Inglis cited the existence of another "recepte" similar to this one attributed to Jean de Lorraine (son of René, and stepson of Jeanne de Laval) in support of this hypothesis. In light of the evidence presented here concerning the close interaction among the women of the French court and Orléans court, as well as the numerous pieces by French court poets surviving in the manuscript, it would seem more likely that a nonspecific reference to "the queen" would be to the queen of France, Marie d'Anjou.

42. See the translation of Tillay's testimony on p. 173 above and in the original French in note 20.

43. S. J. Williams, "The Lady, the Lyrics, and the Letters," *Early Music* 5 (1977), p. 467, quoting *Le Livre du Voir Dit de Guillaume de Machaut,* ed. P. Paris (Paris, 1875), p. 202.

44. See note 5 for the bibliography concerning Margaret of Scotland.

45. P. M. Kendall, *Louis XI: The Universal Spider* (New York, 1971), p. 63.

46. J. Cleugh, *Chant Royal: The Life of King Louis XI of France* (New York, 1970), p. 60.

47. M. G. A. Vale, *Charles VII* (Berkeley, 1974), p. 96. Vale's account is emblematic of the way in which the literary and musical creations of women, even when they have survived, have historically tended to be trivialized or dismissed without a reading or hearing, a subject that has been treated in a witty, polemical, and powerfully sobering work by Dale Spender, *The Writing or the Sex? Or, Why You Don't Have to Read Women's Writing to Know It's No Good* (New York, 1989).

48. P. Champion, "Un 'Liber amicorum' du XVe siècle: Notice d'un manuscrit d'Alain Chartier ayant appartenu à Marie de Clèves, femme de Charles d'Orléans," *Revue des Bibliothèques* 20 (1910): 320–36.

49. [Léon-Emmanuel] le comte de Laborde, *Les Ducs de Bourgogne*, 3 vols., III (Paris, 1852), p. 403, n. 7060.

50. On the poetry albums of Margaret of Austria, see E. Gachet, *Albums poétiques de Marguerite d'Autriche* (Bruxelles, 1849), and M. Françon, *Albums poétiques de Marguerite d'Autriche* (Cambridge, Mass., and Paris, 1934). The names include *demoiselles* Planci, Huclam, Baude, and Vère, whom Françon (p. 55) identifies as ladies-in-waiting. The music-historical importance of Margaret of Austria's court was brought to scholars' attention by M. Picker, ed., *The Chanson Albums of Marguerite of Austria: MSS 228 and 11239 of the Bibliothèque Royale de Belgique, Brussels* (Berkeley, 1965). I wonder, as does Picker, if Margaret might have tried her hand at musical composition.

51. Leeman L. Perkins and Howard Garey, *The Mellon Chansonnier*, 2 vols. (New Haven, 1979), II, p. 74. The remark is attributable to Howard Garey, editor of the chanson texts.

52. W. Calin, *A Poet at the Fountain: Essays on the Narrative Verse of Guillaume de Machaut*, Studies in Romance Languages #9 (Lexington, Ky., 1974), p. 170.

53. Ibid. Calin is summarizing the arguments of G. Hanf, who was the first to attempt to prove that the *Voir-Dit* was entirely a work of fiction. See "Ueber Guillaume de Machauts Voir Dit," *Zeitschrift für romanische Philologie* 22 (1898): 145–96. For an overview of various positions on the "truth or fiction" of Toute Belle, see Calin (1974), pp. 167–72.

54. See Williams (1977), pp. 462–68.

55. See N. Musso, "Comparaison statistique des lettres de Guillaume de Machaut et de Péronne d'Armentière dans le Voir-Dit," *Guillaume de Machaut. Colloque. Table Ronde. Reims, 19–22 avril 1978* (Paris, 1982), pp. 175–93. My thanks to Professor Lawrence Earp for drawing my attention to this article.

56. H. M. Brown, "Women Singers and Women's Songs in Fifteenth-Century Italy," in Bowers and Tick (1986), pp. 67, 83–84, n. 28.

57. Beaucourt (1881–91), IV, p. 189.

58. In fact, all of the texts attributed to women in Paris 9223 and in Paris 15771 are transmitted anonymously in several other poetry anthologies of the period. See note 41 above for these sources.

59. F. Rigolot, "Gender vs. Sex Difference in Louise Labé's Grammar of Love," in Ferguson, Quilligan, and Vickers (1986), p. 298.

60. *Habit le moine ne fait pas*, "Madame d'Orléans," Paris 1104, fol. 94.

61. Poems in a woman's voice make up only 2% of Paris 9223, but about 10% of Roh.

62. D. Munrow, "On the Performance of Late Medieval Music," *Early Music* 1 (1973): 197–98.

63. See especially the documents cited in C. Wright, *Music at the Court of Burgundy, 1364–1419: A Documentary History*, Musicological Studies 28 (Henryville, Pa., 1979), pp. 183–86; Y. Rokseth, "Les Femmes musiciennes du XIIe au XIVe siècle," *Romania* 61 (1935): 464–80; M. V. Coldwell, "Jougleresses and Trobairitz: Secular Musicians in Medieval France," in Bowers and

Tick (1986), pp. 39–61; Brown (1986), pp. 62–89; and C. Page, *Voices and Instruments of the Middle Ages: Instrumental Practice and Songs in France, 1100–1300* (Berkeley and Los Angeles, 1986), pp. 156–59.

64. On publications by women composers in Italy see Bowers (1986), pp. 116–67.

65. Coldwell (1986), pp. 55–56.

66. Brown (1986), pp. 64–65.

67. Ibid., p. 64.

68. A. Yardley, " 'Ful weel she soong the service dyvyne': The Cloistered Musician in the Middle Ages," in Bowers and Tick (1986), pp. 15–38. Still valuable too are the pioneering studies by M. Brenet, "La Musique dans les couvents de femmes depuis le moyen âge à nos jours," *La Tribune de Saint-Gervais* 4 (1898): 25–31, 58–61, 73–81; and Rokseth (1935).

69. Yardley (1986), p. 30.

70. R. Strohm, *Music in Late Medieval Bruges* (Oxford, 1985), pp. 62, 70, 107, 160, nn. 8, 9.

71. Yardley (1986), pp. 26–27.

72. *Anonimi, Notitia del valore delle note del canto misurato,* ed. Armen Carapetyan, Corpus Scriptorum de Musica 5 (n.p., 1957), pp. 13–15, 17–18, 23–26.

73. I am indebted to a member of the staff of the Division Héraldique of the Institut Historique de Recherches de Textes in Paris for pointing this out to me in June 1980.

74. Leeman Perkins made this observation with regard to Beatrice of Aragon, suggesting that she was the terrestrial woman addressed in the two motet texts in the Mellon chansonnier: "The plea for kindness and liberality ostensibly addressed to the virginal Queen of Heaven may actually have been intended for a patron of flesh and blood capable of dispensing more immediately tangible rewards." Perkins and Garey (1979), I, p. 19. One study of women's book ownership worthy of emulating for the history of musical manuscripts is that of S. G. Bell, "Medieval Women Book Owners: Arbiters of Lay Piety and Ambassadors of Culture," in *Women and Power in the Middle Ages,* ed. M. Erler and M. Kowaleski (Athens, Ga., 1988), pp. 149–87.

75. The Tinctoris treatises dedicated to Beatrice of Aragon include *Terminorum musicae diffinitorium,* the first dictionary of musical terms; the *Tractatus de regulari valore notarum,* essentially a notation handbook; and the *Complexus effectuum musices,* a study of the spiritual effects of music. The dedications for the last two can be found in Johannes Tinctoris, *Opera theoretica,* ed. Albert Seay, 2 vols. in 3 (n.p.: American Institute of Musicology, 1975), I:125, II:165–66. The dedication of the *Terminorum* is available in *Dictionary of Musical Terms,* trans. Carl Parrish (Glencoe, Ill., 1963), pp. 2–5.

76. I have recently argued that ladies-in-waiting offer potentially important clues to musical and other creative activity at the courts of medieval and Renaissance female magnates. See Higgins (1991).

77. See especially Coldwell (1986), pp. 39–61. I am thinking in particular of the courts of Eleanor of Aquitaine and of her daughter Marie de Champagne. Examples of musical women at fifteenth-century courts include the woman

named Pacquette, a lady from the household of Isabel of Portugal, duchess of Burgundy, who sang with the two famous blind vielle players at the Burgundian Feast of the Pheasant in 1454. See D. Fallows, "Specific Information on the Ensembles for Composed Polyphony, 1400–1474," in *Studies in the Performance of Late Mediaeval Music*, ed. Stanley Boorman (Cambridge, 1983), p. 139. Similarly, Madame de Beaugrant, the woman who, during the 1468 wedding festivities for Charles the Bold and Margaret of York, sang the chanson *Bien venue la belle bergère* while riding a lion who sang the tenor, was the governess of Charles's daughter Mary of Burgundy. See Strohm (1985), p. 99.

78. See A. Newcomb, "Courtesans, Muses or Musicians? Professional Women Musicians in Sixteenth-Century Italy," in Bowers and Tick (1986), pp. 90–115.

79. Ibid., pp. 93–96.

80. G. Pollock, *Vision and Difference: Femininity, Feminism and the Histories of Art* (London, 1988), p. 42.

81. The composers Baude Cordier, Hayne van Ghizeghem, Robert Morton, and Antoine de Longueval are among the many musicians who served various princes as chamber valets.

82. Williams (1977), p. 462, citing Paris, *Le Livre du Voir-Dit*, p. 4.

83. Unable to keep up with Toute Belle's demands for new music, Machaut sent her an old piece for which he had composed a new tenor and contratenor, but she complained that she had already seen it before and demanded something new. Williams (1977), p. 464, citing Paris, *Le Livre du Voir-Dit*, pp. 242, 250.

84. K. Brownlee, *Poetic Identity in Guillaume de Machaut* (Madison, 1984), p. 239, n. 25.

85. By "feminist" I mean a text in which women are portrayed in a positive light as intelligent, strong willed, gifted, and accomplished, as opposed to negative portrayals of them as stupid, weak, and incompetent. Positive views of women are especially striking within the context of the "viral antifeminism" and its "discourse of misogyny" that according to one leading critic run "like a rich vein throughout the breadth of medieval literature." See R. H. Bloch, "Medieval Misogyny," *Representations* 20 (1987): 1.

86. For a sampling of the extensive literature on the subject, see C. Neuls-Bates, *Women in Music: An Anthology of Source Readings from the Middle Ages to the Present* (New York, 1982), pp. 206–27, 278–302.

87. C. Battersby, *Gender and Genius: Towards a Feminist Aesthetics* (Indianapolis, 1989), p. 151.

88. Ibid., pp. 151–52.

89. Ibid., p. 153.

Notes to Chapter 10

This study is an expansion and revision of the first half of my "Isabella d'Este and Lucrezia Borgia as Patrons of Music: The Frottola at Mantua and Ferrara," which first appeared in the *Journal of the American Musicological Society* 38

(1985): 1–33. I am grateful to the American Musicological Society for permission to republish it here.

1. There were, of course, keyboard players attached to the corps of *bas* instrumentalists as well. A general treatment of music at the north-Italian courts is William F. Prizer, "The North Italian Courts, 1460–1540," in *The Renaissance: From the 1470s to the End of the 16th Century*, ed. Iain Fenlon (Englewood Cliffs, N.J.: Prentice-Hall, 1989), pp. 133–55.

2. Pandolfo's role as a patron of music is surveyed in Allan Atlas, "Pandolfo III Malatesta mecenate musicale: musica e musicisti presso una signoria del primo Quattrocento," *Rivista italiana di musicologia* 23 (1988): 38–92; Ferrara is examined in Lewis Lockwood, *Music in Renaissance Ferrara: The Creation of a Musical Center in the Fifteenth Century* (Cambridge: Harvard University Press, 1984); Prizer, "Music at the Court of the Sforza: The Birth and Death of a Musical Center," *Musica Disciplina* 43 (1989): 141–93, surveys the situation at Milan.

3. Francesco da Barberino, *Del reggimento e costumi di donna*, ed. C. Baudi di Vesne (Bologna: Romagnoli, 1875), pp. 30–31. The role of music and dance in this treatise is examined in Giuseppe Vecchi," Educazione musicale, scuola e società nell'opera didascalica di Francesco da Barberino," *Quadrivium* 7 (1966): 5–29.

4. Barberino (1875), p. 53: "Porrà inprender d'uno mezzo cannone, / O di viuola, o d'altro / Stromento onesto e bello, / E non pur da giullare, / O vuol d'una arpa, ch'è ben da gran donna."

5. Lucrezia's learning to sing a new ballata in three days is documented in Bianca Becherini, "Musica italiana a Firenze nel XV secolo," *Revue belge de musicologie* 8 (1954): 112; and idem, "Antonio Squarcialupi e il Cod. Mediceo-Palatino 87," *Ars Nova italiana del Trecento* 1 (1962): 194 (document 23). The performances of Bianca and Nannina de' Medici are documented in W. F. Prizer, "Games of Venus: Secular Vocal Music in the Late Quattrocento and Early Cinquecento," *Journal of Musicology* 9 (1991): 3–6. A general treatment of women as musicians is Howard M. Brown, "Women Singers and Women's Songs in Fifteenth-Century Italy," in *Women Making Music: The Western Art Tradition, 1150–1950*, ed. Jane Bowers and Judith Tick (Urbana and Chicago: University of Illinois Press, 1986), pp. 62–89.

6. Emilio Motta, "Musicisti alla corte degli Sforza," *Archivio Storico Lombardo*, anno 14 (1887): 59; Guglielmo Barblan, "Vita musicale alla corte sforzesca," in *Storia di Milano*, vol. 9 (Milan: Fondazione Trecani, 1961), p. 814, and Prizer, "Music at the Court of the Sforza" (1989), p. 154n.

7. Motta (1887), p. 59; Luciano Chiappini, *Eleonora d'Aragona, prima duchesssa di Ferrara* (Rovigo: S.T.E.R., 1956), p. 45.

8. Christine de Pisan, *Le Livre des trois vertues*, trans. Charity Cannon Willard as *A Medieval Woman's Mirror of Honor: The Treasury of the City of the Ladies* (Tenafly, N.J.: Bard Hall Press, 1989), pp. 112–28. These rules are discussed in Ruth Kelso, *Doctrine for the Lady of the Renaissance* (Urbana: University of Illinois Press, 1956), pp. 251–54.

9. Ugo Caleffini, *Croniche facte et scripte per Ugo Califfino notaro ferrarexe, commenzando quando Illustrissimo Duca Hercole fu facto Duca et Signore*

de la citade de Ferrara, Vatican Library, MS Chigi I.I.4., fol. 55v, lists Eleonora's court for 1476; the folio is reproduced in Werner Gundersheimer, "Women, Learning, and Power: Eleonora of Aragon and the Court of Ferrara," in *Beyond Their Sex: Learned Women of the European Past,* ed. Patricia H. Labalme (New York and London: New York University Press, 1980), plate 4. Gundersheimer discusses Eleonora's court on pp. 51–52. For the figure of 3.1 *lire marchesane* to the ducat, see note 75 below.

10. Caleffini, *Croniche,* fol. 55v. Lockwood (1984), pp. 319 and 321, lists Nardo in the services of Ercole in 1474 and 1478. Another former musician is also included in Eleonora's court: "Anzolino che fu pifaro," who was the companion of "Jacomo de Zacharia usiero" (gatekeeper). Lockwood, p. 321, includes Anzolino as a gatekeeper ("portonaro") of Ercole in 1478.

11. *Liber continentes testamentum illustrissima Signora Margarita Marchionisque Mantuae, continentes listi eius familie,* fol. 26v. "Laurentio Lavagnolo ducati viginti et libras xiiij per eius provisione—d. 20 l. 14." "Johanni Petro Florentino a viola ducati viginti—d. 20" (ASMN B. 332, fol. 26). Motta (1887), pp. 63–64, discusses Lavagnolo's service in Milan. The following abbreviations are used for archives and sources throughout this essay:

ASMN: Archivio di Stato di Mantova
ASMO: Archivo di Stato di Modena
LASP: Libri d'Amministrazioni dei Singoli Principi (ASMO)
LM: Libro dei Mandati (ASMN)
LD: Libro dei Decreti (ASMN)
L.: Libro
B.: Busta

Unless noted otherwise, all documents from the Archivio di Stato di Mantova come from the Archivio Gonzaga, and all documents from the Archivio di Stato di Modena come from the Archivio Segreto Estense.

12. See the letters concerning her chapel published in Motta (1887), pp. 302–4.

13. Anne's musical establishment is surveyed in Stephen Bonime, "Anne de Bretagne (1477–1514) and Music: An Archival Study" (Ph.D. dissertation, Bryn Mawr, 1975).

14. For what can be said about Beatrice d'Este, see Prizer, "Music at the Court of the Sforza" (1989), pp. 173–74. She sang, played string and keyboard instruments, and may have had at least a *tamborino* and a singer of secular music in her employ. There is at present no study of music at Urbino that would include Elisabetta Gonzaga's patronage.

15. The traditional view of Isabella's education as stated by Alessandro Luzio, *I precettori d'Isabella d'Este,* Nozze Renier-Campostrini (Ancona: Morelli, 1887), has been challenged by Stephen Kolsky, "Images of Isabella d'Este," *Italian Studies* 39 (1984): 47–62.

16. For a recent interpretation of Isabella and her abilities, see Kolsky (1984) as well as Maria Bellonci, "Isabella d'Este a cinquecento anni dalla sua nascita," in *Mantova e i Gonzaga nella civiltà del Rinascimento* (Verona: Mondadori, 1977), pp. 47–56. On Isabella as an administrator, see also A. Luzio, "La reg-

genza d'Isabella d'Este durante la prigionia del marito (1509–1510)," *Archivio storico lombardo*, anno 37 (1910): 5–104.

17. The most reliable and impartial history of the Borgia family is that by Michael Mallett, *The Borgias: The Rise and Fall of a Renaissance Dynasty* (Frogmore: Paladin, 1971).

18. Ferdinand Gregorovius, *Lucrezia Borgia* (Stuttgart, 1874; English trans., London: Phaidon, 1948).

19. Maria Bellonci, *Lucrezia Borgia: La sua vita e i suoi tempi* (Milan, 1939). Throughout this study I use the expanded eleventh edition (Milan: Mondadori, 1967), which includes an appendix of documents from various archives.

20. On this point see Mallett (1971), pp. 137–38.

21. "Et al principio de la cena li cantori cantorno psalmi in voce bassa . . . poi fo sonati liuti, violoni et cornetti." Letter of 2 April 1513 (ASMN B. 1245).

22. On Isabella as a poet, see Luzio (1887), pp. 51–68, and Claudio Gallico, "Poesie musicali di Isabella d'Este," *Collectanea historiae musicae* 3 (1963): 109–19.

23. On the relationship between Bembo and Lucrezia Borgia see Bellonci (1967) and Bernardo Morsolin, "Pietro Bembo e Lucrezia Borgia," *Nuova Antologia* 15 (1885): 388–422.

24. Bembo is indulging in the humanist penchant for referring to modern instruments by obsolete, classical equivalents. In this case *naulia* (*nablium, nablum*) refers to the nabla, an ancient string instrument played with both hands, called by Greek writers "the Phoenician harp." See Sybil Marcuse, *A Survey of Musical Instruments* (New York: Harper and Row, 1975), p. 385, and Charleton T. Lewis and Charles Short, *A Latin Dictionary* (Oxford: Clarendon Press, 1879), s.v. "nablium."

25. *Forte* may be either an adverb, as I have translated it here, or an adjective modifying *arce*. If the latter were selected, then *castle* should be rendered as stronghold. I am grateful to my colleague Alejandro Enrique Planchart for having offered several improvements to my translation of this passage.

26. "Sive refers lingua modulatum carmen Hetrusca / Crederis Hestrusco nata puella solo. / Seu calamo condis numeros & carmina sumto, / Illa novem possunt scripta decere Deas. / Naulia seu, citharamve manu percurrere eburna, / Et varia Ogygios arte ciere modos: / Seu revocare Padi vicinas cantibus undas, / Mulcentem dulci flumina capta sono: / Seu te nexilibus juvat indulgere choreis, / Et facili ad numerum subsiluisse pede: / Quam timeo, ne quis spectans haec forte Deorum, / Te praedam media raptor ab arce petat, / Sublimemque ferat levibus super aethera pennis, / Detque novi caelo sideris esse Deam." *Le rime di messer Pietro Bembo cardinale, colla giunta delle sue poesie latine, e la vita dell'autore descritta da Tommaso Porcacchi* (Verona: Giuseppe Berno, 1750), p. 288. These are internal lines of Bembo's verse. The poem itself, entitled "Ad Lucretiam Borgiam," begins on p. 287.

27. See Bellonci (1967), pp. 252–70. For the music and plays accompanying the celebrations, see Nino Pirrotta, *Music and Theatre from Poliziano to Monteverdi*, trans. Karen Eales (Cambridge: Cambridge University Press, 1982), pp. 51–55.

28. Letter of de' Prosperi to Isabella, 22 January 1502 (ASMN B. 1238, fol. 252). According to this letter, the frugal Ercole was using the same arches he had used during Alfonso's first wedding, in 1491 to Anna Sforza.

29. "Nanti cena, venero li cantori del Illustrissimo Signore Duca, quale cantorono alcune cose bone." Letter of 28 January 1502 from the marchesa of Cotrone [Crotone] to Francesco Gonzaga from Ferrara (ASMN B. 1238, fol. 352).

30. For a detailed discussion of this rivalry, see Bellonci (1967), and Alessandro Luzio, *Isabella d'Este e i Borgia* (Milan: Cogliati, 1916).

31. Il Prete writes on 12 October 1501 and promises to inform Isabella concerning Lucrezia's habits (ASMN B. 1237). In a letter of 19 January 1502, written during the wedding party's journey to Ferrara, Il Prete writes that Lucrezia is a "donna di gran cervello, astuta, bisogna aver la mente a casa" (ASMN B. 855, fol. 23). Nor was Il Prete Isabella's only informant. De' Prosperi in Ferrara copied letters sent to Alfonso d'Este from Rome by Adornino Feruffino and sent them to Isabella. These are valuable descriptions of the Roman proxy wedding of Lucrezia and Alfonso, during which there were mock battles in the streets accompanied by "mille trombe e altri instrumenti," a comedy "in vulgare" in the rooms of the pope, and a parade with floats, on one of which was a Hercules who played a "corno" (ASMN B. 1238, fols. 242–43). Feruffino's letters are partially published in Michele Catalano, *Lucrezia Borgia, Duchessa di Ferrara* (Ferrara: Taddei, 1920), pp. 47–51.

32. "Il se intende anche lei havere de gran zoglie et digne et essere in ordine da regina. Che anche questo vederemo, piacendo a Dio. La Signoria Vostra adoperi mò lo inzegno suo acciò la dimonstri de chi fo figliola, et se la non haverà tante, tante zoglie, che le sue non comparano manco ben poste de quelle de l'altri" (ASMN B. 1237).

33. Letter of Giovanni Lucido Catenei to Francesco Gonzaga, 13 August 1503 (ASMN B. 855, fol. 358).

34. "Dico ben che la sposa non è troppo bella, ma una dolce cera. . . . Portavimo il palio a casa di beleze di Madama mia et di consorte suo" (ASMN, Collezione Volta, B. 1, No. 91).

35. "Son più che certa che lei habi recevuto magiore piacere de le lettere mie ch'io non ho de queste feste, perché non stetti mai in loco alcuno cum magiore fastidio di quello ho facto qui" (ASMN, B. 2115 [*lettere originali*] and B. 2993, L. 13, fols. 42r–v [*copialettere*]).

36. "Per fin qua, questa sposa non s'è tropo desmesticha con Madonna nostra; non ano manzar ancora inseme" (ASMN B. 1238, fol. 392).

37. Although the correspondence from Isabella's agents mentions Lucrezia's skills at the dance, they make no mention of her musical talents. On the other hand, given the widespread inclusion of music in the noblewoman's education, Isabella must have assumed that Lucrezia had at least the rudiments of singing and lute playing.

38. "Lorenzo. . . . Mandiamovi li nostri dui liutti fra quali è quello de hebano che sonno schiappati et getati nel fondo como vedereti. Pregamovi che li vogliati conciare subito et poi portarli cum vui se venireti a Ferrara a queste noze, et non, li mandareti per persone fidate" (ASMN B. 2993, L. 13, fol. 23v);

published in Clifford M. Brown and Anna Maria Lorenzoni, *Isabella d'Este and Lorenzo da Pavia: Documents for the History of Art and Culture in Renaissance Mantua,* Travaux d'Humanisme et Renaissance 189 (Geneva: Librarie Droz, 1982), p. 61.

39. "La Signora Marchesana, vostra consorte, acompagnata di parechie zentildone, andò a la casa del Masaro di Gabella per vedere passare la sposa. [Era] vestita di una bella camora richamata di quella inventione di tempi et pause." Letter of 2 February 1502 (ASMN B. 1283, fols. 355–56).

40. "Madona marchesana, vestita de una camora, recamata a pause di musica." Sanuto, *I diarii* 4, ed. F. Stefani et al. (Venice, 1879–1903; rpt. Bologna: Forni, 1969), col. 224. On Isabella's musical device, see Peter Hirschfeld, *Mäzene: Die Rolle des Auftraggebers in der Kunst,* Kunstwissenschaftliche Studien 40 (Munich: Deutscher Kunstverlag, 1968), pp. 123–26; Volker Scherliess, *Musikalische Noten auf Kunstwerken der italienischen Renaissance,* Hamburger Beiträge zur Musikwissenschaft 8 (Hamburg: Verlag der Musikalienhandlung, 1972), pp. 53–56; idem, "Notizien zur Musikalischen Ikonographie (II): Die Musik-Impresa der Isabella d'Este," *Analecta Musicolgica* 15 (1975): 21–28; Lauriane Fallay-d'Este, "Un Symbole Néo-Platonicien: La devise du silence au Studiolo d'Isabelle d'Este," in *Symboles de la Renaissance* (Paris: Presses de l'École Normale Supérieure, 1976), pp. 79–86; and Ivy Mumford, "Some Decorative Aspects of the Imprese of Isabella d'Este," *Italian Studies* 34 (1979): 60–70.

41. Letter from Alessandro Baesio to Francesco Gonzaga, 6 February 1502 (ASMN B. 1238, fol. 392).

42. "Dopo cena facessimo il ballo dil capello. Finito che'l fu, per tante preghe et croci mi furono facte, fui necessitata fare li mei atti nel cantare in lo lauto." Letter of 7 February 1502 (ASMN, B. 2993, L. 13, fols. 38v–39v). On the necessity for women to adopt a posture that hid their accomplishments, see Joan Ferrante, "Public Postures and Private Maneuvers: Roles Medieval Women Play," in *Women and Power in the Middle Ages,* ed. Mary Elder and Maryanne Kowaleski (Athens: University of Georgia Press, 1988), pp. 213–29. I am grateful to Professor Paula Higgins for having called my attention to this essay.

43. "Dopo cena, la Excellentia de Madama Marchesana, a preghi di questi Signori, Cantò dui soneti e uno capitolo, de che questi Signori forono tanto contenti che più non se potria dire." Letter of 6 February 1502 to Francesco Gonzaga in Mantua (ASMN B. 1238, fols. 359–60).

44. "La continentia et tenore de dicta lettera è che reprende tucti vitii et mancamenti delle donde [donne] lombarde in le noze de Ferrara et dice, fra le altre, della Signora Marchesana, che non era ben conza, che magnava nella festa et multe altre cose, che voleva parere pucto. . . . La Marchesana è in su le furie." Letter of 5 May 1502 (ASMN B. 283). The word *magnava* in this document is difficult to interpret. In Mantuan dialect it means literally *mangiava*. I have given it here a broader interpretation. On Equicola and his service to noblewomen, see Stephen Kolsky, " 'The Good Servant': Mario Equicola. Court and Courtier in the Early Sixteenth Century," *The Italianist* 6 (1986): 34–60; and idem, *Mario Equicola, The Real Courtier,* Travaux d'Humanisme et Renaissance 246 (Geneva: Droz, 1991).

45. "La mia illustrissima Madama hoggi si ha preso gran spasso de la Duchessa di Ferrara, qual per mostrare al marito di esser ben fidel e casta si fa dormire Petro Zorzo da Lampugnano in l'anticamera" (ASMN B. 2475).

46. The eight documents quoted here at length are in an appendix at the end of this essay. Document 1 of the appendix is a transcription of this letter. For Tromboncino as Isabella's personal musician, see the text at note 88 below.

47. Lucrezia's payment registers are extant in ASMO for the years 1506–1508 and 1517–1520, the year after her death.

48. Document 2 in the appendix is a transcription of selected entries from the list of the members of Lucrezia's court for 1506. In order to give an idea of the size of her staff, I have numbered these entries in the order in which they are listed in the full document. The musicians, marked with an asterisk, are Nos. 9, 13, 16, 17, and 66.

49. Isabella requested Ricciardetto from Ippolito d'Este, his employer at the time, on 5 October 1501, saying that "Se la Signoria [Vostra] non me serve de Rizardetto per qualche dì, dubito che remanerò vergognata in questa festa, per haverne scordato tutti li balli francesi, tanto tempo è che non li ho exercitati" (ASMO, Estero, Carteggio di Principe e Signorie, Italia, B. 1196 [Mantova, B. 16]). On Poccino in Mantuan service, see the text at note 67 below.

50. A "Lista de la compagnia de la Illustrissima Signora Madonna Lucretia Estense de Borgia, Duchessa, per lo viagio" from Rome to Ferrara in January 1502 is included in ASMO Casa e Stato, B. 400, fasc. 2051.II.7. On p. 5 of this list is "Nicolò musicho cum uno compagno." Lucrezia also brought Spanish singers with her to Ferrara, although they apparently left in 1502. See W. F. Prizer, "Isabella d'Este and Lucrezia Borgia as Patrons of Music: The Frottola at Mantua and Ferrara, *Journal of the American Musicological Society* 38 (1985): 22–23, on these singers and Lucrezia's Spanish customs.

51. ASMO Archivio per materia, "Musica e musicisti," B. 2. Published in L. Lockwood, "Musicisti a Ferrara all'epoca dell'Ariosto," in *L'Ariosto: La musica, i musicisti*, Quaderni della Rivista italiana di musicologia 5 (1981): 26–29.

52. The list of Lucrezia's employees for 1507 is included in ASMO LASP No. 1131, fols. 84v–86v; those for 1508, in L. 1135, fols. 20–21v.

53. "Madonna Dalida de cantore comenzò a dì primo de settembre per tuto dito ano" (ASMO LASP L. 1131, fol. 86v). Although the documentation is not strong, professional women singers seem to have been a fairly normal part of the court scene in northern Italy. The court of Mantua, for example, employed at least two: Giovanna Moreschi, wife of the frottolist Marchetto Cara, and Paola Poccino, perhaps the wife or sister of Paolo Poccino. See W. F. Prizer, *Courtly Pastimes: The Frottole of Marchetto Cara*, Studies in Musicology 33 (Ann Arbor: UMI Press, 1980), pp. 14, 15, 42–43, as well as Howard M. Brown (1986), p. 69.

54. ASMO LASP L. 1132. fol. 8v and passim (for 1517), and L. 1136bis, fol. 16v, etc. (for 1519).

55. On the financial problems caused by this crisis, see Luciano Chiappini, *Gli Estensi*, 2d ed. (Varese: Dall'Oglio, 1967), pp. 222–33. On the transfer of musicians from Ferrara to Mantua, see W. F. Prizer, "La Cappella di Francesco II Gonzaga e la musica sacra a Mantova nel primo ventennio del Cinquecento,"

in *Mantova e i Gonzaga* (1977), pp. 267–76; and idem, *Courtly Pastimes* (1980), pp. 14–28.

56. ASMN Autografi, B. 3, fol. 9.

57. ASMN B. 2919, L. 220, fol. 73.

58. ASMO LASP No. 783, fol. 33. Poccino, too, seems to have disappeared around this time: the last notice I find of him in Ferrara is in a letter of 28 September 1509, in which Lucrezia informs Isabella that "Pocino, mio servitore," is coming to Mantua (ASMN Autografi B. 2, fol. 137).

59. ASMO LASP No. 782, fol. 99v (14 November 1511). At the standard exchange rate of 20 *soldi* to the *lira*, Tromboncino's salary with Ippolito was 38 *lire*, 15 *soldi* per month. He received L. 116, S. 5 in November 1511; L. 77, S. 10 in February 1512; and L. 38, S. 15 in April, May, and June.

60. ASMO LASP No. 783, fol. 161v (16 June 1512).

61. Mandate of 10 January 1513 (ASMN LM No. 12, fol. 132).

62. For Tromboncino's monthly salary with Lucrezia, see the appendix, Document 2, No. 16.

63. Letter of Giacomo de' Tebaldi to Lucrezia of 19 July 1518 (ASMO, Estero, Ambasciatori, B. 14); published in Prizer (1991), pp. 7–8. I am grateful to Professor Richard Agee for calling this document to my attention.

64. See Document 2 in the appendix for a transcription of these salaries. Dalida de' Putti's salary is given in ASMO LASP No. 1135, fol. 21: "Madonna Dalida di Puti per havere servito tutto lo anno presente in ragione de L. 8 dato il mese—L. 96." Christopher Reynolds, "Musical Careers, Ecclesiastical Benefices, and the Example of Johannes Brunet," *Journal of the American Musicological Society* 37 (1984): 49–97, has offered a salutary warning against equating a musician's salary with his status and total earnings. Although Reynolds is undoubtedly correct in general, this does not seem to be a danger in studying Lucrezia's court. As mentioned above, Niccolò da Padova, who received L. 96 per year, possessed a benefice in 1511. Dalida de' Putti, who received the same amount, was clearly not eligible for benefices, since she was a woman. Conversely, Tebaldeo, Lucrezia's highest-paid servant, was a priest and was therefore eligible for them. It seems that, in this case at least, we may take the salaries paid to retainers as relatively accurate indicators of their status and financial position. I am grateful to Professor Reynolds for having provided me a copy of his study in advance of its publication.

65. On the contents of Petrucci's tenth book of frottole, see Knud Jeppesen, *La Frottola* 1 (Aarhus: Munksgaard, 1968), p. 32.

66. See W. F. Prizer, "Lutenists at the Court of Mantua in the Late Fifteenth and Early Sixteenth Centuries," *Journal of the Lute Society of America* 13 (1980): 7, for a translation of this epitaph.

67. B. 1891, fol. 182 (correspondence with Isabella). There is no date on the letter itself, but the eighteenth-century archivist has written on a folder containing it and other letters, "senza date ma trovate fra le lettere del 1505."

68. See H. Colin Slim, "Musicians on Parnassus," *Studies in the Renaissance* 12 (1965): 149. Two other women singers are also mentioned there: "Marietta" (perhaps Marietta Faliera) and "Lauretta" (perhaps Laura Birago). The singers are identified in ibid., p. 159.

69. "Dalida poi, quale era vestita cum l'altri da pastore, cominciò a cantare cum tri suoi compagni, fra li quali era Trombroncino." Letter of 14 February 1508; ASMN B. 1242, fols. 124–25v. The letter is published in its entirety in Luzio and Rodolfo Renier, *Mantova e Urbino: Isabella d'Este ed Elisabetta Gonzaga* (Turin, 1893; rpt. Bologna: Forni, 1976), pp. 317–19. The unnamed musicians must have included two of her other singers.

70. De' Prosperi writes Isabella on 6 March 1502, saying that Lucrezia wants a court of around 118 to 120 people (ASMN B. 1238, fol. 260). Il Prete informs her on 6 June of the same year that Lucrezia wants a budget of at least 12,000 ducats (ibid., fols. 301–2). De' Prosperi, on 8 July, writes her that Alexander VI is demanding the same figure (ibid., fol. 280).

71. Letter of de' Prosperi to Isabella, 10 January 1503 (ASMN B. 1239, fol. 193).

72. This figure of 66 retainers does not include the Roman and Ferrarese gentlewomen who were Lucrezia's *donzelle*.

73. See Document 1 in the appendix.

74. We are hampered in our search for settings of Tebaldeo's poetry by his preference for not allowing his verses to circulate. On 10 January 1491, for example, he writes to Isabella refusing her copies of his poetry, saying, "I do not give any of my [poems] out because I want to change and improve them from day to day, and, if some were out, my [poems] would be stolen by some of my companions." (Non do cosa alcuna de le mie fuori perché de giorno in giorno vo' mutandole et emendandole et se ne sono alcune andate fuori, le mie sono state robate da qualche mio compagno [ASMN B. 1232, fol. 188]). His cousin, Iacopo Tebaldeo, published his poems with his knowledge in 1498 (*Opere di m. Antonio Thebaldeo da Ferrara* [Modena: Domenico Rocociolo]); the book was dedicated to Isabella d'Este. On Tebaldeo in general see Antonio Rossi, *Serafino Aquilano e la poesia cortigina* (Brescia: Morcelliana, 1980), pp. 106–13, as well as Luigi Coddé, *Notizie biografiche di Antonio Tebaldeo* (Rovigo: Minelli, 1845), and Luzio and Renier, "La coltura e le relazioni letterarie di Isabella d'Este Gonzaga," *Giornale storico della letteratura italiana* 35 (1900): 193–211. Tebaldeo is included in Lucrezia's pay records through December 1507 (ASMO LASP No. 1131, fol. 84v). He may have left her court at this time, for he does not appear again in her registers. On the other hand, de' Prosperi reports on 6 February 1508 that Tebaldeo has written an eclogue glorifying Alfonso and Lucrezia for performance during carnival (ASMN B. 1242, fol. 122), and Equicola reports on 11 August of the same year that Tebaldeo wants to leave Ferrara because of general fears aroused by the assassination of Ercole Strozzi (ibid., fol. 3). On Strozzi's death, see Bellonci (1967), pp. 403–8.

75. See the appendix, Document 2, No. 4. Tromboncino's annual salary of 465 lire was equal, according to the 1508 pay registers, to 150 ducats. There were therefore 3.1 *lire marchesane* per ducat, and Tebaldeo's salary of 620 lire equaled 200 ducats. For Josquin's salary, see Lewis Lockwood, "Josquin at Ferrara: New Documents and Letters," in *Josquin des Prez: Proceedings of the International Josquin Festival-Conference*, ed. Edward E. Lowinsky and Bonnie J. Blackburn (London: Oxford University Press, 1976), pp. 103–37.

76. See the appendix, Document 2, Nos. 23, 40, 48, 3, and 53. Michele Costa,

son of Giovanni Battista Costa and a member of the family of artists whose best-known member was Lorenzo Costa, worked for Lucrezia from 1505 to 1507, when he decorated her rooms in the *castello* in Ferrara. See Ulrich Thieme and Felix Becker, *Allgemeines Lexikon der bildenden Kunstler von der Antike bis zur Gegenwart* 7 (Leipzig: Engelmann, 1912), pp. 531–32, and Giuseppe Campori, *Artisti degli Estensi: I pittori* (Modena, 1875; rpt. Bologna: Forni, 1980), p. 55. Michele had returned to Lucrezia's services by 1517, when he is listed as her "exbursar" (ASMO LASP No. 1132, fol. 2).

77. For loud instruments associated with battle, see W. F. Prizer, "Bernardino Piffaro e i pifferi e tromboni di Mantova: strumenti a fiato in una corte italiana," *Rivista italiana di musicologia* 16 (1981): 151–84. For the belief that women should not be associated with loud instruments, see idem, "Isabella d'Este and Lorenzo da Pavia, 'Master Instrument Maker,'" *Early Music History* 2 (1982): 112–16.

78. On the cost of the musical chapel, see Prizer, "North Italian Courts" (1989), pp. 135–36.

79. "10 marzo 1506. Speza la Illustrissima Domina nostra per d'oro in oro . . . dati a Nichola Piva con trj compagnj pivj per havere sona in questo carneval in sala a la festa che ge dona Sua Signoria" (ASMO LASP No. 1130, fol. 14v).

80. "A Vizenzo Tanborino del Gardenal nostro ducati cinque. . . . A li tronbeti e pifari del Ducha nostro, ducati quatordexe d'oro." At the same time Lucrezia gave gifts to her own musicians, to "Tromboncino cantore e li soi compagnj," to "Rizardetto Tanborino," and to the musicians of others: "cinque sonadori del Gardenal nostro," and to "li tronbeti del Papa [Julius II], zoè Mascharelo e compagni" (ASMO LASP No. 1130, fol. 96).

81. Appendix, Document 3.

82. That is, Isabella's *donzelle*, whose equivalent were not included in Lucrezia's list.

83. Appendix, Document 4.

84. See above for the details of Lucrezia's budget.

85. Appendix, Document 5.

86. Letter of 27 July 1490 (ASMN B. 2904, fol. 47).

87. For further biographical detail on Tromboncino and Cara, see Prizer, *Courtly Pastimes* (1980), pp. 35–61. On Cara see also idem, "Marchetto Cara at Mantua: New Documents on the Life and Duties of a Renaissance Court Musician," *Musica Disciplina* 32 (1978): 87–110. The point that Tromboncino was Isabella's musician and that Cara was Francesco's is made in neither study, however.

88. There are three such documents for Tromboncino: 21 July 1497, 30 March 1501, and 23 or 24 January 1502 (ASMN LD No. 30, fol. 10; LM No. 1, fol. 57v; and LM No. 2, fol. 83v).

89. During the years in which Tromboncino was probably in Mantua, 1489 to 1504, there are seven such decrees and mandates from Francesco for Cara. These are published in Prizer, *Courtly Pastimes* (1980), Documents 6–10, 12, and 19.

90. Letter of 21 July 1499 (ASMN B. 2113 [Lettere originali dei Gonzaga] and B. 2993, L. 10, fol. 34v [Copialettere]); published in Jeppesen (1968), p. 146,

where through a typographical error the date is given as 1599. Also published in Francesco Luisi, *La musica vocale del Rinascimento* (Turin: Edizioni Radiotelivisione Italiana, 1977), p. 71. An English translation of the letter is included in Prizer, *Courtly Pastimes* (1980), p. 57.

91. See Prizer, *Courtly Pastimes* (1980), pp. 56–60, for a selection of these letters.

92. Appendix, Document 6.

93. ASMN B. 2992, L. 5, fol. 72. Published in Prizer, *Courtly Pastimes* (1980), Document 3.

94. Giulio's letter is found in ASMN B. 1187 and is published in Prizer, *Courtly Pastimes* (1980), Document 7. That of Isabella is in B. 2993, L. 10, fol. 15v, and is partially published in Prizer, *Courtly Pastimes* (1980), pp. 187–88.

95. Appendix, Document 7.

96. Without court pay registers, it is impossible to give a full list of Isabella's musicians. It is possible, however, to give an indication of the kinds of musicians she employed.

97. Appendix, Document 8.

98. On Charles, see Stefano Davari, "La musica a Mantova," *Rivista storica mantovana* 1 (1885): 63–67, and Prizer, *Courtly Pastimes* (1980), pp. 6–12.

99. Antonia del Balzo, Marchesa of Bozzolo, writes to Isabella on 23 June 1501, suggesting that the latter raise Testagrossa's salary by a ducat a month (ASMN B. 1801). For further information on Testagrossa and Isabella, see Davari (1885), pp. 67–71, and Prizer, "Lutenists at the Court of Mantua" (1980), pp. 5–34.

100. On 21 August 1490 Isabella sent a son of "Alessandro dal Organo, mio familiare," to study singing and organ in Ferrara (ASMN B. 2904, L. 136, fol. 51). Alessandro died by 1506 and was replaced in Isabella's court by another Alessandro (letter of 16 June 1510, ASMN B. 1065), probably the "Alessandro Mantovano" who contributed fourteen works to Antico's third book of frottole (RISM 1513[1]). On 20 May 1496, Niccolò da Correggio writes Isabella and gives the "Tamburino de la Signoria Vostra" permission to sell land that Niccolò had given him (ASMN B. 1313).

101. On Isabella as a player of keyboard instruments, see Prizer (1982), pp. 92–94.

102. There are many documents that indicate Isabella did not speak French; see, for example, the letter from Luigi Gonzaga to the Marchese Federico Gonzaga of 12 November 1528, in which the meeting of Isabella and Renée of France is described; Luigi reports that Isabella accompanied Renée without speaking because neither knew the other's language: "non sapendosi intertenire l'una l'altra per la diversità de le lingue" (ASMN B. 1292).

103. For Isabella as a player of string instruments, see Prizer (1982), pp. 103–8; on her disdain for wind instruments, see ibid., pp. 112–16.

104. Punctuation, capitalization, and diacritical marks have been added and abbreviations realized by the author, both in the appendix and throughout this essay. For the meaning of the sigla used for archives and sources, see note 11 above. The asterisks in Document 2 denote musicians. I should like to thank Dottoressa Adele Bellù, former Director of the Archivio di Stato of Mantua,

and Dottor Angelo Spaggiari, Director of the Archivio di Stato of Modena, for their kind aid in my research in their archives. I should also like to thank Signorina Anna Maria Lorenzoni of the Archivio di Stato of Mantua, who checked my transcriptions of the documents in this appendix.

105. Page torn. The entire letter is water-stained and torn, making it difficult to be sure of the exact transcription of several words.

Notes to Chapter 11

The research for this essay was completed with the help of a National Endowment for the Humanities Fellowship for Independent Scholars in 1990–91. It originally appeared in slightly different form in *Musical Quarterly* 77, no. 3. I would like to acknowledge the heroic research help of Dr. Sergio Nerli of the Archivio di Stato in Lucca and Dr. Antonio Corsaro at the Casa Buonarotti in Florence. An earlier version was presented at the Fifth Biennial Conference on Baroque Music at the University of Durham, U.K., July 1992; I should like to thank Tim Carter, Carolyn Gianturco, Colleen Reardon, and Michael Tilmouth for their helpful comments on that draft. Finally, I should like to thank Bridget Kelly Black and Margaret McFadden for invaluable contributions to the conception and completion of this essay.

1. Alessandro Ademollo, *La bell'Adriana ed altre virtuose del suo tempo alla corte di Mantova* (Citta di Castello, 1888), p. 151. The entire footnote reads as follows: "Un *ricordo* contemporaneo dice di lei: '—Nel 1626 li morì il marito; si rimaritò in un lucchese, lasciando il servizio di queste Altezze (Toscana) et morì di cancro in bocca. Eccellente nel cantare, sonare e comporre.'"

2. Maria G. Masera, "Una musicista fiorentina del seicento, Francesca Caccini," *Rassegna musicale* 5 (1941): 195–207; 6 (1941): 237–44; and 7 (1942): 249–66.

3. Doris Silbert, "Francesca Caccini, called La Cecchina," *Musical Quarterly* 32 (1946): 50–62.

4. Carolyn Raney, "Francesca Caccini, Musician to the Medici, and her *Primo Libro* (1618)" (Ph.D. diss., New York University, 1971).

5. Jane Bowers, "The Emergence of Women Composers in Italy, 1566–1700," in *Women Making Music: The Western Art Tradition, 1150–1950*, ed. Jane Bowers and Judith Tick (Urbana: University of Illinois Press, 1986), p. 124.

6. Tim Carter, *Jacopo Peri, 1561–1633: His Life and Works* (New York and London: Garland, 1989), p. 99, n. 75. Carter's source for the 1627 payroll information was I-Fas, Depositeria Generale 1523, fol. 91; for Caccini's 1635 return, he cites a letter from Medici secretary Ugo Cacciotti to Michelangelo Buonarotti the younger, I-Fl, Buonarotti 44, n.o 460.

7. Caccini's first known stage work was the *torneo* (musically accompanied joust) *La Stiava*, to words of Michelangelo Buonarotti the younger, performed at Pisa for the Medici princes during carnival 1607. See Carter (1989), p. 53, n. 21.

8. Sandra Harding, *Whose Science? Whose Knowledge? Thinking from Women's Lives* (Ithaca: Cornell University Press, 1991).

9. Ademollo (1888), p. 142. "Nel complesso, Vittoria Archilei mi fa l'effetto di una *virtuosa* di buona pasta e molto tranquilla, che viveva contenta e lasciava

gli altri vivere in pace. Tutto l'opposto cioè della *fiera ed irrequieta* Francesca Caccini, altra cantatrice in quel tempo addetta alla corte di Toscana."

10. Ibid., p. 146. Ferdinando Saracinelli was *Balì* (bailiff) in charge of musical and theatrical events at the Medici court until his death in 163?. An experienced if mediocre creator of poetry-for-music, he had collaborated with Caccini at least once before, contributing the libretto for the *balletto* of 1615 *Il ballo delle zigane.* While there is considerable documentary evidence that Caccini and Salvadori were at odds during the preparations for the 1625 season, in which *La Liberazione* was produced, there is no evidence that he was ever charged with writing the libretto for the latter work. On *La Liberazione*, see my "Of Women, Music, and Power; A Model from *Seicento* Florence" in *Musicology and Difference*, ed. Ruth Solie (Berkeley: University of California Press, 1993). On the 1625 season, see Kelly Harness, "Amazon of God: The Musical Patronage of Archduchess Maria Maddalena in Florence, 1621–28" (Ph.D. diss., University of Illinois, in progress).

11. Ademollo (1888), p. 162. ". . . cioè quarant'anni più tardi del tempo in cui quel melodramma servì così bene al desiderio di vendetta della *fiera ed irrequieta* Cecchina" (italics original). Caccini's nickname at court had been "La Cecchina" (the songbird).

12. I-Fr, Codex 2270, fol. 288–89v.

13. I-Fn, MS II.102–6. Caccini and Signorini are in MS II.105, fol. 83v and 84r.

14. Florence, Opera di S. Maria dei Fiori, *Battesimi Femmine* 1587–88.

15. Florence, Archivio Arcivescovile. Parocchia S. Maria Novella. Registri di Morti dal 1556 al 1668.

16. I-Fas, Notarile Moderno. 13734–37, fol. 31r–34r, Testamento del 23.xii.1626—G. B. Signorini.

17. According to the cross-referenced deed, I-Fas, Notarile Moderno. 10609–10622 [Niccolo Minacci], fol. 62r–64r, on 17 April 1610 Signorini paid 1455 lire for property bounded by the via Valfonda, by property belonging to the monks at S. Maria Novella, by property of Lorenzo Cavalcanti, and by property of Raffaello di Stefano. The previous owner was Benedetto (di Francesco) Landi.

18. See Nino Tamassia, *La famiglia italiana nei secoli decimoquinto e decimosesto* (Milan: Remo Sandron, 1910), and Christiane Klapisch-Zuber, *Women, Family, and Ritual in Renaissance Italy* (Chicago: University of Chicago Press, 1985), for descriptions of dowry practices in early modern Italy.

19. Florence, Opera di S. Maria dei Fiori, *Battesimi Femmine*, 1621–22.

20. I-Fl, Buonarotti 44, n.o 455, 456. Caccini's letters to Buonarotti from 1614 to 1626 have been transcribed and reprinted by M. G. Masera in "Alcune lettere inedite di Francesca Caccini," *Rassegna musicale* 4 (1940): 173–82, and M. G. Masera, *Michelangelo Buonarotti il giovane* (Turin, 1941), Appendix I. Unfortunately, Masera's transcriptions contain a number of errors in dates and text.

21. These letters are preserved in I-Fl, Archivio Buonarotti 52, n.o 1543–47.

22. I-Fas, Mediceo del Principato 2828, inserto 1, letter of 23 July 1627: "La tardanza che o fatto a scriverli e state perché desideravo di poterli dire qualche cose sustanziale della S.a Ciechina la quale è come maritata nel S.re Tomaso

raffaelli zio paterno del S.r Cav. Raffaelli che solo è di età 56 in cirche vive d'entrate musico piu che cag.le A una villa regalata che si domanda a monte S. quilici lontano un miglio dalla citta in luogo che vi sono molte bellissime ville di gentiluomini e vi sta in grandissime conversazione e per quello si sente in breve settimane ne doverra seguire lo sposalizio."

23. I-Fas, Mediceo del Principato 2828, inserto 1, letter of 13 August 1627: "le sirene si crede di certo che a settembre prossimo di doverr.o Congiungere insieme e perché il Gentiluomo è suggetto in quella professione stimata assai . . . Lucca si convertire in nuovo parnaso."

24. I-Fas, Mediceo del Principato 2828, inserto 1, letter of 15 September 1627: "Lamicho che mi tiene avisato delli affari della S.ra Francesca mi a detto che la mandato molte robe in Casa del S.r sposo e che non passare questo mese che si faranno le nozze che lo credo senza dubbio alcuneo perche avendo visto questo giorno lo sposo che me parso un Ganimede se bene assai grisigo ma però molto attillato e grazioso."

25. On the common use of the Ganymede image as code for an effeminate homosexual man, see James M. Saslow, "Homosexuality in the Renaissance: Behavior, Identity, and Artistic Expression," in *Hidden from History: Reclaiming the Gay and Lesbian Past*, ed. Martin Duberman, Martha Vicinus, and George Chauncy, Jr. (New York: Meridian, 1990), p. 99.

26. The location of Raffaelli's holdings is drawn from the contracts Caccini, acting as his widow-executrix, made with *fattori* in these areas. The contracts are preserved in I-Las, Notari 2492, fol. 183r–207v, and 250r.

27. Bernardino Baroni, *Alberi di Famiglie* (I-Las, Bibl. MSS 22), vol. 3, p. 109, and B. Baroni, *Famiglie Lucchesi* (I-Las, Bibl. MSS 127), vol. IV, p. 136.

28. I-Las, Anziani al tempo della libertà 420, p. 52.

29. Baroni, *Famiglie Lucchesi* IV, p. 136.

30. The identity of Raffaelli's nearest neighbors is established in the aforementioned contracts Caccini made in June 1630. See note 26 above. For their social status in Lucchese society and commerce, see Rita Mazzei, *La Società Lucchese del Seicento* (Lucca: Maria Pacini Fazzi, 1977).

31. Baroni, *Famiglie Lucchesi* IV, p. 136.

32. This according to Raffaelli's will, the last codicil to which is dated 13 April 1630. The will is in I-Las, Notari 188, fol. 822–34v.

33. Mazzei (1977), ch. 5, "La serrata del 1628."

34. I-Las, Libri di corredo alle arte della Signoria 83 (*Libbro delle Famiglie Nobili della Republica di Lucca e loro Stemmi formato l'anno 1628 per decreto dell'ecc.mo consiglio li 21 gennaro detto anno*), p. 170.

35. This discussion is drawn from Bernardo Bertacchi, *Le accademie di Lucca* (Lucca, 1885), pp. iv–xxxi.

36. Carter (1989), p. 26, n. 75, and p. 28.

37. Adriano Banchieri, *Lettere Armoniche* (Bologna: Girolamo Mascheroni, 1628), p. 66.

38. I-Las, Anziani al tempo della libertà 641, lettere di Firenze 1 gennaio 1622 a 12 ottobre 1630.

39. Lucca, Biblioteca Governativa, MS 36, fol. 457.

40. Carter (1989), p. 99, n. 73 notes that Brunelli used Francesca Caccini's

name as a potential witness to his skill as a teacher in the rather defensive preface to his *Parte Prima delli Fioretti spirituali* (Venice, 1626). Brunelli was maestro di cappella to the Cavalieri di S.o Stefano in Pisa, as well as a teacher of musical nuns at the Monasterio di S. Matteo there. Evidently Caccini, too, taught singing in Pisa, presumably during her frequent sojourns there with the Medici court between 1608 and 1626, and had heard Brunelli's pupils perform at S. Matteo. At some point, Brunelli sought Michelangelo Buonarotti's help in obtaining appointment as rector of S. Frediano in Lucca—the Raffaelli's parish church. See I-Fl, Archivio Buonarotti 40, n.o 228, for Buonarotti's notes for a letter on his behalf.

41. On intangible dowries, see Tamassia (1910), ch. 9. For evidence of how a father understood the musical training of daughters as a form of endowment, see Lorenzo Parigi's 1617 letters on behalf of his daughters to Don Paolo Giordano Orsini in Rome, Archivio Capitolino, Fondo Orsini 161/1, n.o 53, 53, 57, 59, 72, 73; and Fondo Orsini 161/2 n.o 249, 251, 256, 258, and 264.

42. The idea that the young Tomaso Raffaelli may not have been Cacccini's biological child has been suggested to me by a number of scholars, including Judith C. Brown, Stephanie Siegmund, Rebecca Harris-Warrick, and Elizabeth Wood.

43. Carter (1989), p. 53, n. 21.

44. I-Las, Notari 188 (Fabritio Calcei), fol. 822–33v.

45. Carter (1989), p. 99, n. 75, based on I-Fl, Buonarotti 44, n.o 460.

46. I-Fas, Ufficiali poi Magistrato della Grascia 195. Morti 1626–69 lists "Margherita della Scala, widow (who) was wife of Giulio Caccini" as buried in S. Michele Bisdomini in February 1635. The same source lists "Settimia widow (who) was wife of Alessandro Grezzani" as buried in S. Ambrogio in June 1661. No Francesca Caccini, widow of either Signorini or Raffaelli, is listed. See Frederick Hammond, "Musicians at the Medici Court in the Mid-Seventeenth Century," *Analecta Musicologica* 14 (1974): 151–69, for Settimia's presence on the grand duke's payroll. A 1635 letter from Margherita de' Medici ne' Farnese to her grandmother Granduchess Cristina asks that the aging Settimia be given a pension upon her return to Florence. See I-Fas, Mediceo del Principato 6042, fol. 23.

47. I-Fl, Buonarotti 52, n.o 1543–47.

48. Hammond (1974).

49. Emilia Grazii's one surviving letter, asking for more canzonette, is at I-Fl, Archivio Buonarotti 48, n.o 1001.

50. Carter (1989), pp. 22–24 and nn. 62, 63, 71. The castrati hired to replace women were Giovanni Bocherino and Fabio Fabri, accompanied initially by Troselli, and later by Horazio Benvenuti, Jacopo Peri, and Gio. Batt.a Signorini.

51. Carter (1989), p. 24, n. 72. Margherita's payment as a lady-in-waiting is documented in I-Fas, Depositeria Generale 389, appendix 30, and I-Fas, Carte Strozziane, I, 51, fol. 4v.

52. I-Fas, Mediceo del Principato 6044, fol. 147.

53. I-Fas, Depositeria Generale Antica 561. Salariati della Ser.ma Vittoria, dal 1635, opening 36.

54. I-Fas, Depositeria Generale Antica 1034, n.o 182, order of 27 February 1636 from the grand duke to paymaster Cosimo Sera.

55. Ibid., unnumbered sheet two leaves after n.o 210.

56. Ibid., n.o 30, contains three receipts signed by Forti, dated 20 December 1636, 1 April 1637, and 10 November 1637. Forti matriculated in the Arte della Lana on 16 March 1635 (I-Fas, Arte della Lana 22, fol. 200). He had apparently been ill enough to make his will the previous year; from that document we know that he owned two houses, one in Borgo Pinti and one that was his mother's dowry in via del Moro (I-Fas, Notarile Moderno. Protocolli dal 11727 a 11759, Testamento di Francesco Forti, 20 settembre 1634, fol. 30). On 18 August 1630, Forti had been among the wool merchants who received a cash advance of 400 lire for cloth to be produced for the grand duke (I-Fas, Depositeria Generale Antica 1019, n.o 312 lists the merchants; n.o 326 is Forti's signed receipt).

57. I-Fas, Mediceo del Principato 6026, letter of 4 April 1635.

58. I-Fas, Mediceo del Principato 6044, fol. 185.

59. I-Fas, Mediceo del Principato 6026, letter of 6 December 1636 to the "Arciduchessa," presumably Vittoria della Rovere.

60. A series of letters or notes for letters from Granduchess Cristina in I-Fas, Mediceo del Principato 6026, refers to comedies of Adimari and Buonarotti being performed at La Crocetta in February 1635.

61. I-Fl, Buonarotti 52, n.o 1545.

62. These letters are at I-Fl, Buonarotti 52, n.o 1544 and 1546.

63. I-Fas, Mediceo del Principato 6026, letter of 27 January 1637, and undated letter immediately following.

64. Many such poems are cited in whole or in part by Ademollo. For poetic praises of first-generation *virtuose*, see the appendix to E. Durante and A. Martelloti, *Cronistoria del Concerto delle Dame* (Florence: Studio di edizioni rari, 1979). The poem about Caccini alluded to here is in [G. B. Basile], *Delle Rime di Gianfrancesco Maia Materdona, Parte Seconda* (Venice: Vangelista Denchino, 1629), p. 65.

65. Dominic La Capra, "Rethinking Intellectual History and Reading Texts," in *Rethinking Intellectual History: Texts and Contexts* (Ithaca: Cornell University Press, 1983), pp. 23–71.

List of Contributors

SUZANNE G. CUSICK teaches music history and criticism at the University of Virginia. Her essays of feminist criticism have appeared in music journals. She is writing a book on Francesca Caccini and gender in early modern music.

PAULA HIGGINS is Associate Professor of Music at the University of Notre Dame. She is the 1987 recipient of the Alfred Einstein Award of the American Musicological Society. Her forthcoming book is *Princes, Prelates, Priests and Poets*.

ROBERT L. KENDRICK took degrees in musicology and ethnomusicology from the University of Pennsylvania and New York University, receiving his Ph.D. from NYU with a dissertation on nuns' music in Seicento Milan. He is currently a Junior Fellow at Harvard University.

KIMBERLY MARSHALL is Dean of Postgraduate Studies at the Royal Academy of Music in London and Assistant Professor and University Organist at Stanford University. She is the author of *Iconographical Evidence for the Late-Medieval Organ* and has published numerous articles in journals. Her compact disc recordings feature music of the Italian and Spanish Renaissance, French Classical and Romantic periods, and works by J. S. Bach. She has recently completed a recording of organ music by women composers entitled *Divine Euterpe*, released on the Gamut label.

CAROL MEYERS is Professor of Biblical Studies and Archaeology and Associate Director of the Women's Studies Program at Duke University. She currently co-directs the Sepphoris Regional Project and is also Vice President of the Albright Institute of Archaeological Research in Jerusalem. She is the author of *Discovering Eve: Ancient Israelite Women in Context,* and co-author of numerous books on aspects of the Bible and archaeology.

HELEN PAYNE specializes in Australian Aboriginal music. She has published widely in international journals and anthologies, and currently lectures in both Music and Women's Studies at the University of Queensland. She is making a film about the importance of ritual in the lives of Australian Aboriginal women.

WILLIAM F. PRIZER is Professor of Musicology at the University of California, Santa Barbara. He was named as a fellow by the National Humanities Center for 1984–1985. He is the author of *Courtly Pastimes: The Frottole of Marchetto Cara,* as well as many articles.

NANCY SULTAN is Assistant Professor of Humanities and Classical Studies at Illinois Wesleyan University. She has published many journal articles, including several on women in ancient Greek music.

EMILY TEETER is Assistant Curator of the Oriental Institute Museum at the University of Chicago. She was a Fellow of the American Research Center in Egypt in 1985 and 1986, and has published a wide variety of articles on ancient Egypt in journals.

DIANE TOULIATOS is Professor of Musicology at the University of Missouri, St. Louis. She is the author of two books, *The Byzantine Amomos Chant of the Fourteenth and Fifteenth Centuries* and *Catalogue of the Byzantine Musical Manuscripts in the Vatican,* as well as many journal articles. She is the recipient of the 1993 Phi Kappa Phi Faculty Scholar/Artist Award for the University of Missouri–St. Louis campus.

SARAH WEISS is Visiting Scholar in the Music Department at the University of Sydney, Australia, to which she has recently returned from the field. She is completing her dissertation on female *gender* players from Central Java for a Ph.D. from New York University.

Index

Index

Index

Landini, Francesco, 154, 161
Lapi, Paolo, 212
Latria, 154, 156–57, 159
Lavagnolo, Lorenzo, 188
Laws (Plato), 95
Lemaire, Jehan, 166
Lent, 157
lesbianism, 112–14; in *Hagesichora*, 114; in Sappho, 112–13
Lesbos, 113; Sappho of, 112–13, 123
Lettere Armoniche, 215, 217
Liberazione di Ruggiero, La (Caccini), 208–9, 216
Libbro d'Oro, 215
Life of Solon (Plutarch), 95
lira da braccio, 202
Litta, Archbishop Alfonso, 127–28
Livre du Voir-Dit (Machaut), 167–68, 177, 183
Lodi, 126
Lombardy, 126; musicians in seventeenth-century, 124, 127–28, 130, 134
Louis VI (king), 169, 175
Louis XI (king), 178
Louis XII (king), 181
Lucca, xxiv, 212, 214–19, 224
Lucchesini, Orazio, 215
lute, 68, 79, 82–84, 90, 126, 143, 187, 190, 192–93, 196, 201–2; *rebab*, 21, 37
lyre, 53, 55, 59–60, 79, 82–84, 88, 104, 115, 117, 153

Machaut, Guillaume de, 175; *Livre du Voir-Dit*, 167–68, 177, 183, 277n83
Maddalena, Maria (archduchess), 217
Mademoiselle de Beau Chastel, 175
madrigal, xxiv
Magliabecchi, Antonio, 210
Mahabharata, 25, 29
Malatesta, Pandolfo, III, 186
Malatesta, Parisina, 187
mallets, used with cymbals, 150
Mani, 101 103, 247n13
Mantua, 164, 188–90, 192–95, 198–99, 201, 214
Margaret (Marguerite) of Austria, 166–67, 176, 181
Margaret of Orleans, 181
Margaret of Scotland, 170–71, 174–76, 178, 184
Margherita von Wittelsbach, 188
Maria of Burgundy, 166–167

Maria of Cleves, Madame d'Orleans, 174–76, 179
Marie d'Anjou, 174–75, 274n41
Marshall, Joane, 158
Marshall, William, 158
Martha, mother of Symeon the Stylite, 118–19
Martin le Franc, 175, 178; *Le Champion des Dams*, 169
Martini, Johannes, 201
Mary, the Virgin, 119, 131, 133–34, 139, 165, 181–82; worship of, 125, 128–29
Mary Magdalen, 125
Mascherata di ninfe di Senna, 164
Mass: Ordinary, 130; Proper, 127
Materdona, G. F., 223
mayu, 11
Medea (Euripides), 111
Medici, Anna de', 219, 221
Medici, Bianca de', 160–62, 187
Medici, Ferdinand I de', 219–20
Medici, Maria de', 220
Medici, Piero de', 187
Medici, Nannina de', 187
Medici, Selvaggia Guasconi, 220
Mei, Filippo, 217
Meir, 78–79, 87
Mellon Chansonnier, 166, 176, 181
membranophone, 53, 57–58
menat, 75–76, 85–86
Mendelssohn, Abraham, xxvi
Mendelssohn, Fanny, xv, xxvi
Mendelssohn, Felix, xxvi
Menelaos, 100, 109
Mereruka, 70–71
Merlin de Cordebeuf, 169
Mersyankh III, 72
Meryre, 84
Mesopotamia, 59
metallophone, 21
Metami (Ovid), 108
Milan, xxii, 124–28, 130–31, 186–88; nuns living in the area of, 124, 139
mimes, 85
mimic dancers (*tragodos* and *tragode*), 85, 117
Miriam (sister of Moses), xx–xxi, xxvi, 61, 156; Song of, 61
Mnemosyne, xix
Modena, 164
moira, 109, 247n9
moirologia, 105, 247n9

Index

Mon cuer chante joyeusement (Binchois),
161
monochord, 143, 147
monody, 113; trouvère, 158
monophony: in chant, 147; in song, 140–
41, 158
Montefeltro, Guidobaldo di, 188
Montefeltro, Teodoro da, 160–62
Monteverdi, Claudio, 164
Monti, Archbishop Cesare, 130
Montu, 85
Moses, 63
motet, 127–29, 131, 134, 139, 181
Mount Athos monastery, 122
mousikê, 114
Muses, xix–xx, xxvii, 93, 102, 112, 142–
43, 156, 167, 190, 223
Musica, 142–45, 147, 149–51, 152–54,
156–57, 159, 162, 165, 167
Musgrave Ranges, 2, 4, 7
Mut, 85, 89
mysticism, 124–25, 128, 139

Nakht, 83
Nakhtamuh, 88
Naples, 133, 181, 189
nay, 69
Nefertiti, 84, 86
Nenchefka, 72
Neolithic period, 50
Nephthys, 88
Nepoti, Govard, 166
Niccolò de Correggio, 191
Niccolò da Padova, 194–95, 196, 203
Nikawre, 70, 76, 87
Nivelle de La Chaussée, 174
Nossis, 113
notation, 140–41, 160; diastematic neu-
matic, 115; of Javanese music, 233n36;
unnotated music, xvi–xvii, xxiii
Notitia del valore delle note del canto
misurato, 181
Novara, 126
nudity, xxi, 56–57, 90
Nyai Jlamprang, 34–36, 45
Nyai Lara Kidul, 34–36, 45
Nyai Panjang Mas, 32, 33, 45

O pulcherrima mulierum (from the Pixérécourt chansonnier), 181–82
O quam bonus es (Cozzolani), 131, 136–
39, 259n46
oboe, 69, 72–75, 90, 242n56; double, 79,

80, 82–84, 242n63; long, 45, 85; single,
79; zummara, 69
Oclata, 157
Oddi, Mutio, 216
Odysseus, 98, 100, 109
Odyssey, 93, 97, 99–100, 102, 108
Oedipus Coloneus (Sophocles), 101
Old Testament, 128
On Ecstatic and Delusional Women (Bor-
romeo), 125
orchestras, xxi, 49, 60–61, 63, 68, 72, 74–
76, 78, 82, 88; integration, 74–75, 78–
80, 84, 90–91; segregation, 72–74, 84,
90–91
Ordinary (of the Mass), 130
Orestes (Ovid), 110
organ, 150–51, 152–57, 159, 160–61, 164,
166; bellows, 153, 161, 187; portative,
152–53, 156; sliders, 150
organist, 134, 186, 265n43, 266n54
organum, 147
Orleans, Charles d', 175–76
Orleans, Madame d' (Marie of Cleves),
174–76, 179
Orleans, Margaret of, 181
Orpheus, 223
Orsini, Leonora, 220
Osiris, 85, 88–89
Ovid: Metami, 108; Orestes, 110

Padua, 126
Palaeologina, 118, 122–23
palaran, 37
Paleologo, Guglielmo (marchese of Ca-
sale), 200, 204
Pan, 104–5
Pandora, 111, 115
"Papino" (Dionisio de Mantova), 194,
196, 202
Papyrus Anastasi IV, 88, 239n12
Papyrus Westcar, 88
Partheneia, 113–14
pasindhen, xxiv, 43–44, 46–47, 233–
34n38
Passion (of Christ), 125, 129, 133–34, 139
pathet, 39–42
Patroklos, 102
Paul, 116
Paumann, Conrad; attributions in the
Buxheimer Orgelbuch, 160; Funda-
mentum organisandi, 160
Pavia, Lorenzo, 192

Index

Index